Outlook® 2002 -In an Instant™-

by Nancy Buchanan

From
maranGraphics®

&

Wiley Publishing, Inc.

Outlook® 2002 In an Instant™

Published by
Wiley Publishing, Inc.
909 Third Avenue
New York, NY 10022

Published simultaneously in Canada

maranGraphics, Inc.
5755 Coopers Avenue
Mississauga, Ontario, Canada
L4Z 1R9

Library of Congress Control Number: 2001098036

ISBN: 0-7645-3669-9

Manufactured in the United States of America

10 9 8 7 6 5 4 3 2

1B/TQ/QY/QS/IN

Trademark Acknowledgments

Important Numbers

For U.S. corporate orders, please call maranGraphics at 800-469-6616 or fax 905-890-9434.

Permissions

For general information on our other products and services or to obtain technical support please contact our Customer Care Department within the U.S. at 800-762-2974, outside the U.S. at 317-572-3993 or fax 317-572-4002.

maranGraphics

Certain text and Illustrations by maranGraphics, Inc., used with maranGraphics' permission.

Wiley also publishes its books in a variety of electronic formats. Some content that appears in print may not be available in electronic books.

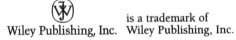

Wiley Publishing, Inc. is a trademark of Wiley Publishing, Inc.

U.S. Corporate Sales

Contact maranGraphics at (800) 469-6616 or fax (905) 890-9434.

U.S. Trade Sales

Contact Wiley at (800) 762-2974 or fax (317) 572-4002.

Some comments from our readers...

"I have to praise you and your company on the fine products you turn out. I have twelve of the *Teach Yourself VISUALLY* and *Simplified* books in my house. They were instrumental in helping me pass a difficult computer course. Thank you for creating books that are easy to follow."

–Gordon Justin (Brielle, NJ)

"I commend your efforts and your success. I teach in an outreach program for the Dr. Eugene Clark Library in Lockhart, TX. Your *Teach Yourself VISUALLY* books are incredible and I use them in my computer classes. All my students love them!"

–Michele Schalin (Lockhart, TX)

"Thank you so much for helping people like me learn about computers. The Maran family is just what the doctor ordered. Thank you, thank you, thank you."

–Carol Moten (New Kensington, PA)

"I would like to take this time to compliment maranGraphics on creating such great books. Thank you for making it clear. Keep up the good work."

–Kirk Santoro (Burbank, CA)

"I write to extend my thanks and appreciation for your books. They are clear, easy to follow, and straight to the point. Keep up the good work!"

–Seward Kollie (Dakar, Senegal)

"What fantastic teaching books you have produced! Congratulations to you and your staff. You deserve the Nobel prize in Education in the Software category. Thanks for helping me to understand computers."

–Bruno Tonon (Melbourne, Australia)

"Over time, I have bought a number of your 'Read Less – Learn More' books. For me, they are THE way to learn anything easily."

–José A. Mazón (Cuba, NY)

"I was introduced to maranGraphics about four years ago and YOU ARE THE GREATEST THING THAT EVER HAPPENED TO INTRODUCTORY COMPUTER BOOKS!"

–Glenn Nettleton (Huntsville, AL)

"Compliments To The Chef!! Your books are extraordinary! Or, simply put, Extra-Ordinary, meaning way above the rest! THANK YOU THANK YOU THANK YOU! for creating these."

–Christine J. Manfrin (Castle Rock, CO)

"I'm a grandma who was pushed by an 11-year-old grandson to join the computer age. I found myself hopelessly confused and frustrated until I discovered the Visual series. I'm no expert by any means now, but I'm a lot further along than I would have been otherwise. Thank you!"

–Carol Louthain (Logansport, IN)

"Thank you, thank you, thank you...for making it so easy for me to break into this high-tech world. I now own four of your books. I recommend them to anyone who is a beginner like myself. Now... if you could just do one for programming VCRs, it would make my day!"

–Gay O'Donnell (Calgary, Alberta, Canada)

"You're marvelous! I am greatly in your debt."

–Patrick Baird (Lacey, WA)

maranGraphics is a family-run business located near Toronto, Canada.

At maranGraphics, we believe in producing great computer books—one book at a time.

Each maranGraphics book uses the award-winning communication process that we have been developing over the last 25 years. Using this process, we organize screen shots and text in a way that makes it easy for you to learn new concepts and tasks.

We spend hours deciding the best way to perform each task, so you don't have to!

Our clear, easy-to-follow screen shots and instructions walk you through each task from beginning to end.

We want to thank you for purchasing what we feel are the best computer books money can buy. We hope you enjoy using this book as much as we enjoyed creating it!

Sincerely,

The Maran Family

Please visit us on the Web at:

www.maran.com

CREDITS

Project Editors:
Rev Mengle
Sarah Hellert

Acquisitions Editor:
Jen Dorsey

Product Development Supervisor:
Lindsay Sandman

Technical Editor:
Lee Musick

Editorial Manager:
Rev Mengle

Editorial Assistant:
Amanda Foxworth

Book Design:
maranGraphics®

Production Coordinator:
Nancee Reeves

Layout:
LeAndra Johnson
Kristin McMullan
Jill Piscitelli
Erin Zeltner

Screen Artists:
Mark Harris
Jill A. Proll

Proofreaders:
David Faust
Andy Hollandbeck
Henry Lazarek
Carl Pierce

Indexer:
Sherry Massey

GENERAL AND ADMINISTRATIVE

Wiley Technology Publishing Group: Richard Swadley, Vice President and Executive Group Publisher; Bob Ipsen, Vice President and Group Publisher; Joseph Wikert, Vice President and Publisher; Barry Pruett, Vice President and Publisher; Mary Bednarek, Editorial Director; Mary C. Corder, Editorial Director; Andy Cummings, Vice President and Publisher

Wiley Manufacturing: Carol Tobin, Director of Manufacturing

Wiley Marketing: John Helmus, Assistant Vice President, Director of Marketing

Wiley Composition Services: Gerry Fahey, Vice President of Production Services; Debbie Stailey, Director of Composition Services

ABOUT THE AUTHOR

Nancy Buchanan is a freelance high-tech marketing consultant and writer who has been in technical marketing and sales for more than 18 years. Most recently she was in product marketing for almost eight years for Microsoft Corporation, where she worked in marketing for Microsoft Office, Microsoft FrontPage, for Windows-based streaming media, and for marketing Microsoft products sold to attorneys. Prior to joining Microsoft, Nancy was in sales and marketing for over six years at Novell, Inc.

Nancy holds a Bachelor of Arts degree in Business Administration from the University of Washington in Seattle and lives in Washington state with her husband, her four children ranging in age from 3 to 12, her golden retriever Jake, and her cat Mocha.

AUTHOR'S ACKNOWLEDGMENTS

I'd like to thank the folks from Hungry Minds, Inc. who were so great to work with on this project. Barry Pruett and Ruth Maran were kind enough to allow me to work on this, Jen Dorsey helped me get started, Lee Musick kept us technically on track, and last but not least, Rev Mengle kept the whole project humming along with his talent and skill and generous sense of humor to make this project fun.

This book is dedicated to my husband Doug, the avid (or should I say rabid?) fly fisherman mentioned throughout. I could not have done this book without his love and patience and willingness to take care of our 3-ring circus while I was busy writing.

TABLE OF CONTENTS

1 Understanding Outlook Basics

2 Working with Your Inbox

3 Sending E-mail

4 Working with Attachments

5 Deleting E-mail

6 Organizing Your Inbox

7 Storing E-mail in Folders

8 Managing Your Schedule

TABLE OF CONTENTS

OUTLOOK OVERVIEW

Microsoft Outlook 2002 helps you simplify e-mail communication, streamline group planning and scheduling, and access the information you need — all in one place.

OUTLOOK OVERVIEW

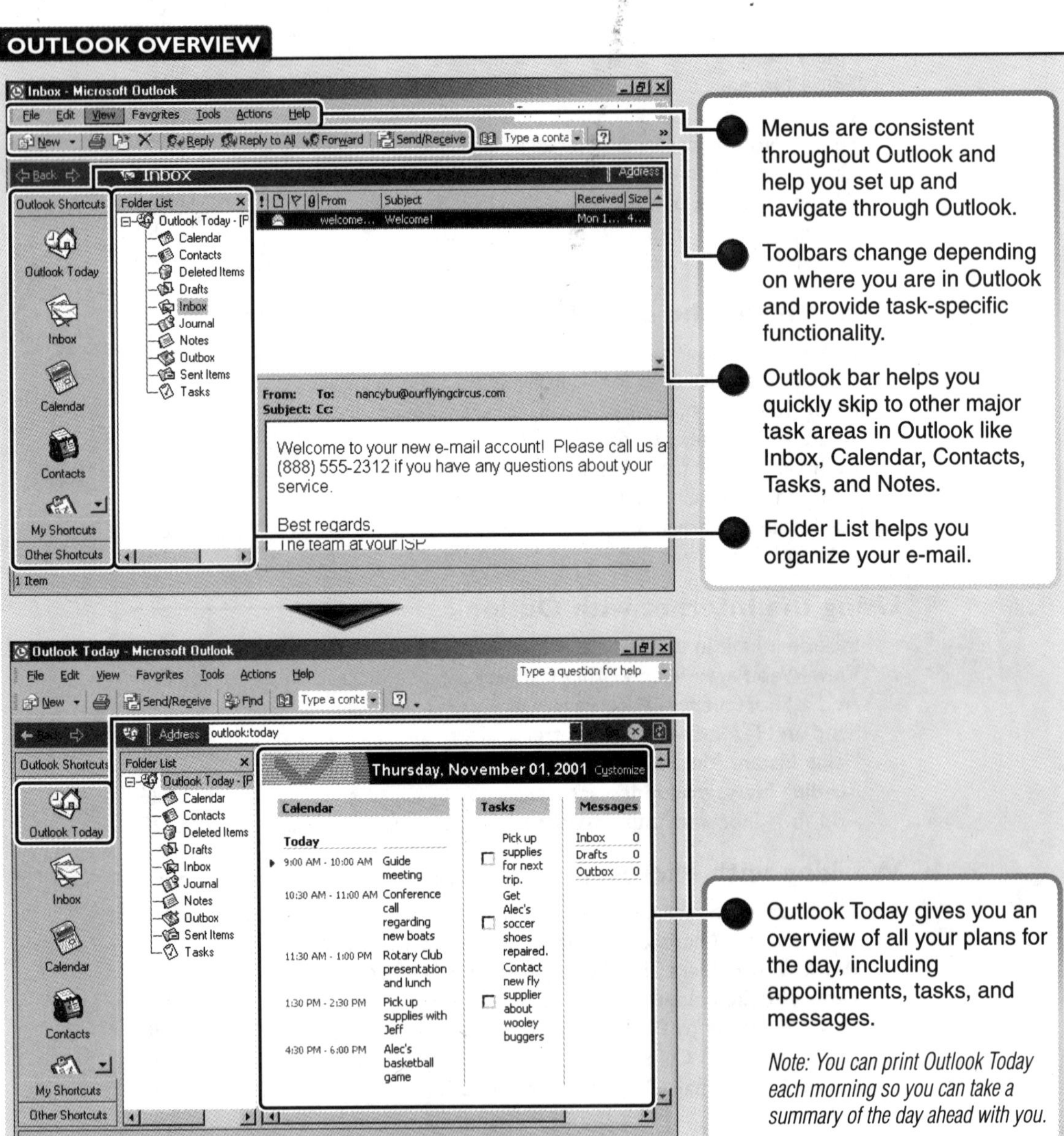

Menus are consistent throughout Outlook and help you set up and navigate through Outlook.
Toolbars change depending on where you are in Outlook and provide task-specific functionality.
Outlook bar helps you quickly skip to other major task areas in Outlook like Inbox, Calendar, Contacts, Tasks, and Notes.
Folder List helps you organize your e-mail.
Outlook Today gives you an overview of all your plans for the day, including appointments, tasks, and messages.
Note: You can print Outlook Today each morning so you can take a summary of the day ahead with you.

in an instant

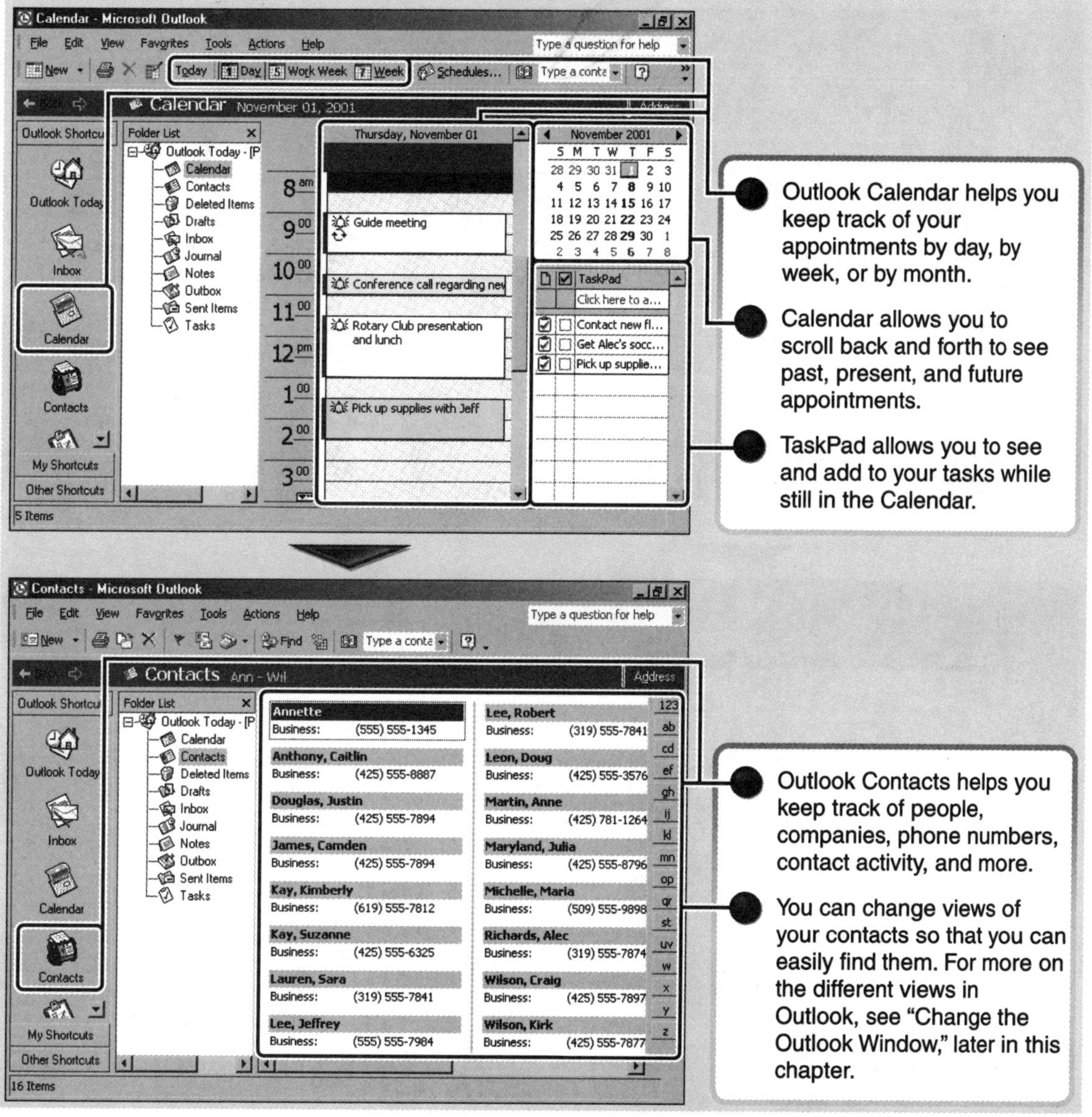

Calendar - Microsoft Outlook
Outlook Calendar helps you keep track of your appointments by day, by week, or by month.
Calendar allows you to scroll back and forth to see past, present, and future appointments.
TaskPad allows you to see and add to your tasks while still in the Calendar.
Contacts - Microsoft Outlook
Outlook Contacts helps you keep track of people, companies, phone numbers, contact activity, and more.
You can change views of your contacts so that you can easily find them. For more on the different views in Outlook, see "Change the Outlook Window," later in this chapter.

CONNECT TO YOUR MAIL SERVER

Outlook 2002 serves as the mail client to your mail server. Once you give Outlook some key information about the e-mail service you subscribe to, you can get started. You won't have to enter this information again unless your e-mail service changes.

CONNECT TO YOUR MAIL SERVER

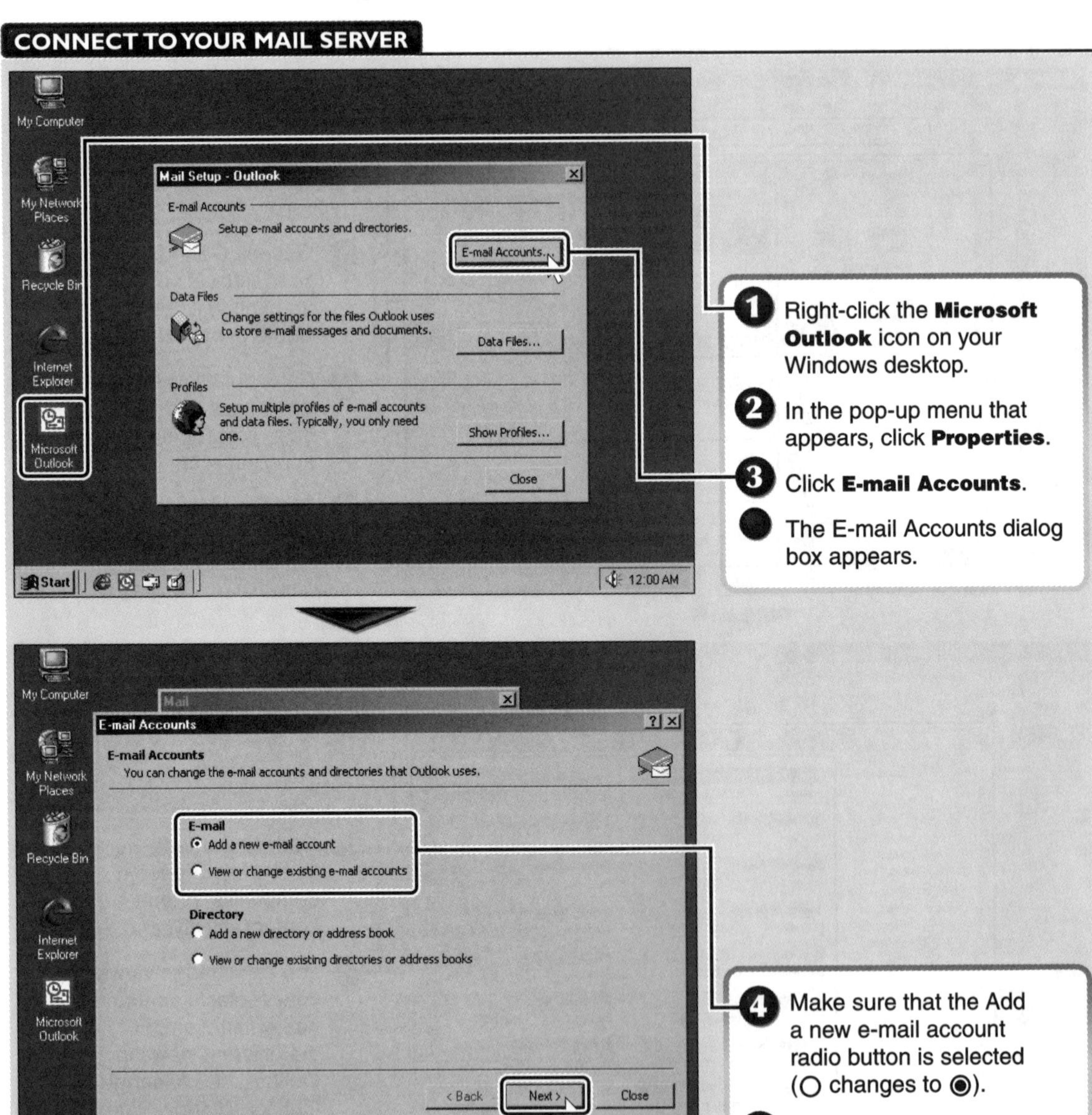

1. Right-click the **Microsoft Outlook** icon on your Windows desktop.
2. In the pop-up menu that appears, click **Properties**.
3. Click **E-mail Accounts**.

- The E-mail Accounts dialog box appears.

4. Make sure that the Add a new e-mail account radio button is selected (○ changes to ◉).
5. Click **Next**.

in an instant

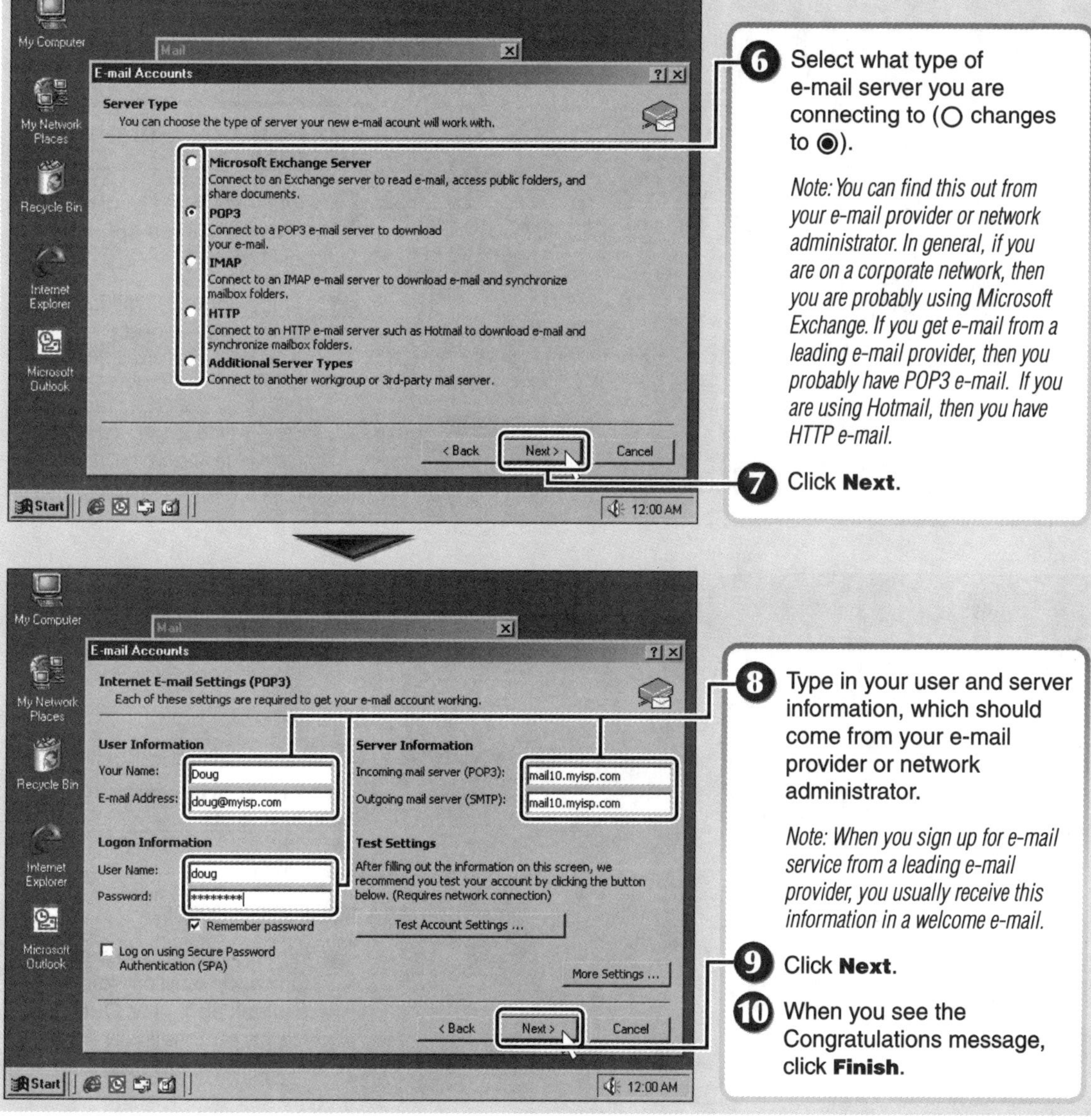

6. Select what type of e-mail server you are connecting to (○ changes to ◉).

   Note: You can find this out from your e-mail provider or network administrator. In general, if you are on a corporate network, then you are probably using Microsoft Exchange. If you get e-mail from a leading e-mail provider, then you probably have POP3 e-mail. If you are using Hotmail, then you have HTTP e-mail.

7. Click **Next**.

8. Type in your user and server information, which should come from your e-mail provider or network administrator.

   Note: When you sign up for e-mail service from a leading e-mail provider, you usually receive this information in a welcome e-mail.

9. Click **Next**.

10. When you see the Congratulations message, click **Finish**.

START OUTLOOK

You can start Outlook several ways: using the Outlook icon on the desktop, the Outlook icon on the Windows taskbar, the Start button menu, or the Start menu's Run dialog box.

START OUTLOOK

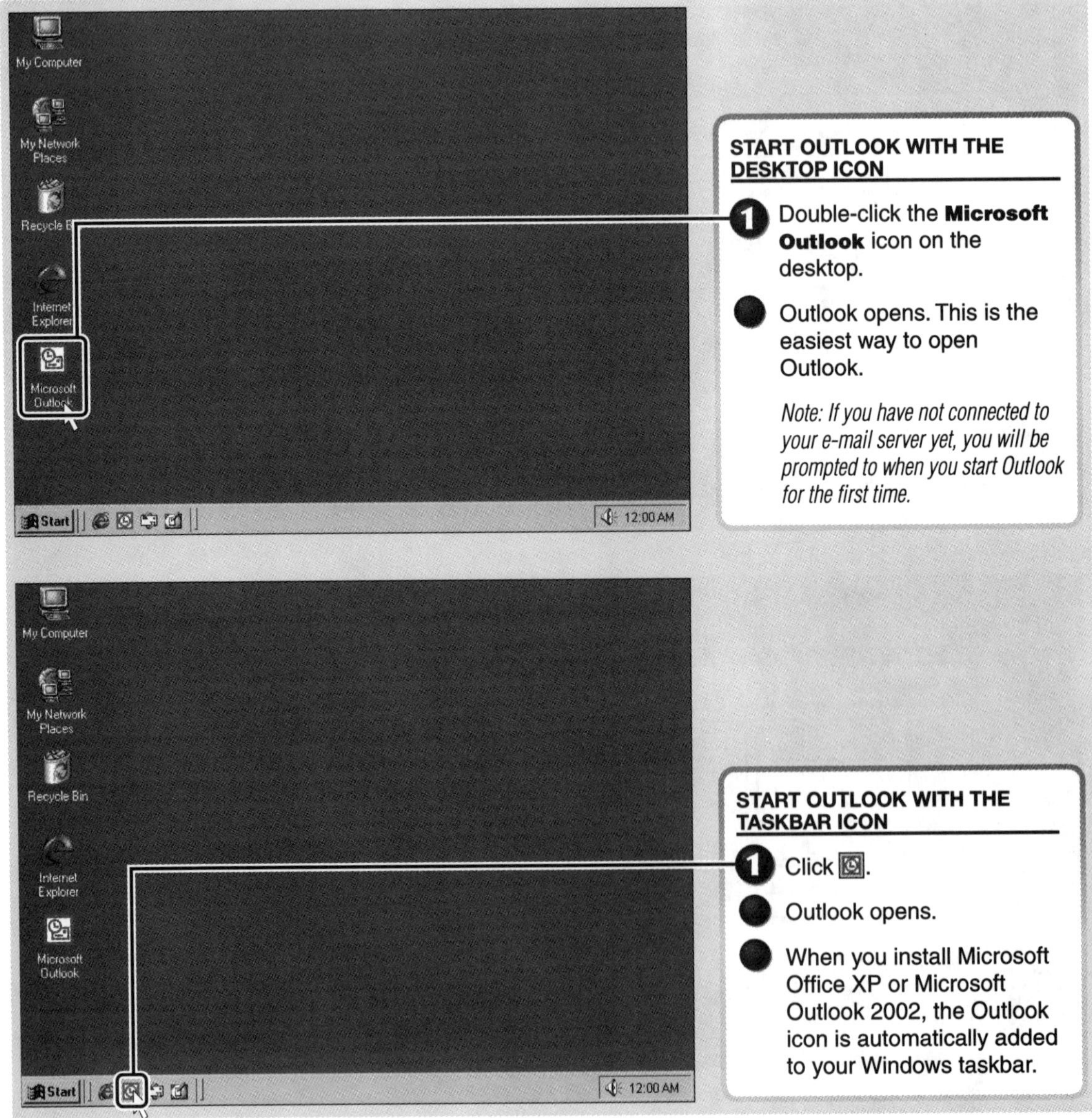

START OUTLOOK WITH THE DESKTOP ICON

1. Double-click the **Microsoft Outlook** icon on the desktop.

- Outlook opens. This is the easiest way to open Outlook.

Note: If you have not connected to your e-mail server yet, you will be prompted to when you start Outlook for the first time.

START OUTLOOK WITH THE TASKBAR ICON

1. Click [icon].

- Outlook opens.
- When you install Microsoft Office XP or Microsoft Outlook 2002, the Outlook icon is automatically added to your Windows taskbar.

in an instant

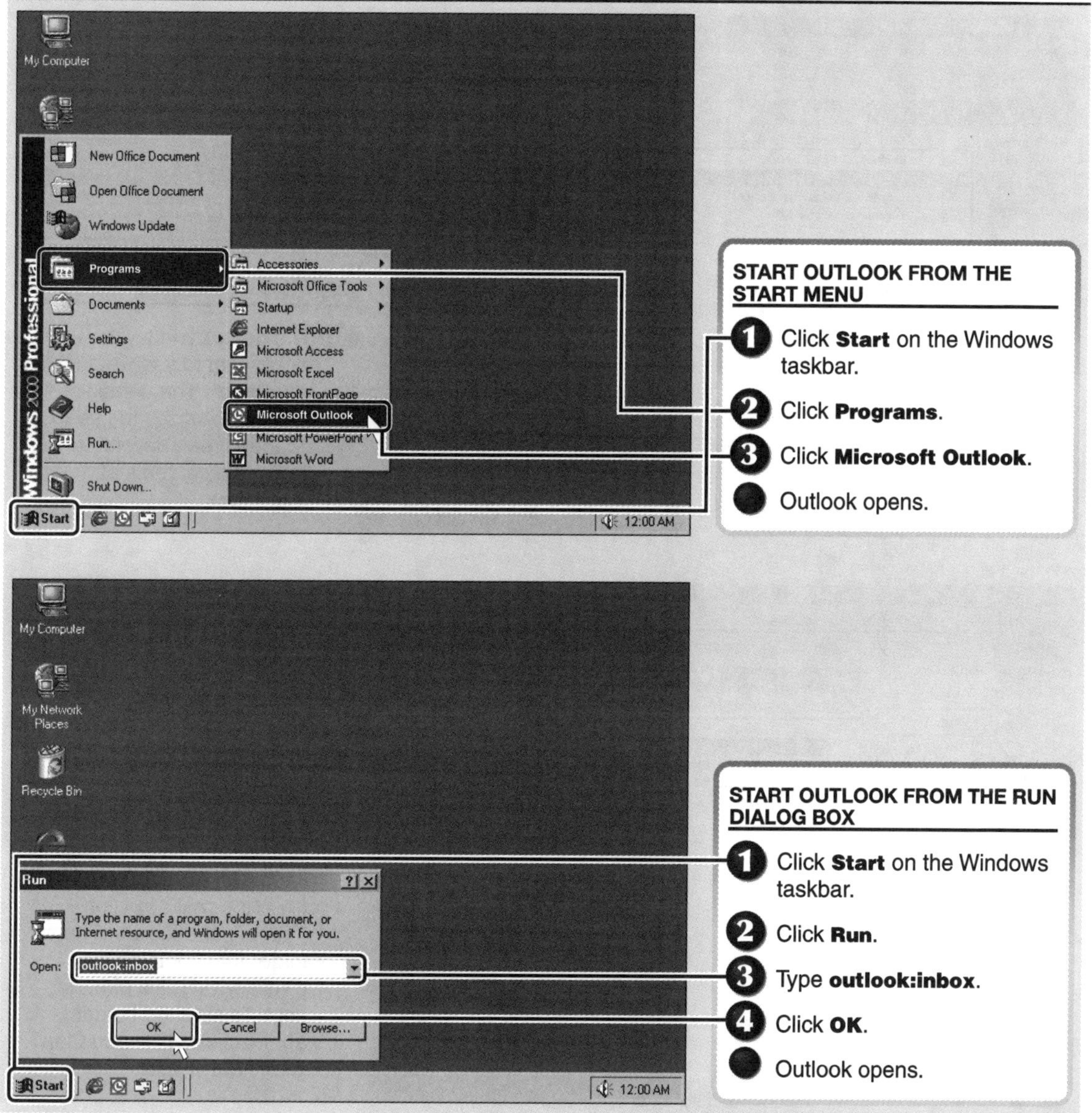

START OUTLOOK FROM THE START MENU

1. Click **Start** on the Windows taskbar.
2. Click **Programs**.
3. Click **Microsoft Outlook**.

- Outlook opens.

START OUTLOOK FROM THE RUN DIALOG BOX

1. Click **Start** on the Windows taskbar.
2. Click **Run**.
3. Type **outlook:inbox**.
4. Click **OK**.

- Outlook opens.

CHANGE THE OUTLOOK WINDOW

Change the Outlook window so that you can find just what you want. You can maximize the amount of screen space dedicated to individual e-mail messages, give up some of that space and get quick access to deleted, draft, or sent messages, or you can choose to preview messages before you open them.

CHANGE THE OUTLOOK WINDOW

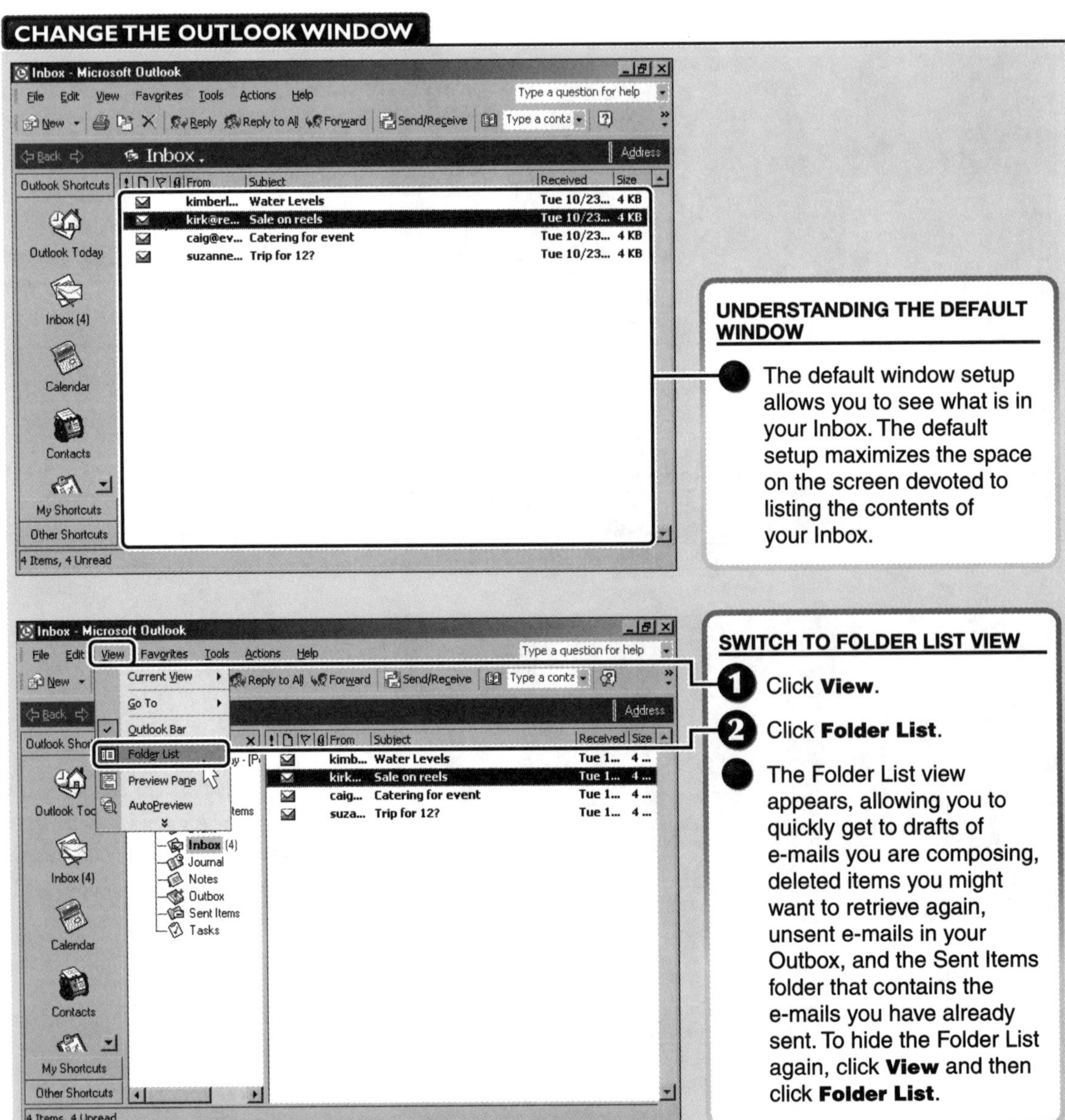

UNDERSTANDING THE DEFAULT WINDOW

- The default window setup allows you to see what is in your Inbox. The default setup maximizes the space on the screen devoted to listing the contents of your Inbox.

SWITCH TO FOLDER LIST VIEW

1. Click **View**.
2. Click **Folder List**.

- The Folder List view appears, allowing you to quickly get to drafts of e-mails you are composing, deleted items you might want to retrieve again, unsent e-mails in your Outbox, and the Sent Items folder that contains the e-mails you have already sent. To hide the Folder List again, click **View** and then click **Folder List**.

in an instant

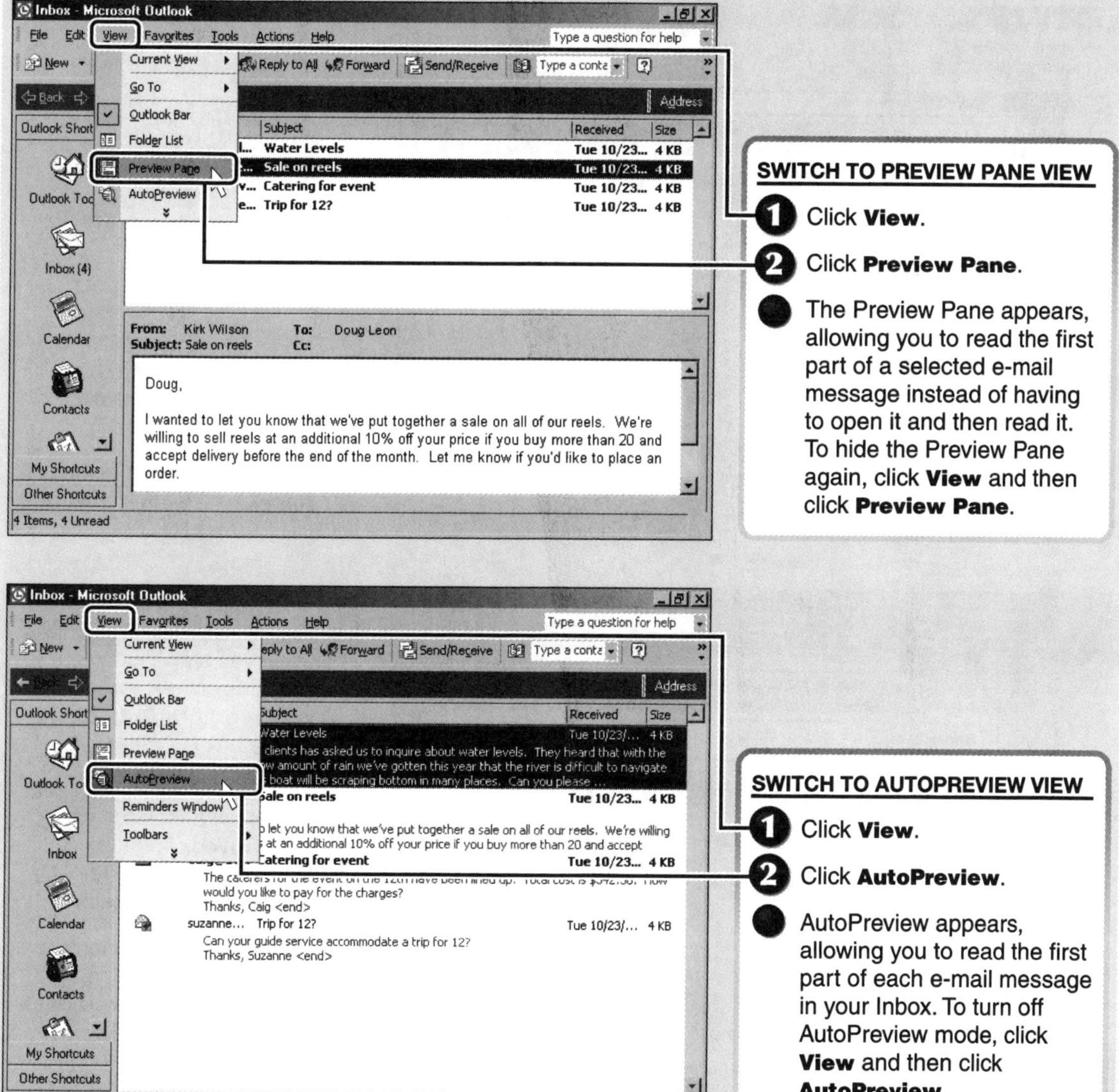

SWITCH TO PREVIEW PANE VIEW

1. Click **View**.
2. Click **Preview Pane**.

- The Preview Pane appears, allowing you to read the first part of a selected e-mail message instead of having to open it and then read it. To hide the Preview Pane again, click **View** and then click **Preview Pane**.

SWITCH TO AUTOPREVIEW VIEW

1. Click **View**.
2. Click **AutoPreview**.

- AutoPreview appears, allowing you to read the first part of each e-mail message in your Inbox. To turn off AutoPreview mode, click **View** and then click **AutoPreview**.

CUSTOMIZE OUTLOOK TODAY

Outlook Today gives you a snapshot of your appointments, your tasks, and your Inbox in one glance, and by clicking on any of those items, you can open them up. Even better, you can customize Outlook Today to suit your needs.

CUSTOMIZE OUTLOOK TODAY

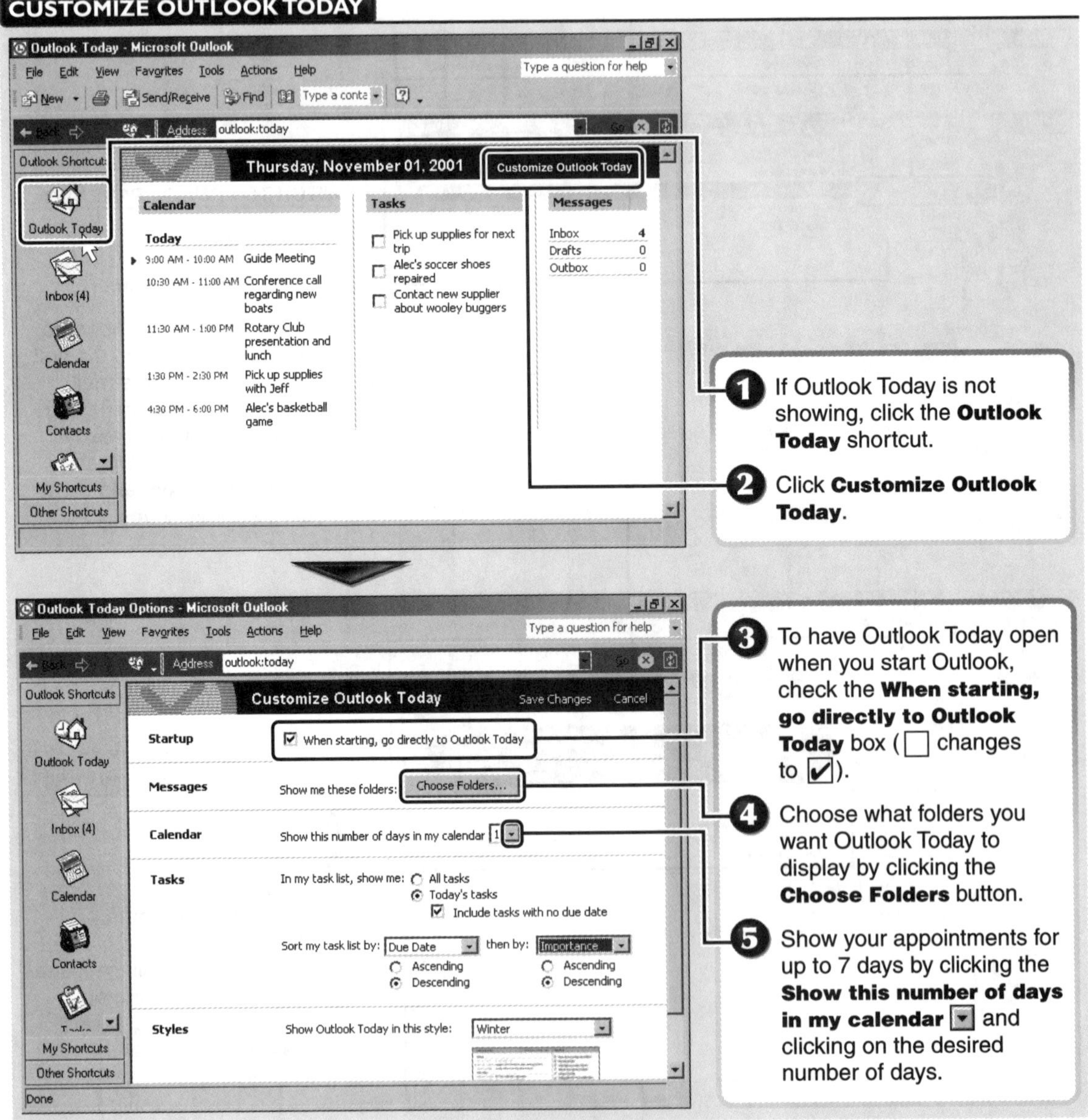

1. If Outlook Today is not showing, click the **Outlook Today** shortcut.

2. Click **Customize Outlook Today**.

3. To have Outlook Today open when you start Outlook, check the **When starting, go directly to Outlook Today** box (☐ changes to ☑).

4. Choose what folders you want Outlook Today to display by clicking the **Choose Folders** button.

5. Show your appointments for up to 7 days by clicking the **Show this number of days in my calendar** ▾ and clicking on the desired number of days.

in an instant

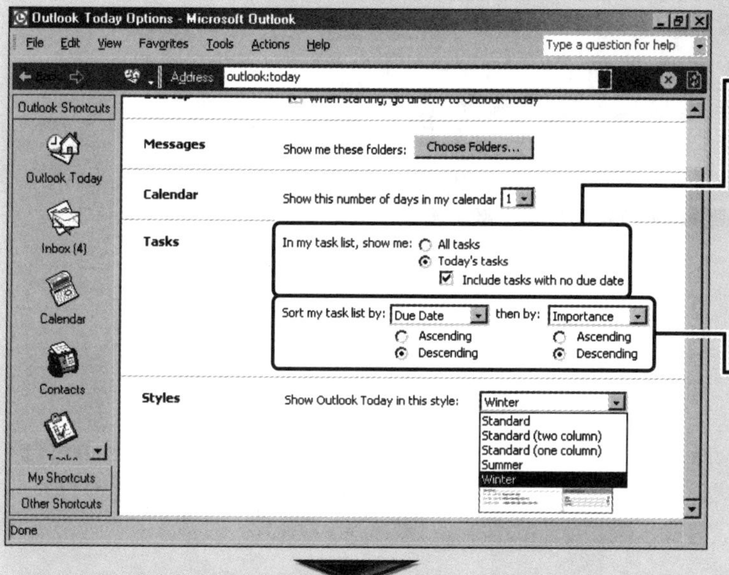

6 Click the appropriate option box to specify how you want your tasks to appear (○ changes to ◉).

- Click **All tasks** if you want every task you have to appear. Click **Today's tasks** if you want just your tasks for today to appear.

7 Specify how you want your tasks to be sorted in Outlook Today by clicking the **Sort my task list by** ▾ and clicking on the desired setting.

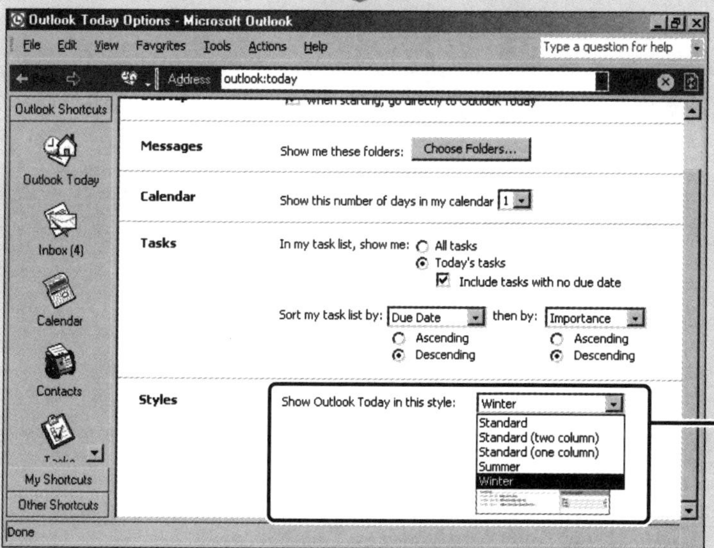

8 Change the style of your Outlook Today by clicking the **Show Outlook Today in this style** ▾ and clicking on the desired style.

9 Click **Save Changes**.

- The Outlook Today window reappears with the new settings.

CHANGE ICON SIZE

You can make Microsoft Outlook easier to navigate by changing the size of Outlook program icons.

CHANGE ICON SIZE

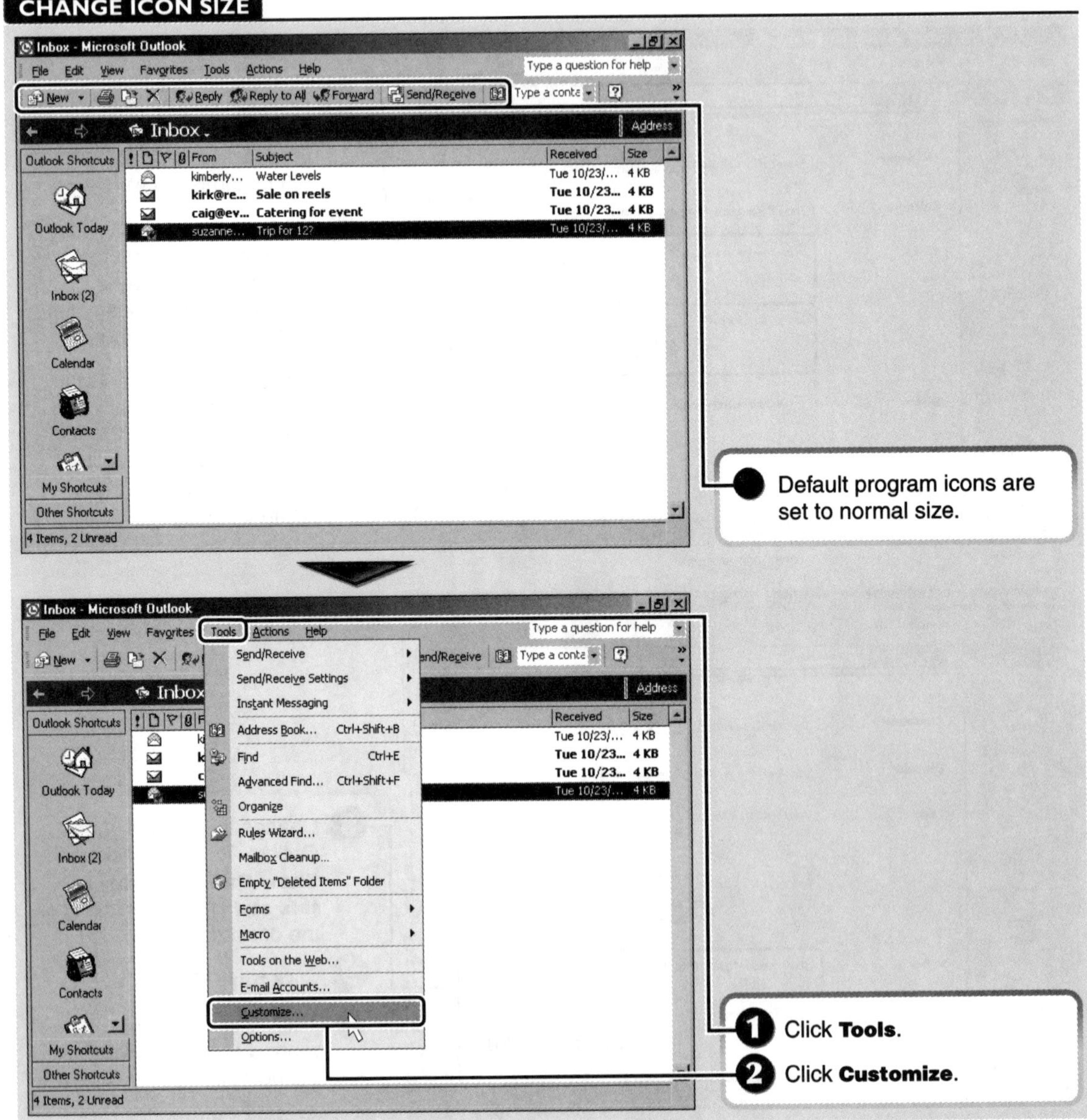

● Default program icons are set to normal size.

1 Click **Tools**.

2 Click **Customize**.

in an instant

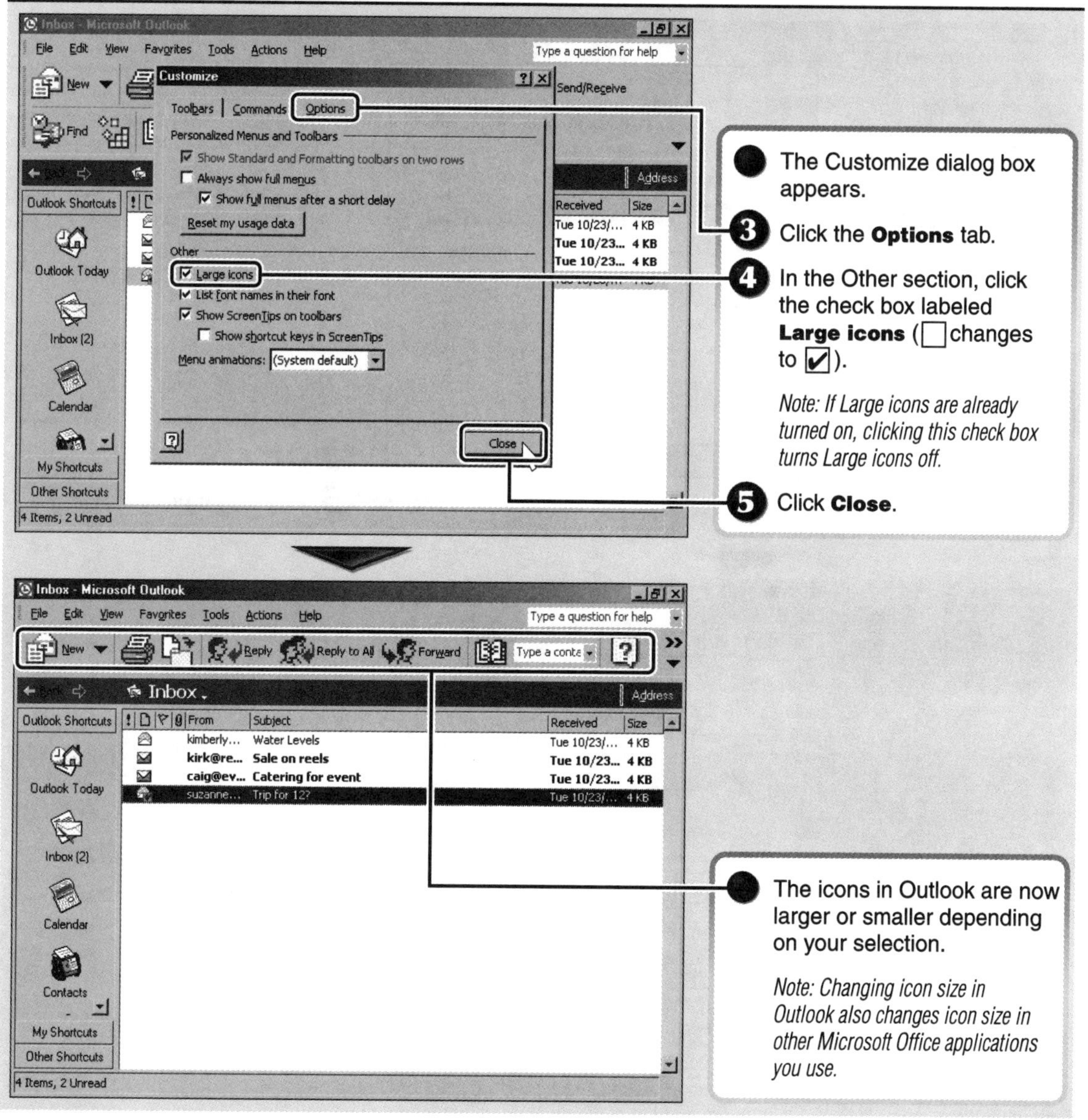

- The Customize dialog box appears.

3 Click the **Options** tab.

4 In the Other section, click the check box labeled **Large icons** (☐ changes to ☑).

Note: If Large icons are already turned on, clicking this check box turns Large icons off.

5 Click **Close**.

- The icons in Outlook are now larger or smaller depending on your selection.

Note: Changing icon size in Outlook also changes icon size in other Microsoft Office applications you use.

CHANGE E-MAIL FONTS

You can easily change the fonts with which you view and send e-mail. You can change the font you use when composing a new message, when replying and forwarding a message, and when composing and reading plain text.

CHANGE E-MAIL FONTS

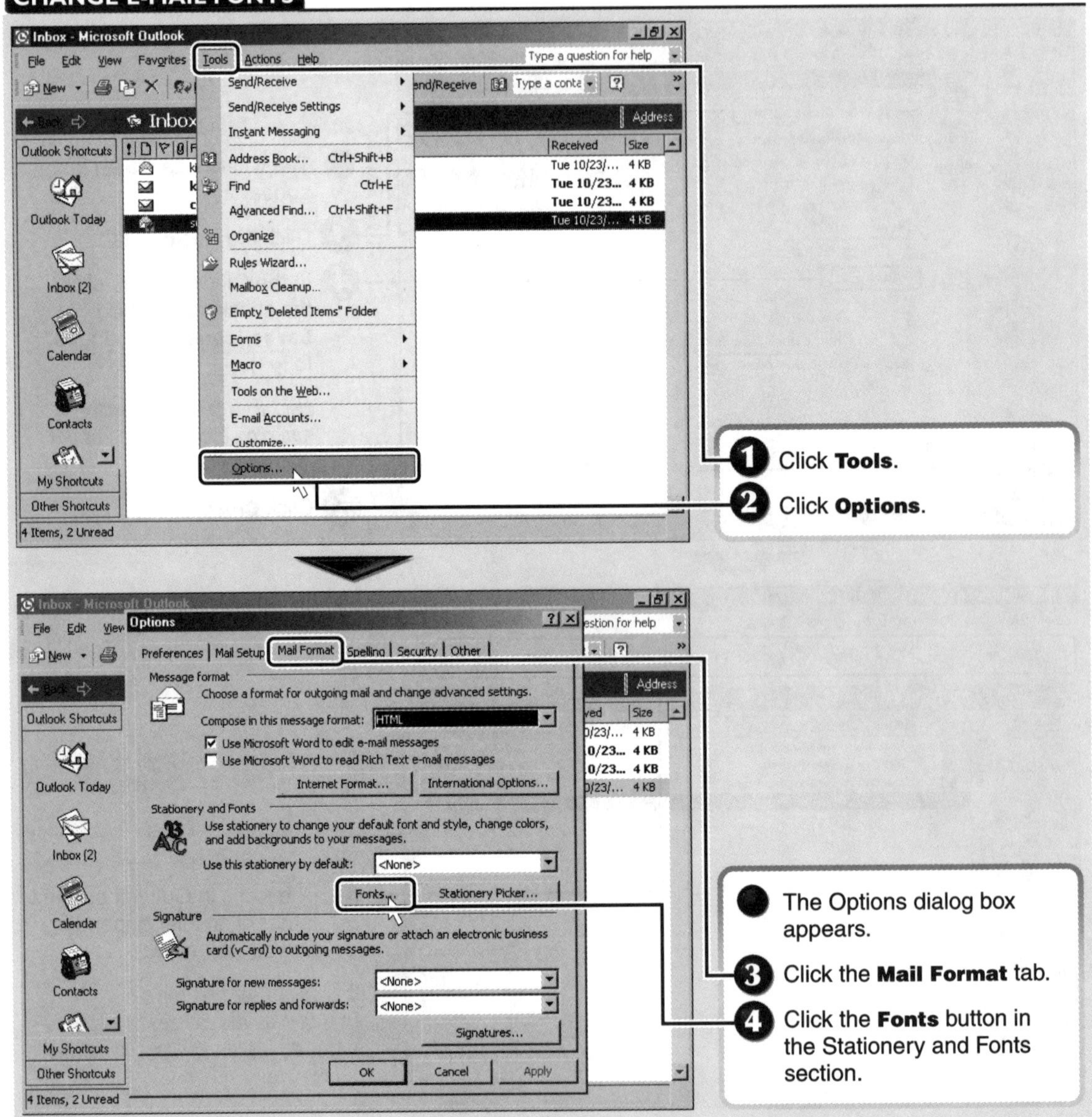

1 Click **Tools**.
2 Click **Options**.
The Options dialog box appears.
3 Click the **Mail Format** tab.
4 Click the **Fonts** button in the Stationery and Fonts section.

in an instant

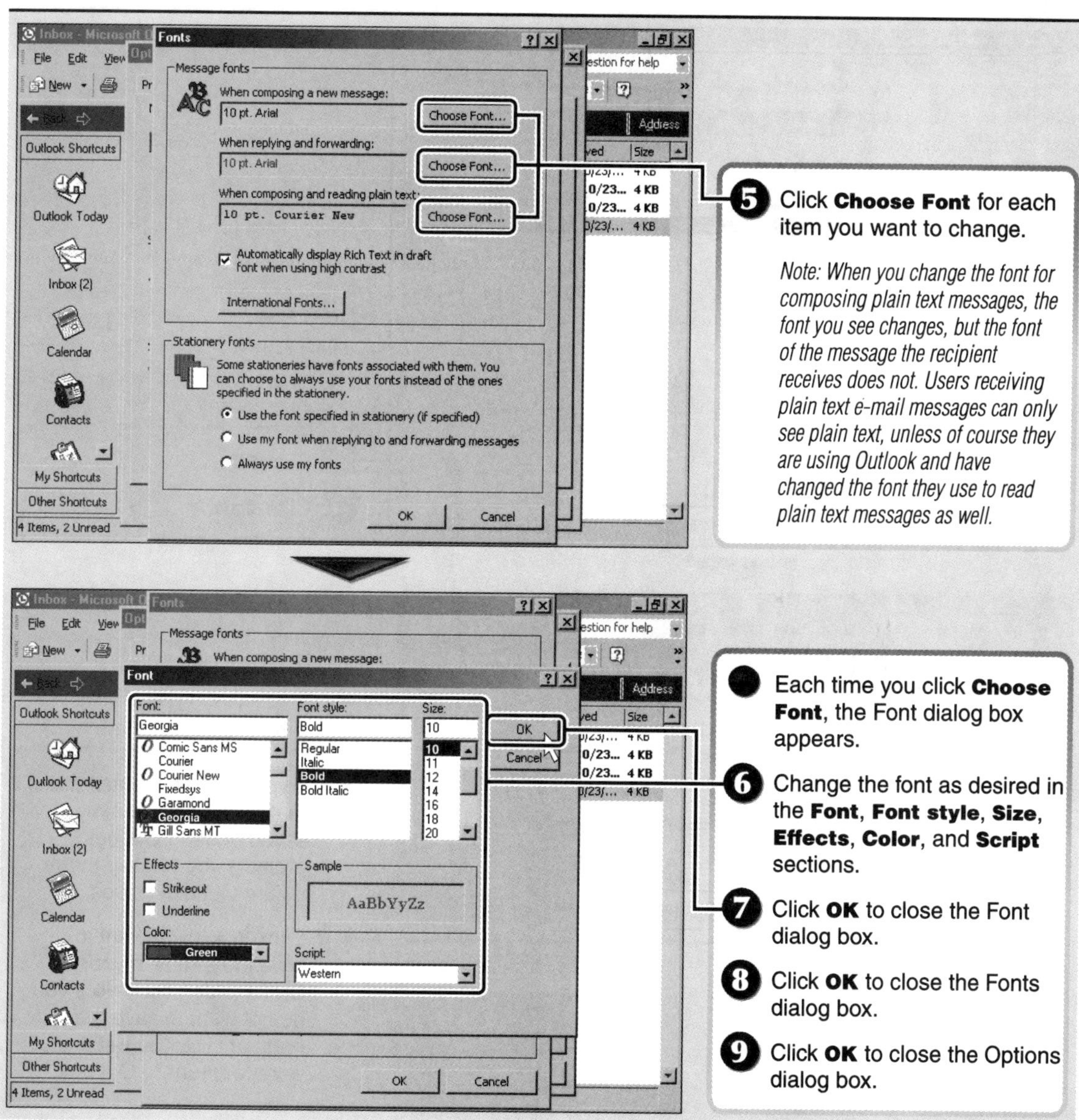

5 Click **Choose Font** for each item you want to change.

Note: When you change the font for composing plain text messages, the font you see changes, but the font of the message the recipient receives does not. Users receiving plain text e-mail messages can only see plain text, unless of course they are using Outlook and have changed the font they use to read plain text messages as well.

- Each time you click **Choose Font**, the Font dialog box appears.

6 Change the font as desired in the **Font**, **Font style**, **Size**, **Effects**, **Color**, and **Script** sections.

7 Click **OK** to close the Font dialog box.

8 Click **OK** to close the Fonts dialog box.

9 Click **OK** to close the Options dialog box.

CLOSE OUTLOOK

Close Outlook when you are finished working with the program. Outlook prompts you to save any e-mail drafts before shutting down.

CLOSE OUTLOOK

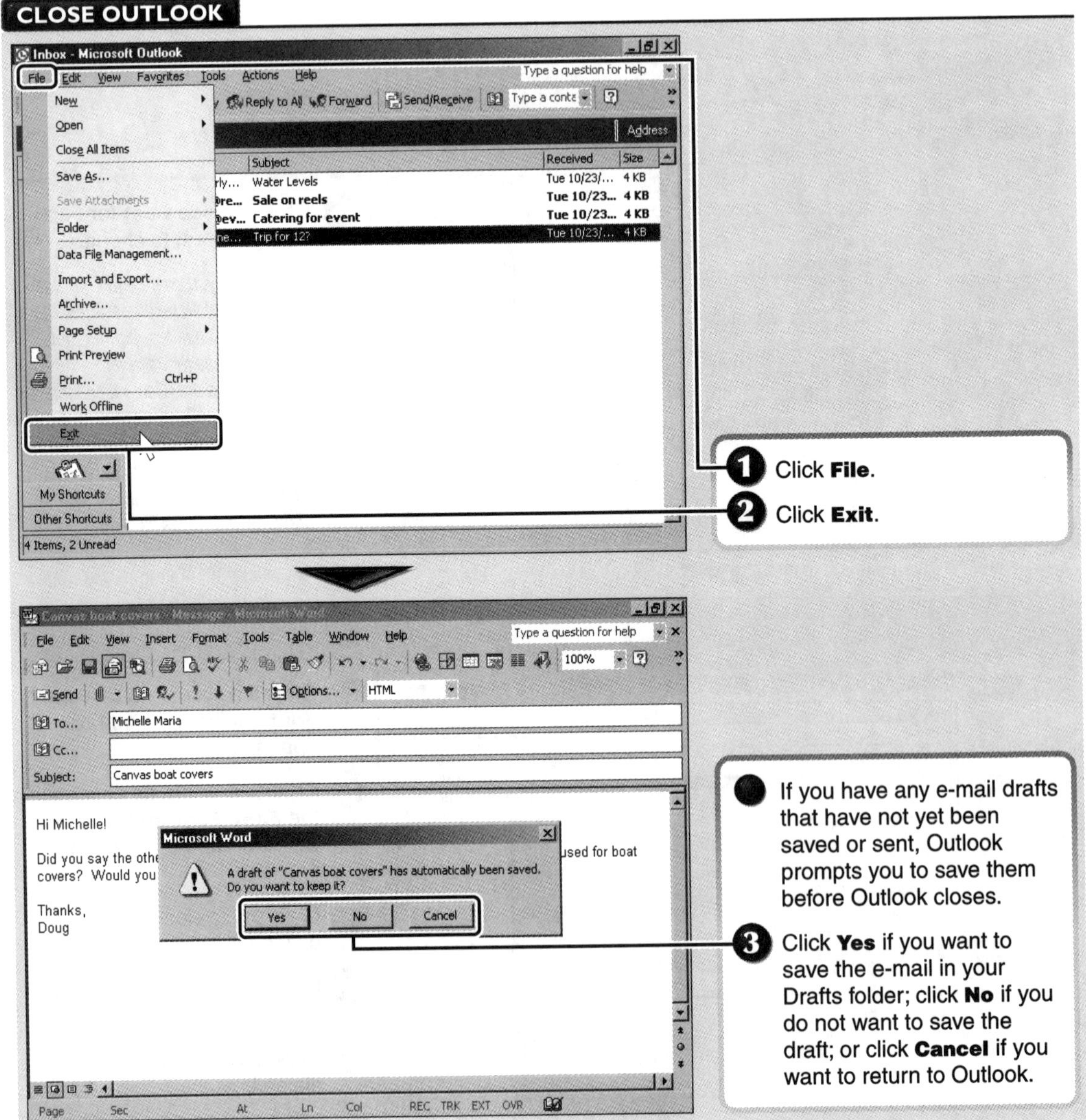

1. Click **File**.
2. Click **Exit**.

- If you have any e-mail drafts that have not yet been saved or sent, Outlook prompts you to save them before Outlook closes.

3. Click **Yes** if you want to save the e-mail in your Drafts folder; click **No** if you do not want to save the draft; or click **Cancel** if you want to return to Outlook.

GETTING HELP

You can get assistance in using Outlook at any time with Outlook 2002 Help. Pressing the F1 key on your keyboard brings up Outlook Help quickly, and you can also use the animated Office Assistants to help you as you use Outlook.

GETTING HELP

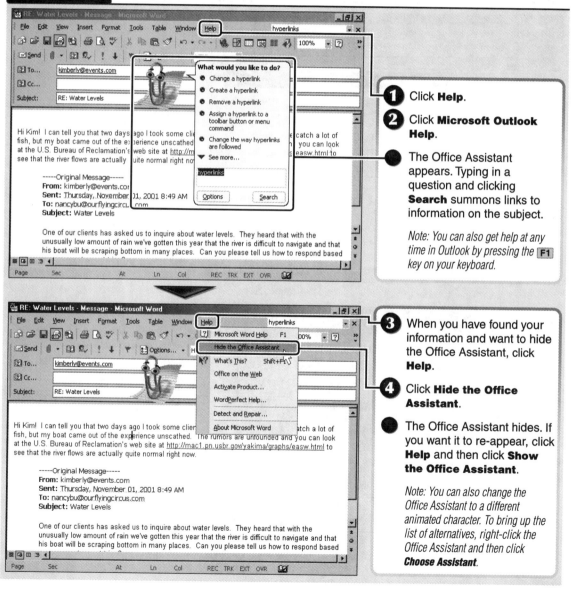

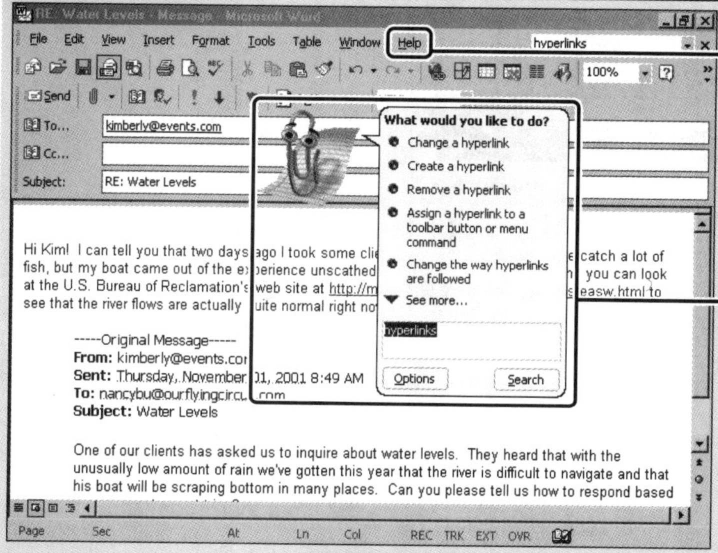

1. Click **Help**.
2. Click **Microsoft Outlook Help**.

- The Office Assistant appears. Typing in a question and clicking **Search** summons links to information on the subject.

Note: You can also get help at any time in Outlook by pressing the F1 *key on your keyboard.*

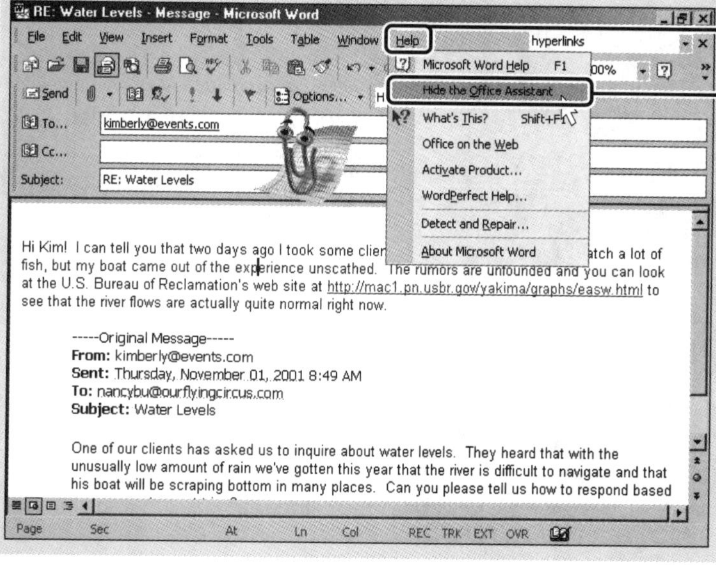

3. When you have found your information and want to hide the Office Assistant, click **Help**.
4. Click **Hide the Office Assistant**.

- The Office Assistant hides. If you want it to re-appear, click **Help** and then click **Show the Office Assistant**.

Note: You can also change the Office Assistant to a different animated character. To bring up the list of alternatives, right-click the Office Assistant and then click ***Choose Assistant****.*

OPEN YOUR INBOX

You can quickly open your Inbox from the Outlook bar once you are in Outlook. You can also open your Inbox from the Windows command prompt if you do not have Outlook opened yet.

OPEN YOUR INBOX

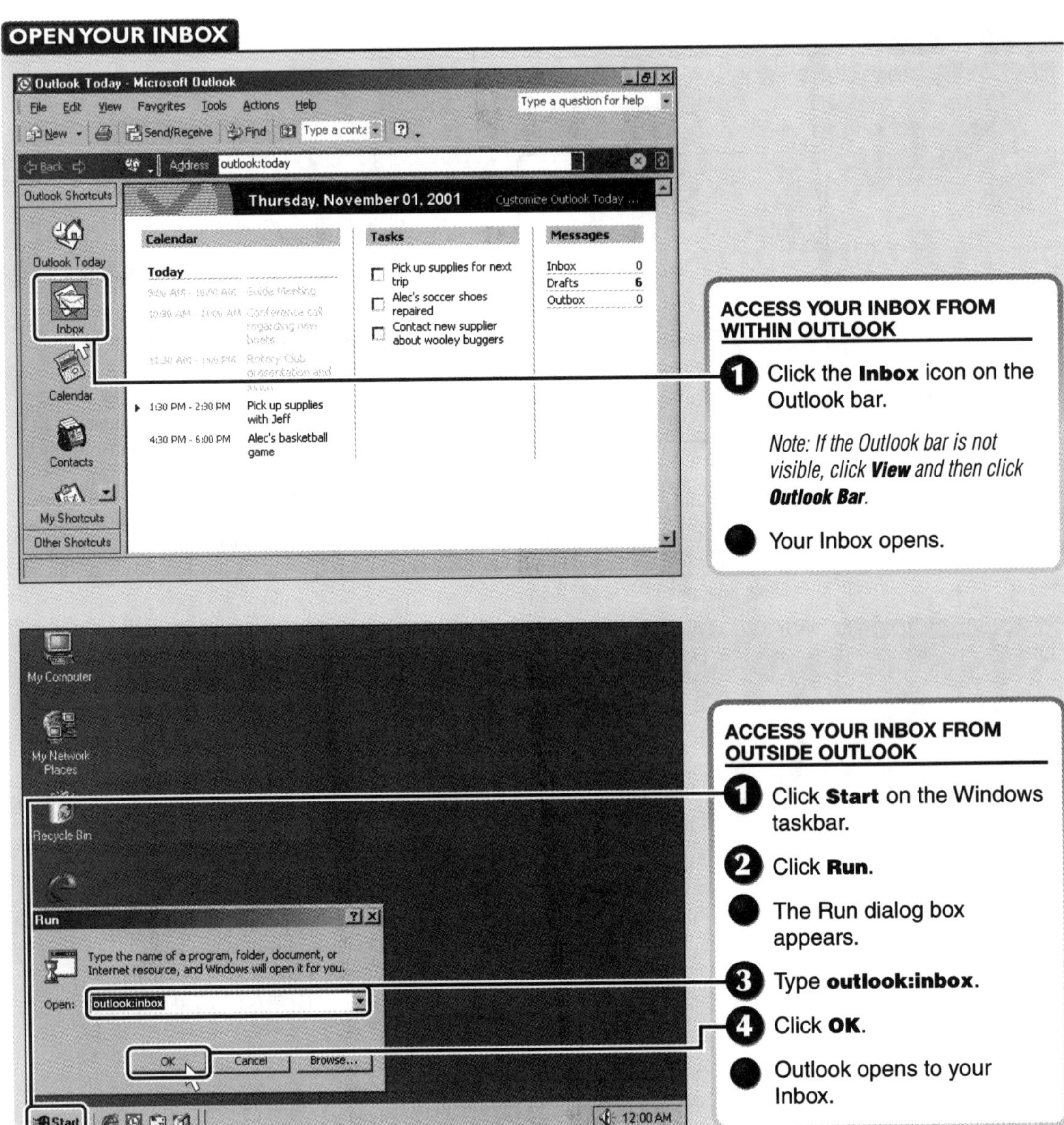

ACCESS YOUR INBOX FROM WITHIN OUTLOOK

1. Click the **Inbox** icon on the Outlook bar.

   *Note: If the Outlook bar is not visible, click **View** and then click **Outlook Bar**.*

- Your Inbox opens.

ACCESS YOUR INBOX FROM OUTSIDE OUTLOOK

1. Click **Start** on the Windows taskbar.
2. Click **Run**.
- The Run dialog box appears.
3. Type **outlook:inbox**.
4. Click **OK**.
- Outlook opens to your Inbox.

READ AN E-MAIL MESSAGE

You can open an e-mail message from your Outlook Inbox. For more on how to open your Inbox, see "Open Your Inbox," earlier in this chapter.

READ AN E-MAIL MESSAGE

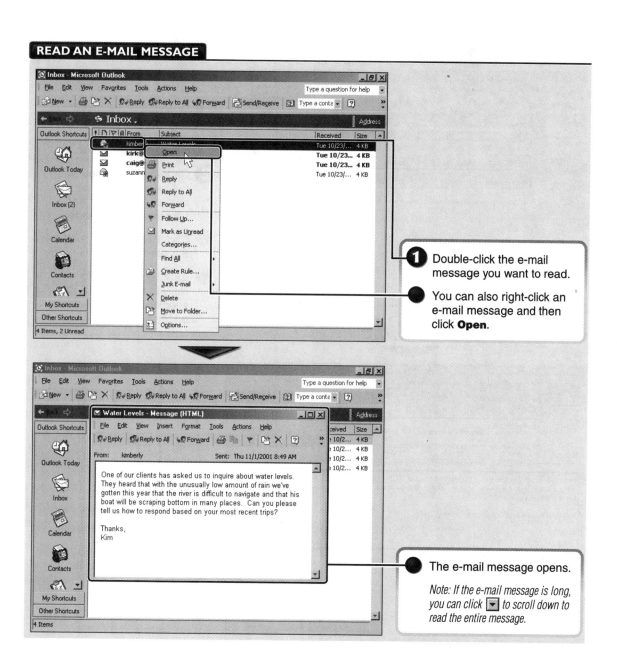

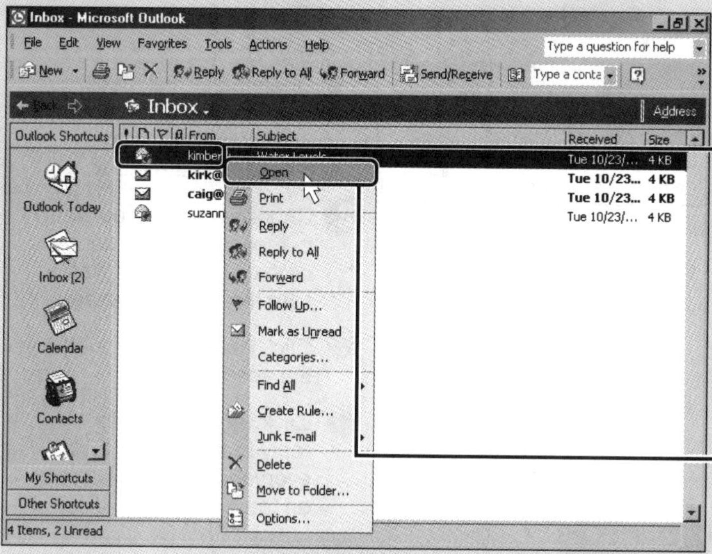

1. Double-click the e-mail message you want to read.

- You can also right-click an e-mail message and then click **Open**.

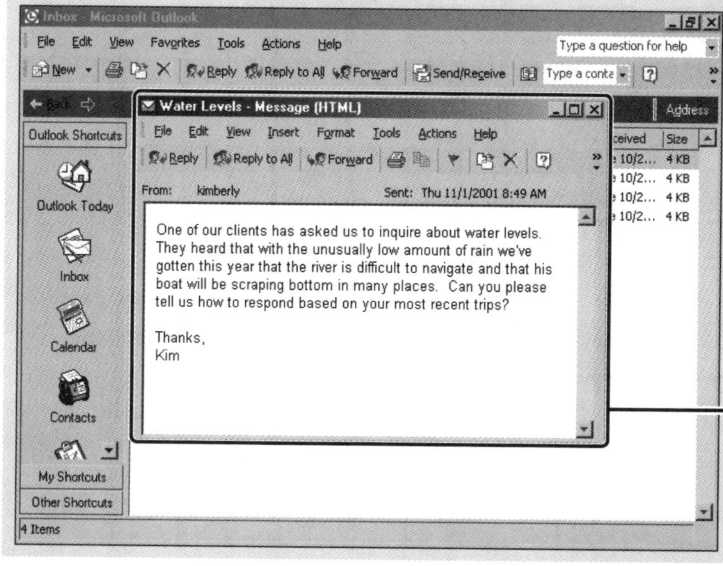

- The e-mail message opens.

Note: If the e-mail message is long, you can click ▾ to scroll down to read the entire message.

ANSWER AN E-MAIL MESSAGE

You can easily reply to an e-mail message you have received. For more on how to open an e-mail message, see "Read an E-mail Message," earlier in this chapter.

ANSWER AN E-MAIL MESSAGE

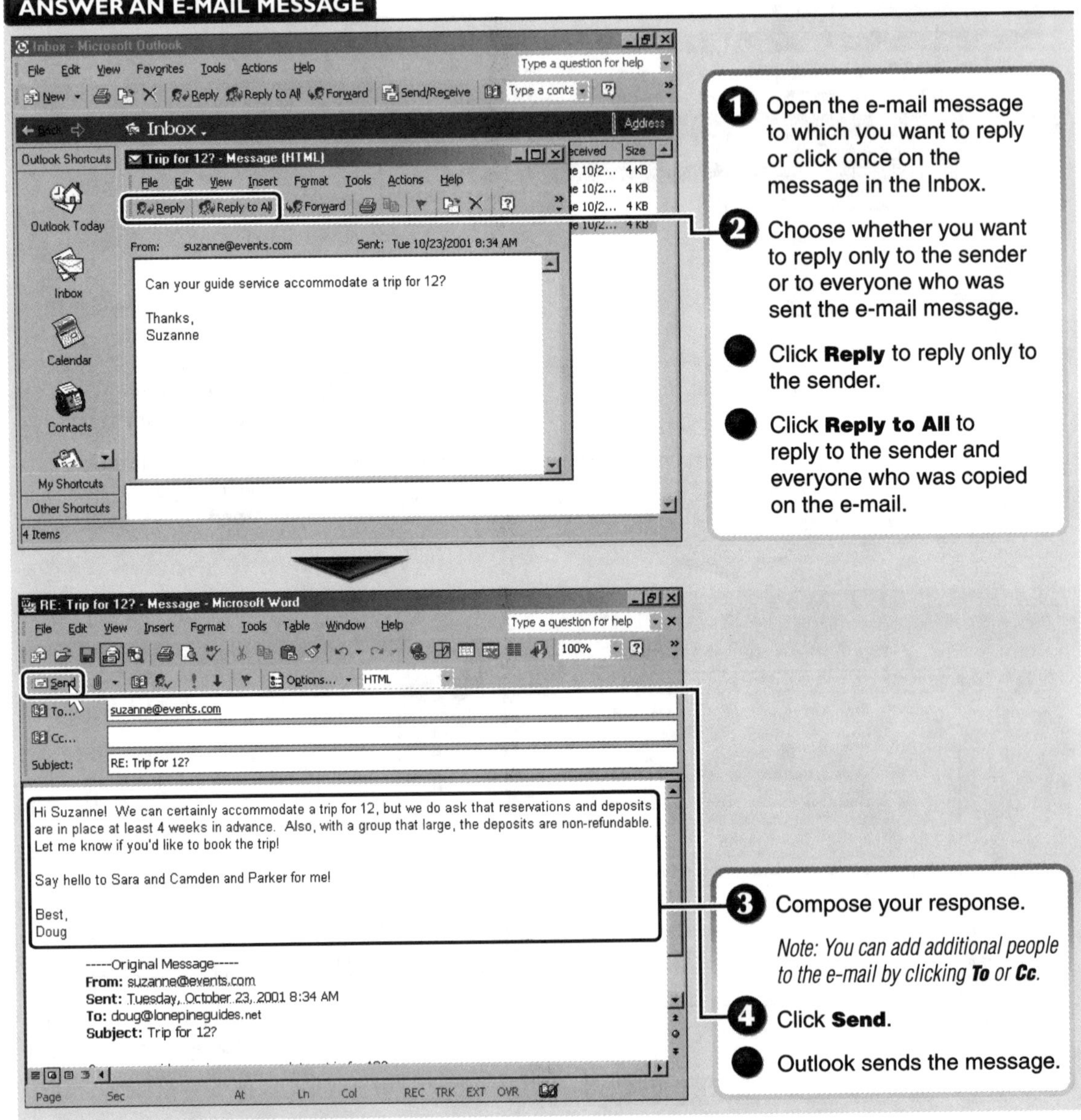

1. Open the e-mail message to which you want to reply or click once on the message in the Inbox.
2. Choose whether you want to reply only to the sender or to everyone who was sent the e-mail message.

- Click **Reply** to reply only to the sender.
- Click **Reply to All** to reply to the sender and everyone who was copied on the e-mail.

3. Compose your response.

*Note: You can add additional people to the e-mail by clicking **To** or **Cc**.*

4. Click **Send**.

- Outlook sends the message.

FORWARD AN E-MAIL MESSAGE

You can easily send an e-mail message you have received to someone else. For more on how to open an e-mail message, see "Read an E-mail Message," earlier in this chapter.

FORWARD AN E-MAIL MESSAGE

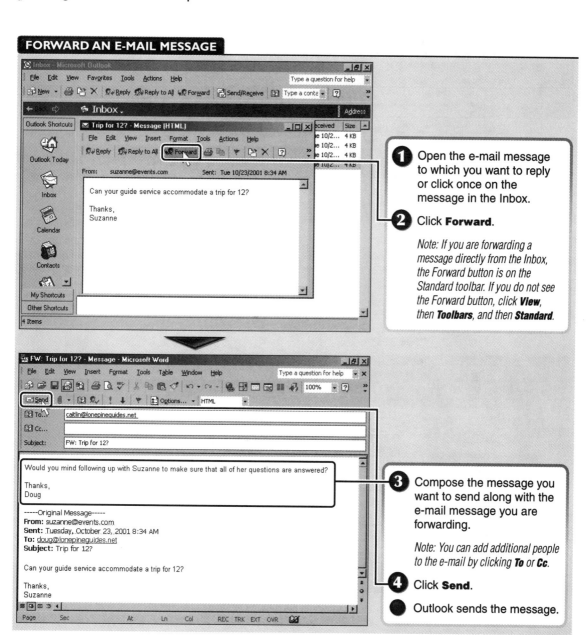

1. Open the e-mail message to which you want to reply or click once on the message in the Inbox.
2. Click **Forward**.

Note: If you are forwarding a message directly from the Inbox, the Forward button is on the Standard toolbar. If you do not see the Forward button, click ***View****, then* ***Toolbars****, and then* ***Standard****.*

3. Compose the message you want to send along with the e-mail message you are forwarding.

Note: You can add additional people to the e-mail by clicking ***To*** *or* ***Cc****.*

4. Click **Send**.

- Outlook sends the message.

CREATE A NEW E-MAIL MESSAGE

You can create a new e-mail message with just a few clicks of the mouse. Outlook gives you the option of either typing an e-mail address directly into the message or choosing an address from your personal list of contacts. If you are working on a company e-mail system, you can also choose from any company address list.

CREATE A NEW E-MAIL MESSAGE

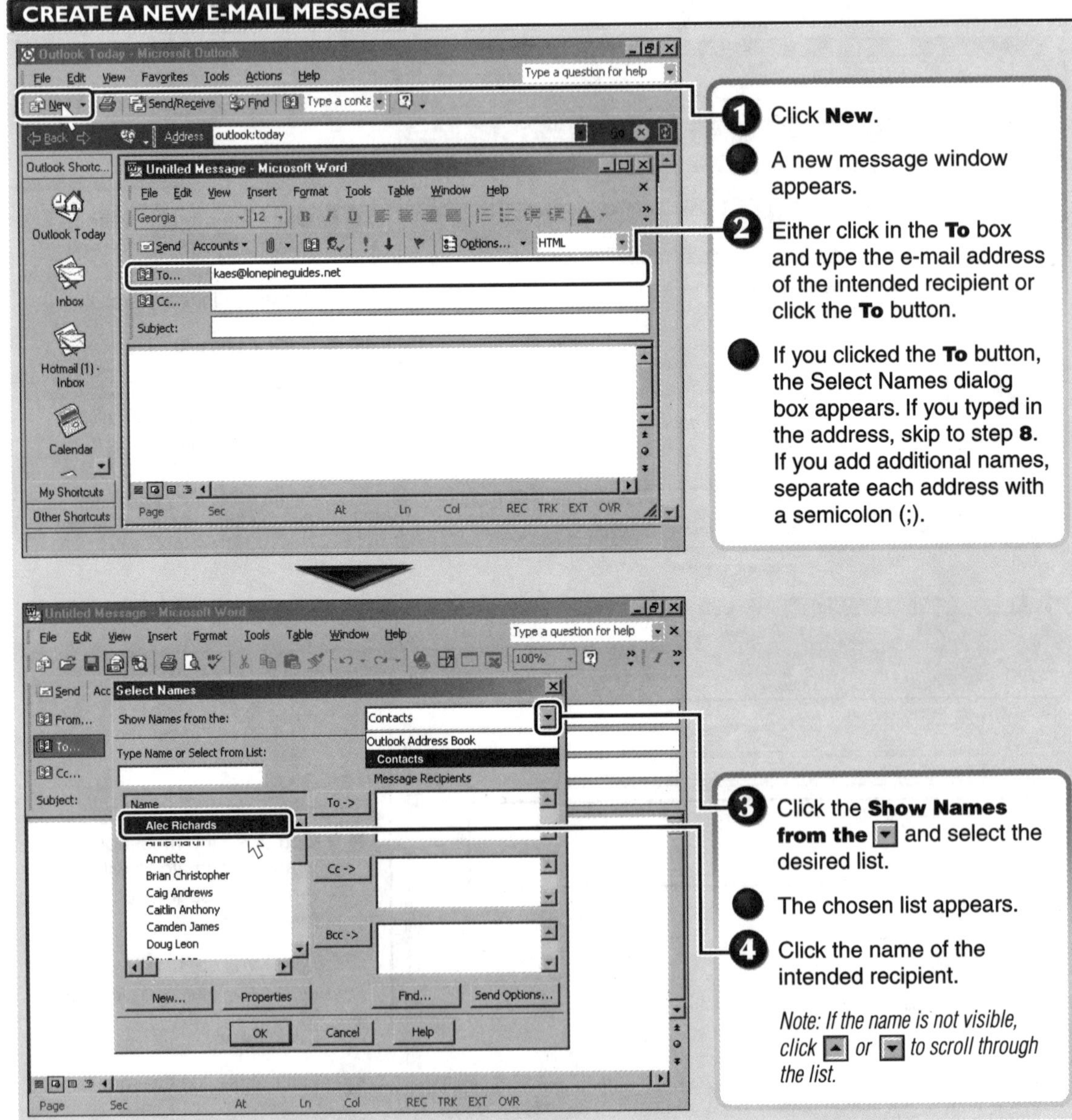

1. Click **New**.

- A new message window appears.

2. Either click in the **To** box and type the e-mail address of the intended recipient or click the **To** button.

- If you clicked the **To** button, the Select Names dialog box appears. If you typed in the address, skip to step **8**. If you add additional names, separate each address with a semicolon (;).

3. Click the **Show Names from the** ▾ and select the desired list.

- The chosen list appears.

4. Click the name of the intended recipient.

Note: If the name is not visible, click ▴ or ▾ to scroll through the list.

in an instant

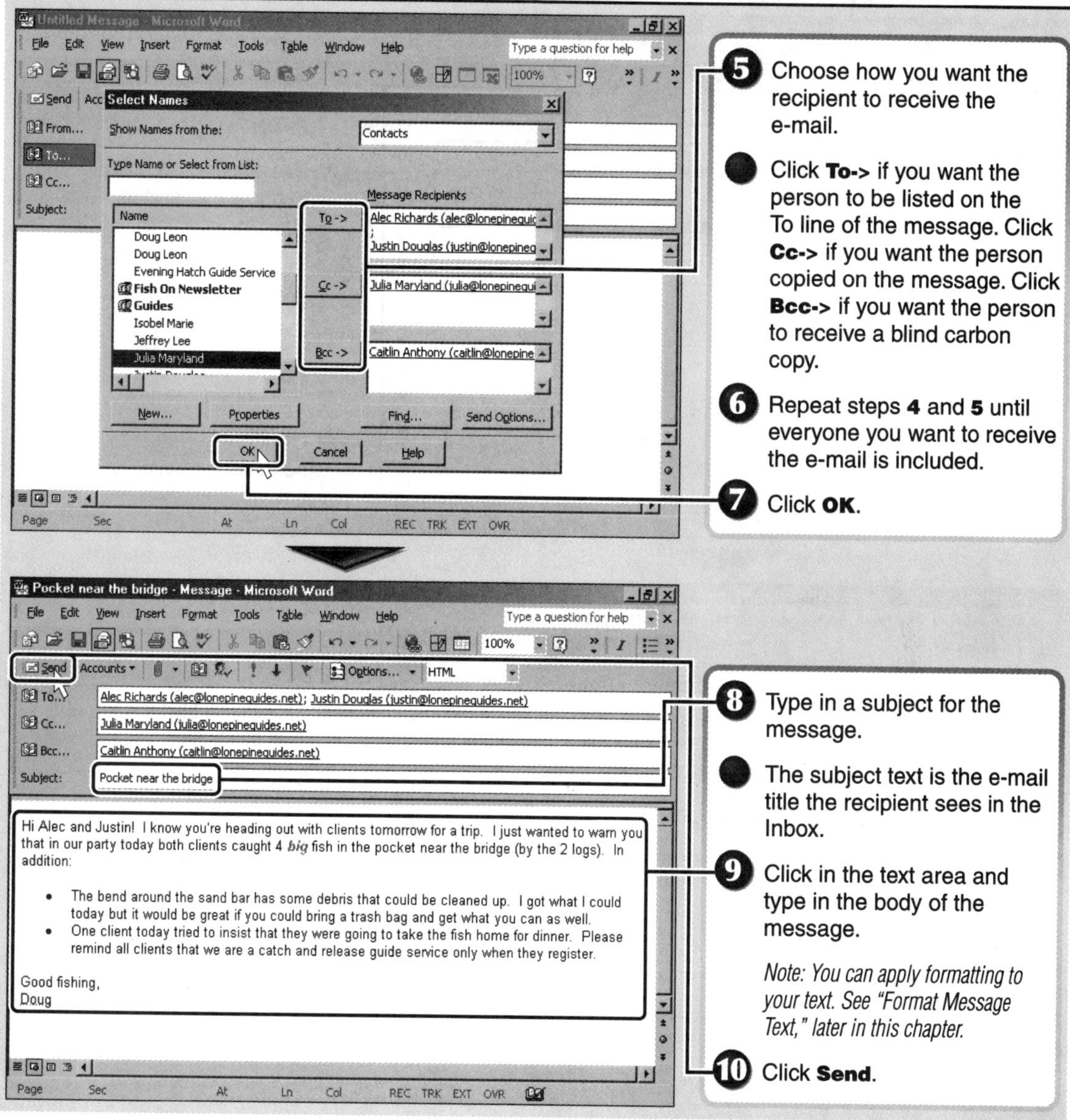

5 Choose how you want the recipient to receive the e-mail.

- Click **To->** if you want the person to be listed on the To line of the message. Click **Cc->** if you want the person copied on the message. Click **Bcc->** if you want the person to receive a blind carbon copy.

6 Repeat steps **4** and **5** until everyone you want to receive the e-mail is included.

7 Click **OK**.

8 Type in a subject for the message.

- The subject text is the e-mail title the recipient sees in the Inbox.

9 Click in the text area and type in the body of the message.

Note: You can apply formatting to your text. See "Format Message Text," later in this chapter.

10 Click **Send**.

FORMAT MESSAGE TEXT

Outlook offers you several formatting options for your message text. To use the formatting buttons, simply select the text and then click the appropriate button on the Formatting toolbar. You can also click where you want the special formatting to begin and click the formatting button before typing the text. Formatting buttons appear depressed when activated; to turn them off, just click the button again.

FORMAT MESSAGE TEXT

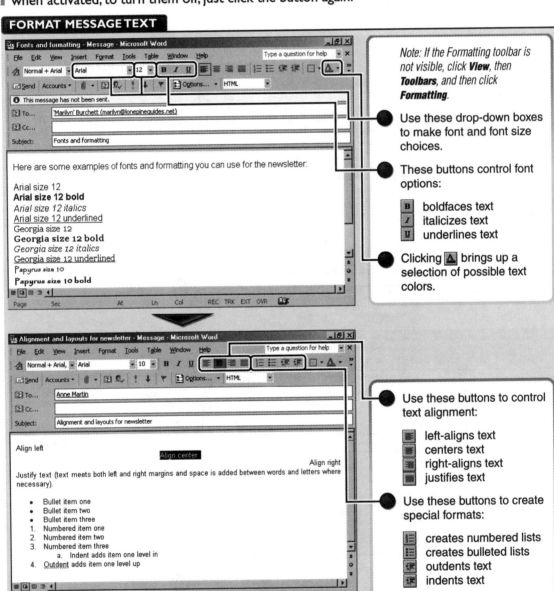

*Note: If the Formatting toolbar is not visible, click **View**, then **Toolbars**, and then click **Formatting**.*

- Use these drop-down boxes to make font and font size choices.
- These buttons control font options:
  - B boldfaces text
  - I italicizes text
  - U underlines text
- Clicking A brings up a selection of possible text colors.

- Use these buttons to control text alignment:
  - left-aligns text
  - centers text
  - right-aligns text
  - justifies text
- Use these buttons to create special formats:
  - creates numbered lists
  - creates bulleted lists
  - outdents text
  - indents text

SAVE A MESSAGE AS A FILE

You can save e-mail messages as files if you want to access them from non-Microsoft Office XP applications. Saving e-mail messages as HTML allows you to link to them from Web pages or other documents.

SAVE A MESSAGE AS A FILE

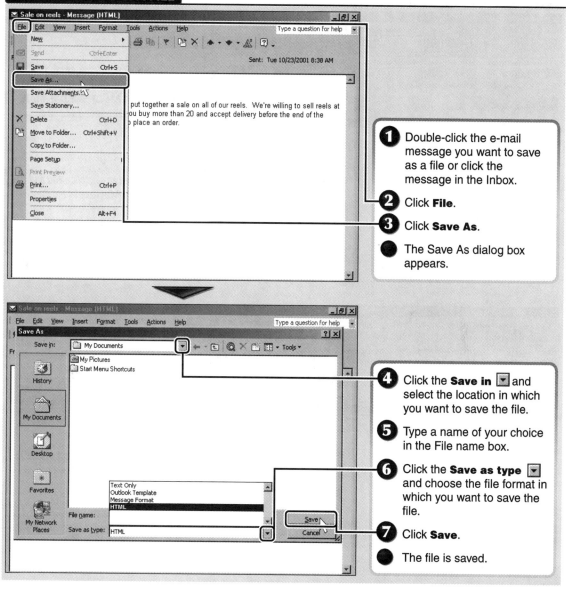

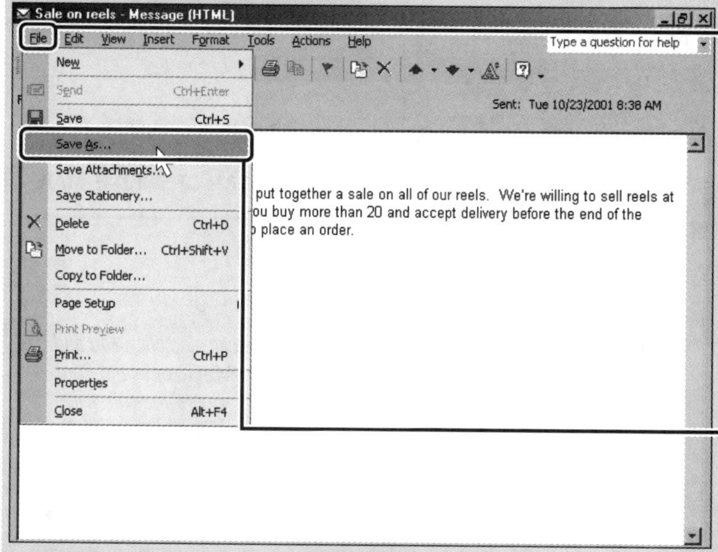

1. Double-click the e-mail message you want to save as a file or click the message in the Inbox.
2. Click **File**.
3. Click **Save As**.

- The Save As dialog box appears.

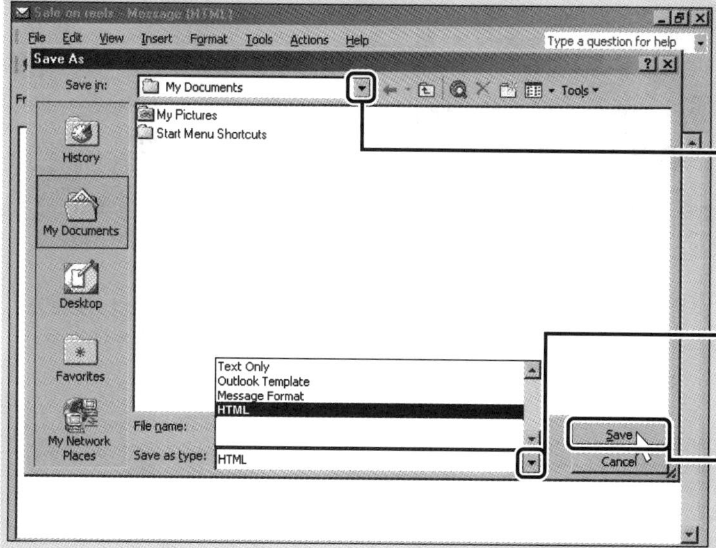

4. Click the **Save in** ▾ and select the location in which you want to save the file.
5. Type a name of your choice in the File name box.
6. Click the **Save as type** ▾ and choose the file format in which you want to save the file.
7. Click **Save**.

- The file is saved.

PRINT A MESSAGE

Outlook allows you to print messages in a variety of ways. You can print a message while it is open; you can print single or multiple e-mail messages from the Inbox; and you can print by right-clicking from the Inbox. You can even print a summary of the number of e-mail messages you have from Outlook Today.

PRINT A MESSAGE

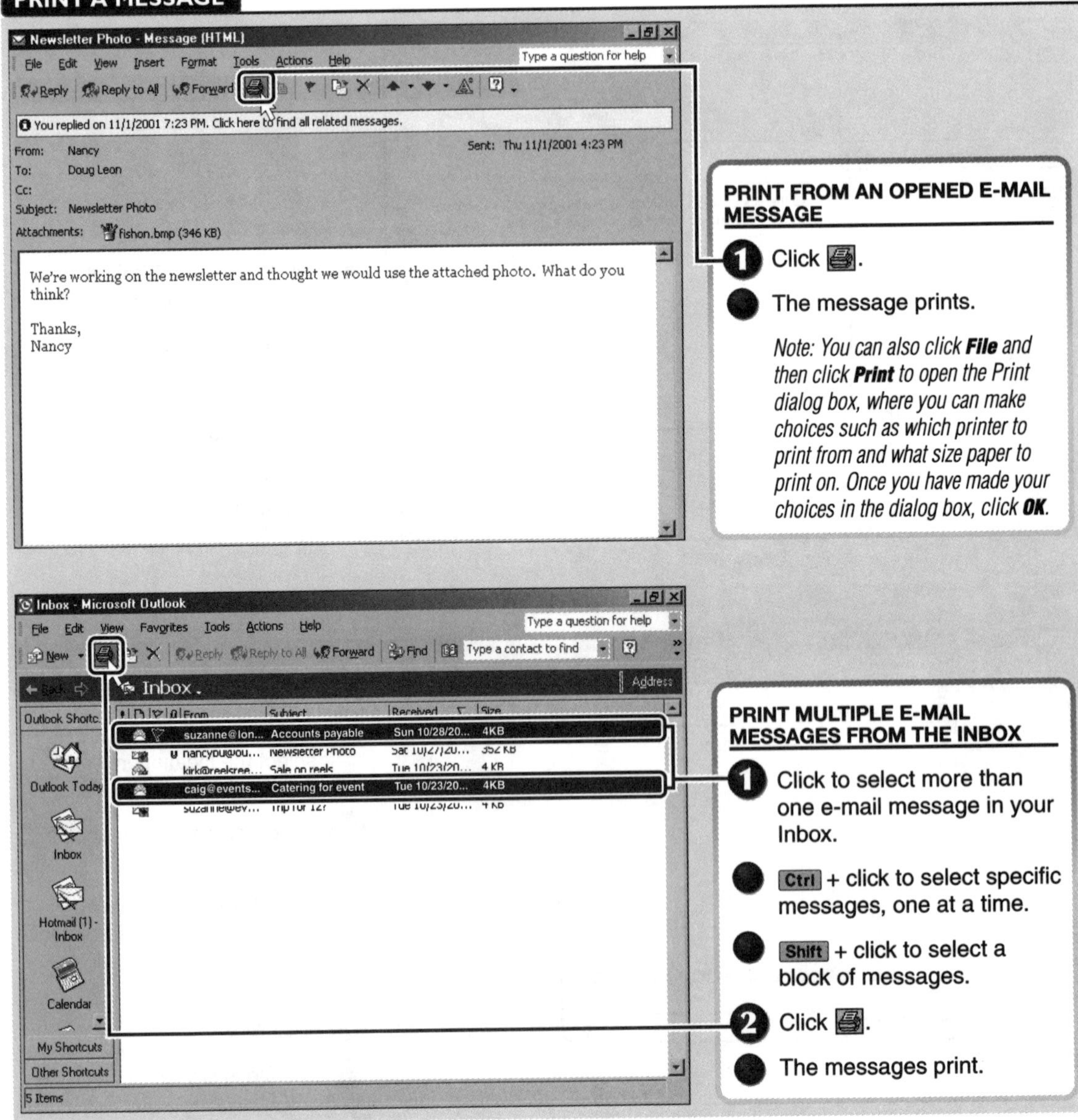

PRINT FROM AN OPENED E-MAIL MESSAGE

1. Click 🖨.

- The message prints.

*Note: You can also click **File** and then click **Print** to open the Print dialog box, where you can make choices such as which printer to print from and what size paper to print on. Once you have made your choices in the dialog box, click **OK**.*

PRINT MULTIPLE E-MAIL MESSAGES FROM THE INBOX

1. Click to select more than one e-mail message in your Inbox.

- **Ctrl** + click to select specific messages, one at a time.
- **Shift** + click to select a block of messages.

2. Click 🖨.

- The messages print.

in an instant

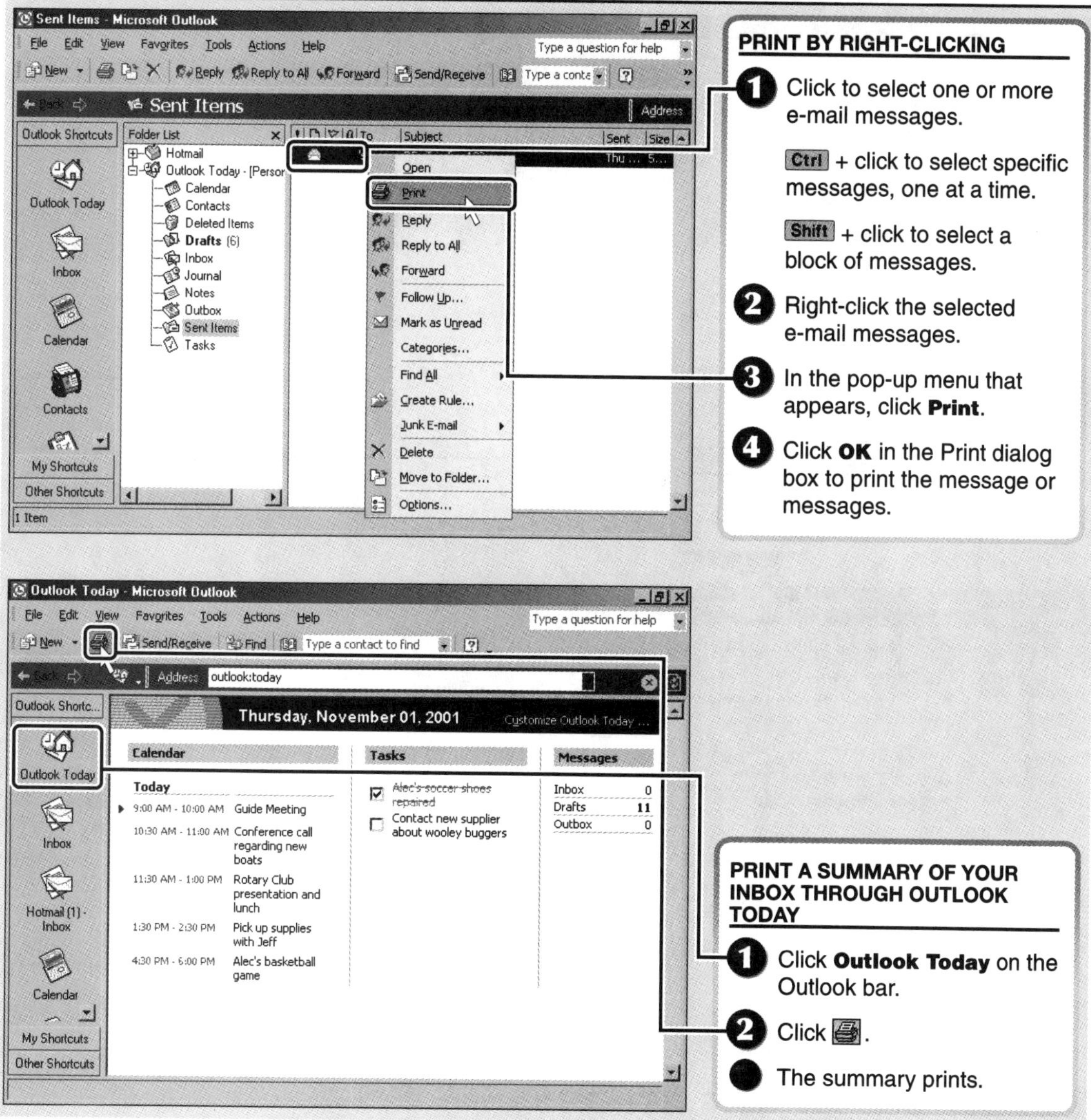

PRINT BY RIGHT-CLICKING

1. Click to select one or more e-mail messages.

   Ctrl + click to select specific messages, one at a time.

   Shift + click to select a block of messages.

2. Right-click the selected e-mail messages.

3. In the pop-up menu that appears, click **Print**.

4. Click **OK** in the Print dialog box to print the message or messages.

PRINT A SUMMARY OF YOUR INBOX THROUGH OUTLOOK TODAY

1. Click **Outlook Today** on the Outlook bar.

2. Click the Print button.

- The summary prints.

CHANGE NEW E-MAIL NOTIFICATIONS

You can easily change how you find out that new e-mail messages have arrived. If you work primarily in applications other than Outlook, you probably keep Outlook open but minimize it. You can tell Outlook to play a sound, briefly change the mouse cursor, or show an envelope icon in the Windows taskbar so that you know when new e-mail messages have arrived.

CHANGE NEW E-MAIL NOTIFICATIONS

1 Click **Tools**.

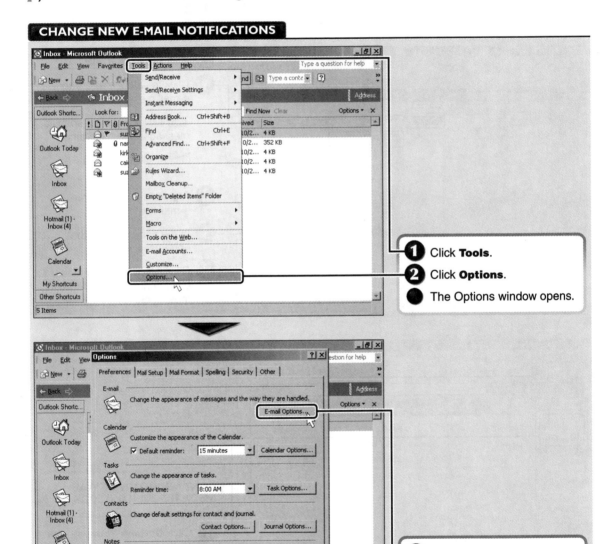

2 Click **Options**.

- The Options window opens.

3 Click **E-mail Options**.

- The E-mail Options window opens.

in an instant

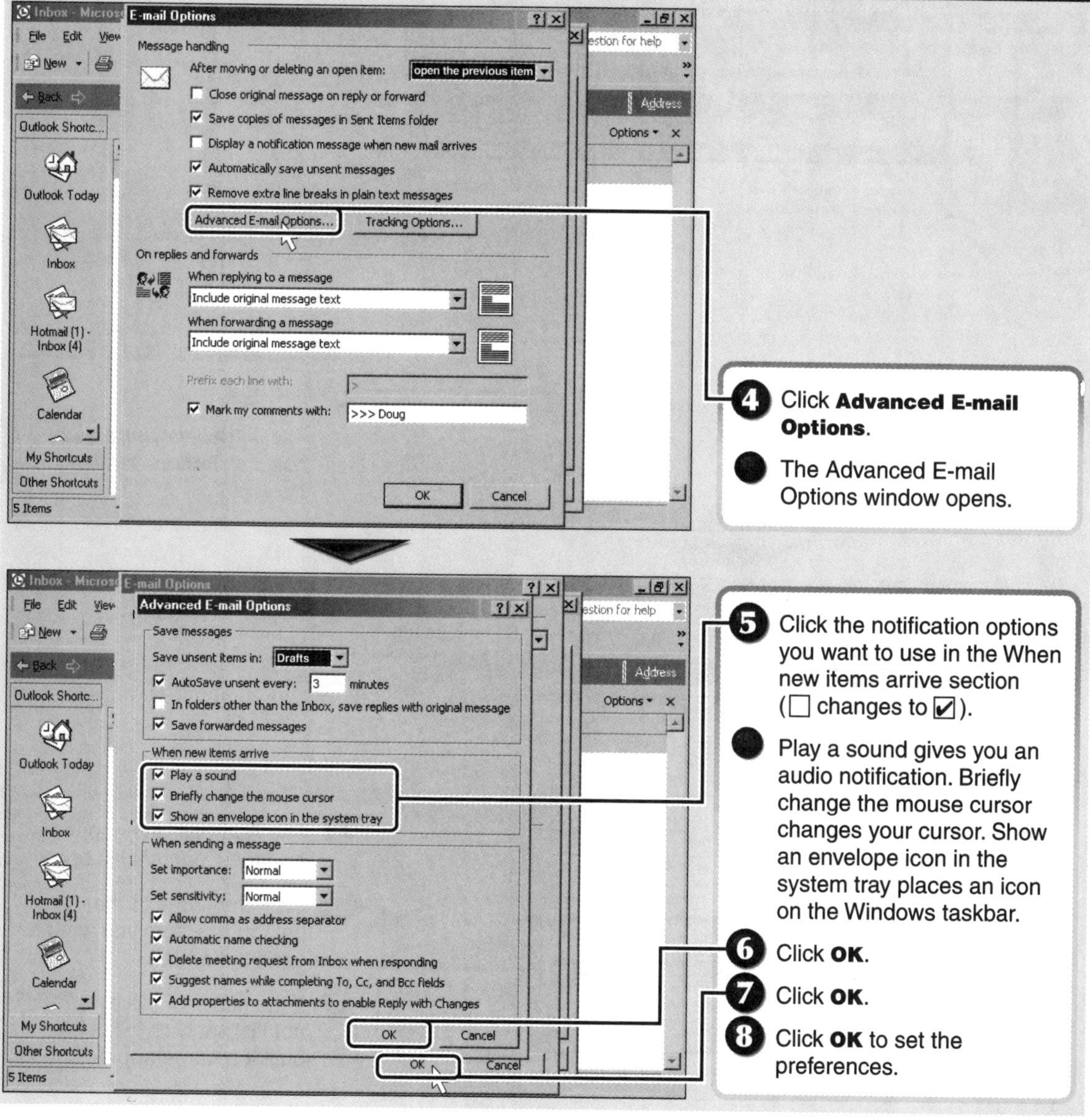

4. Click **Advanced E-mail Options**.
   - The Advanced E-mail Options window opens.

5. Click the notification options you want to use in the When new items arrive section (☐ changes to ☑).
   - Play a sound gives you an audio notification. Briefly change the mouse cursor changes your cursor. Show an envelope icon in the system tray places an icon on the Windows taskbar.

6. Click **OK**.

7. Click **OK**.

8. Click **OK** to set the preferences.

SEND E-MAIL TO A CONTACT

You can access your Outlook contacts while you are still in your Inbox. Sending an e-mail to a contact without opening Contacts view takes only a few easy clicks.

SEND E-MAIL TO A CONTACT

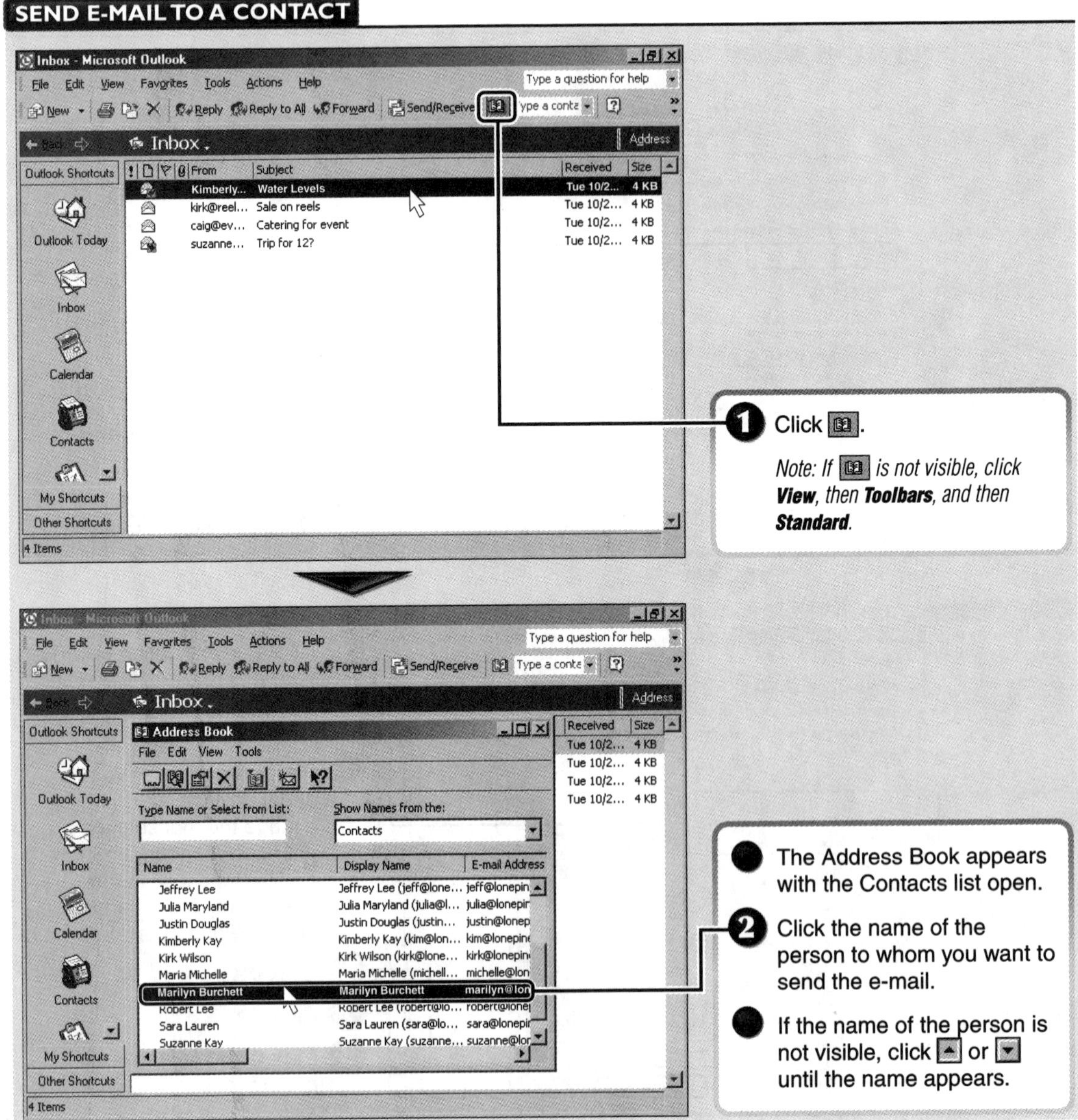

1. Click [icon].

   *Note: If [icon] is not visible, click **View**, then **Toolbars**, and then **Standard**.*

- The Address Book appears with the Contacts list open.

2. Click the name of the person to whom you want to send the e-mail.

- If the name of the person is not visible, click [up] or [down] until the name appears.

in an instant

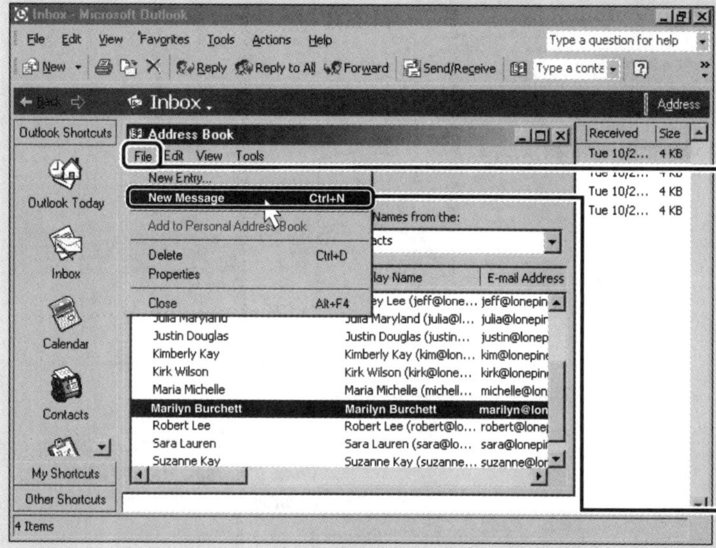

3 Click **File**.

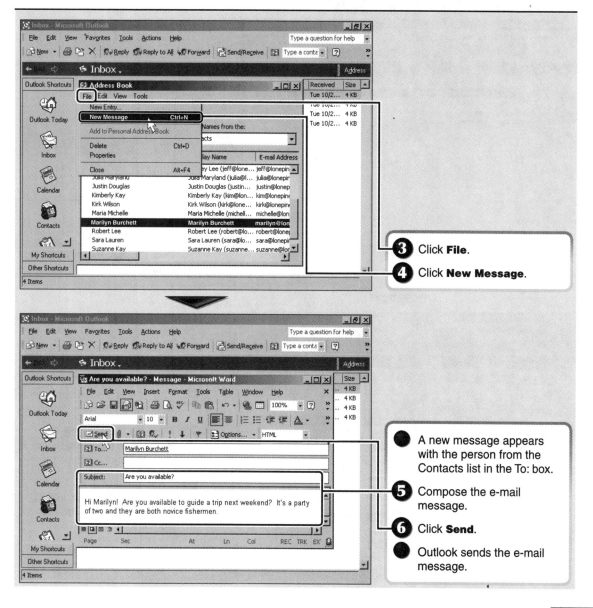

4 Click **New Message**.

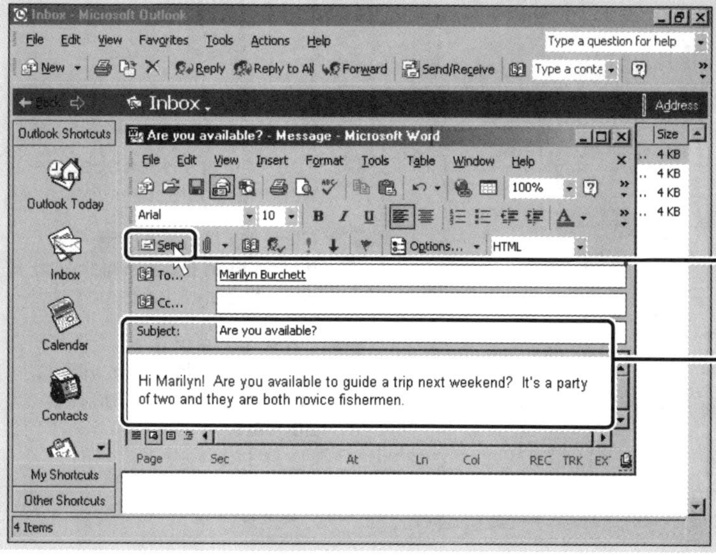

- A new message appears with the person from the Contacts list in the To: box.

5 Compose the e-mail message.

6 Click **Send**.

- Outlook sends the e-mail message.

SEND E-MAIL TO A DISTRIBUTION LIST

You can send e-mail to a group of people at one time instead of individually adding them to an e-mail message. You can do this by creating what Outlook calls a *distribution list* and sending the e-mail to the distribution list. For information on how to create a distribution list, see Chapter 9.

SEND E-MAIL TO A DISTRIBUTION LIST

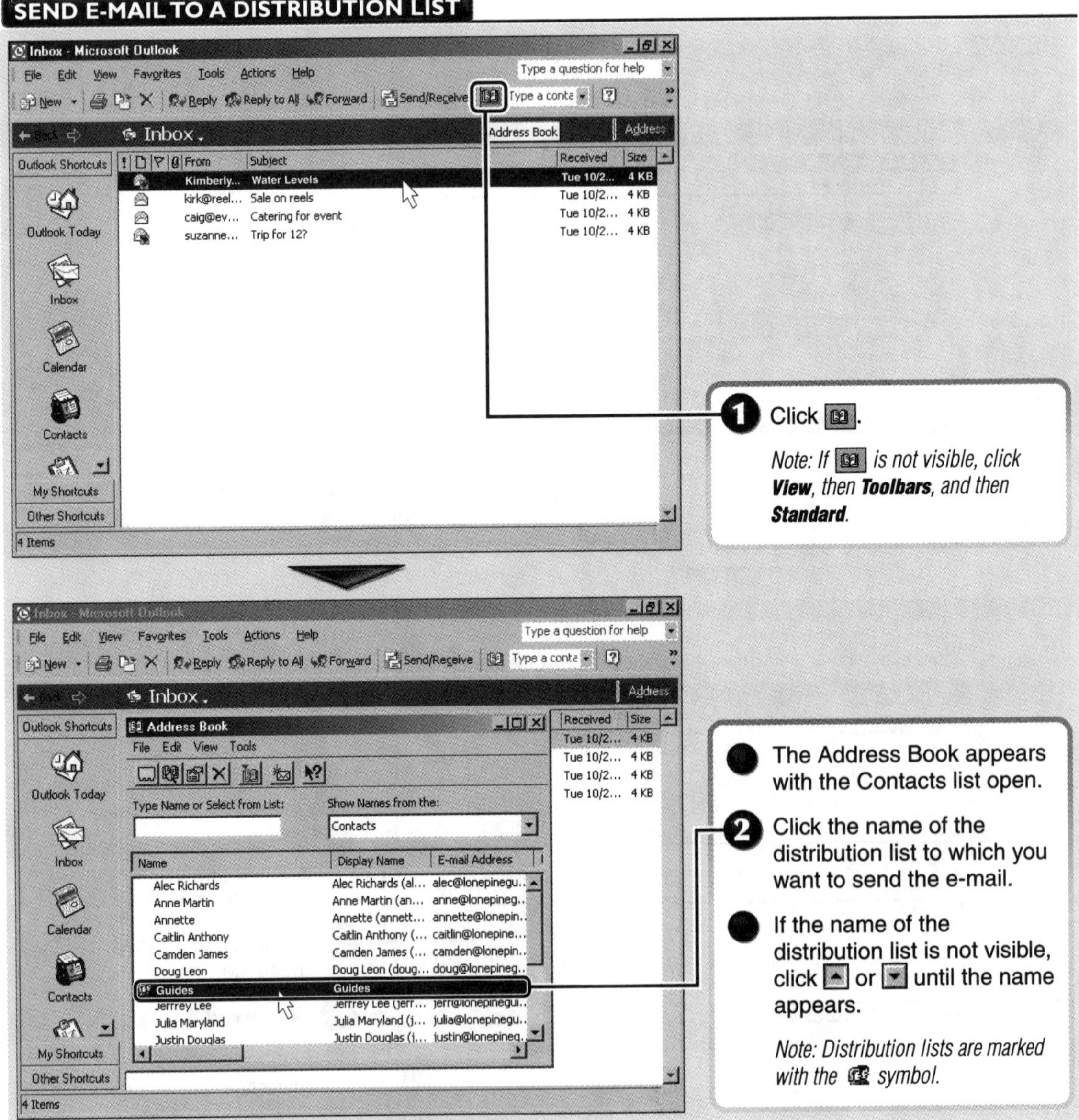

1 Click .

Note: If is not visible, click ***View****, then* ***Toolbars****, and then* ***Standard****.*

- The Address Book appears with the Contacts list open.

2 Click the name of the distribution list to which you want to send the e-mail.

- If the name of the distribution list is not visible, click or until the name appears.

Note: Distribution lists are marked with the symbol.

in an instant

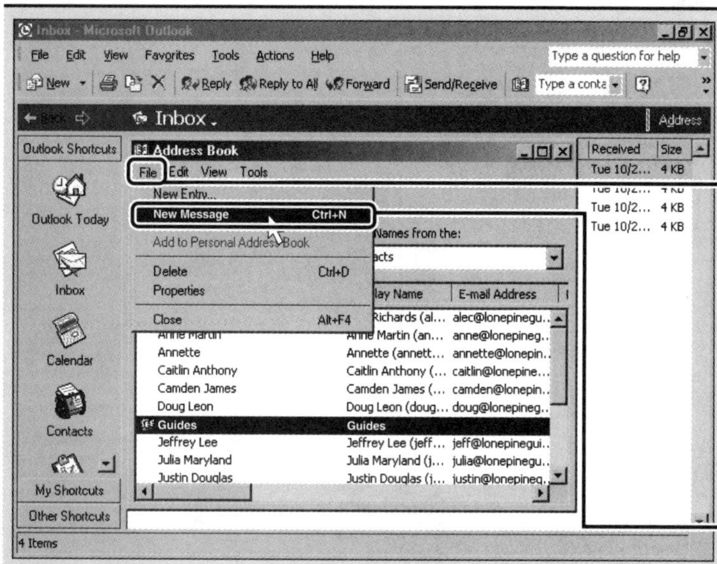

3 Click **File**.

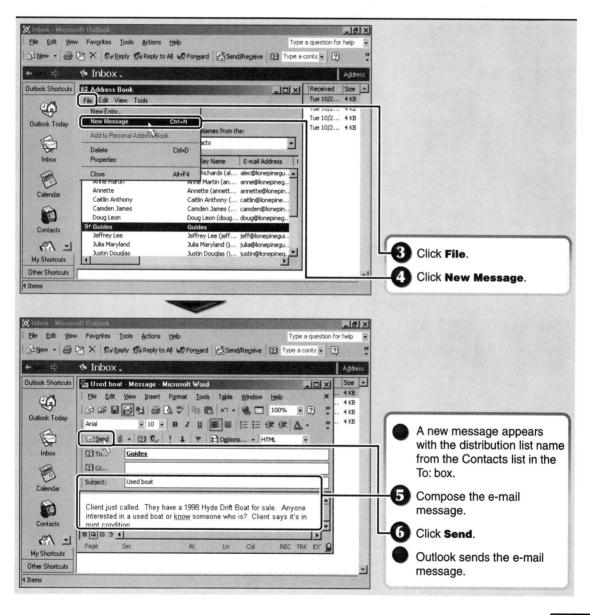

4 Click **New Message**.

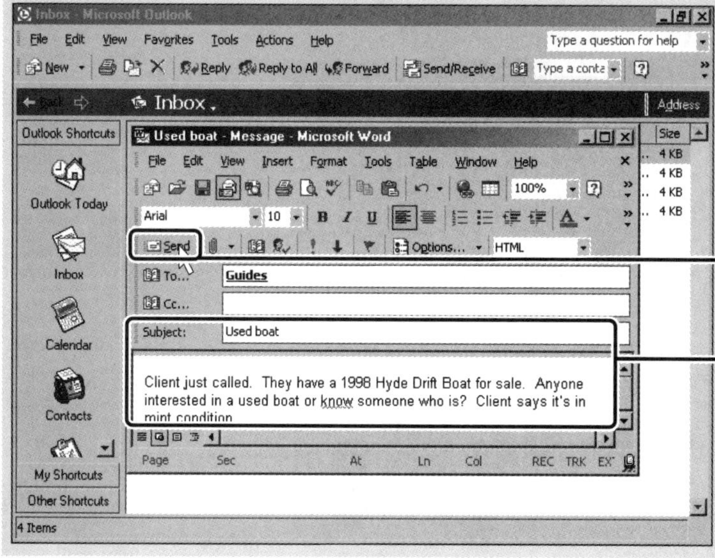

- A new message appears with the distribution list name from the Contacts list in the To: box.

5 Compose the e-mail message.

6 Click **Send**.

- Outlook sends the e-mail message.

SET FREQUENCY FOR SEND/RECEIVE

Outlook routinely sends and receives e-mail without much fanfare. Should you need to prompt Outlook to send an outgoing message or check for incoming messages, simply click the Send/Receive button on the Standard toolbar. Outlook also offers you the option of specifying exactly at what intervals it should send or receive e-mail.

SET FREQUENCY FOR SEND/RECEIVE

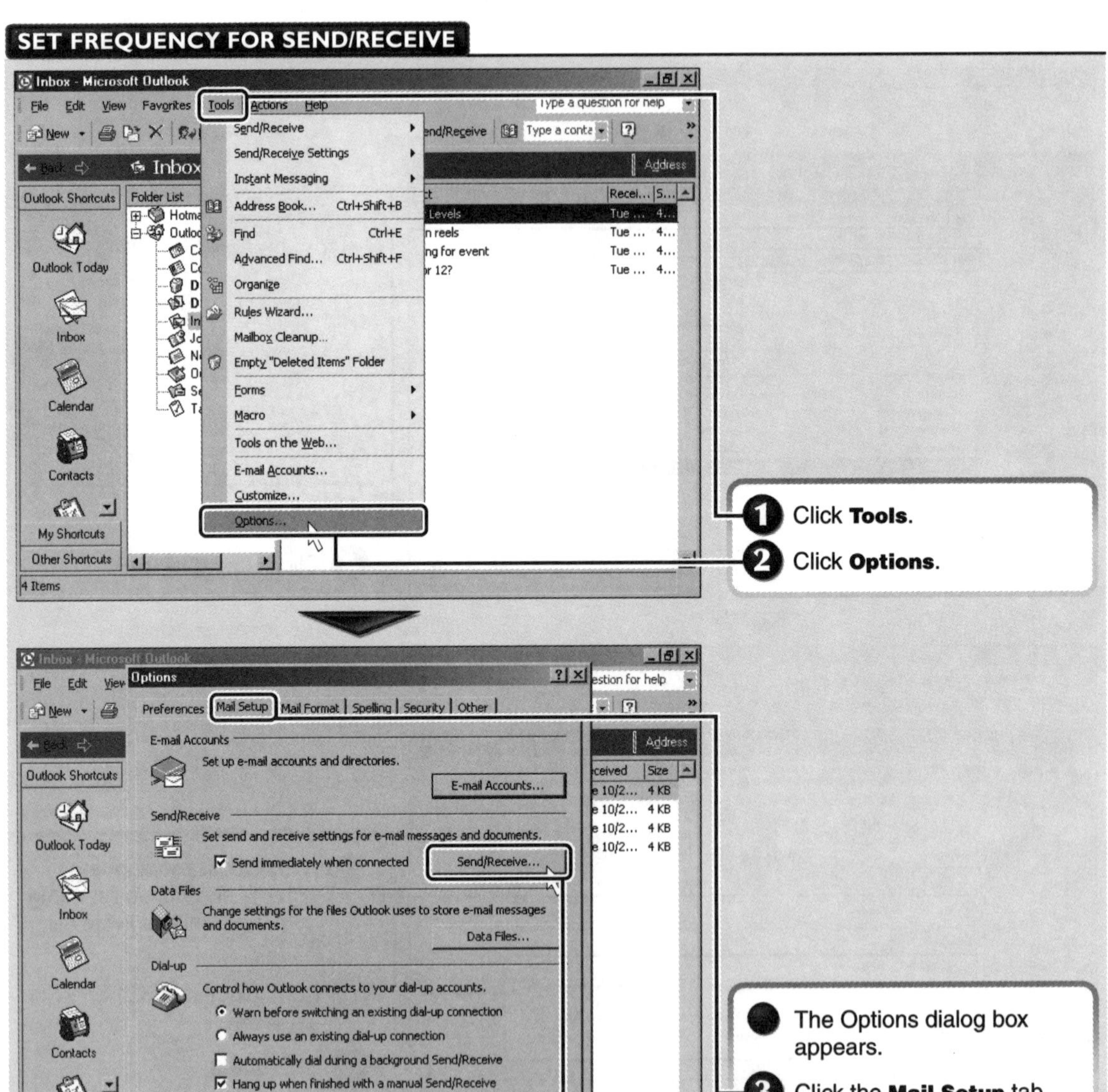

1 Click **Tools**.

2 Click **Options**.

- The Options dialog box appears.

3 Click the **Mail Setup** tab.

4 Click **Send/Receive**.

in an instant

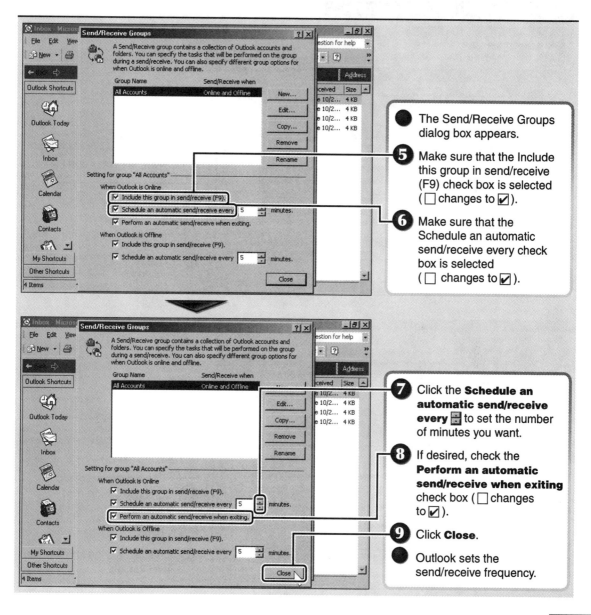

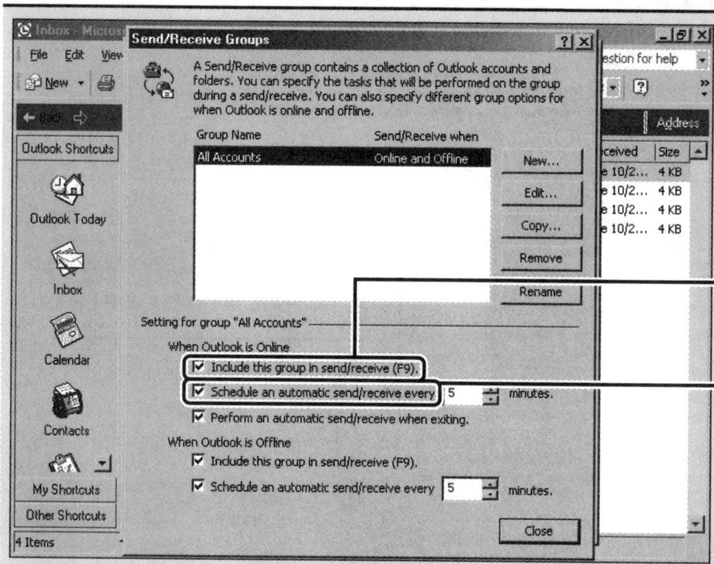

- The Send/Receive Groups dialog box appears.

5 Make sure that the Include this group in send/receive (F9) check box is selected (☐ changes to ☑).

6 Make sure that the Schedule an automatic send/receive every check box is selected (☐ changes to ☑).

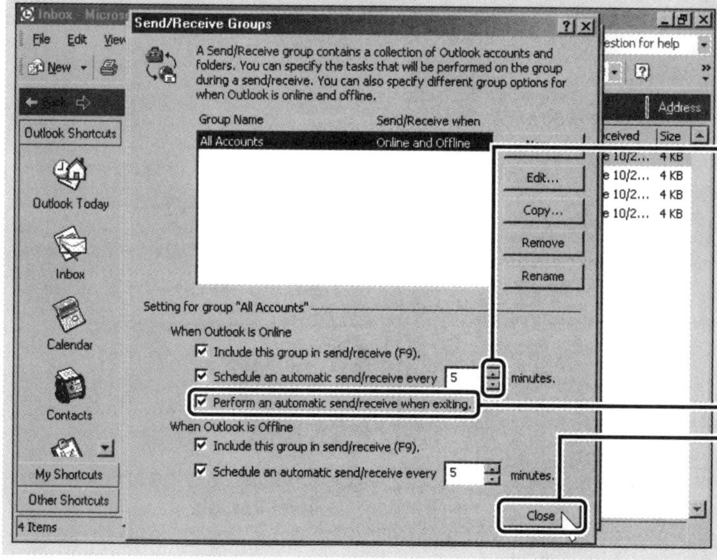

7 Click the **Schedule an automatic send/receive every** ⬍ to set the number of minutes you want.

8 If desired, check the **Perform an automatic send/receive when exiting** check box (☐ changes to ☑).

9 Click **Close**.

- Outlook sets the send/receive frequency.

SET AND IDENTIFY E-MAIL IMPORTANCE

You can alert recipients of your e-mail message to the importance of the contents by setting the importance level. By default, e-mails are set to normal importance, but you can also set e-mail to low or high importance levels. Once you have received a message, you can easily identify the importance level by checking the Inbox or the message itself.

SET AND IDENTIFY E-MAIL IMPORTANCE

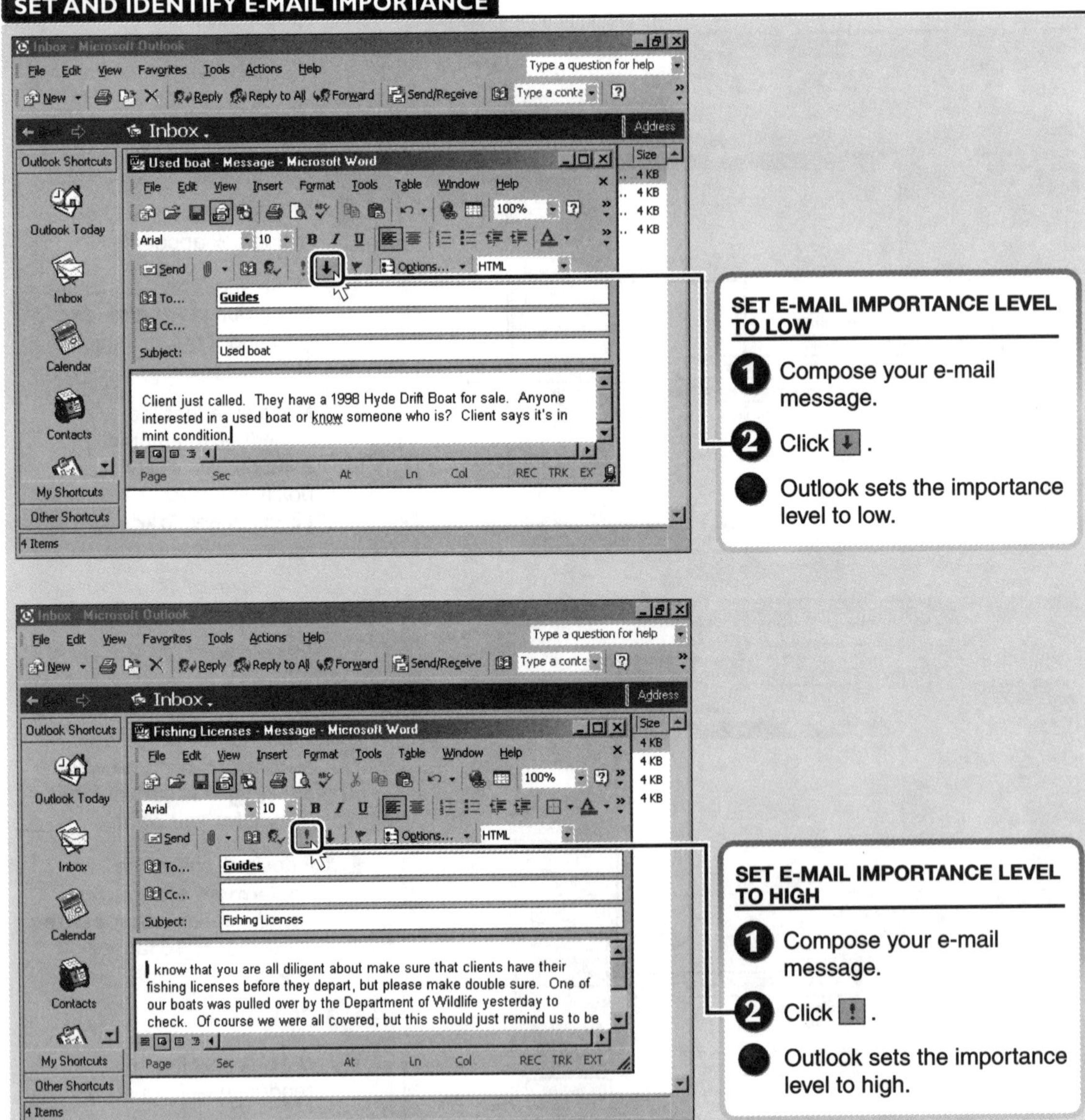

SET E-MAIL IMPORTANCE LEVEL TO LOW

1. Compose your e-mail message.
2. Click ↓.

- Outlook sets the importance level to low.

SET E-MAIL IMPORTANCE LEVEL TO HIGH

1. Compose your e-mail message.
2. Click !.

- Outlook sets the importance level to high.

in an instant

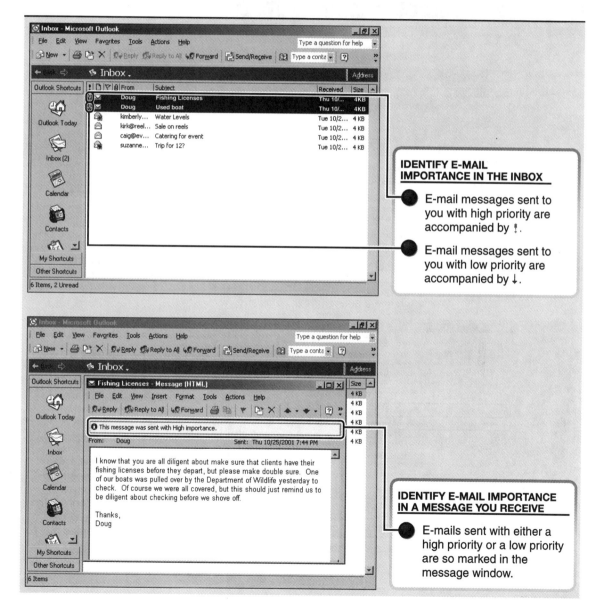

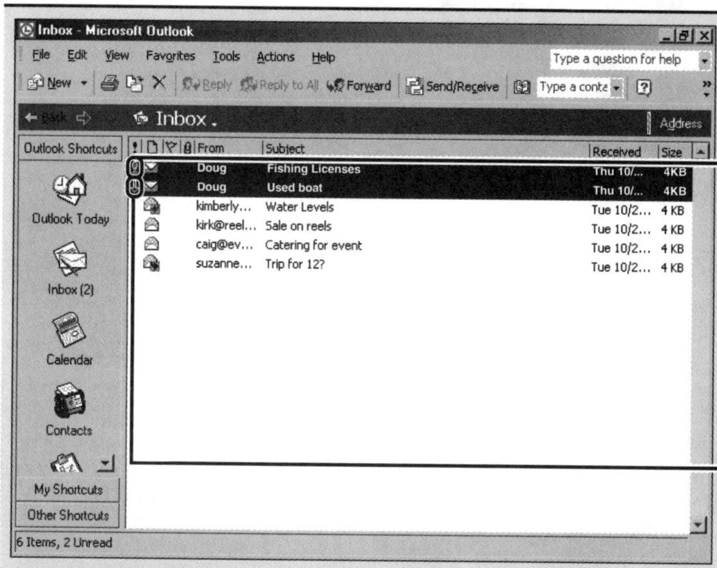

IDENTIFY E-MAIL IMPORTANCE IN THE INBOX

- E-mail messages sent to you with high priority are accompanied by !.
- E-mail messages sent to you with low priority are accompanied by ↓.

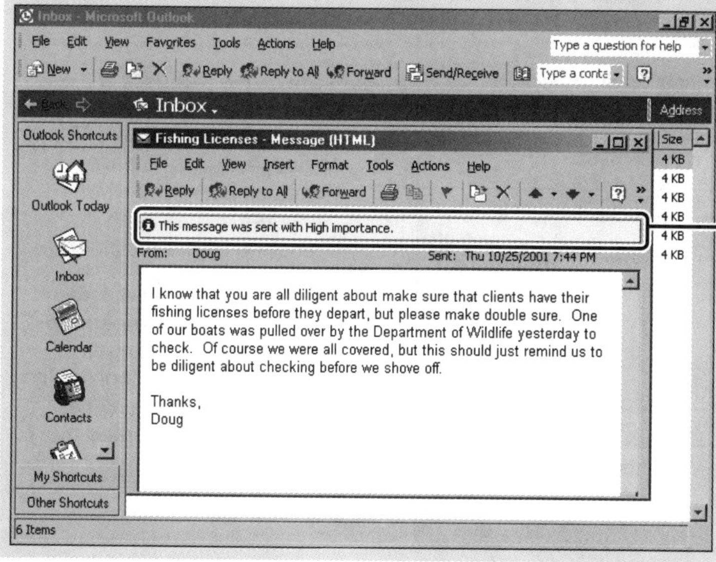

IDENTIFY E-MAIL IMPORTANCE IN A MESSAGE YOU RECEIVE

- E-mails sent with either a high priority or a low priority are so marked in the message window.

REQUEST OR RESPOND TO READ OR DELIVERY RECEIPT

When a message you send is really important, you can request an e-mail notification when the message has been received or read by the recipient. You may also be asked to respond to a read or delivery receipt request by the sender of an e-mail addressed to you.

REQUEST OR RESPOND TO READ OR DELIVERY RECEIPT

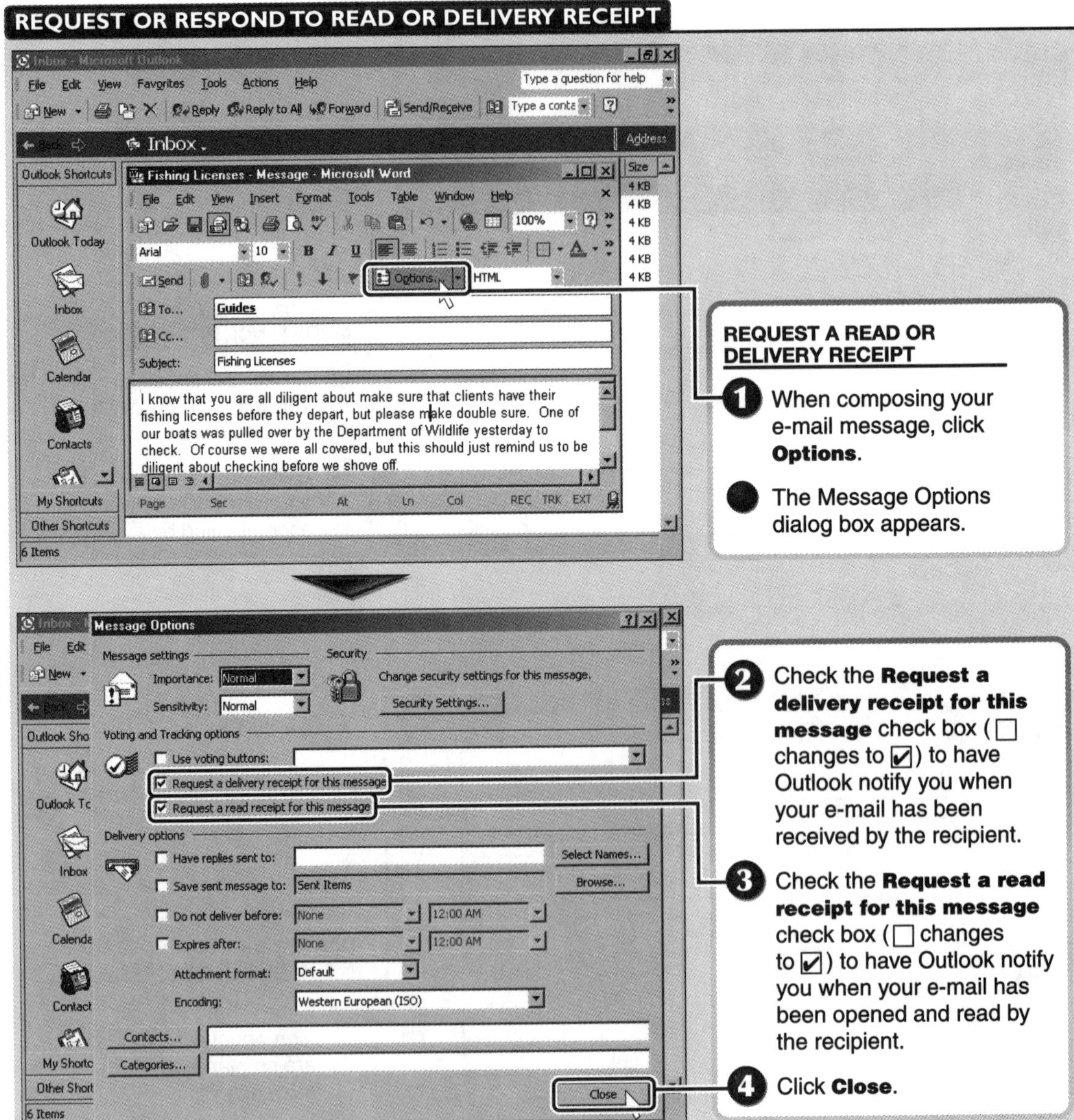

REQUEST A READ OR DELIVERY RECEIPT

1. When composing your e-mail message, click **Options**.

- The Message Options dialog box appears.

2. Check the **Request a delivery receipt for this message** check box (☐ changes to ☑) to have Outlook notify you when your e-mail has been received by the recipient.

3. Check the **Request a read receipt for this message** check box (☐ changes to ☑) to have Outlook notify you when your e-mail has been opened and read by the recipient.

4. Click **Close**.

in an instant

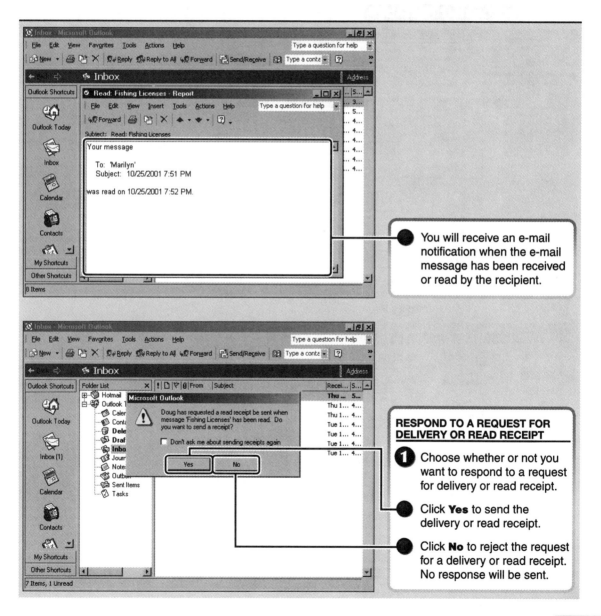

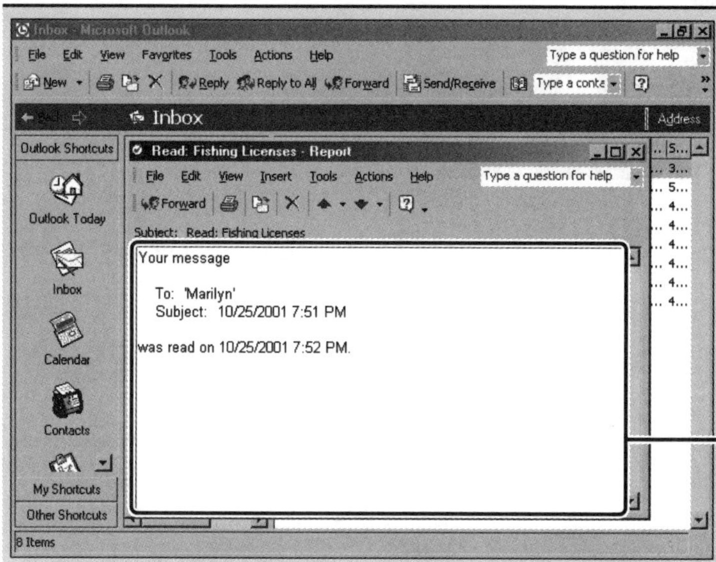

- You will receive an e-mail notification when the e-mail message has been received or read by the recipient.

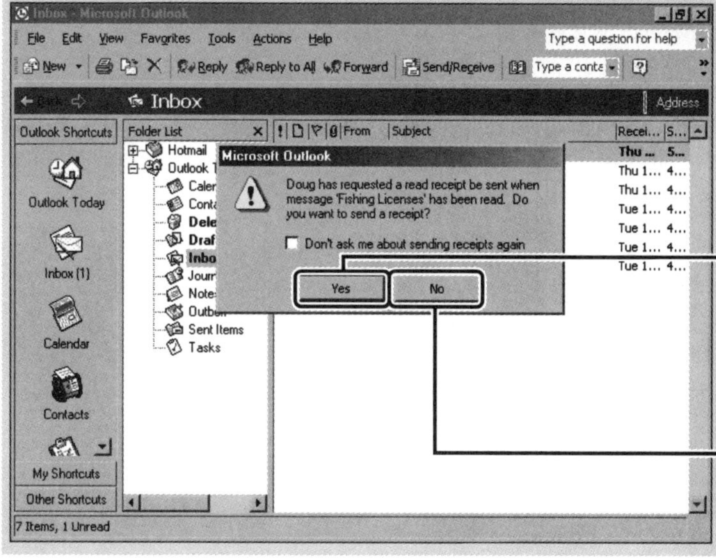

RESPOND TO A REQUEST FOR DELIVERY OR READ RECEIPT

1. Choose whether or not you want to respond to a request for delivery or read receipt.

- Click **Yes** to send the delivery or read receipt.
- Click **No** to reject the request for a delivery or read receipt. No response will be sent.

SAVE A COPY OF SENT MESSAGES

You can choose to automatically save e-mail messages that you send. Saved messages are collected in the Sent Mail folder. Automatically saving e-mails you send is a convenient way to keep a record of your messages.

SAVE A COPY OF SENT MESSAGES

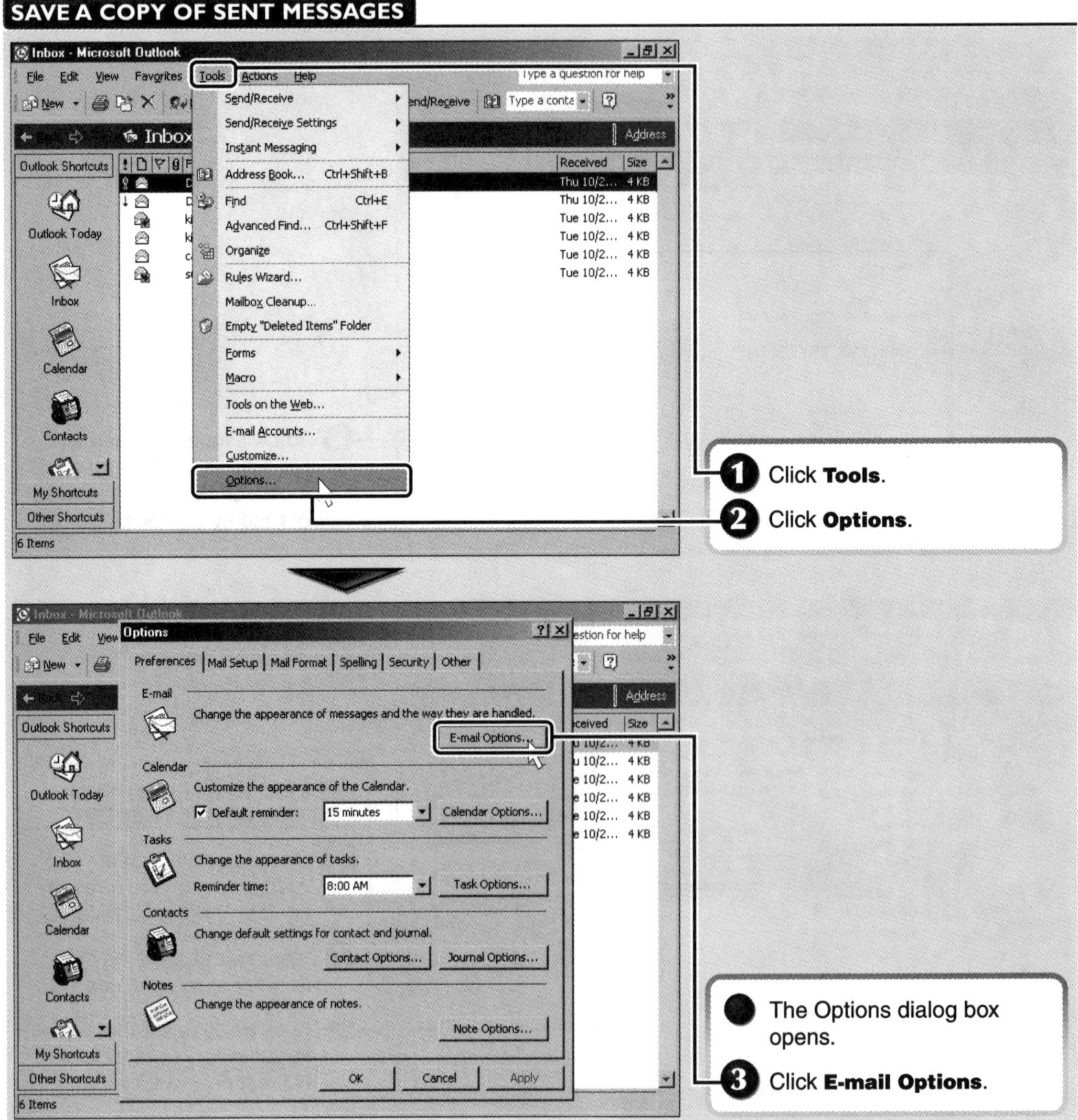

1. Click **Tools**.
2. Click **Options**.

- The Options dialog box opens.

3. Click **E-mail Options**.

in an instant

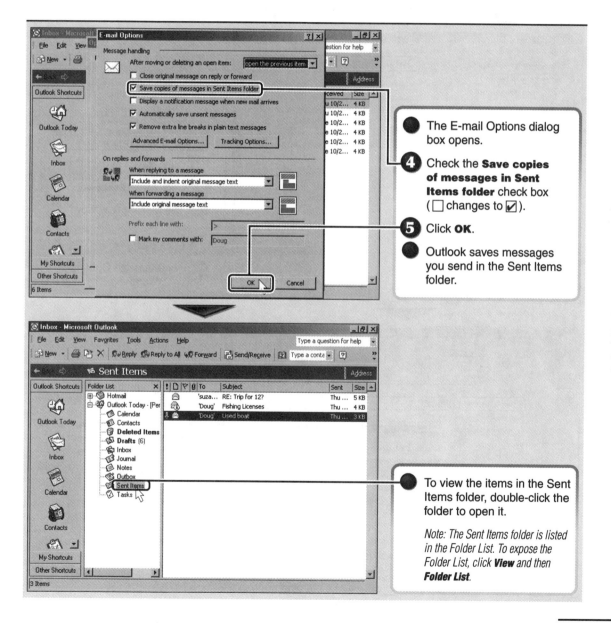

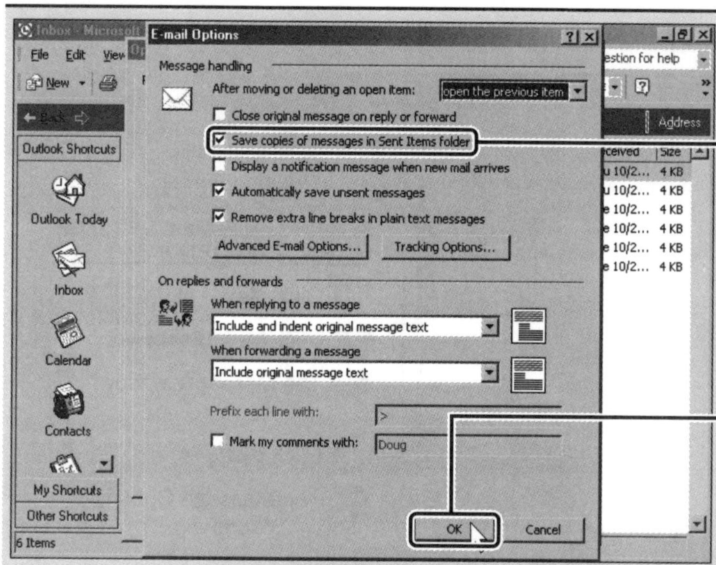

- The E-mail Options dialog box opens.

4 Check the **Save copies of messages in Sent Items folder** check box (☐ changes to ☑).

5 Click **OK**.

- Outlook saves messages you send in the Sent Items folder.

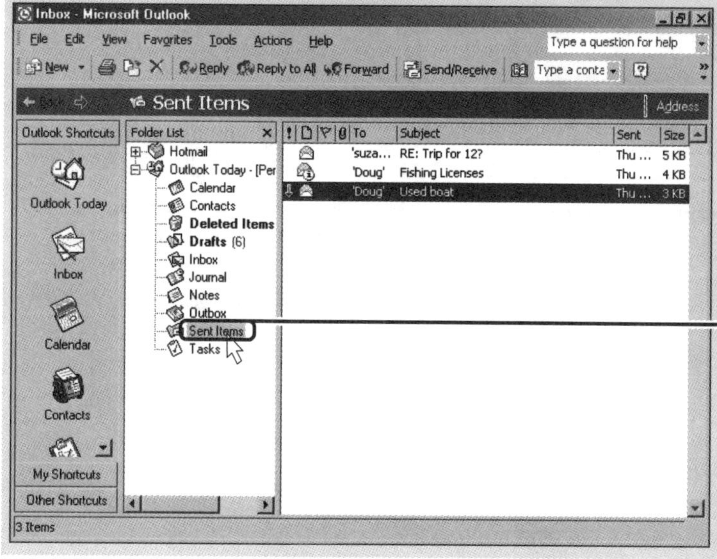

- To view the items in the Sent Items folder, double-click the folder to open it.

*Note: The Sent Items folder is listed in the Folder List. To expose the Folder List, click **View** and then **Folder List**.*

TAKE A VOTE

You may just want to get a quick answer to a specific question instead of reading detailed responses to an e-mail message. Outlook makes it easy for you to send an e-mail message with voting option buttons. The recipient clicks an answer to your question and sends an e-mail response to you. Users on Microsoft Exchange servers can take advantage of enhanced voting features like the ability to add customized response buttons and use Exchange to tally the votes.

TAKE A VOTE

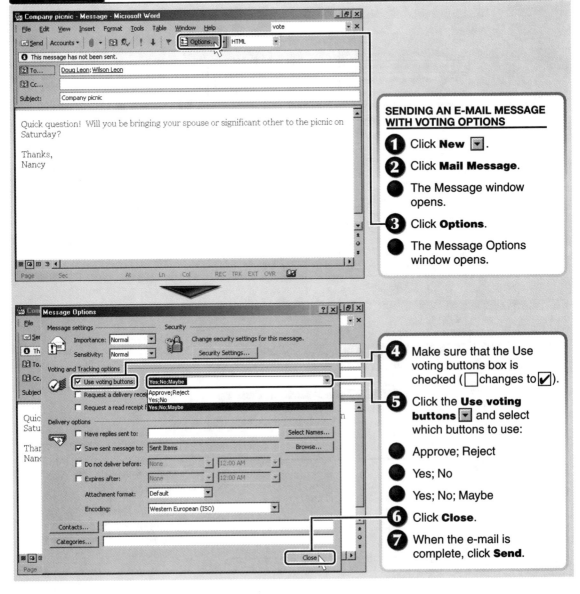

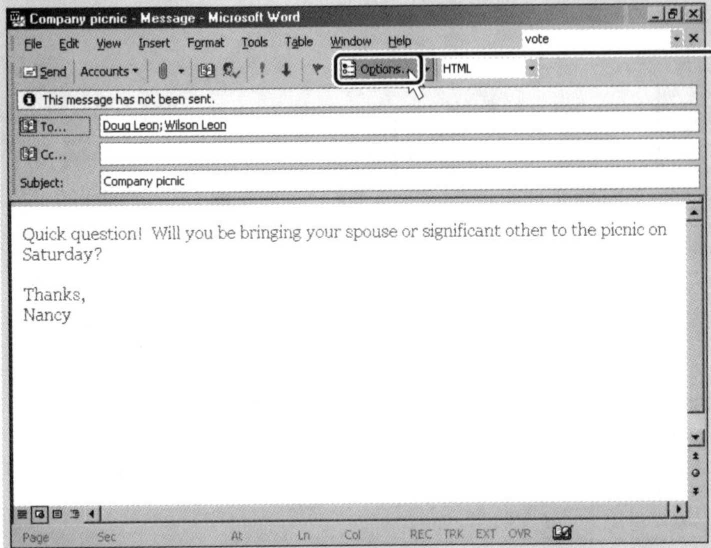

SENDING AN E-MAIL MESSAGE WITH VOTING OPTIONS

1. Click **New** ▾.
2. Click **Mail Message**.
   - The Message window opens.
3. Click **Options**.
   - The Message Options window opens. 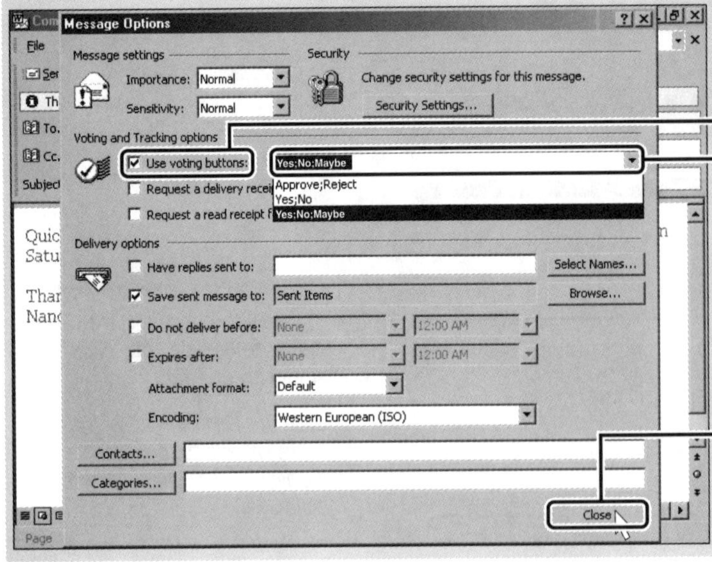
4. Make sure that the Use voting buttons box is checked (☐ changes to ☑).
5. Click the **Use voting buttons** ▾ and select which buttons to use:
   - Approve; Reject
   - Yes; No
   - Yes; No; Maybe
6. Click **Close**.
7. When the e-mail is complete, click **Send**.

in an instant

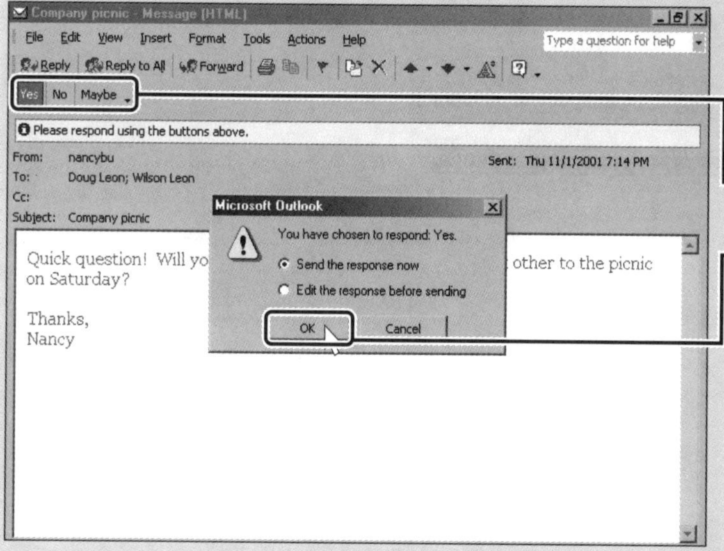

RESPONDING TO A REQUEST FOR A VOTE

1. Open the e-mail message with the vote request.
2. Click the option that suits you.
3. Confirm your response by clicking **OK**.

- Click **Cancel** to cancel the option and change your selection.
- Outlook sends an e-mail message to the sender of the vote request with your response.

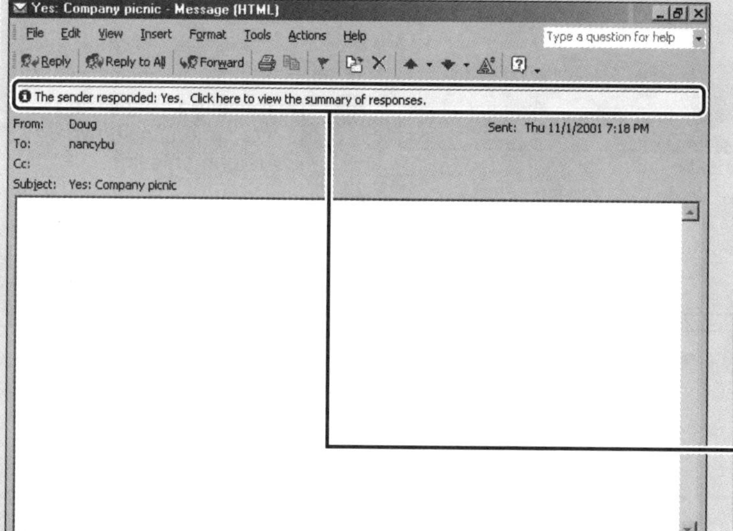

RECEIVING VOTE RESPONSES

1. Open the e-mail message with the vote response.

- The e-mail message indicates the recipient's response to the vote request.

OPEN AN ATTACHMENT YOU RECEIVE

You can open attachments you receive in e-mail messages in just a few clicks of the mouse. Attachments can include files, e-mail messages, contacts, notes, and more.

OPEN AN ATTACHMENT YOU RECEIVE

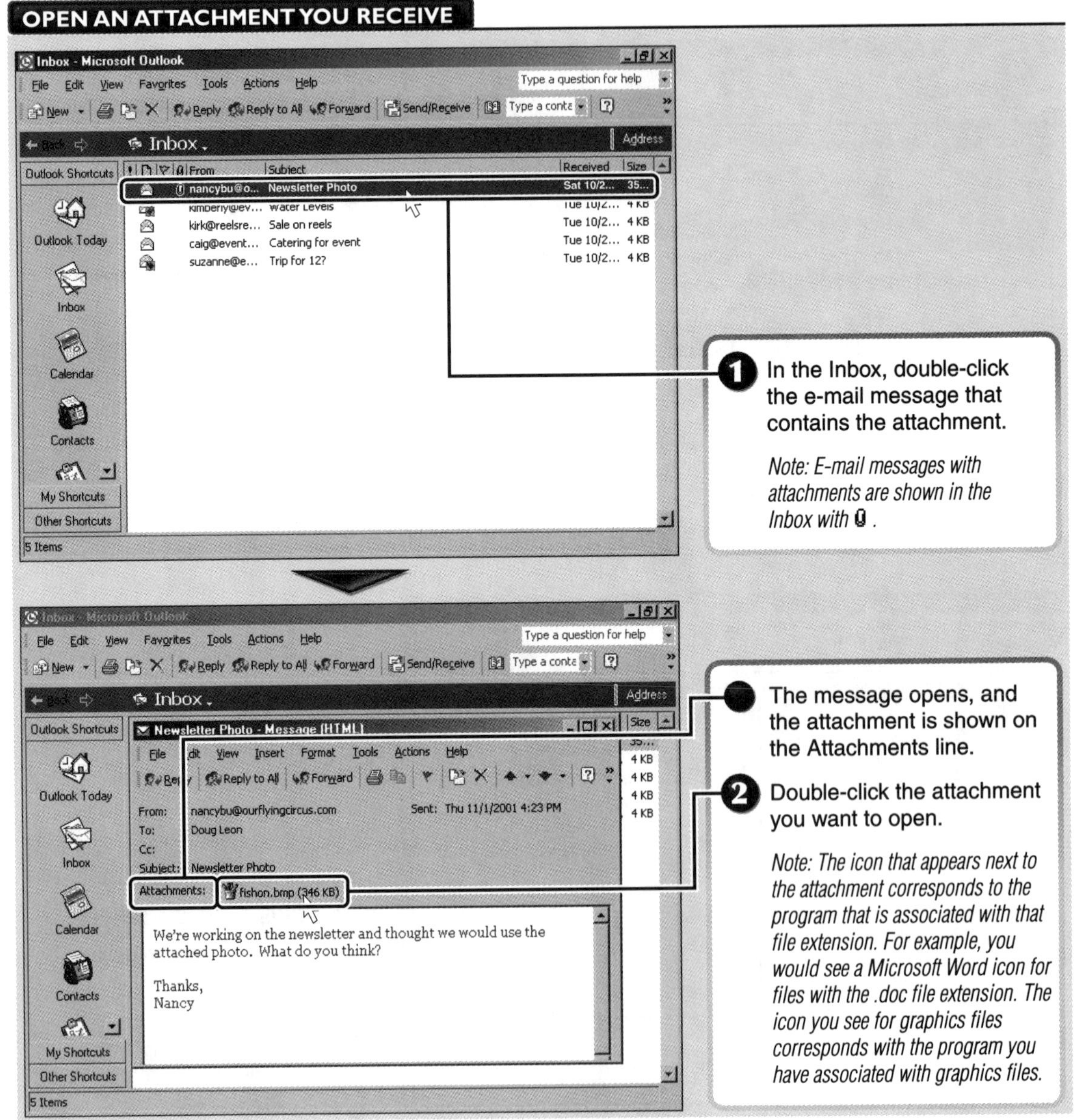

1. In the Inbox, double-click the e-mail message that contains the attachment.

Note: E-mail messages with attachments are shown in the Inbox with 📎.

- The message opens, and the attachment is shown on the Attachments line.

2. Double-click the attachment you want to open.

Note: The icon that appears next to the attachment corresponds to the program that is associated with that file extension. For example, you would see a Microsoft Word icon for files with the .doc file extension. The icon you see for graphics files corresponds with the program you have associated with graphics files.

in an instant

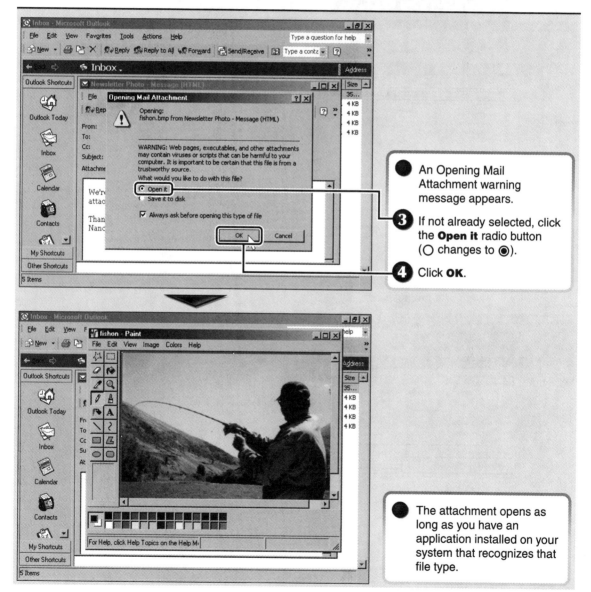

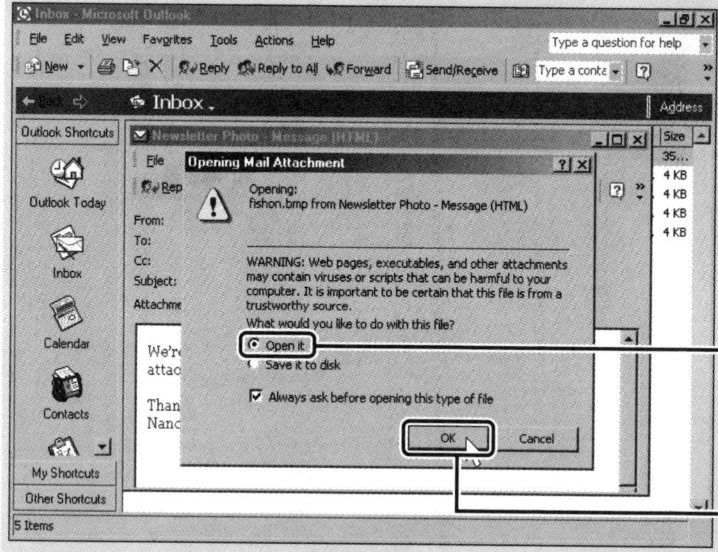

- An Opening Mail Attachment warning message appears.
- **3** If not already selected, click the **Open it** radio button (○ changes to ◉).
- **4** Click **OK**.

- The attachment opens as long as you have an application installed on your system that recognizes that file type.

SAVE AN ATTACHMENT YOU RECEIVE

You can save an attachment that you have received on your hard drive or network drive so that you can access it from outside of Outlook. As an example, you can save a report or graphics file you have received as an e-mail attachment to your company's network for others to access.

SAVE AN ATTACHMENT YOU RECEIVE

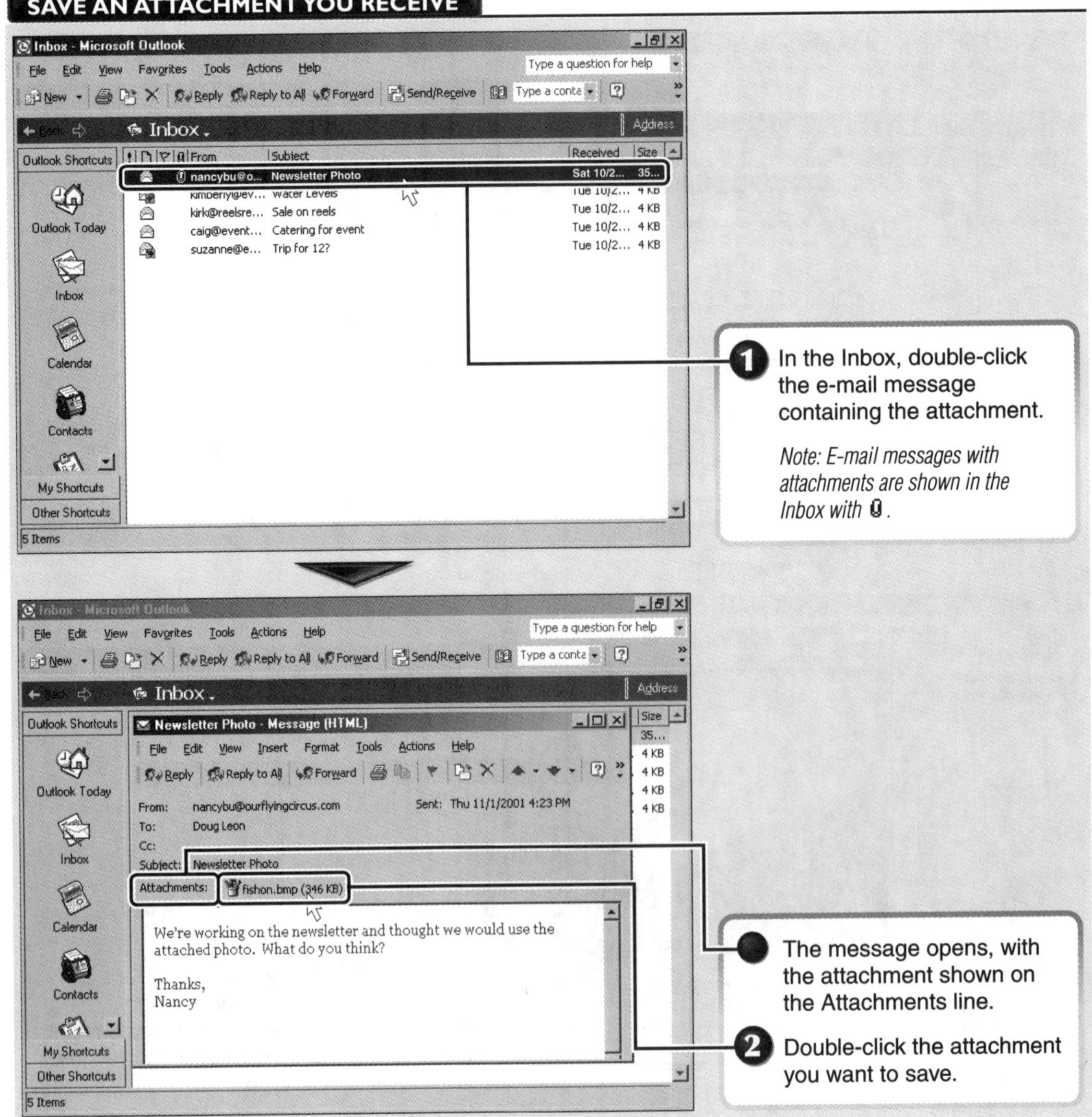

1. In the Inbox, double-click the e-mail message containing the attachment.

   Note: E-mail messages with attachments are shown in the Inbox with (📎).

- The message opens, with the attachment shown on the Attachments line.

2. Double-click the attachment you want to save.

in an instant

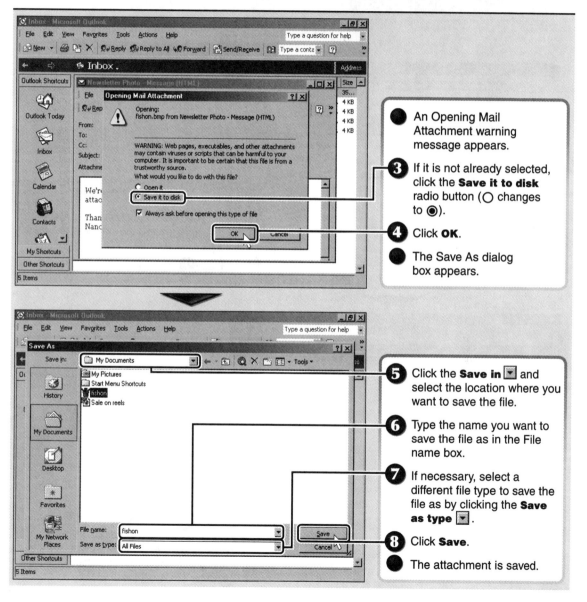

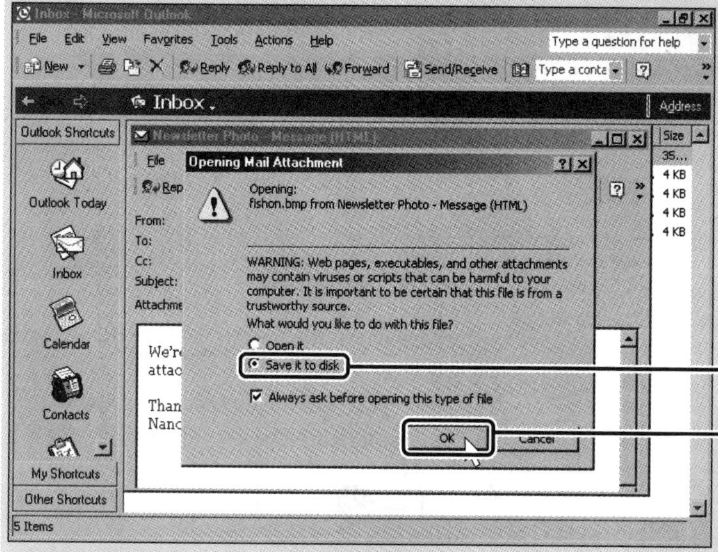

- An Opening Mail Attachment warning message appears.

3. If it is not already selected, click the **Save it to disk** radio button (○ changes to ◉).
4. Click **OK**.

- The Save As dialog box appears.

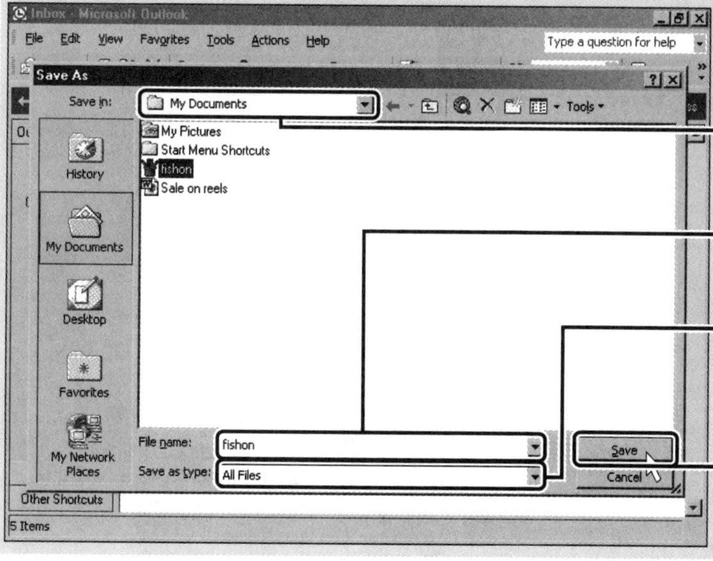

5. Click the **Save in** ▼ and select the location where you want to save the file.
6. Type the name you want to save the file as in the File name box.
7. If necessary, select a different file type to save the file as by clicking the **Save as type** ▼.
8. Click **Save**.

- The attachment is saved.

SEND A FILE WITH YOUR MESSAGE

You can easily send a file attached to an e-mail message. Do keep in mind that some virus protection programs may strip certain file types (mostly macros and executable files) from incoming e-mail messages, and that many e-mail systems limit the size of e-mail messages that can be sent or received.

SEND A FILE WITH YOUR MESSAGE

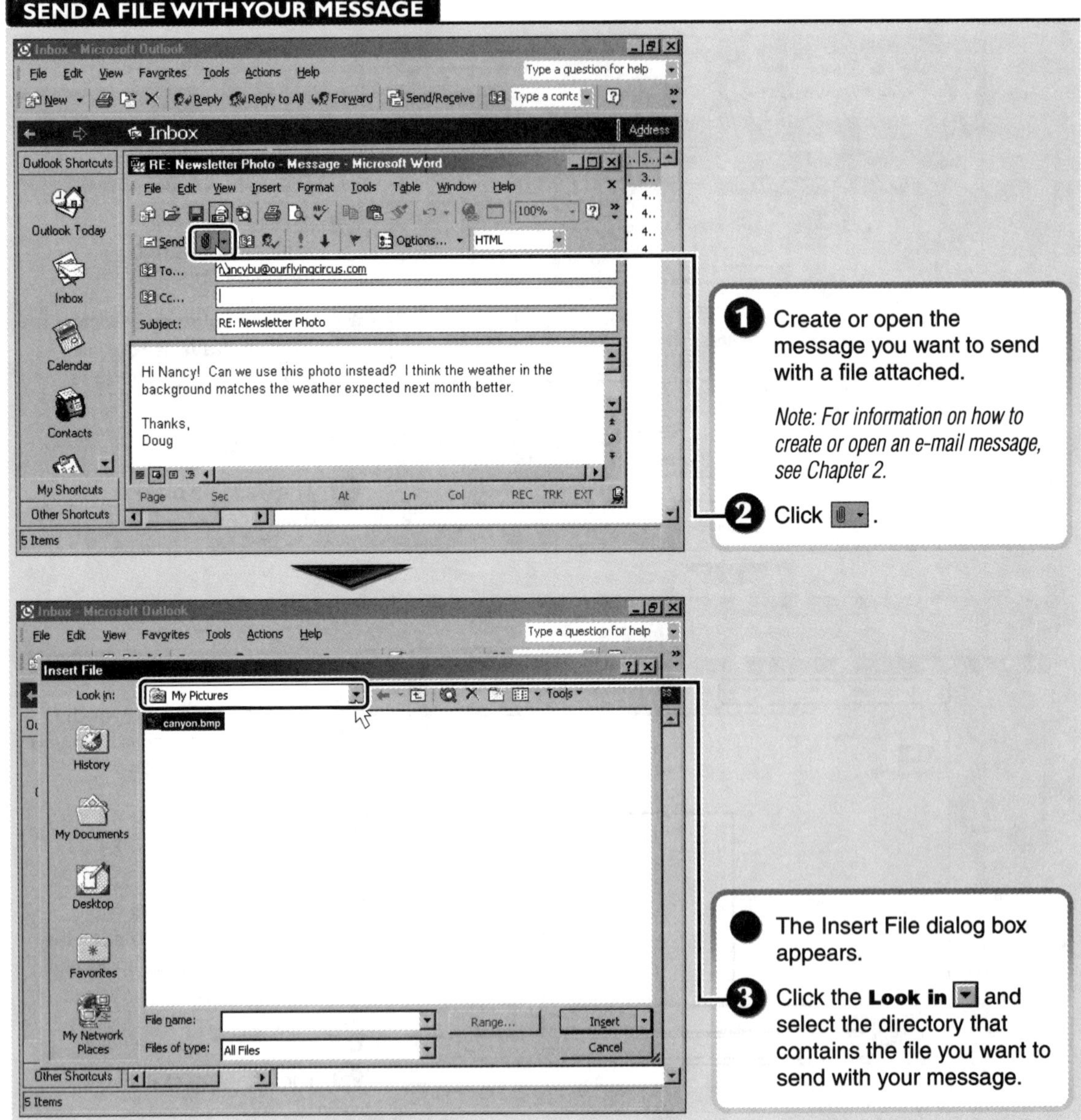

1 Create or open the message you want to send with a file attached.

Note: For information on how to create or open an e-mail message, see Chapter 2.

2 Click .

- The Insert File dialog box appears.

3 Click the **Look in** and select the directory that contains the file you want to send with your message.

in an instant

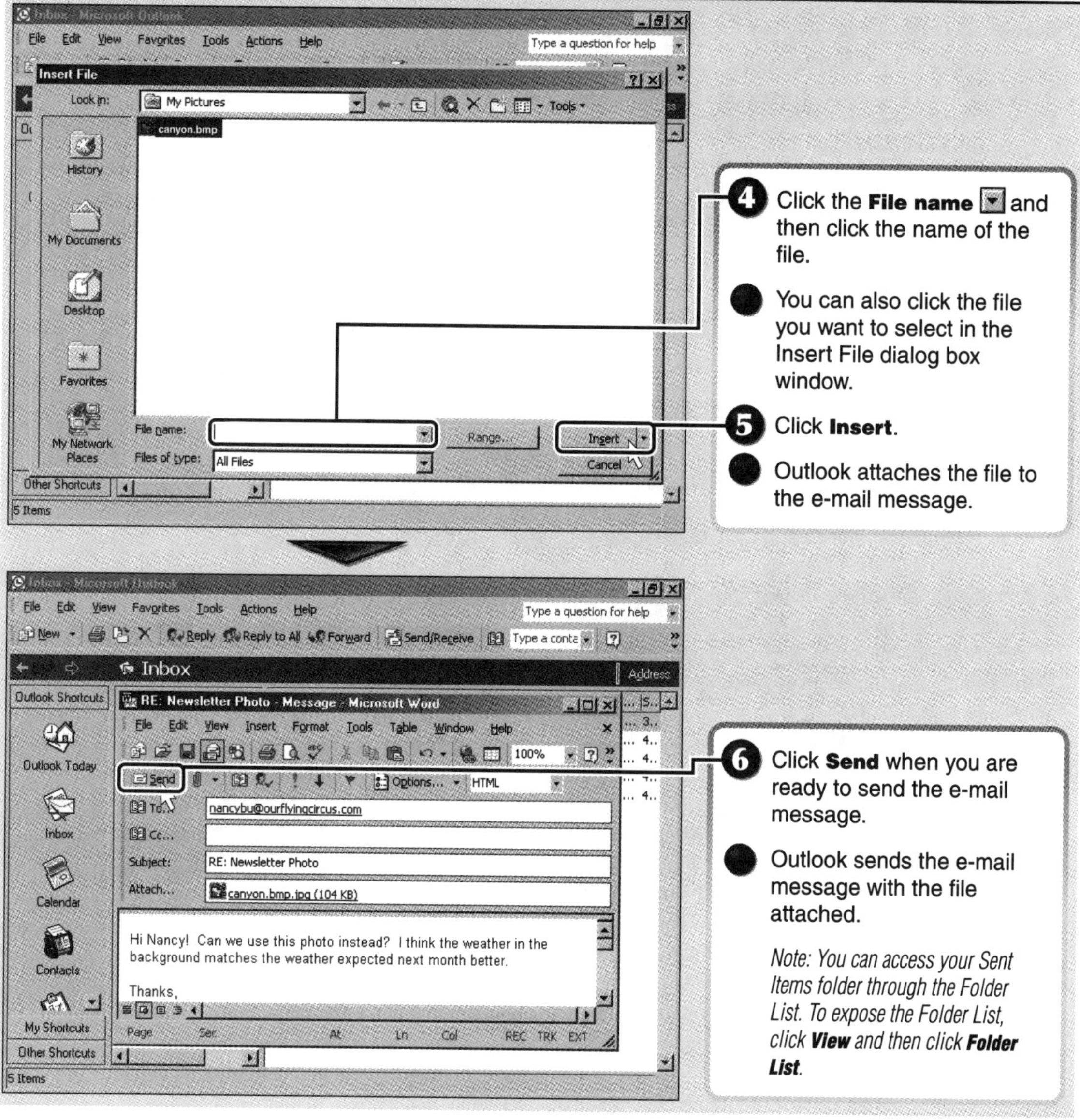

4 Click the **File name** ▾ and then click the name of the file.

- You can also click the file you want to select in the Insert File dialog box window.

5 Click **Insert**.

- Outlook attaches the file to the e-mail message.

6 Click **Send** when you are ready to send the e-mail message.

- Outlook sends the e-mail message with the file attached.

*Note: You can access your Sent Items folder through the Folder List. To expose the Folder List, click **View** and then click **Folder List**.*

SEND A LINK TO A FILE WITH YOUR MESSAGE

You can include links to files or Web pages in e-mail messages simply by typing them into the message area in Outlook. You can also browse to files, folders, and Web pages to make the process of including links in your messages even easier.

SEND A LINK TO A FILE WITH YOUR MESSAGE

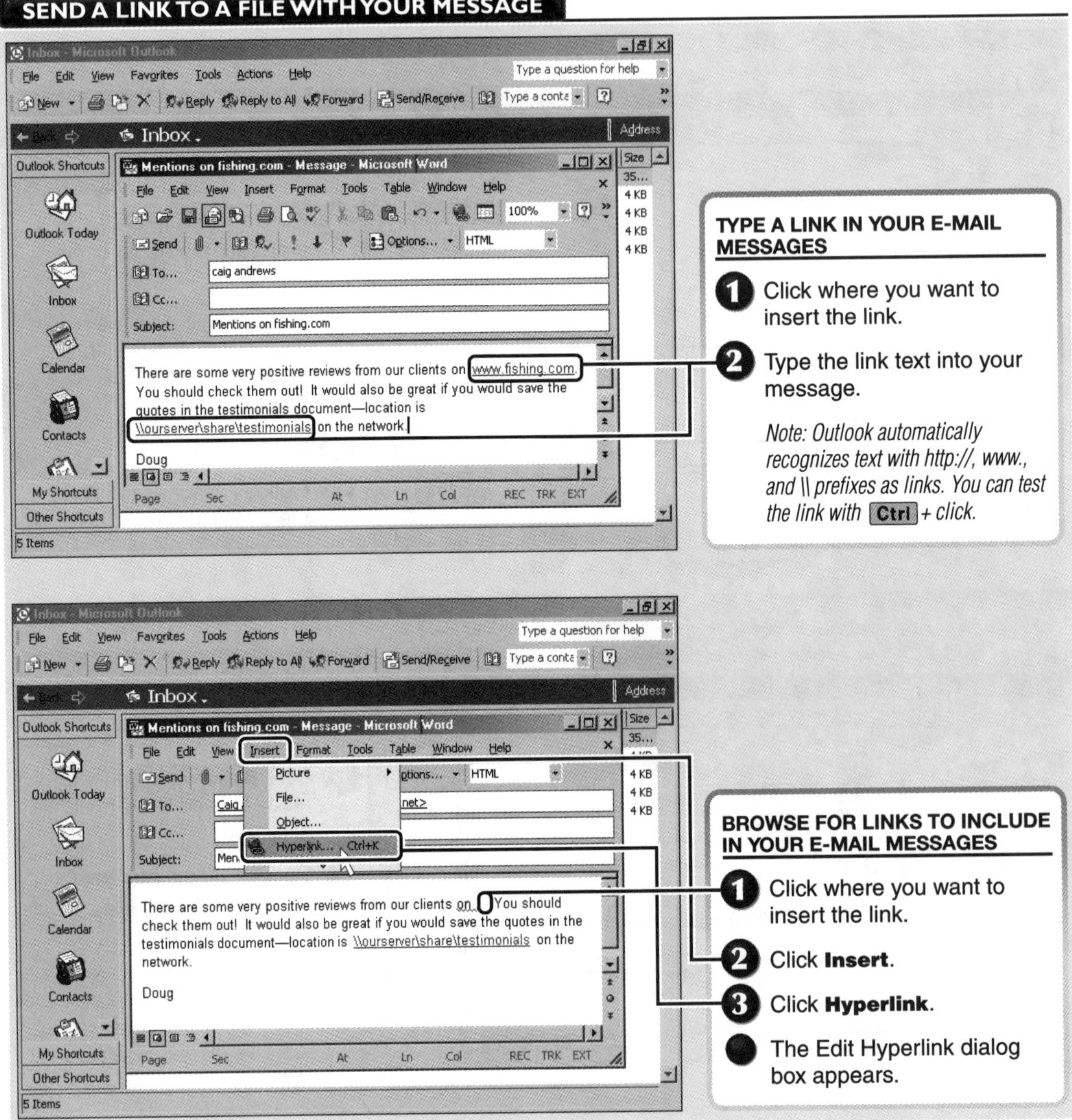

TYPE A LINK IN YOUR E-MAIL MESSAGES

1. Click where you want to insert the link.
2. Type the link text into your message.

Note: Outlook automatically recognizes text with http://, www., and \\ prefixes as links. You can test the link with **Ctrl** *+ click.*

BROWSE FOR LINKS TO INCLUDE IN YOUR E-MAIL MESSAGES

1. Click where you want to insert the link.
2. Click **Insert**.
3. Click **Hyperlink**.

- The Edit Hyperlink dialog box appears.

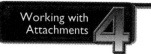

in an instant

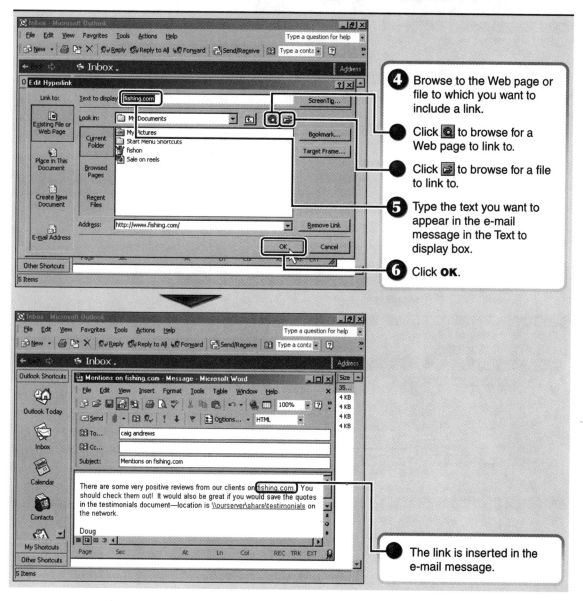

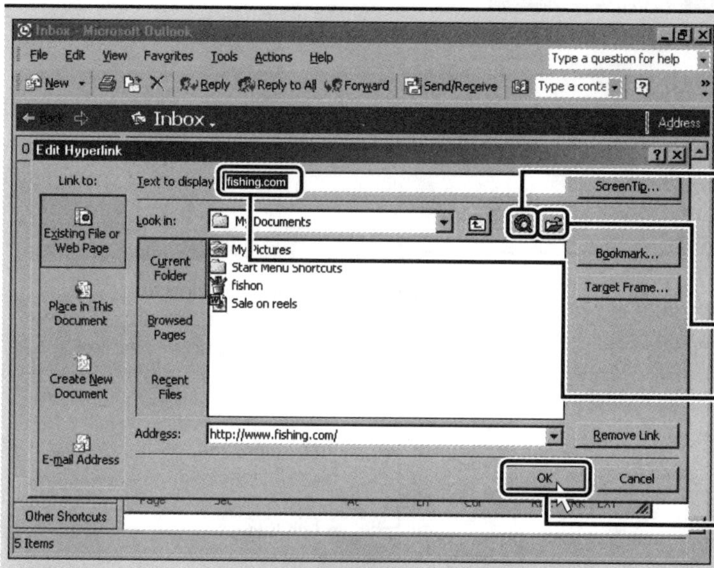

4 Browse to the Web page or file to which you want to include a link.

- Click to browse for a Web page to link to.

- Click to browse for a file to link to.

5 Type the text you want to appear in the e-mail message in the Text to display box.

6 Click **OK**.

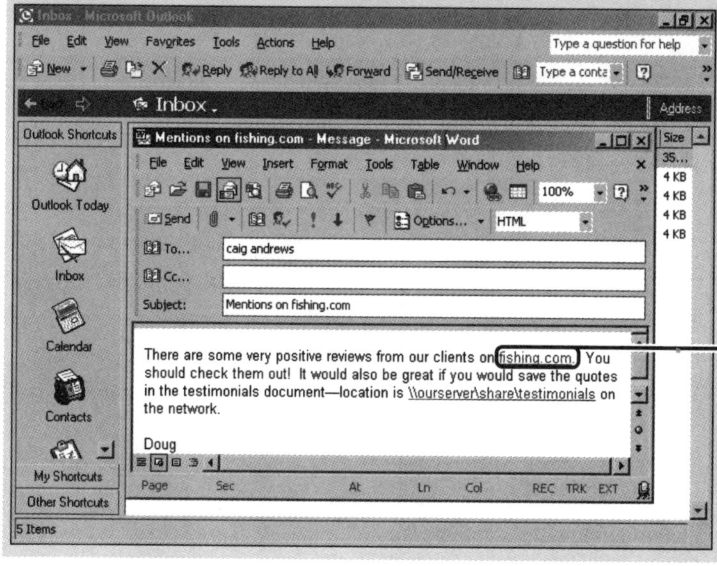

- The link is inserted in the e-mail message.

SEND AN E-MAIL MESSAGE WITH YOUR MESSAGE

You can insert an e-mail message you have sent or received into an e-mail message you are composing. Attaching an e-mail message often saves time over copying and pasting between e-mail messages. Additionally, when you want to send multiple e-mail messages to someone, you can keep them all in one e-mail message by attaching them instead of forwarding each message separately.

SEND AN E-MAIL MESSAGE WITH YOUR MESSAGE

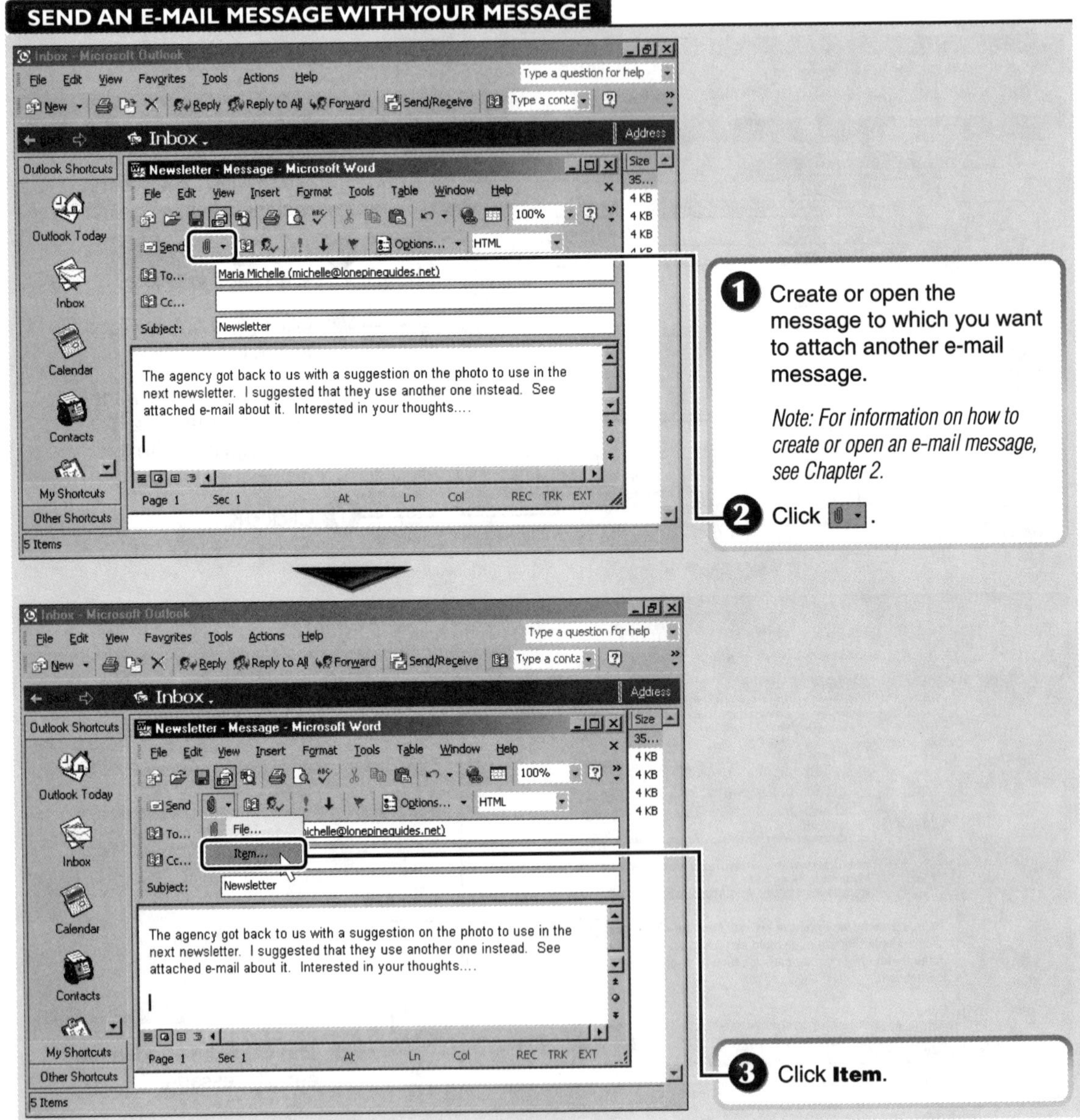

1. Create or open the message to which you want to attach another e-mail message.

   Note: For information on how to create or open an e-mail message, see Chapter 2.

2. Click the attachment button.

3. Click **Item**.

in an instant

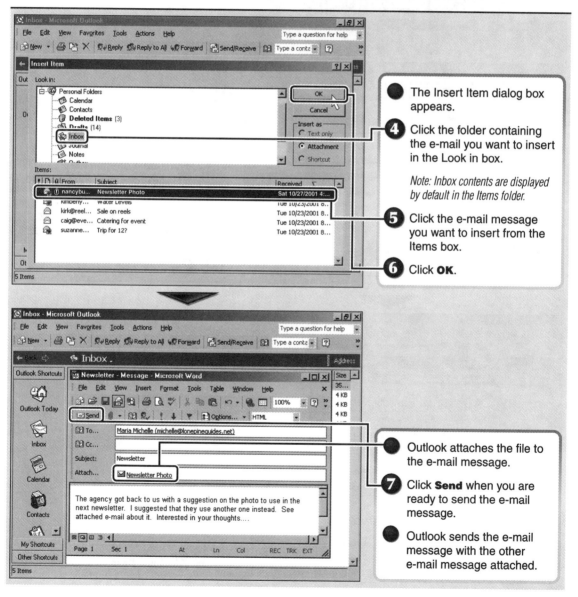

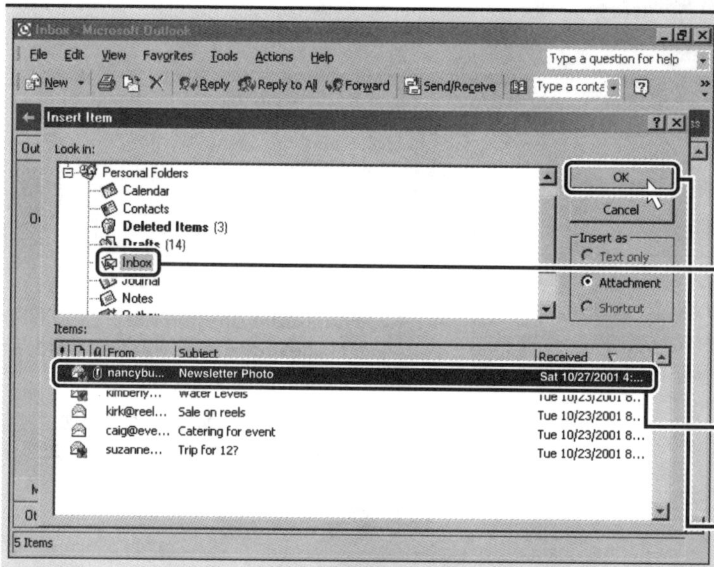

- The Insert Item dialog box appears.

4. Click the folder containing the e-mail you want to insert in the Look in box.

   Note: Inbox contents are displayed by default in the Items folder.

5. Click the e-mail message you want to insert from the Items box.

6. Click **OK**.

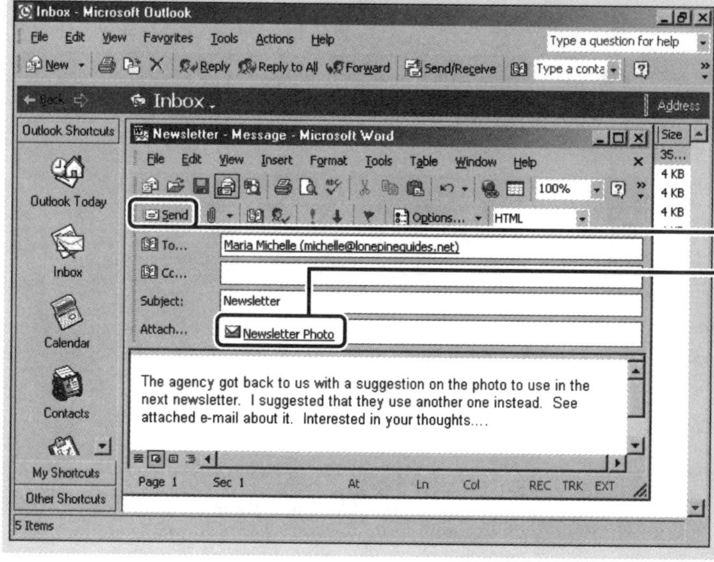

- Outlook attaches the file to the e-mail message.

7. Click **Send** when you are ready to send the e-mail message.

- Outlook sends the e-mail message with the other e-mail message attached.

SEND A CONTACT WITH YOUR MESSAGE

You do not need to cut and paste information from your Outlook contacts list to e-mail messages. You can simply insert a contact card directly into your e-mail messages and send the contact card as an attachment. For more on contacts, see Chapter 9.

SEND A CONTACT WITH YOUR MESSAGE

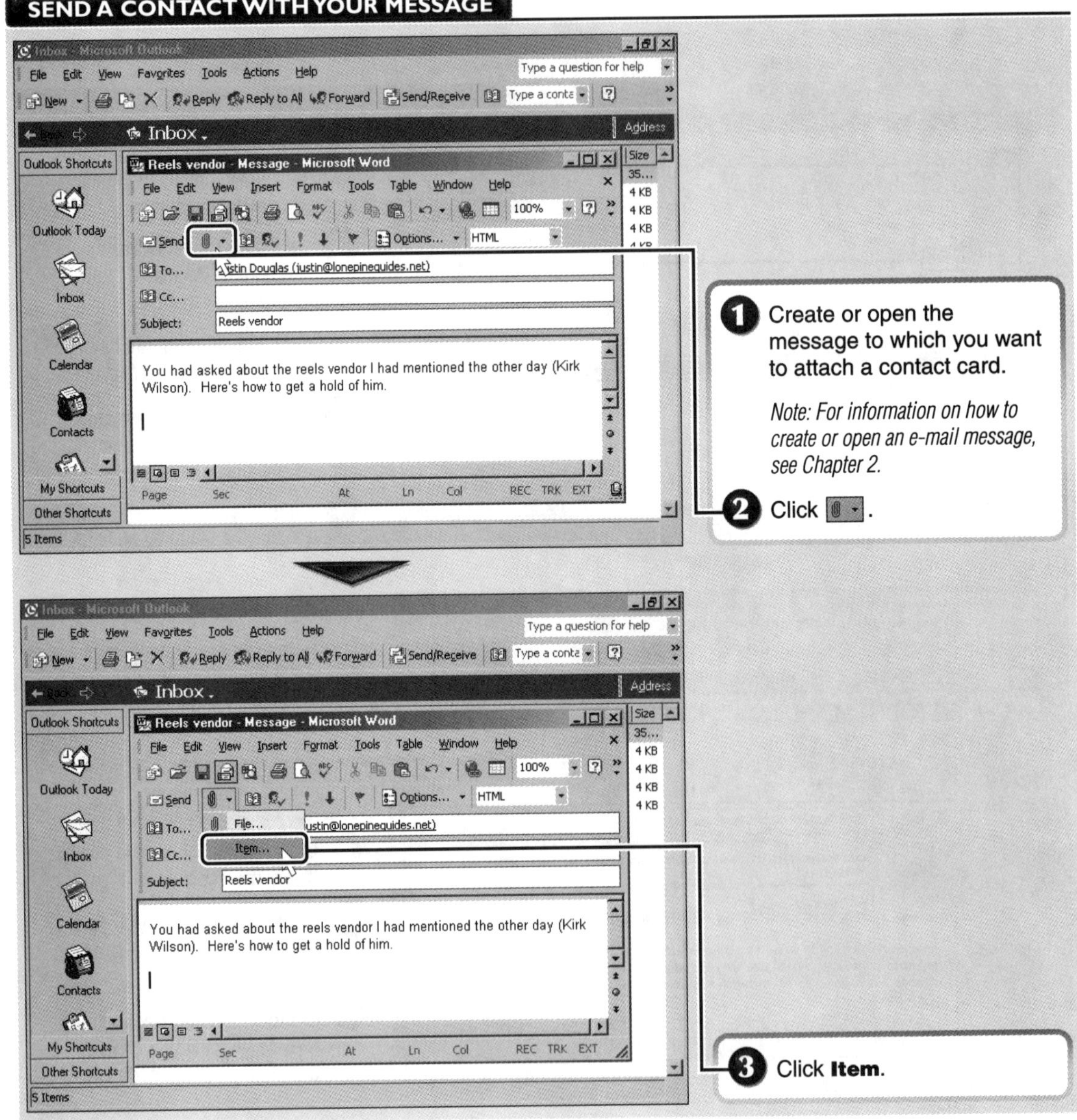

1 Create or open the message to which you want to attach a contact card.
Note: For information on how to create or open an e-mail message, see Chapter 2.
2 Click [attachment button].
3 Click Item.

in an instant

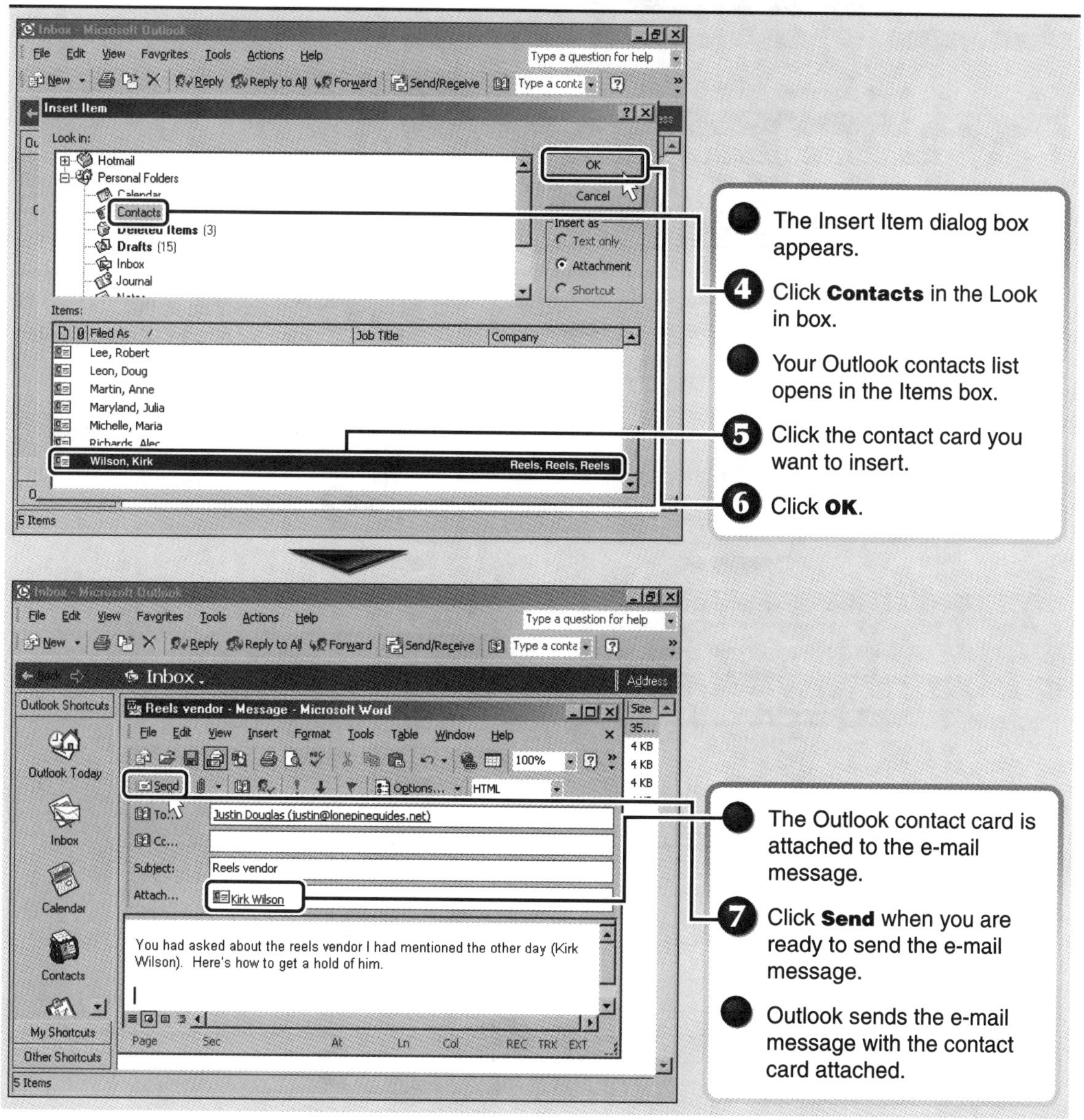

- The Insert Item dialog box appears.
4. Click **Contacts** in the Look in box.
- Your Outlook contacts list opens in the Items box.
5. Click the contact card you want to insert.
6. Click **OK**.

- The Outlook contact card is attached to the e-mail message.
7. Click **Send** when you are ready to send the e-mail message.
- Outlook sends the e-mail message with the contact card attached.

SEND A NOTE WITH YOUR MESSAGE

Outlook notes are a great way to store odd bits of information. You can easily send Outlook notes to someone else by including them in an e-mail message. For more information on Outlook notes, see Chapter 12.

SEND A NOTE WITH YOUR MESSAGE

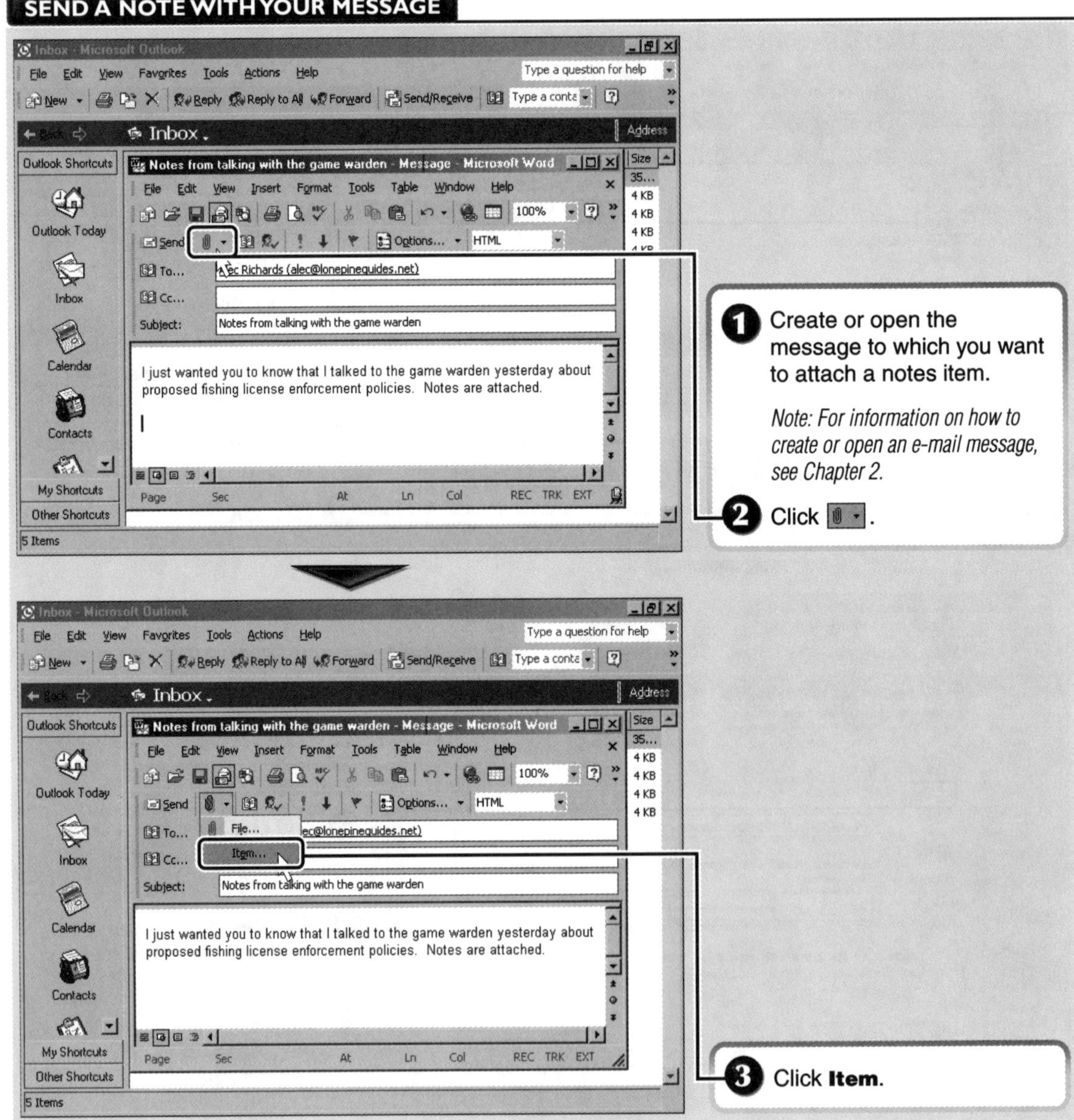

1 Create or open the message to which you want to attach a notes item.

Note: For information on how to create or open an e-mail message, see Chapter 2.

2 Click 📎 ▾.

3 Click **Item**.

in an instant

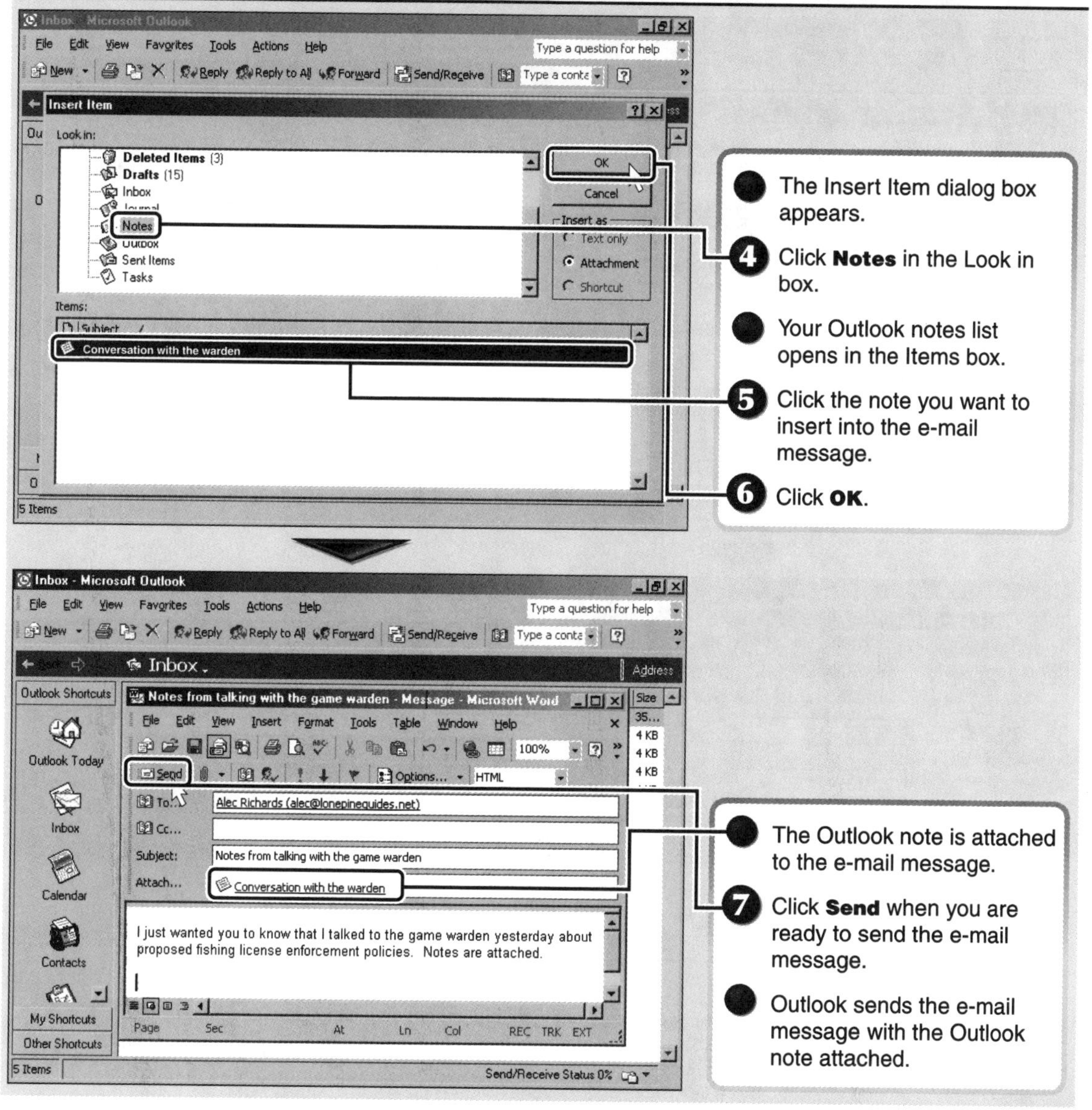

- The Insert Item dialog box appears.
4. Click **Notes** in the Look in box.
- Your Outlook notes list opens in the Items box.
5. Click the note you want to insert into the e-mail message.
6. Click **OK**.

- The Outlook note is attached to the e-mail message.
7. Click **Send** when you are ready to send the e-mail message.
- Outlook sends the e-mail message with the Outlook note attached.

SEND YOUR BUSINESS CARD WITH YOUR MESSAGE

You can save time for the people receiving your e-mail messages by sending your contact information as an attachment or in vCard format. Recipients of your e-mail who use Outlook can save your electronic business card directly into their Outlook contacts list. Recipients of your e-mail message who use a vCard-compatible e-mail application can also save your electronic business card directly to their vCard-compatible application.

SEND YOUR BUSINESS CARD WITH YOUR MESSAGE

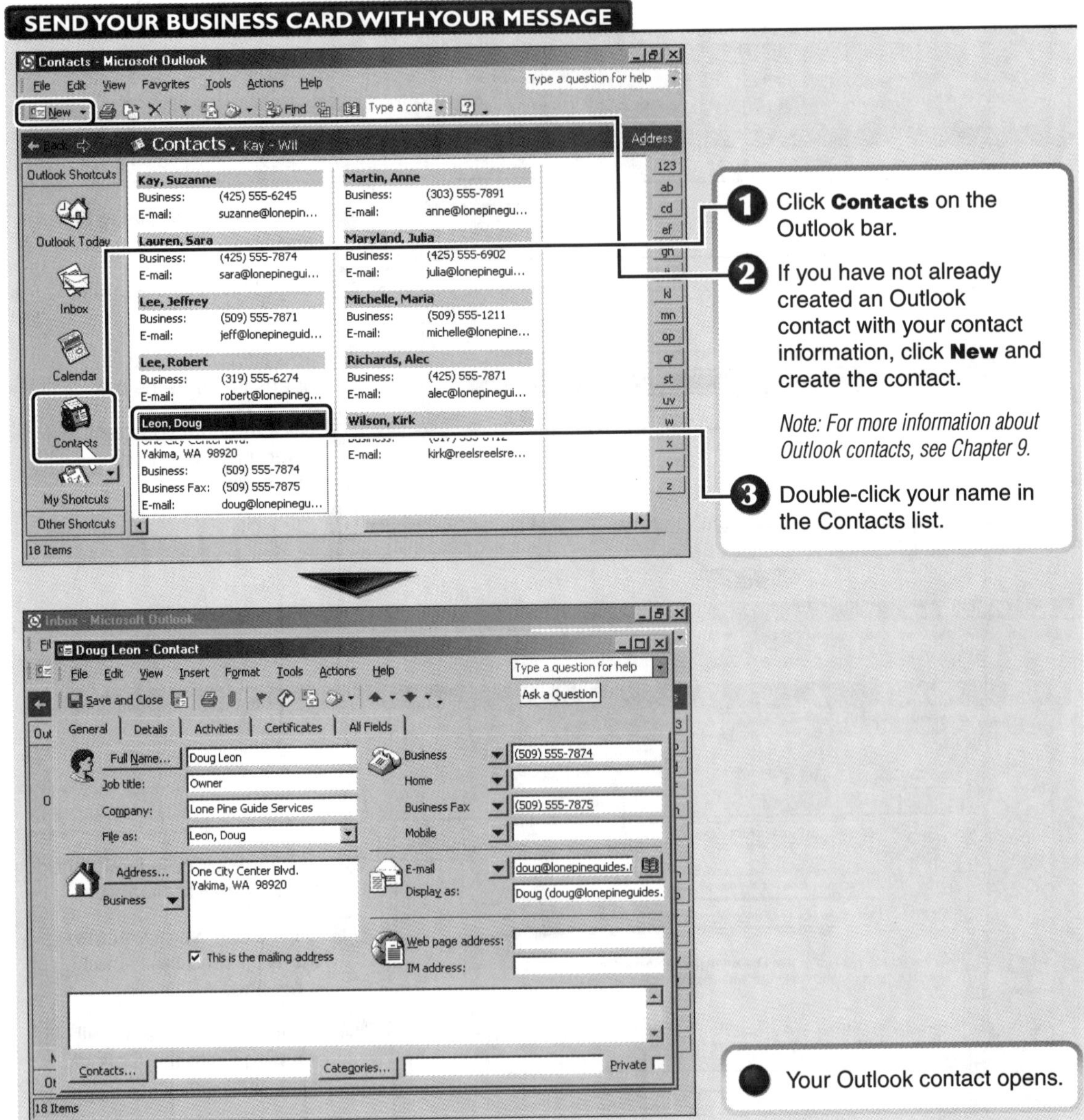

1. Click **Contacts** on the Outlook bar.

2. If you have not already created an Outlook contact with your contact information, click **New** and create the contact.

   Note: For more information about Outlook contacts, see Chapter 9.

3. Double-click your name in the Contacts list.

- Your Outlook contact opens.

in an instant

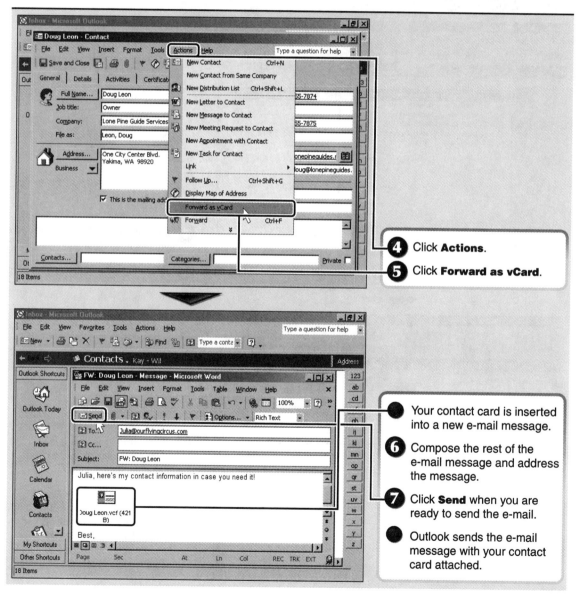

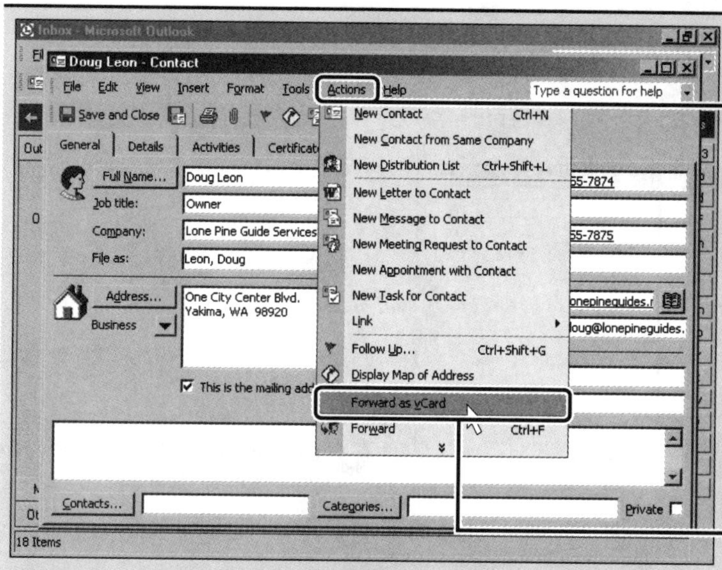

4 Click **Actions**.

5 Click **Forward as vCard**.

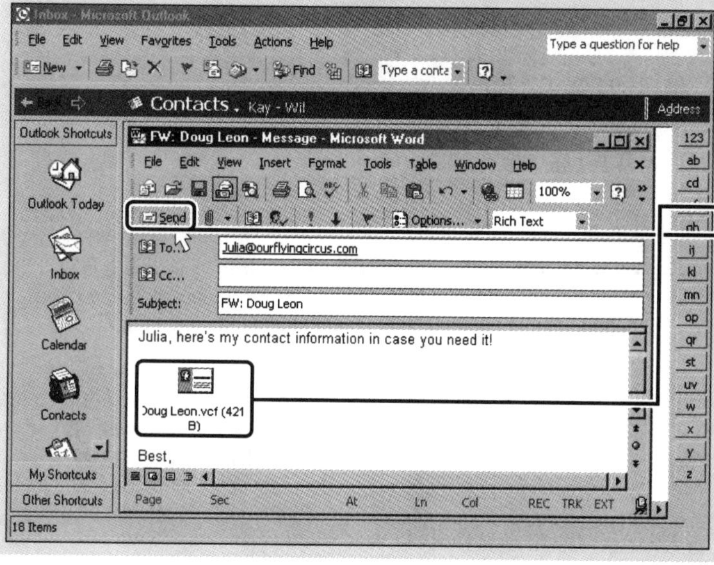

- Your contact card is inserted into a new e-mail message.

6 Compose the rest of the e-mail message and address the message.

7 Click **Send** when you are ready to send the e-mail.

- Outlook sends the e-mail message with your contact card attached.

DELETE A MESSAGE

You can easily delete messages from your Inbox or other folders. Deleted messages are stored in the Deleted Items folder until they are permanently deleted, giving you a chance to change your mind.

DELETE A MESSAGE

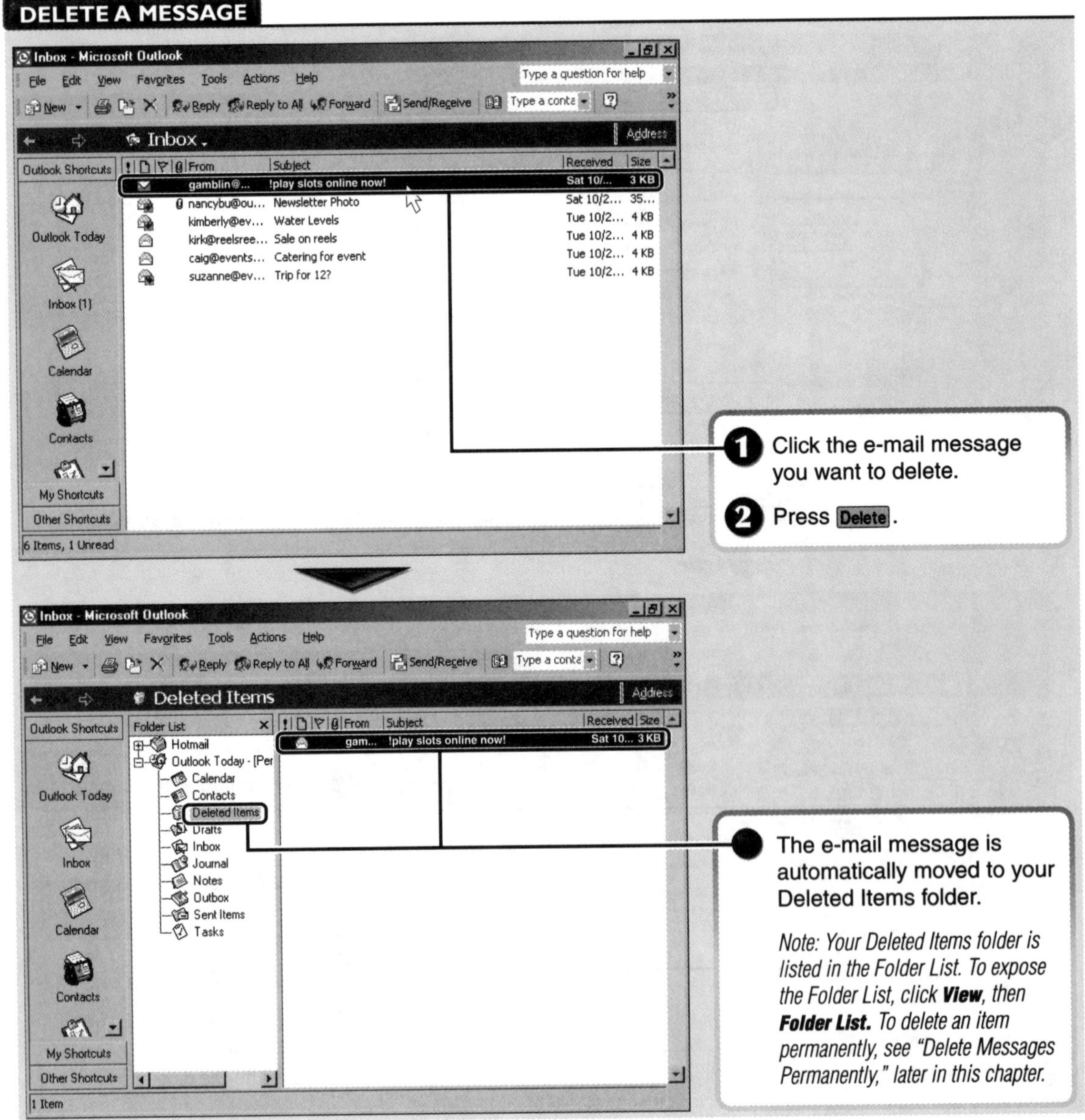

1. Click the e-mail message you want to delete.
2. Press **Delete**.

- The e-mail message is automatically moved to your Deleted Items folder.

Note: Your Deleted Items folder is listed in the Folder List. To expose the Folder List, click ***View****, then* ***Folder List.*** *To delete an item permanently, see "Delete Messages Permanently," later in this chapter.*

DELETE MORE THAN ONE MESSAGE

You do not have to delete messages one at a time; you can delete multiple e-mail messages at once. As an example, you can sort your Inbox by subject or sender, block select a group of e-mail messages, and then quickly delete them all at once.

DELETE MORE THAN ONE MESSAGE

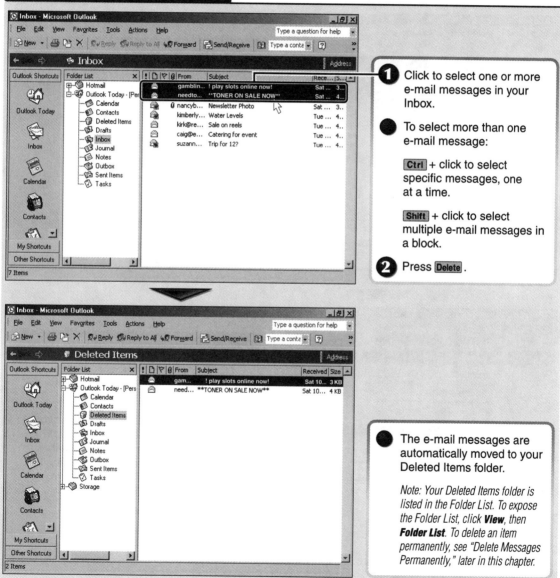

1. Click to select one or more e-mail messages in your Inbox.

- To select more than one e-mail message:

  Ctrl + click to select specific messages, one at a time.

  Shift + click to select multiple e-mail messages in a block.

2. Press Delete.

- The e-mail messages are automatically moved to your Deleted Items folder.

Note: Your Deleted Items folder is listed in the Folder List. To expose the Folder List, click ***View****, then* ***Folder List****. To delete an item permanently, see "Delete Messages Permanently," later in this chapter.*

DELETE MESSAGES PERMANENTLY

Some e-mail messages you know you will never want. You can delete these messages permanently from your Inbox without sending them to the Deleted Items folder.

DELETE MESSAGES PERMANENTLY

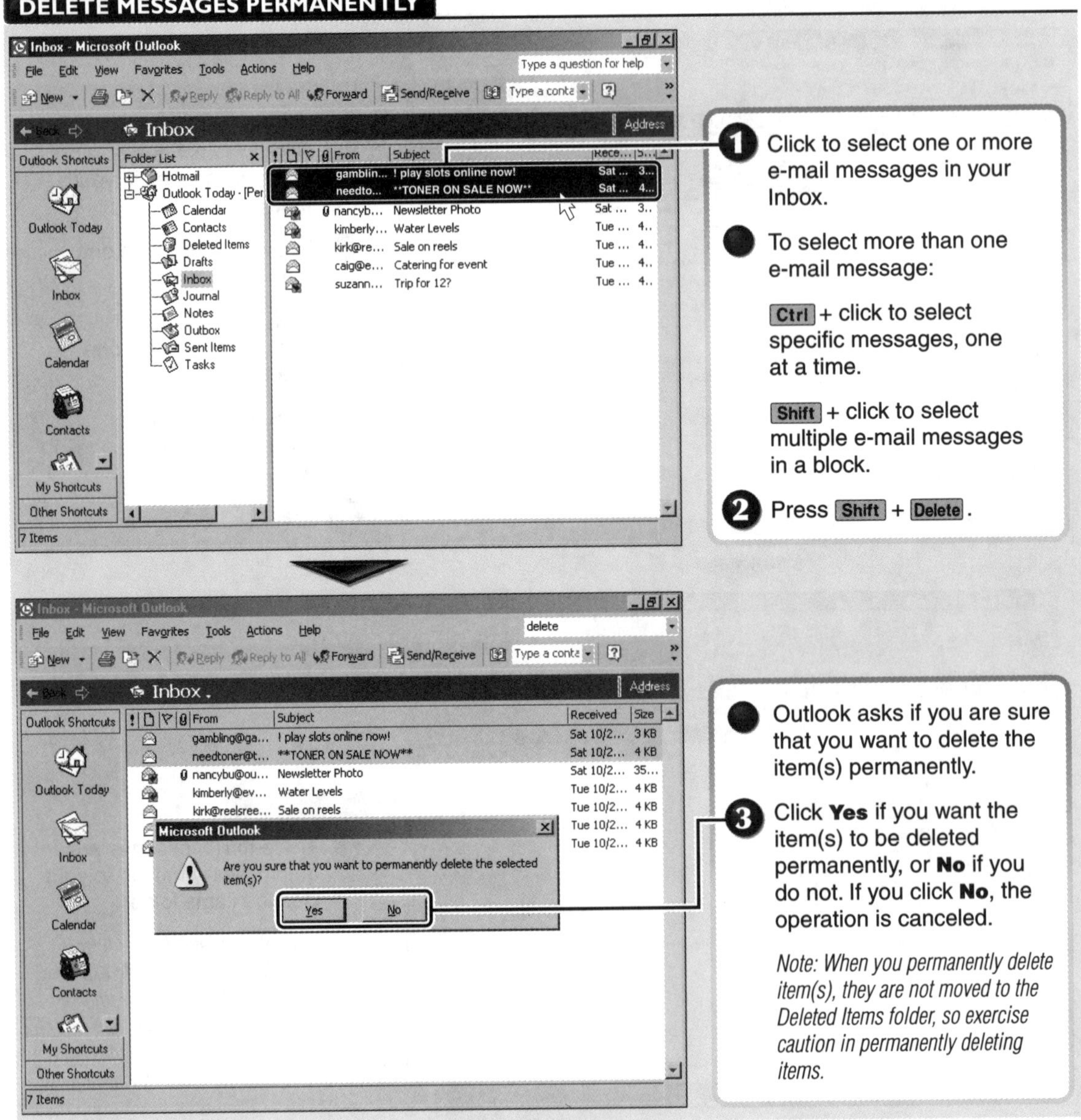

1. Click to select one or more e-mail messages in your Inbox.

- To select more than one e-mail message:

  Ctrl + click to select specific messages, one at a time.

  Shift + click to select multiple e-mail messages in a block.

2. Press **Shift** + **Delete**.

- Outlook asks if you are sure that you want to delete the item(s) permanently.

3. Click **Yes** if you want the item(s) to be deleted permanently, or **No** if you do not. If you click **No**, the operation is canceled.

Note: When you permanently delete item(s), they are not moved to the Deleted Items folder, so exercise caution in permanently deleting items.

REMOVE DELETED MESSAGES

Rather than select individual items to delete, you can empty the entire Deleted Items folder with just a few clicks of the mouse. The e-mail messages in the Deleted Items folder are permanently deleted when the folder is emptied.

REMOVE DELETED MESSAGES

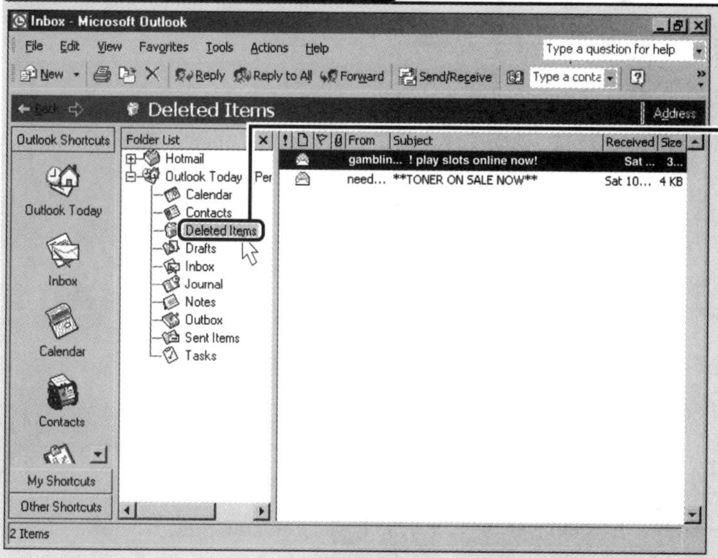

1. Click the **Deleted Items** folder in the Folder List.

Note: If the Folder List is not exposed, click ***View*** *and then click* ***Folder List****.*

- Outlook displays the contents of the Deleted Items folder. If you change your mind about deleting an item, select the item and move it to another folder. See Chapter 7 for more about moving items between folders.

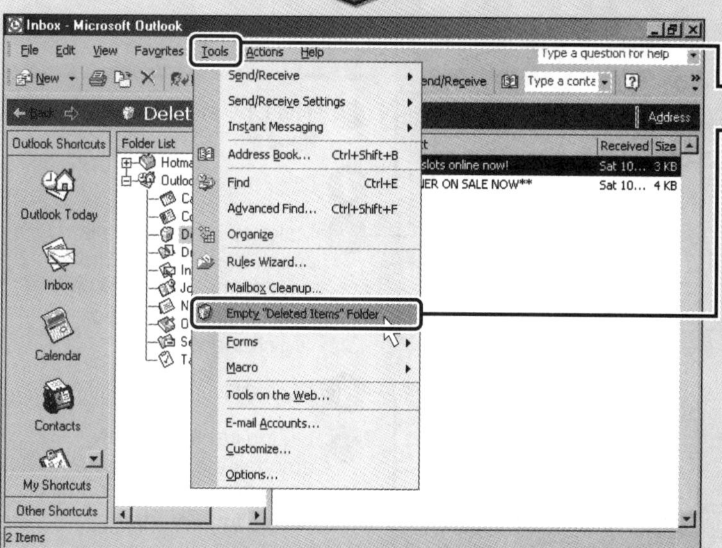

2. Click **Tools**.
3. Click **Empty "Deleted Items" Folder**.

- Outlook asks if you are sure that you want to delete the item(s) permanently.

4. Click **Yes** if you want the item(s) to be deleted permanently, or **No** if you do not.

- If you click Yes, Outlook permanently deletes the items in the Deleted Items folder.

REMOVE DELETED MESSAGES UPON EXIT

Outlook can be set to automatically empty the Deleted Items folder when you exit Outlook. The e-mail messages in the Deleted Items folder are permanently deleted when the Deleted Items folder is emptied.

REMOVE DELETED MESSAGES UPON EXIT

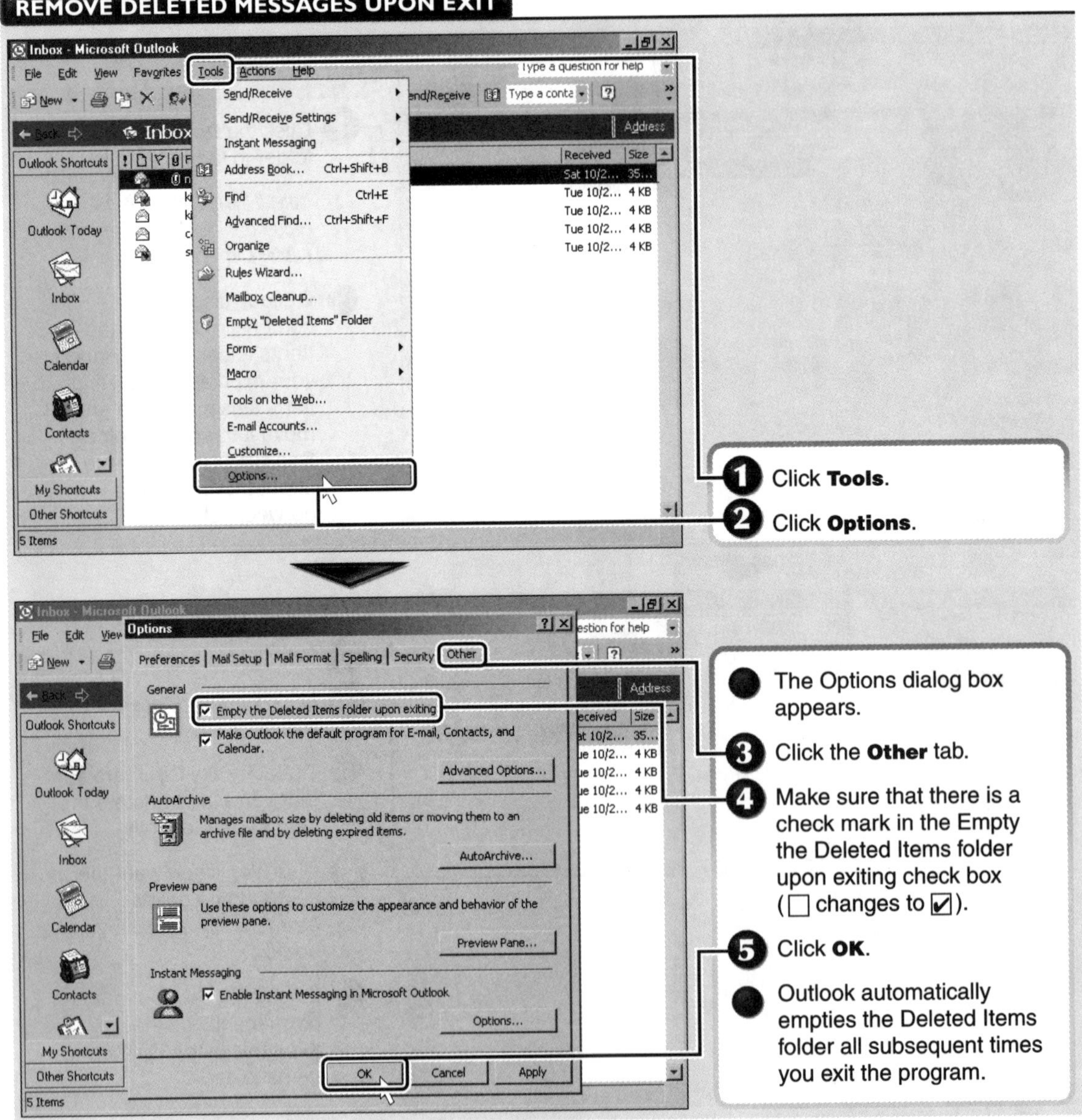

1. Click **Tools**.
2. Click **Options**.

- The Options dialog box appears.

3. Click the **Other** tab.
4. Make sure that there is a check mark in the Empty the Deleted Items folder upon exiting check box (☐ changes to ☑).
5. Click **OK**.

- Outlook automatically empties the Deleted Items folder all subsequent times you exit the program.

GET RID OF JUNK MAIL

You can instruct Outlook to automatically color code or move junk or adult content e-mail messages. Outlook uses a predetermined set of key words to filter junk or adult content e-mail messages, so this functionality should be considered helpful but not necessarily 100% accurate. For example, you may sometimes want to keep e-mail messages containing key words that trigger the junk or adult filters.

GET RID OF JUNK MAIL

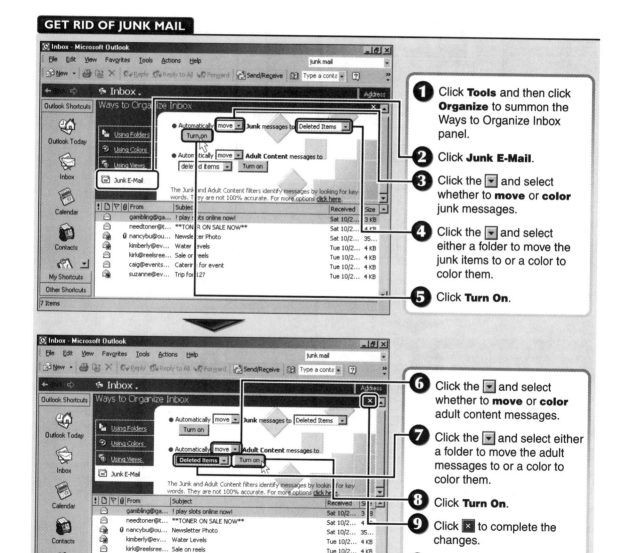

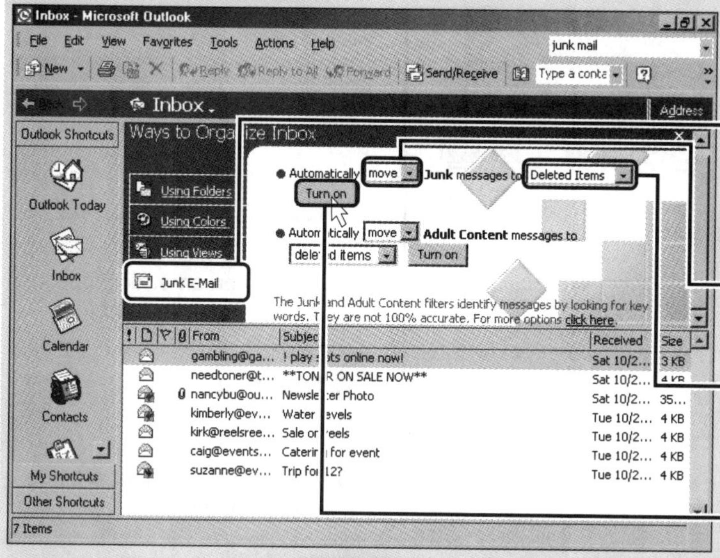

1. Click **Tools** and then click **Organize** to summon the Ways to Organize Inbox panel.
2. Click **Junk E-Mail**.
3. Click the ▾ and select whether to **move** or **color** junk messages.
4. Click the ▾ and select either a folder to move the junk items to or a color to color them.
5. Click **Turn On**.
6. Click the ▾ and select whether to **move** or **color** adult content messages. 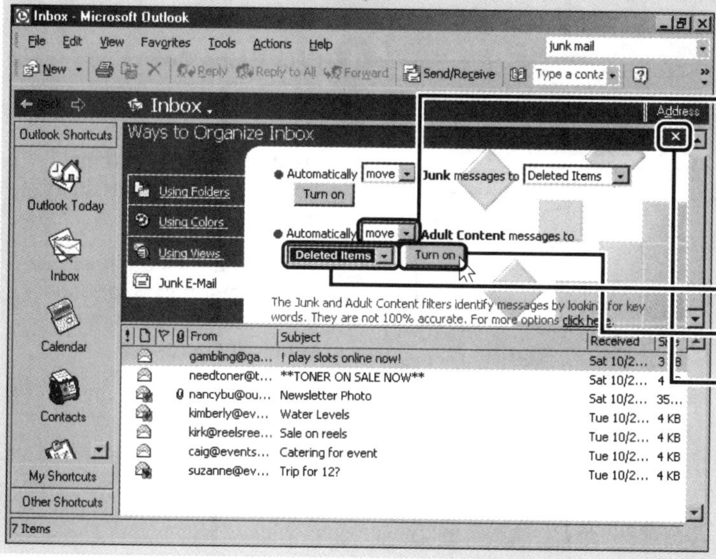
7. Click the ▾ and select either a folder to move the adult messages to or a color to color them.
8. Click **Turn On**.
9. Click ✖ to complete the changes.

- Outlook automatically moves or color codes junk or adult content e-mail.

COLOR CODE MESSAGES

You can color code e-mail messages you receive to help you determine which ones need your immediate attention and which ones do not. For example, you can choose to color all e-mail messages from your boss or spouse, or color all e-mail messages sent directly to you.

COLOR CODE MESSAGES

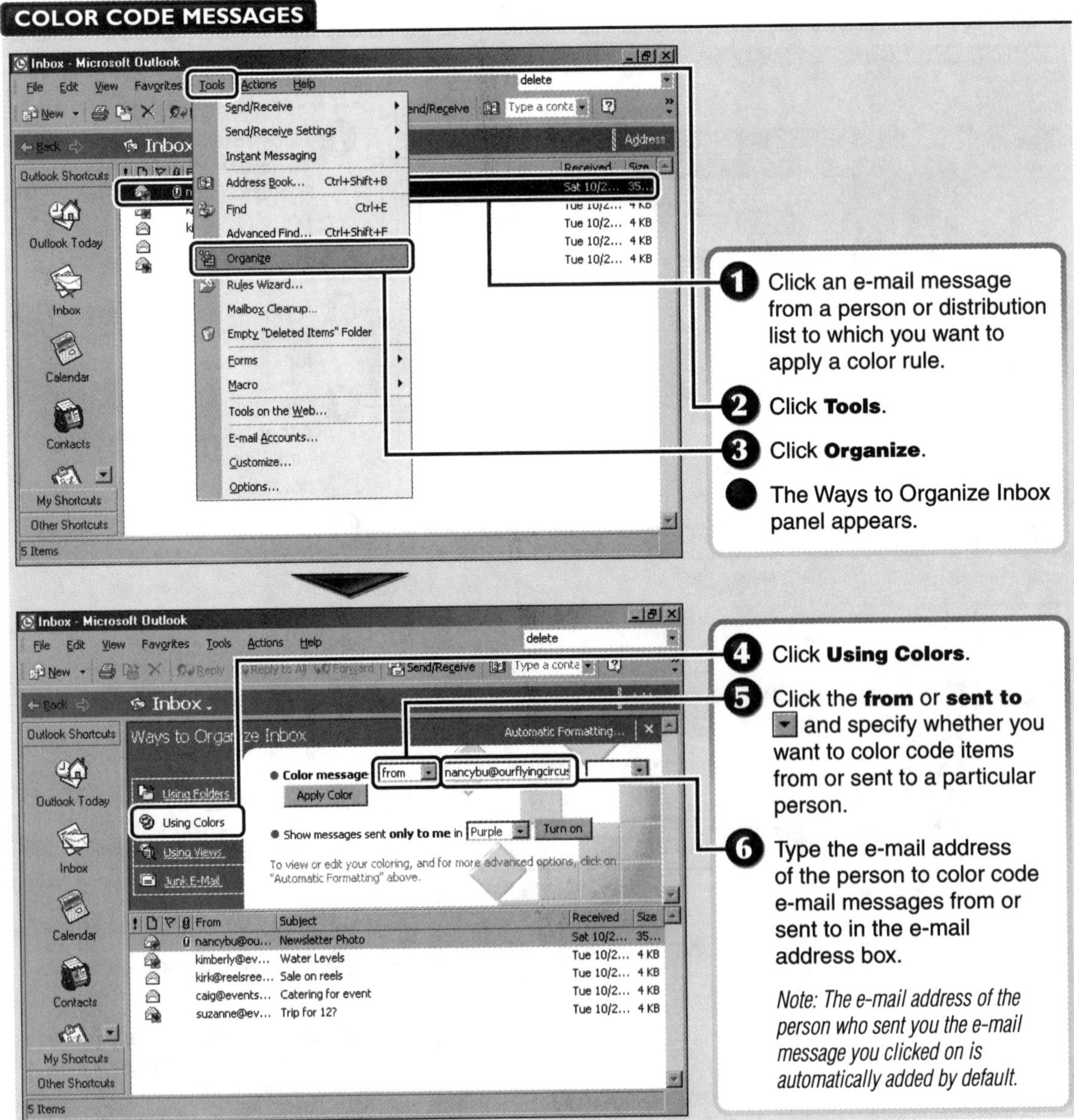

1. Click an e-mail message from a person or distribution list to which you want to apply a color rule.
2. Click **Tools**.
3. Click **Organize**.

- The Ways to Organize Inbox panel appears.

4. Click **Using Colors**.
5. Click the **from** or **sent to** ▾ and specify whether you want to color code items from or sent to a particular person.
6. Type the e-mail address of the person to color code e-mail messages from or sent to in the e-mail address box.

Note: The e-mail address of the person who sent you the e-mail message you clicked on is automatically added by default.

in an instant

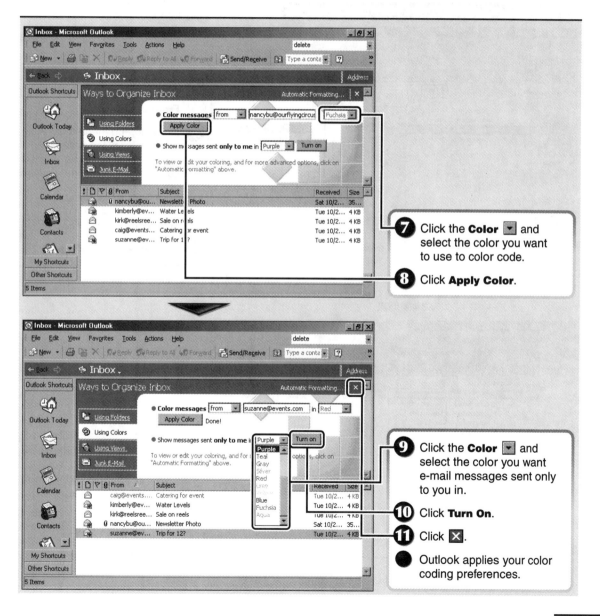

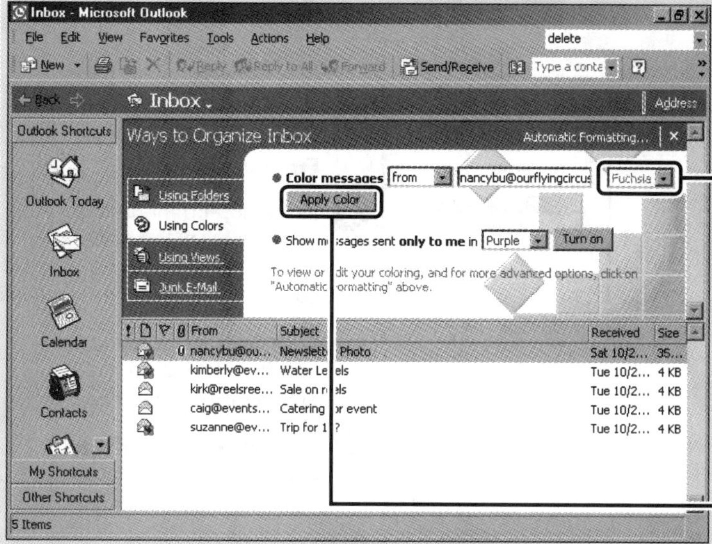

7 Click the **Color** ▾ and select the color you want to use to color code.

8 Click **Apply Color**.

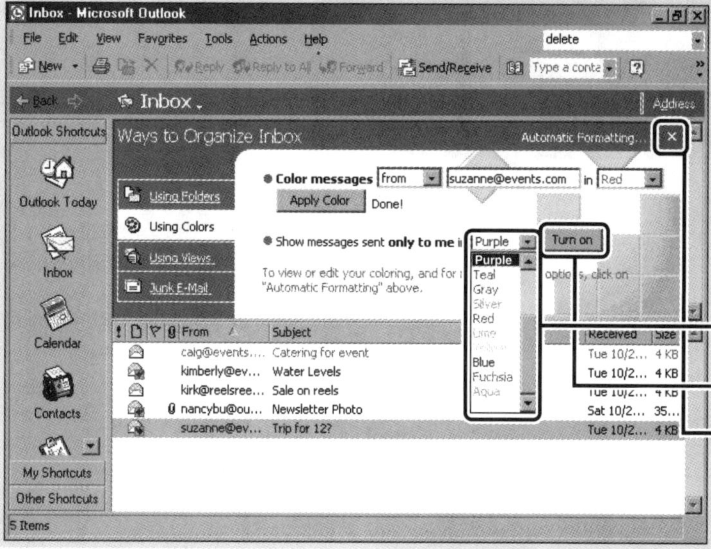

9 Click the **Color** ▾ and select the color you want e-mail messages sent only to you in.

10 Click **Turn On**.

11 Click ✕.

- Outlook applies your color coding preferences.

SORT MESSAGES

You can easily sort e-mail messages in ascending or descending order in your Inbox or any folder. You can also change the way you see the contents of your Inbox or folder by changing the view. Views allow you to organize and sort your Outlook items in a variety of ways. For example, you can tell Outlook to sort your messages by subject.

SORT IN ASCENDING OR DESCENDING ORDER

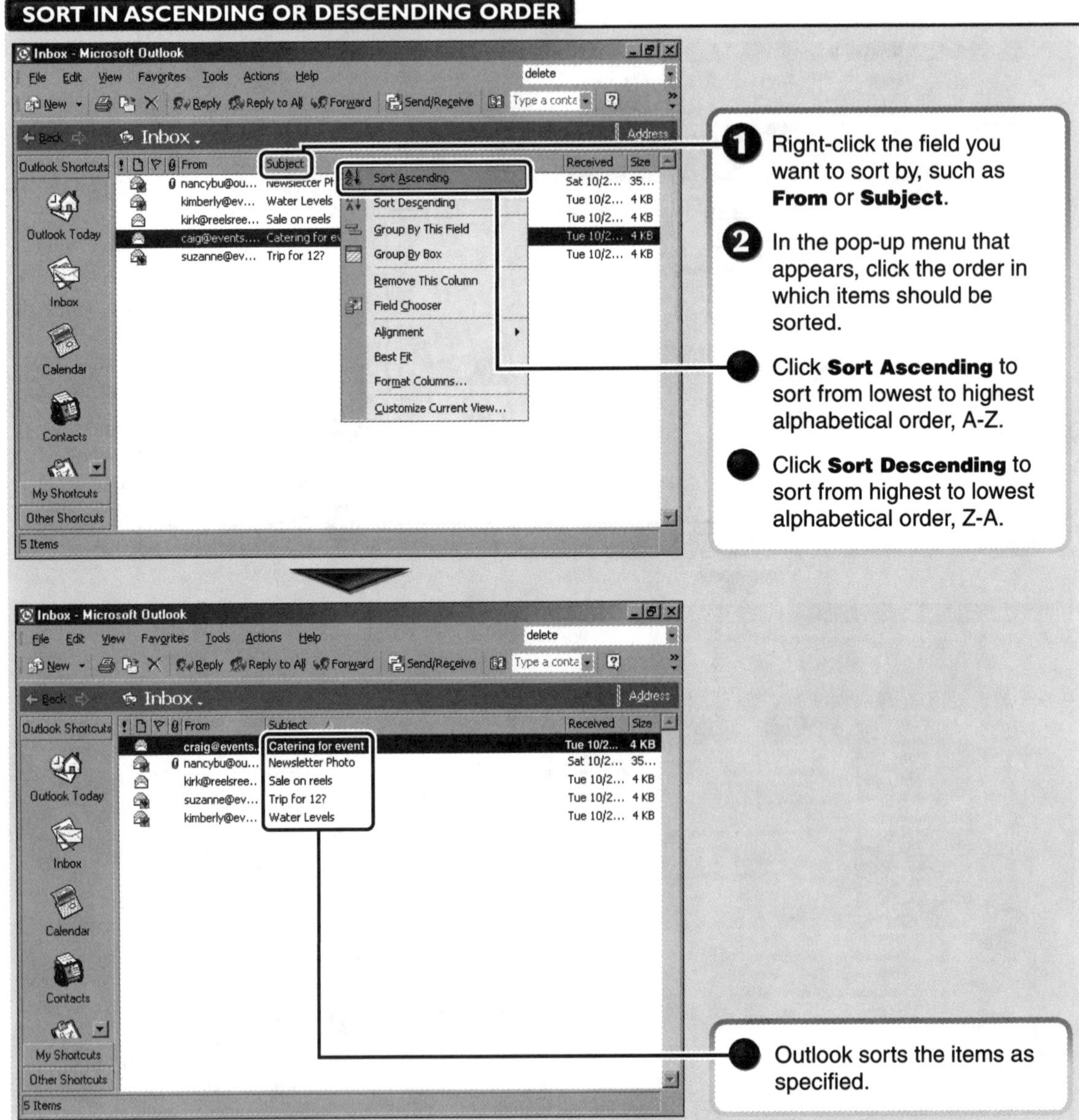

1. Right-click the field you want to sort by, such as **From** or **Subject**.

2. In the pop-up menu that appears, click the order in which items should be sorted.

- Click **Sort Ascending** to sort from lowest to highest alphabetical order, A-Z.
- Click **Sort Descending** to sort from highest to lowest alphabetical order, Z-A.

- Outlook sorts the items as specified.

in an instant

SORT BY CHANGING VIEWS

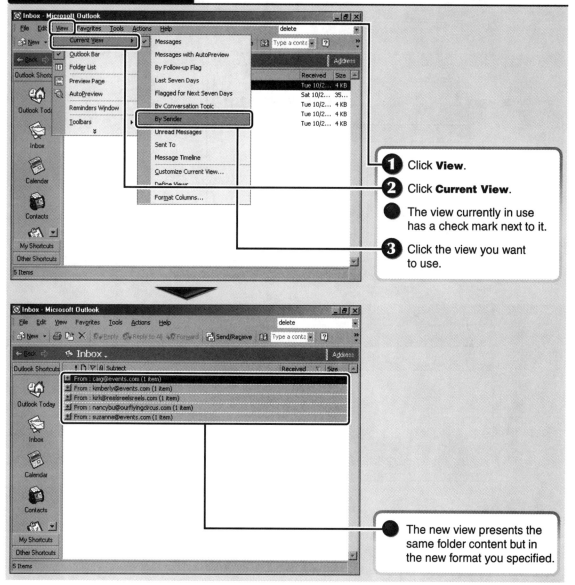

1. Click **View**.
2. Click **Current View**.
   - The view currently in use has a check mark next to it.
3. Click the view you want to use.

- The new view presents the same folder content but in the new format you specified.

USING RULES

You can use rules to help manage and organize the e-mail messages you send or receive. For example, you can use rules to automatically move e-mail messages received by or sent to a specific person or containing certain content. You can also use rules to flag messages for later follow-up.

USING RULES

1 Click **Tools**.

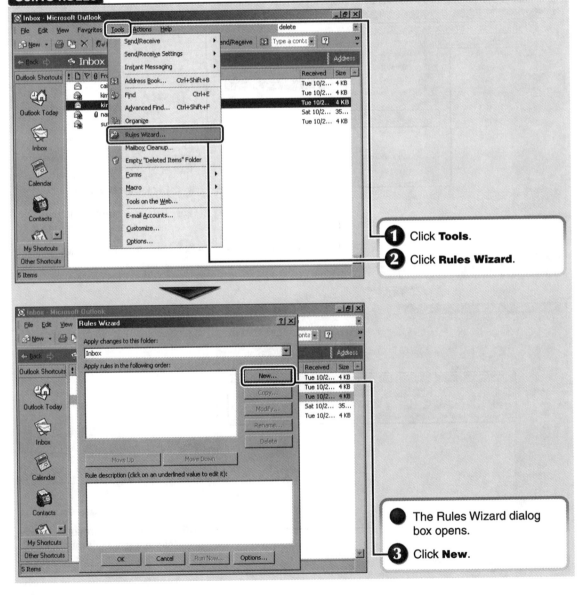

2 Click **Rules Wizard**.

- The Rules Wizard dialog box opens.

3 Click **New**.

in an instant

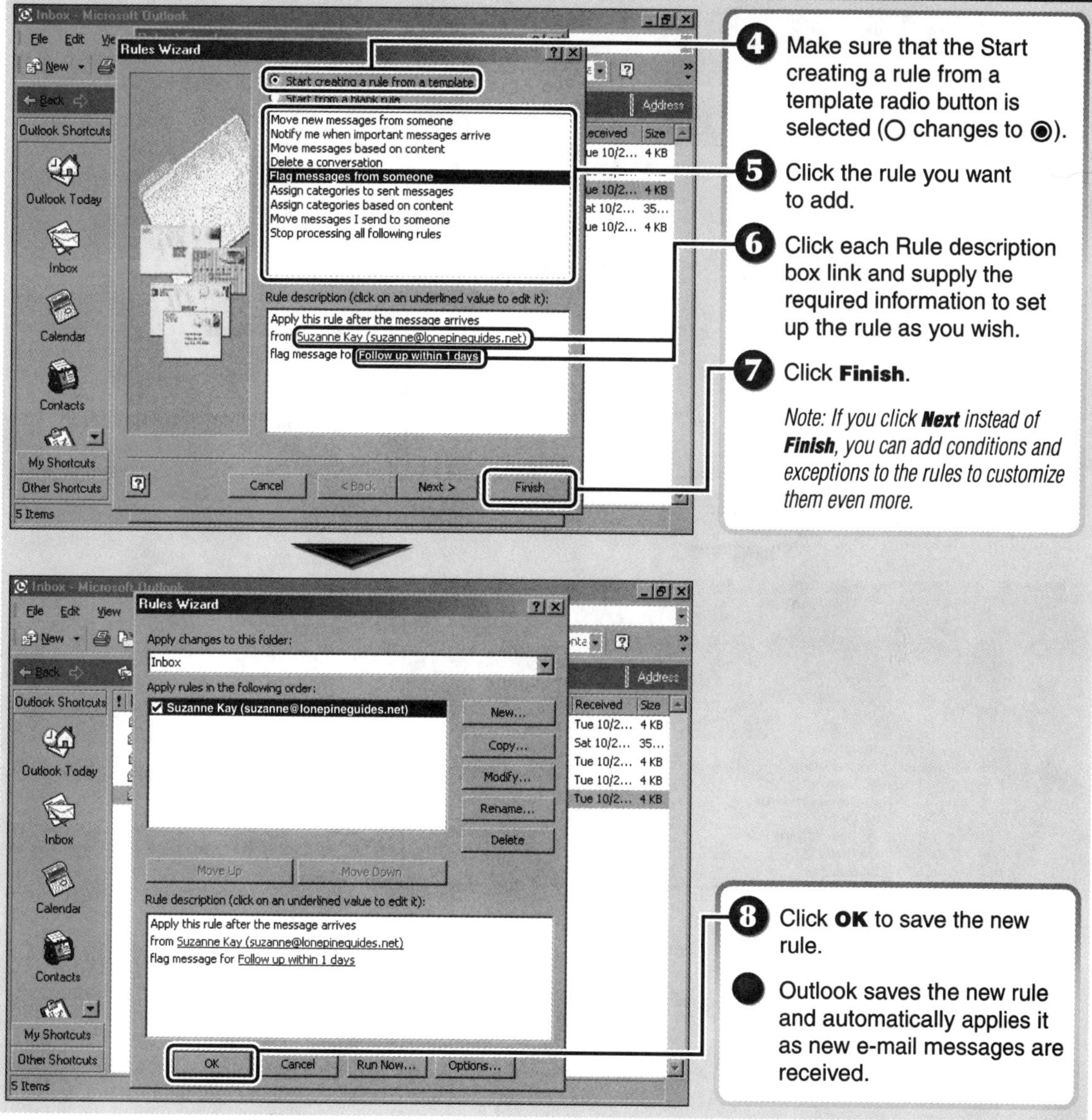

4. Make sure that the Start creating a rule from a template radio button is selected (○ changes to ◉).
5. Click the rule you want to add.
6. Click each Rule description box link and supply the required information to set up the rule as you wish.
7. Click **Finish**.

*Note: If you click **Next** instead of **Finish**, you can add conditions and exceptions to the rules to customize them even more.*

8. Click **OK** to save the new rule.

- Outlook saves the new rule and automatically applies it as new e-mail messages are received.

RUN RULES NOW

You can use rules to specify what actions Outlook should take automatically after receiving e-mail messages, such as automatically moving or flagging messages. However, if you want to apply rules to messages that have already been received, you can use the Outlook Run Rules Now feature to apply rules to your Inbox or any other folder.

RUN RULES NOW

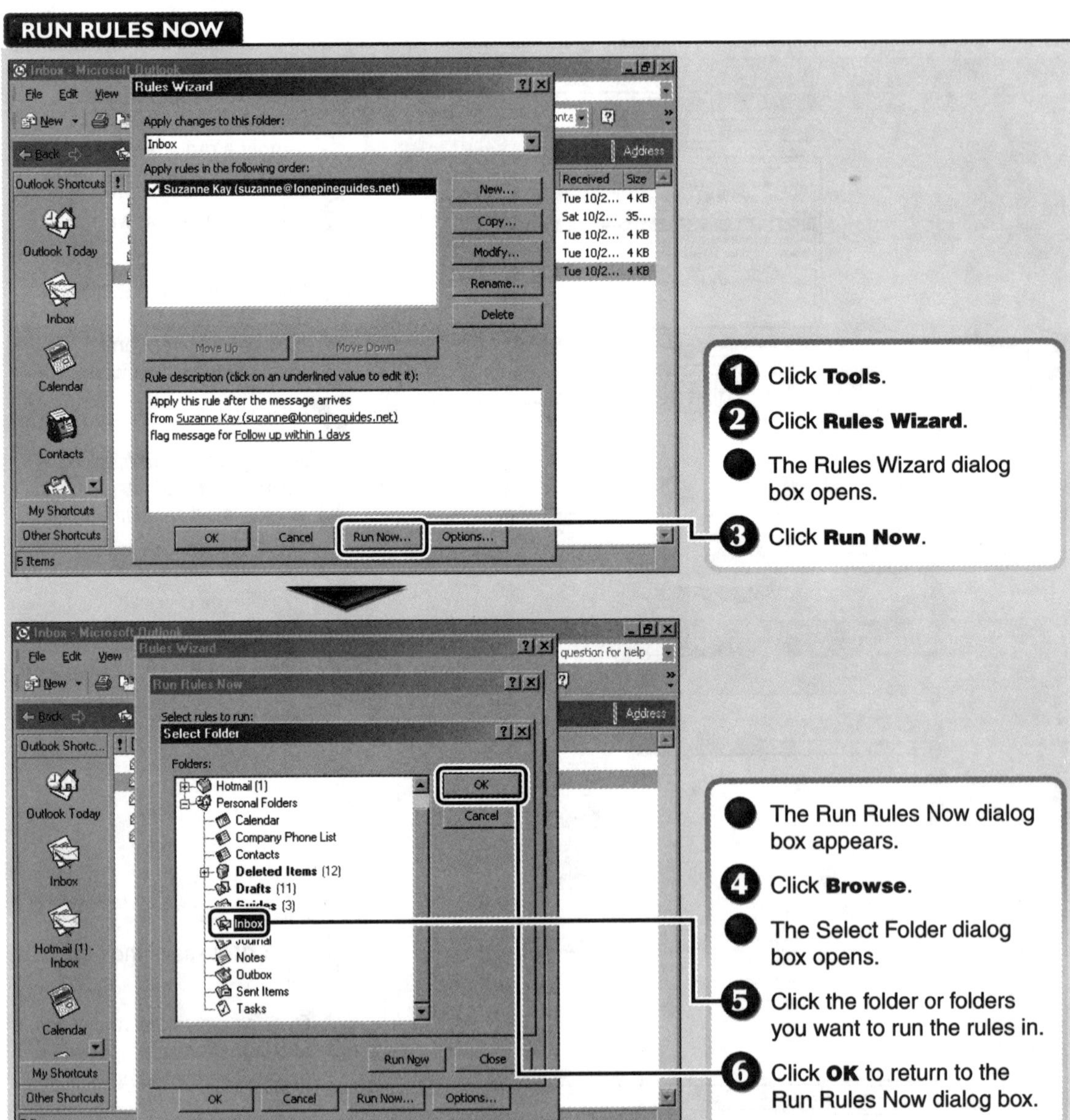

in an instant

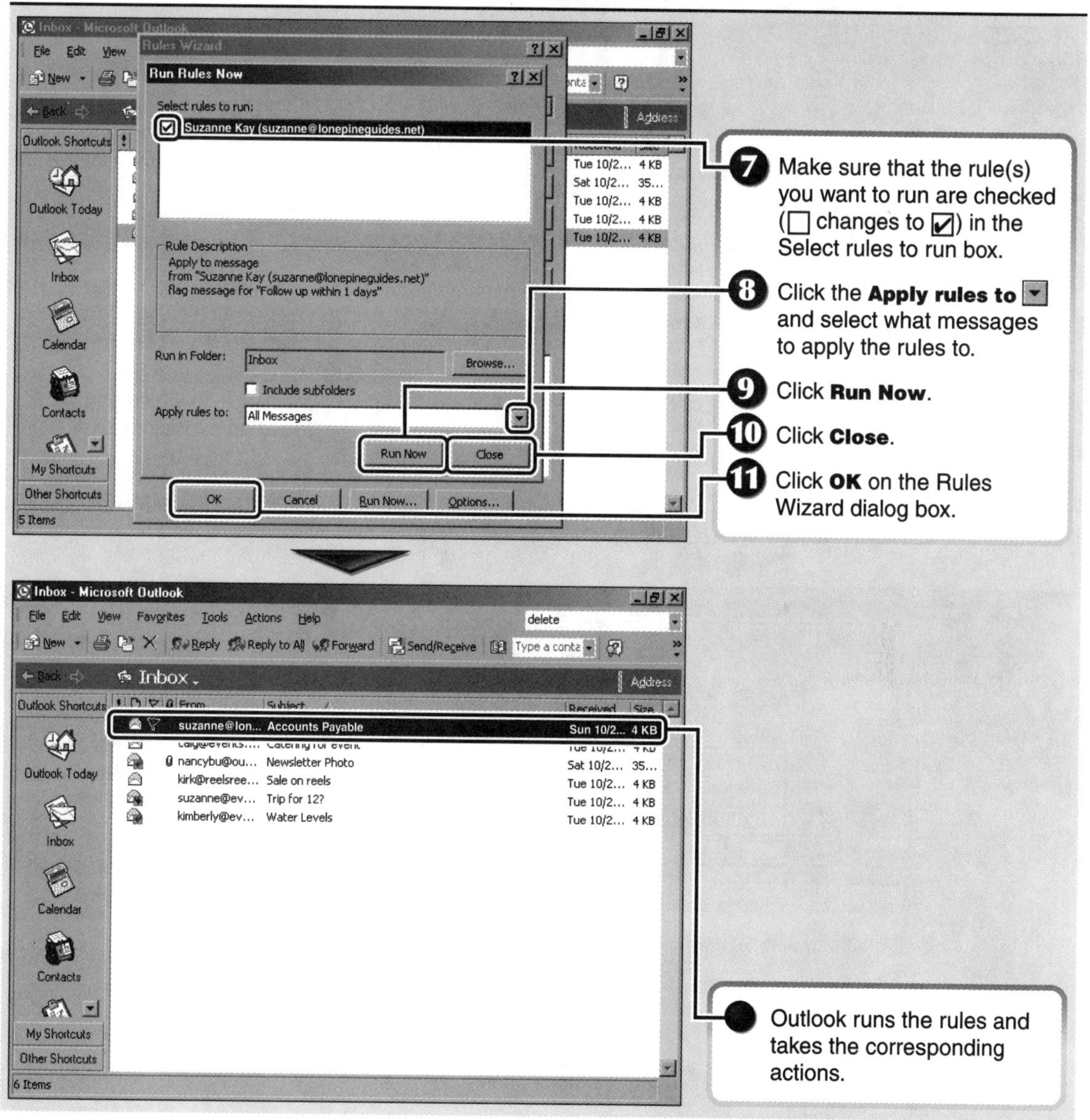

7 Make sure that the rule(s) you want to run are checked (☐ changes to ☑) in the Select rules to run box.

8 Click the **Apply rules to** ▼ and select what messages to apply the rules to.

9 Click **Run Now**.

10 Click **Close**.

11 Click **OK** on the Rules Wizard dialog box.

- Outlook runs the rules and takes the corresponding actions.

USING AUTOARCHIVE

You can help keep your Inbox and other folders from containing old and outdated content by using AutoArchive. AutoArchive, which is on by default, periodically moves old and expired content to an archive file. AutoArchive uses customizable rules to determine when content becomes old, and you can also flag e-mail messages with an expiration date for archival after a specific date.

ASSIGN AN EXPIRATION DATE TO MESSAGES

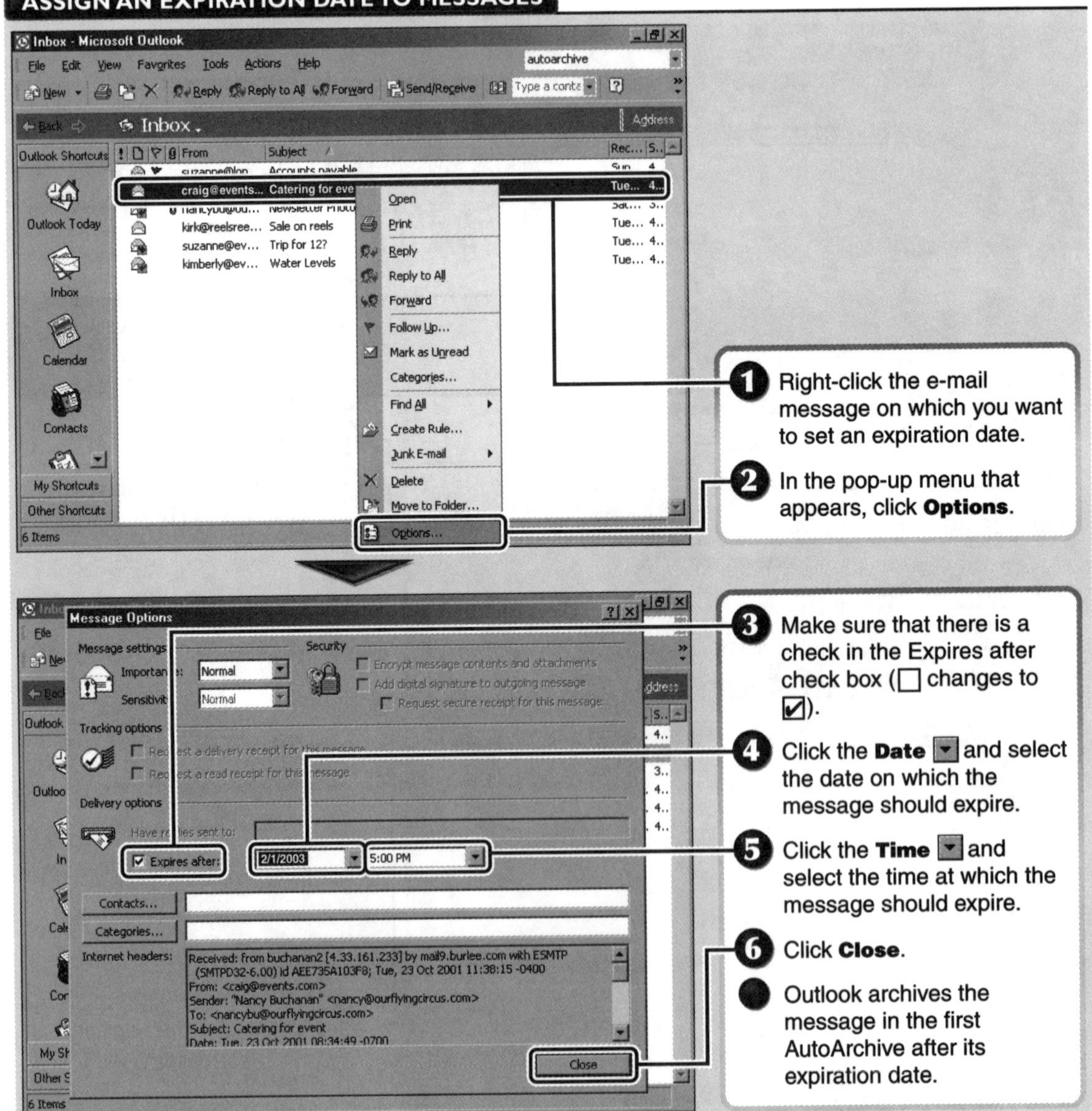

1 Right-click the e-mail message on which you want to set an expiration date.
2 In the pop-up menu that appears, click **Options**.
3 Make sure that there is a check in the Expires after check box (☐ changes to ☑).
4 Click the **Date** ▾ and select the date on which the message should expire.
5 Click the **Time** ▾ and select the time at which the message should expire.
6 Click **Close**.
● Outlook archives the message in the first AutoArchive after its expiration date.

in an instant

SET AUTOARCHIVE PREFERENCES

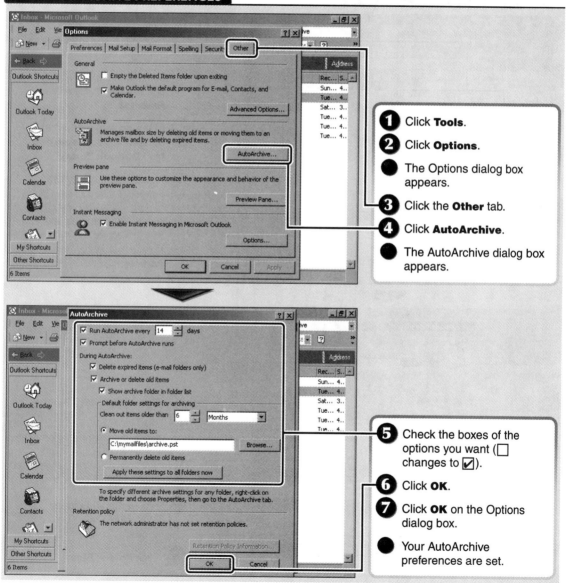

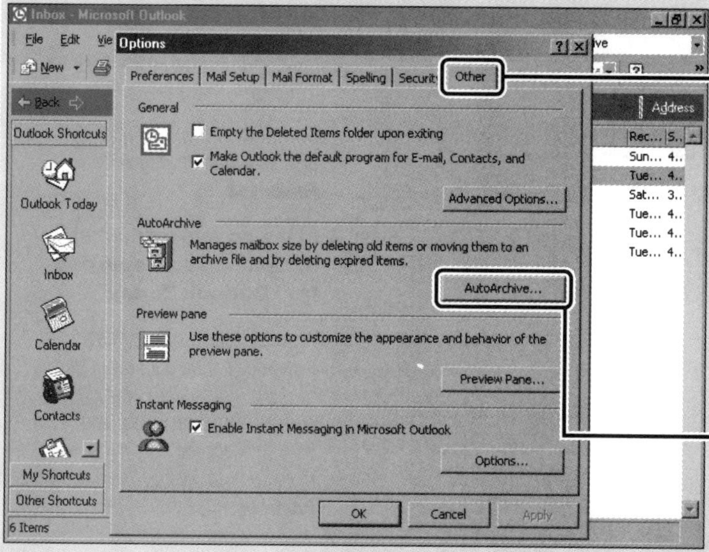

1. Click **Tools**.
2. Click **Options**.
   - The Options dialog box appears.
3. Click the **Other** tab.
4. Click **AutoArchive**.
   - The AutoArchive dialog box appears.
5. Check the boxes of the options you want (☐ changes to ☑). 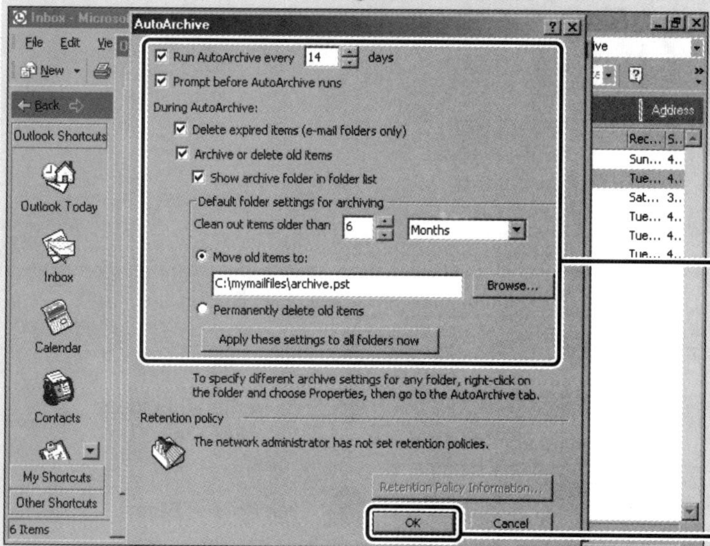
6. Click **OK**.
7. Click **OK** on the Options dialog box.
   - Your AutoArchive preferences are set.

FIND THE SIZE OF YOUR MAILBOX

You can find out how large your mailbox or even specific folders are from within Outlook. The ability to find out how large your mail files are is important because most e-mail providers limit mailbox file sizes, and when limits are reached, incoming e-mail messages are often rejected.

FIND THE SIZE OF YOUR MAILBOX

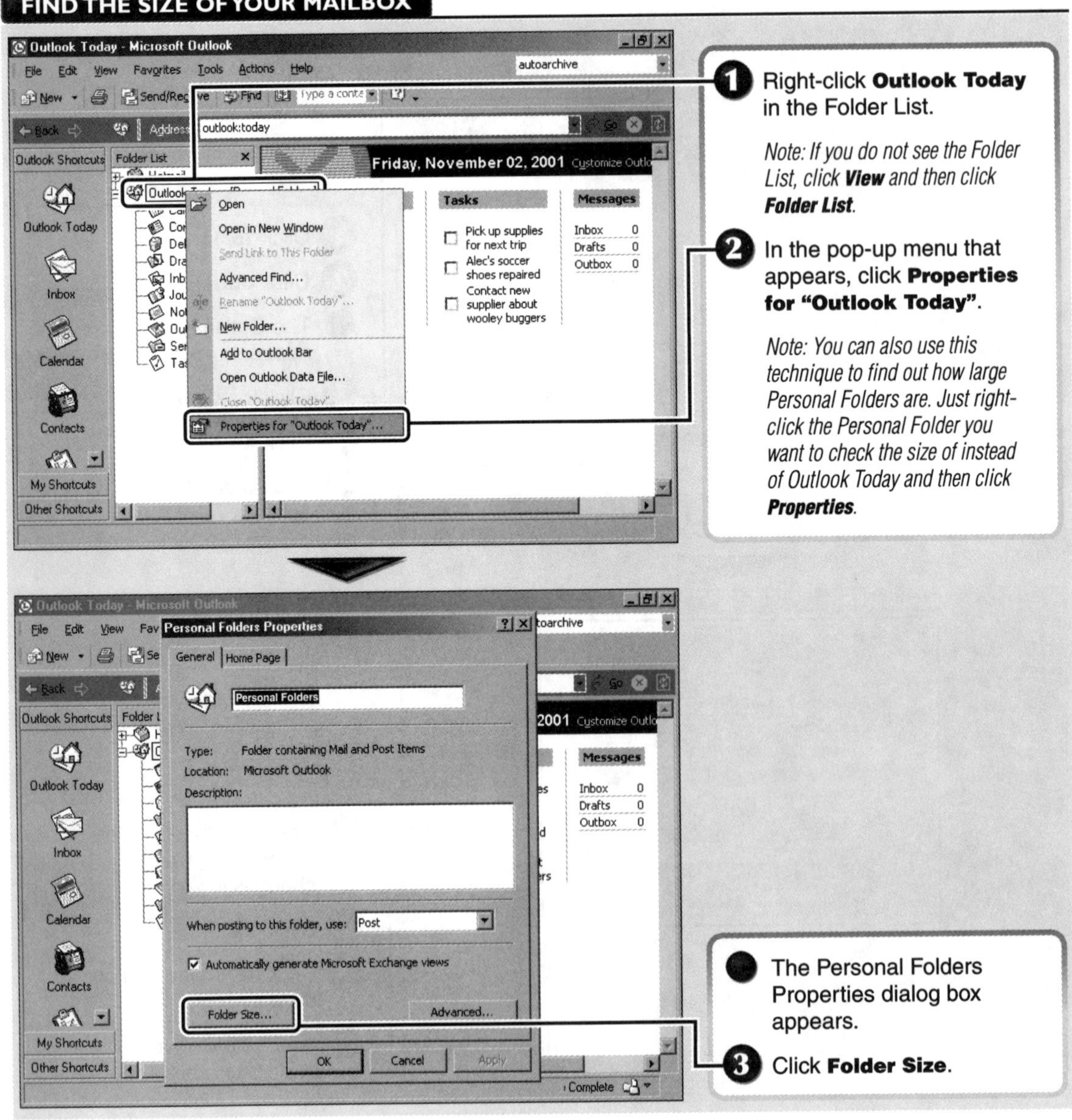

1. Right-click **Outlook Today** in the Folder List.

   *Note: If you do not see the Folder List, click **View** and then click **Folder List**.*

2. In the pop-up menu that appears, click **Properties for "Outlook Today"**.

   *Note: You can also use this technique to find out how large Personal Folders are. Just right-click the Personal Folder you want to check the size of instead of Outlook Today and then click **Properties**.*

- The Personal Folders Properties dialog box appears.

3. Click **Folder Size**.

in an instant

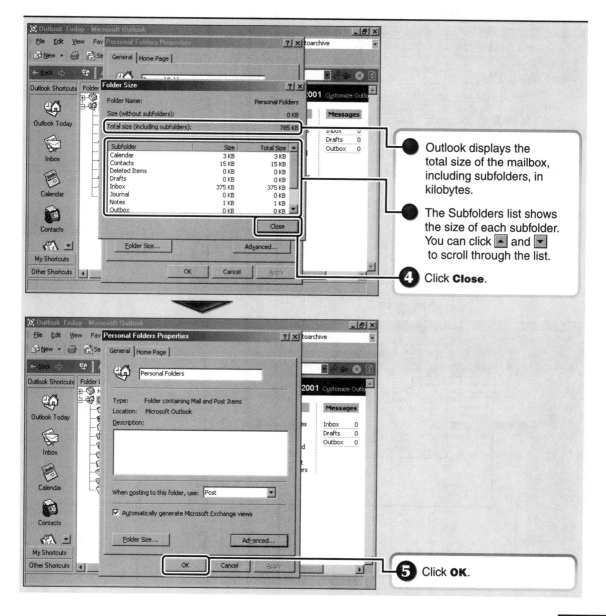

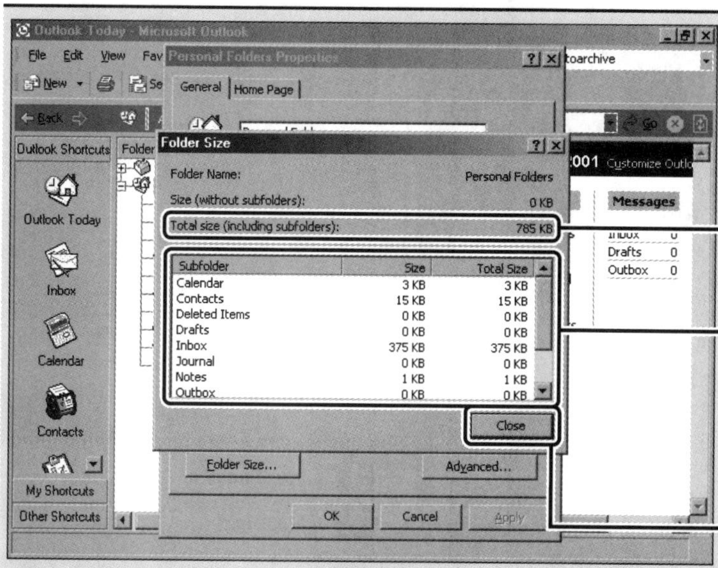

- Outlook displays the total size of the mailbox, including subfolders, in kilobytes.
- The Subfolders list shows the size of each subfolder. You can click ▲ and ▼ to scroll through the list.

4 Click **Close**.

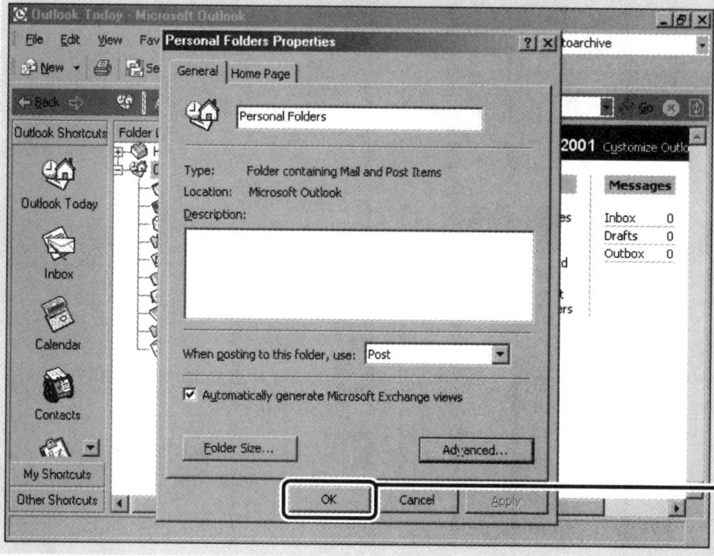

5 Click **OK**.

FIND E-MAIL MESSAGES

You can use Outlook to quickly find e-mail messages containing any text that you specify. Outlook also has a more advanced search procedure; for information on that, see "Using Advanced Find," later in this chapter.

FIND E-MAIL MESSAGES

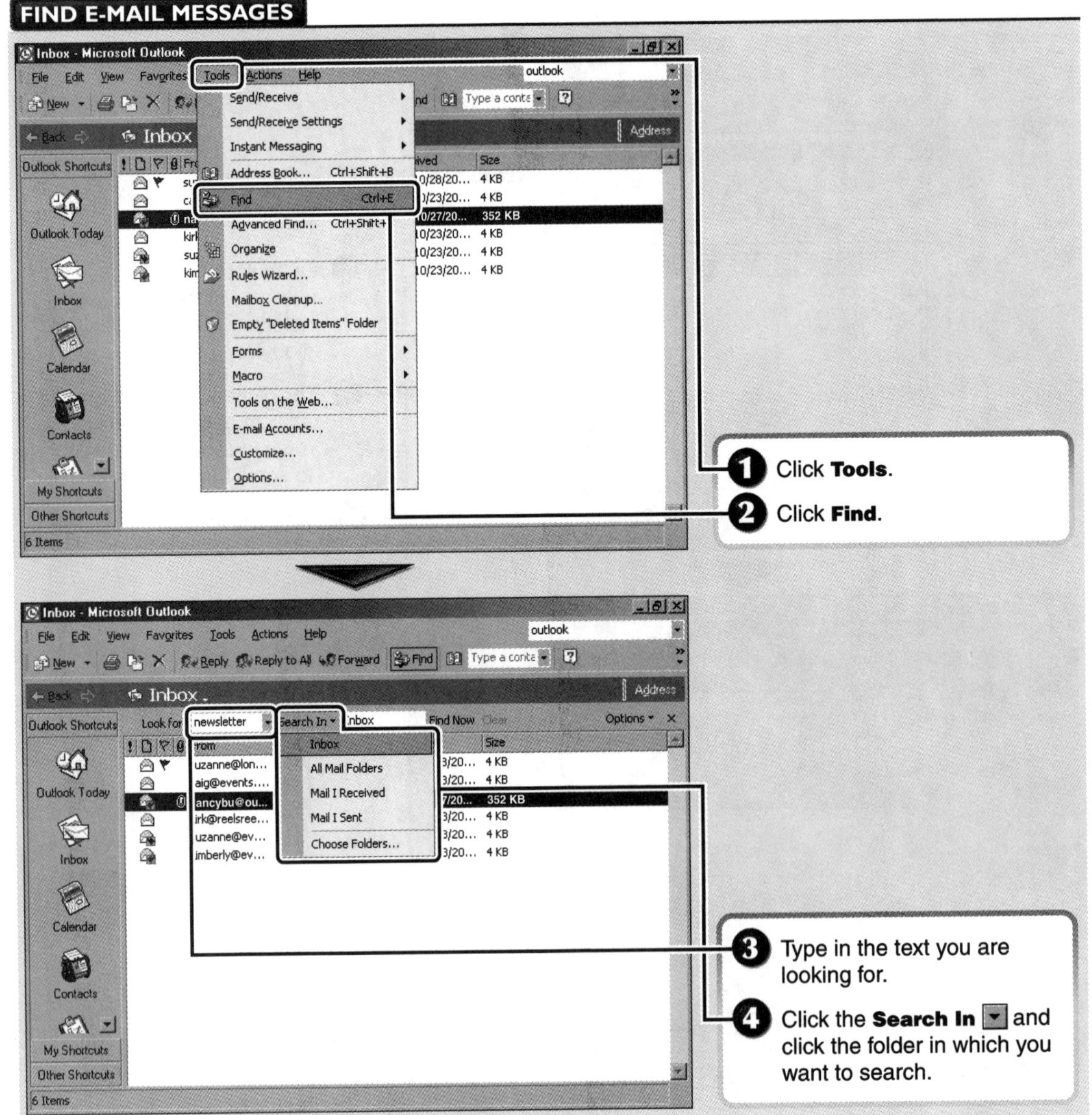

1 Click **Tools**.
2 Click **Find**.
3 Type in the text you are looking for.
4 Click the **Search In** ▾ and click the folder in which you want to search.

in an instant

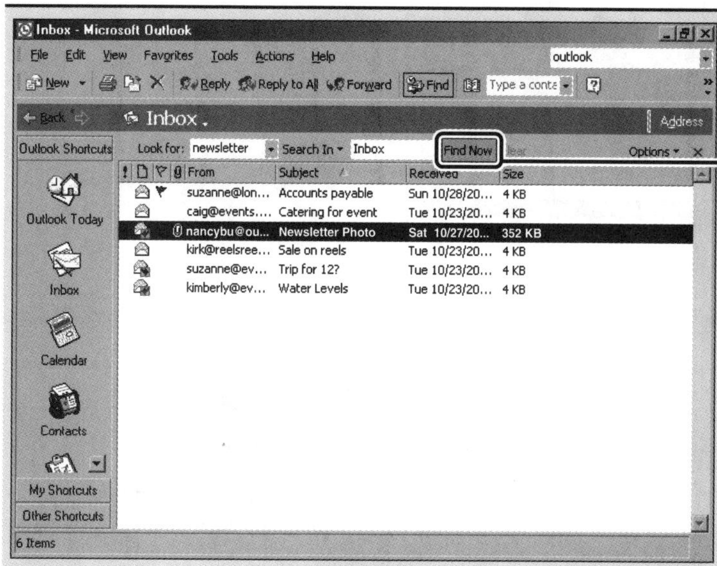

5 Click **Find Now**.

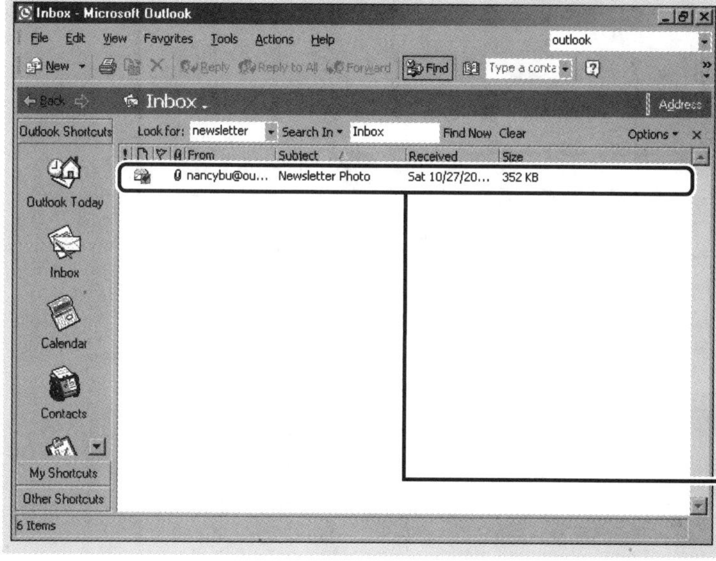

Outlook displays the search results.

USING ADVANCED FIND

You can use the Outlook Advanced Find dialog box to search across all types of Outlook items by a wide variety of criteria.

USING ADVANCED FIND

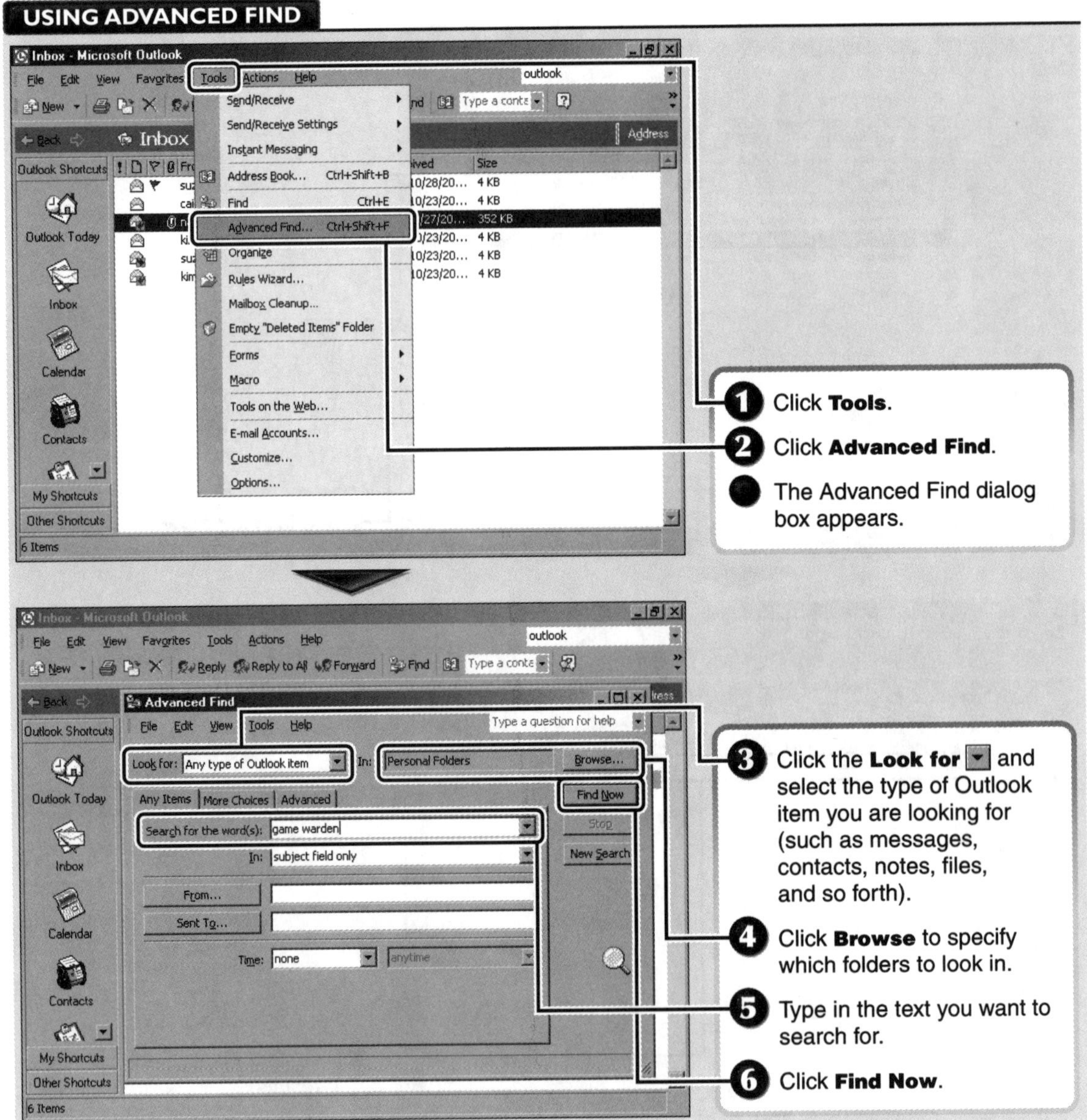

1. Click **Tools**.
2. Click **Advanced Find**.

- The Advanced Find dialog box appears.

3. Click the **Look for** ▼ and select the type of Outlook item you are looking for (such as messages, contacts, notes, files, and so forth).
4. Click **Browse** to specify which folders to look in.
5. Type in the text you want to search for.
6. Click **Find Now**.

in an instant

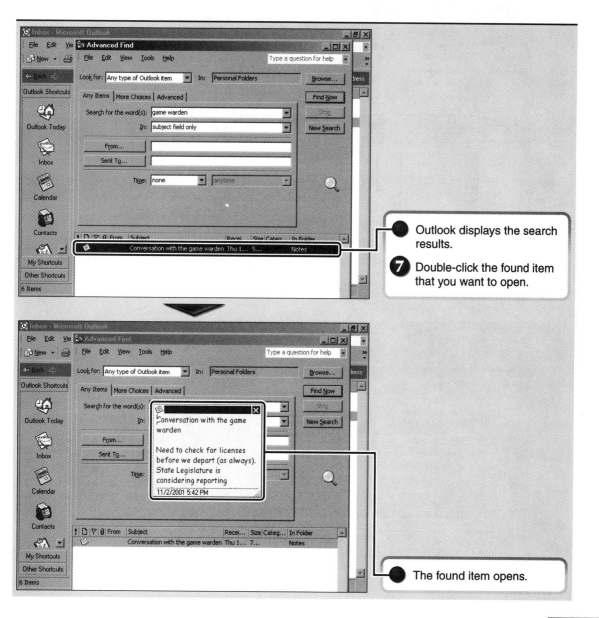

- Outlook displays the search results.
7. Double-click the found item that you want to open.

- The found item opens.

FIND E-MAIL MESSAGES BY SIZE

You can use the Advanced Find dialog box to find Outlook items that are less than, equal to, or greater than a particular size. This is often useful if your mailbox is getting large in size and you want to find items that might need to be moved or deleted. This is particularly helpful in finding e-mail messages that include large attachments.

FIND E-MAIL MESSAGES BY SIZE

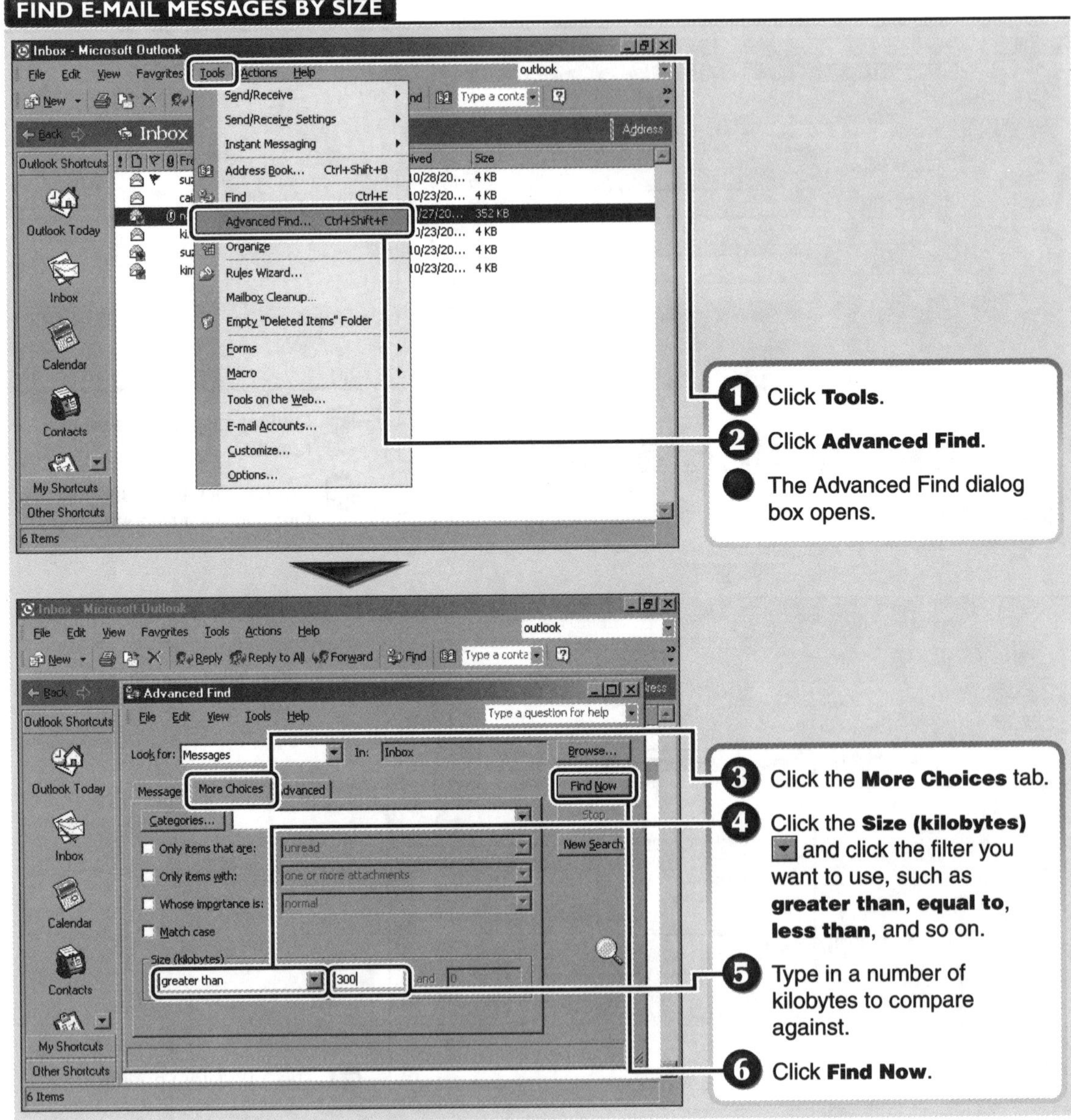

1. Click **Tools**.
2. Click **Advanced Find**.
- The Advanced Find dialog box opens.

3. Click the **More Choices** tab.
4. Click the **Size (kilobytes)** ▾ and click the filter you want to use, such as **greater than**, **equal to**, **less than**, and so on.
5. Type in a number of kilobytes to compare against.
6. Click **Find Now**.

in an instant

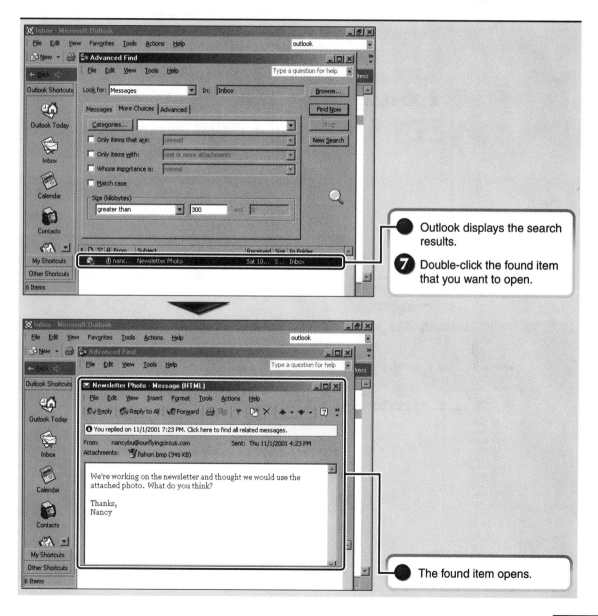

- Outlook displays the search results.
- 7 Double-click the found item that you want to open.
- The found item opens.

VIEW FOLDERS

Outlook stores similar items in folders, which work much like file folders in your office or home office. You can use the Folder List to quickly view your available folders. Default folders include Sent Items, Drafts, Deleted Items, and more.

VIEW FOLDERS

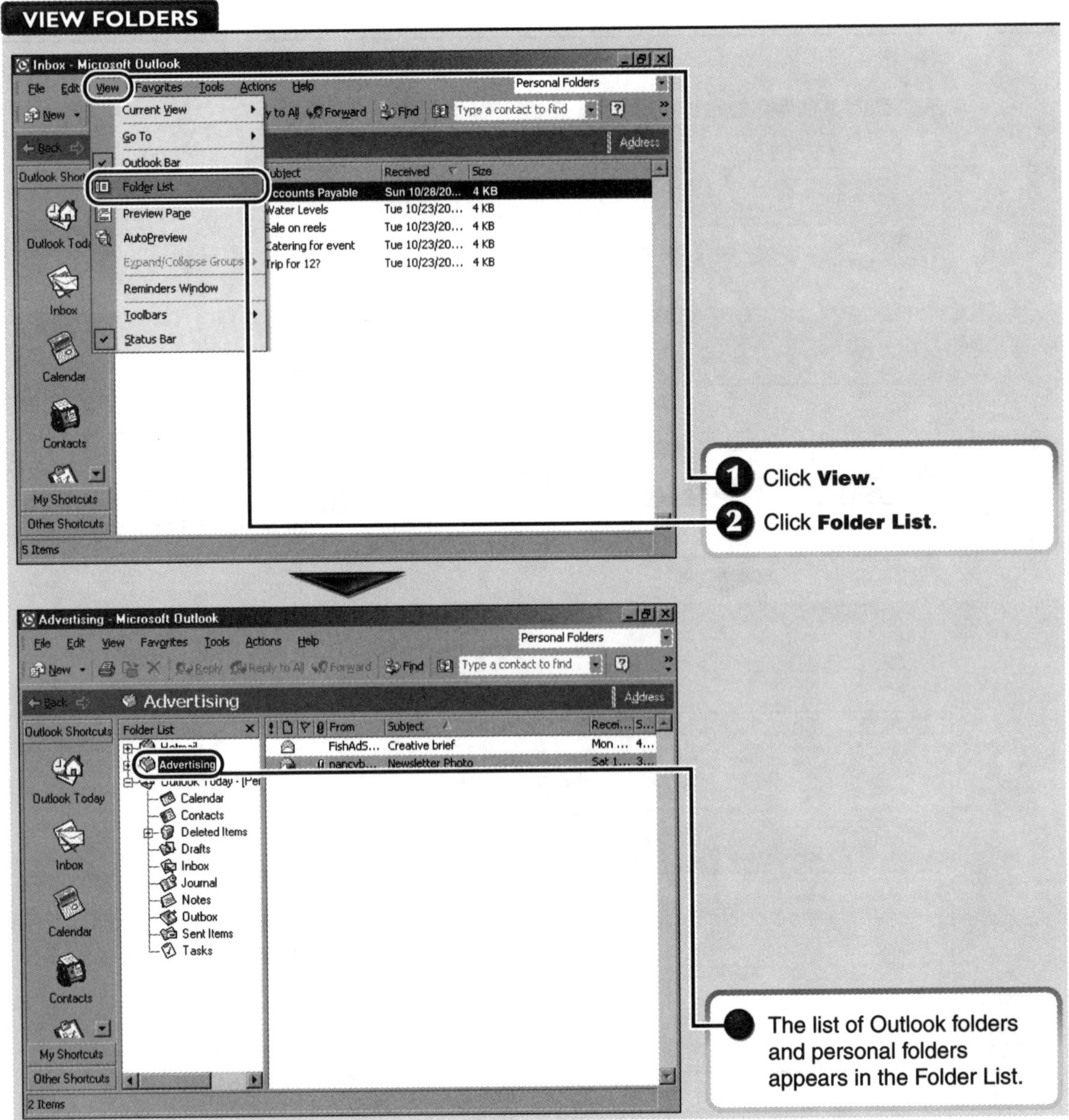

1 Click **View**.

2 Click **Folder List**.

- The list of Outlook folders and personal folders appears in the Folder List.

CREATE A NEW OUTLOOK FOLDER

Outlook has two types of folders: Outlook folders and personal folders. *Outlook folders* are stored along with the rest of your folders on your e-mail server. Creating a new Outlook folder is easy.

CREATE A NEW OUTLOOK FOLDER

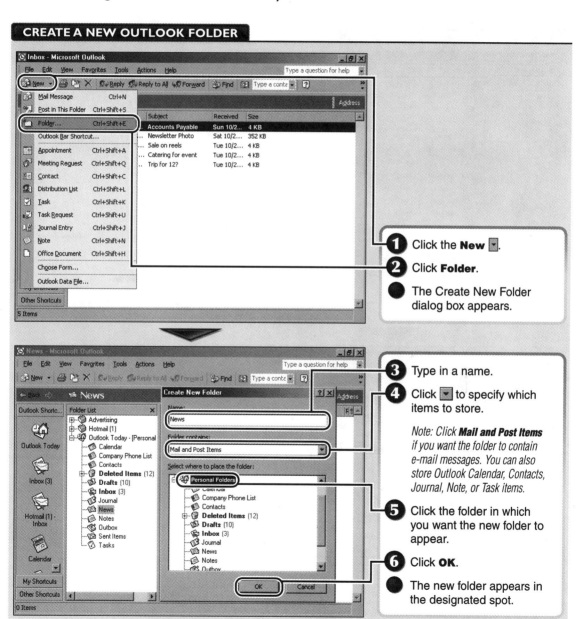

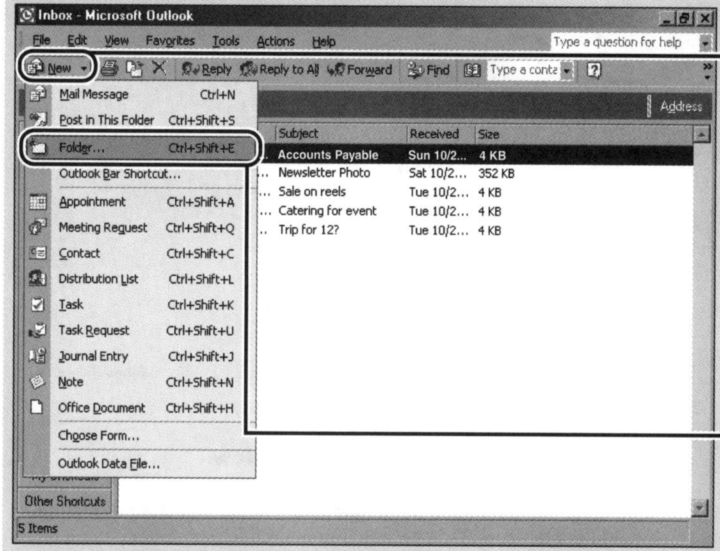

1. Click the **New** ▾.
2. Click **Folder**.

- The Create New Folder dialog box appears.

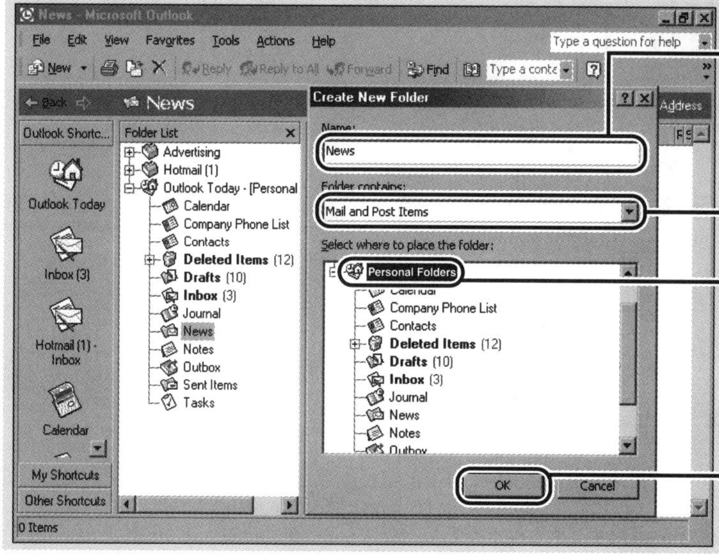

3. Type in a name.
4. Click ▾ to specify which items to store.

*Note: Click **Mail and Post Items** if you want the folder to contain e-mail messages. You can also store Outlook Calendar, Contacts, Journal, Note, or Task items.*

5. Click the folder in which you want the new folder to appear.
6. Click **OK**.

- The new folder appears in the designated spot.

CREATE A NEW PERSONAL FOLDER

Personal folders are created on your workstation or on a network drive instead of in your Outlook Mailbox on the server. Personal folders provide a convenient way to store collections of e-mail messages in separate files. Even though the folder may not be on the server, you can still access the folder through the Folder List.

CREATE A NEW PERSONAL FOLDER

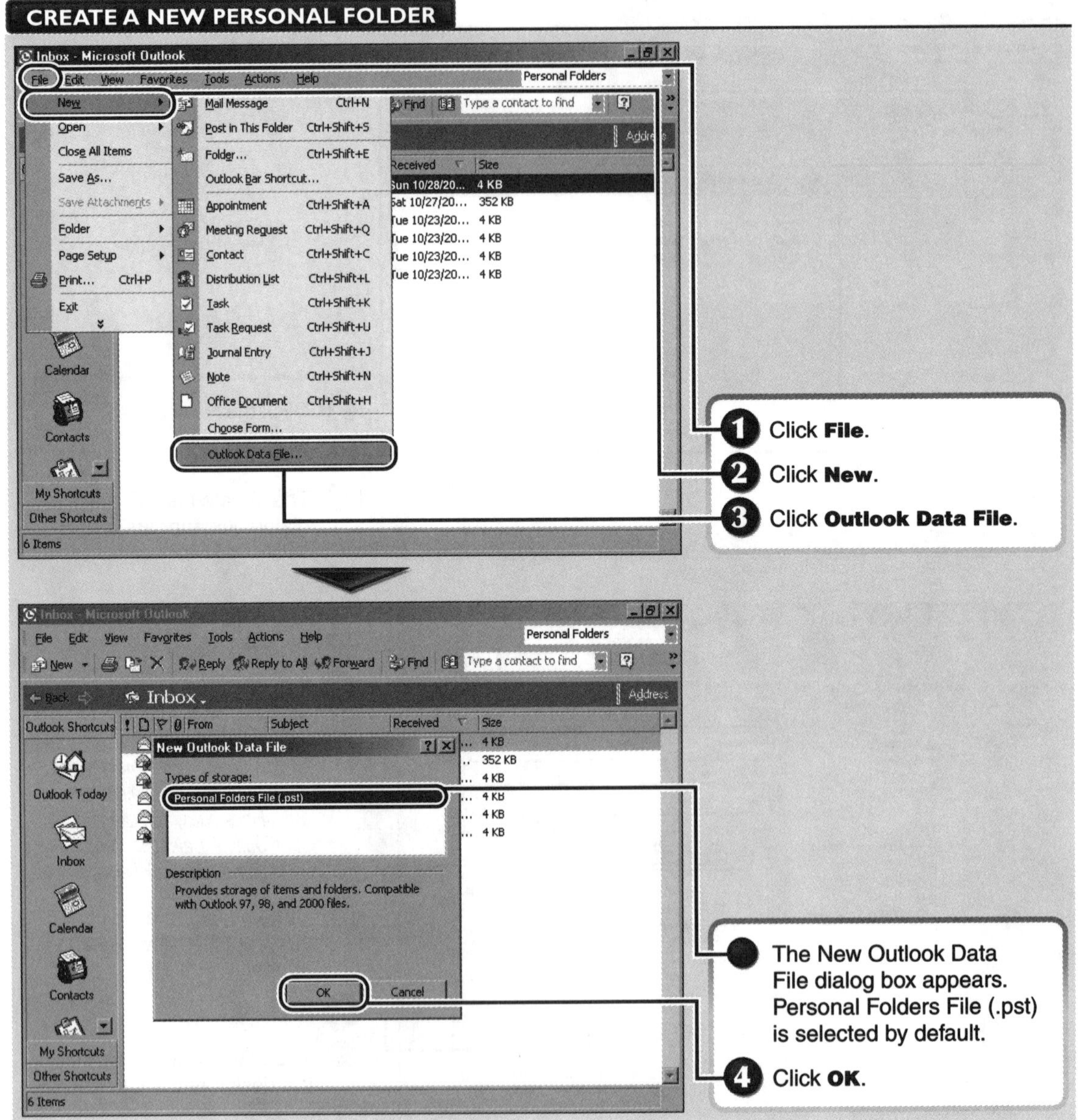

1. Click **File**.
2. Click **New**.
3. Click **Outlook Data File**.

- The New Outlook Data File dialog box appears. Personal Folders File (.pst) is selected by default.

4. Click **OK**.

in an instant

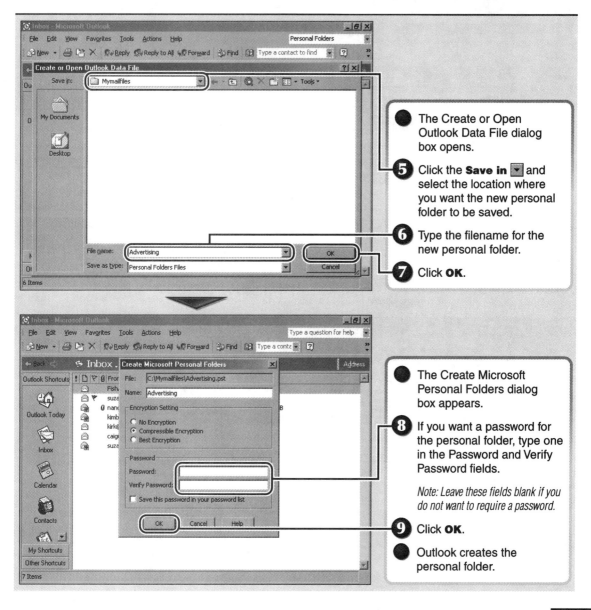

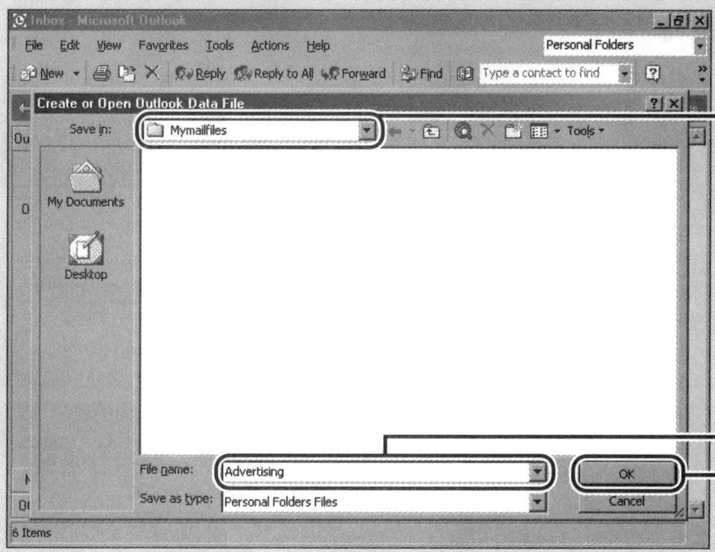

- The Create or Open Outlook Data File dialog box opens.

5. Click the **Save in** ▾ and select the location where you want the new personal folder to be saved.

6. Type the filename for the new personal folder.

7. Click **OK**.

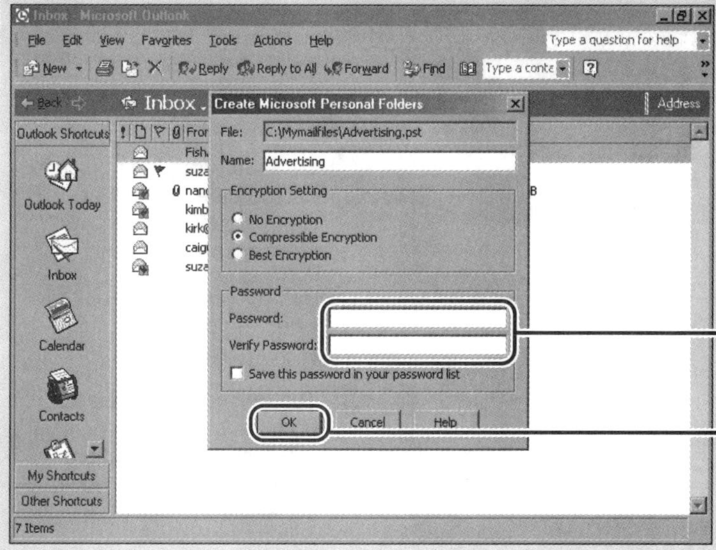

- The Create Microsoft Personal Folders dialog box appears.

8. If you want a password for the personal folder, type one in the Password and Verify Password fields.

   Note: Leave these fields blank if you do not want to require a password.

9. Click **OK**.

- Outlook creates the personal folder.

MOVE E-MAIL TO A FOLDER

You can keep your Inbox organized by moving e-mail messages to different folders. For example, if you are working on a special project, you might want to move all the e-mails about the project to one folder. Moving messages between folders is a simple drag-and-drop operation.

MOVE E-MAIL TO A FOLDER

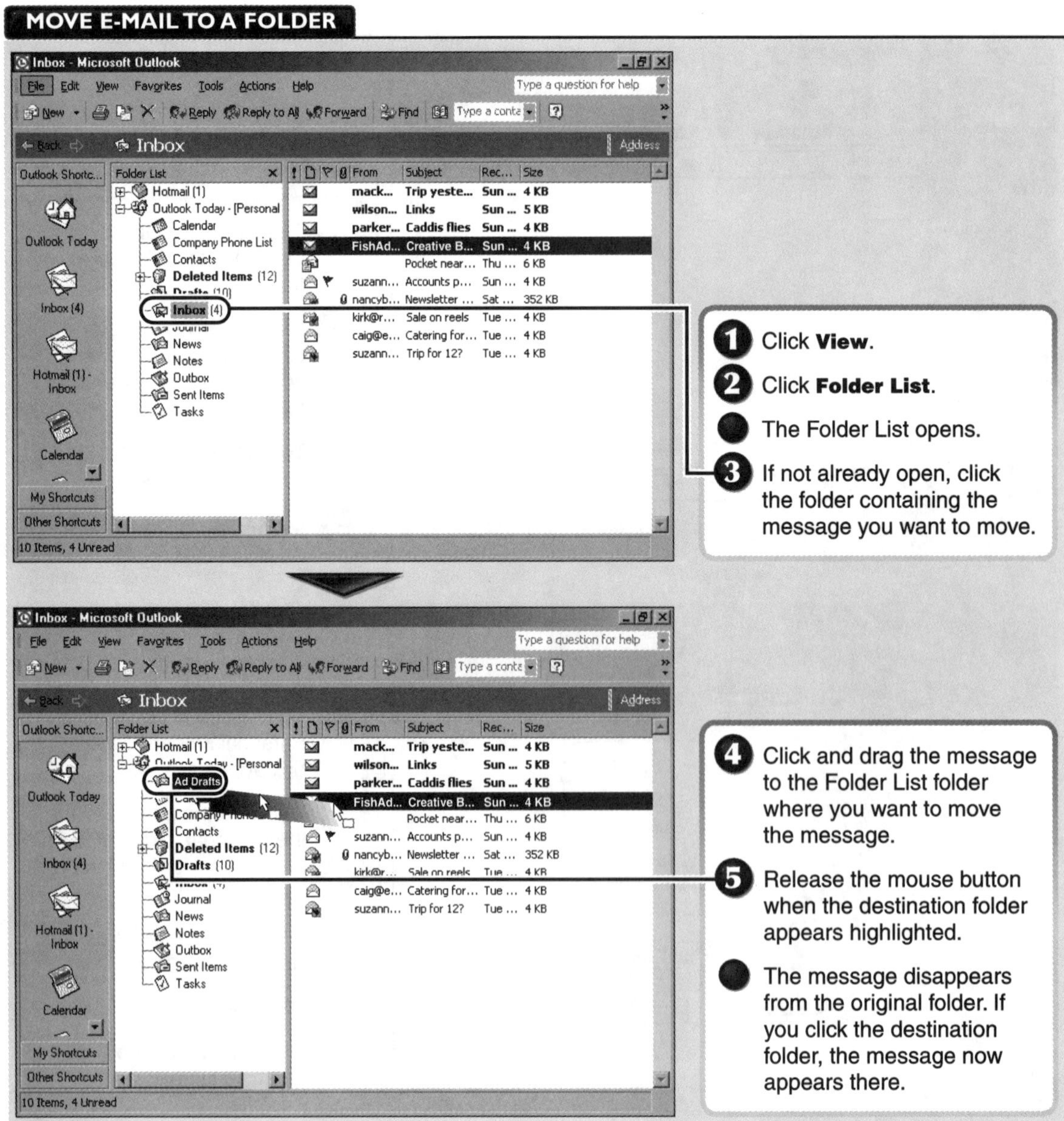

1. Click **View**.
2. Click **Folder List**.

- The Folder List opens.

3. If not already open, click the folder containing the message you want to move.
4. Click and drag the message to the Folder List folder where you want to move the message.
5. Release the mouse button when the destination folder appears highlighted.

- The message disappears from the original folder. If you click the destination folder, the message now appears there.

MOVE A FOLDER

You can easily move folders from one Outlook folder to another, or even from one personal folder to another. For example, you might have a folder for completed tasks into which you can drag project folders after you finish the projects.

MOVE A FOLDER

1 Click **View**.

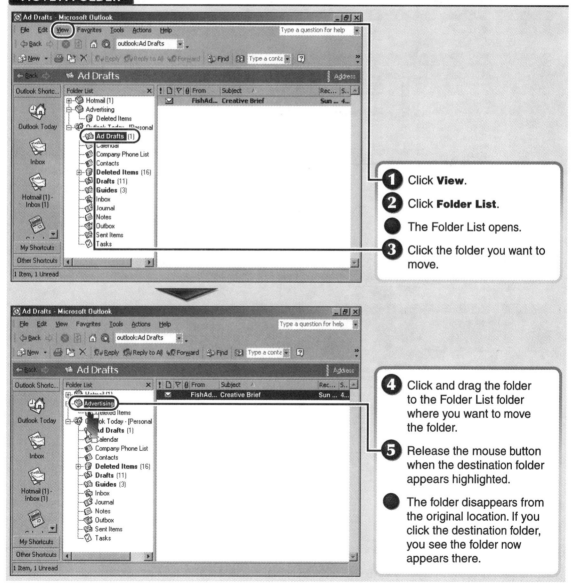

2 Click **Folder List**.

● The Folder List opens.

3 Click the folder you want to move.

4 Click and drag the folder to the Folder List folder where you want to move the folder.

5 Release the mouse button when the destination folder appears highlighted.

● The folder disappears from the original location. If you click the destination folder, you see the folder now appears there.

RENAME A FOLDER

You can rename folders easily in Outlook. You can either rename the folder directly in the Folder List, or you can rename the folder using the Properties dialog box. Personal folders should be renamed using the Properties dialog box.

RENAME IN THE FOLDER LIST

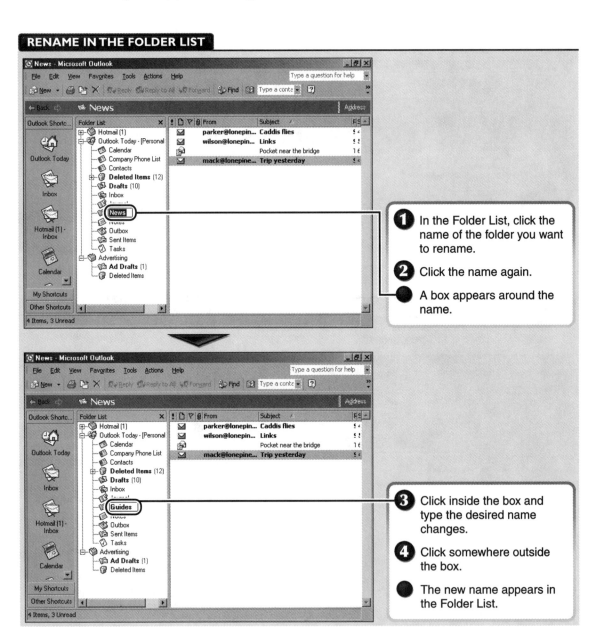

1. In the Folder List, click the name of the folder you want to rename.
2. Click the name again.

- A box appears around the name.

3. Click inside the box and type the desired name changes.
4. Click somewhere outside the box.

- The new name appears in the Folder List.

in an instant

RENAME USING THE PROPERTIES DIALOG BOX

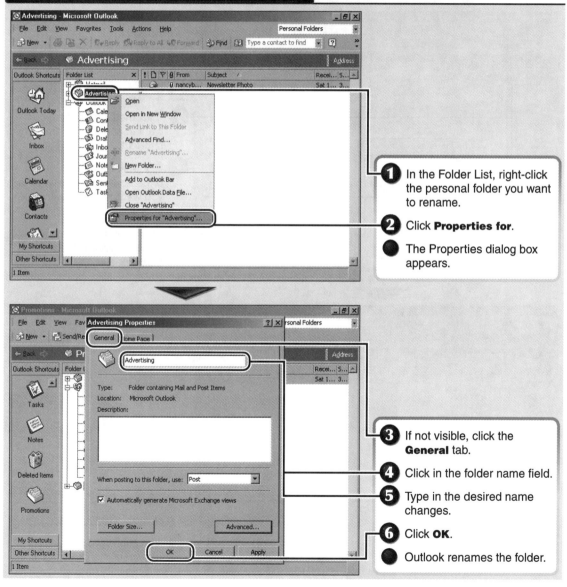

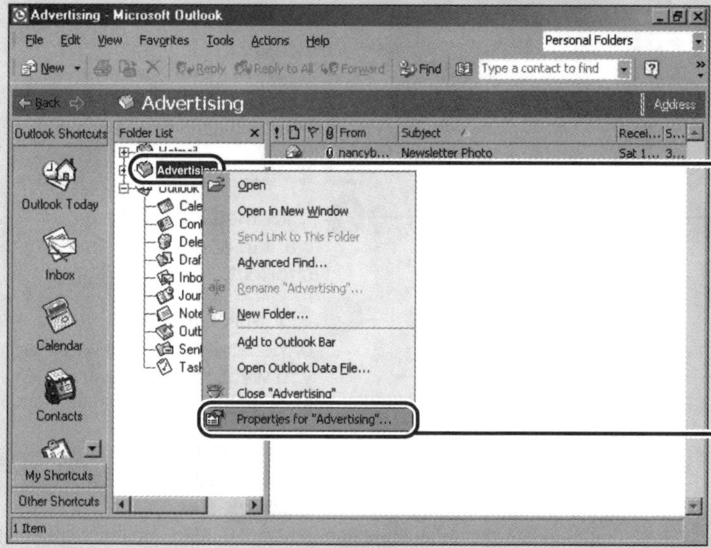

1 In the Folder List, right-click the personal folder you want to rename.

2 Click **Properties for**.

- The Properties dialog box appears.

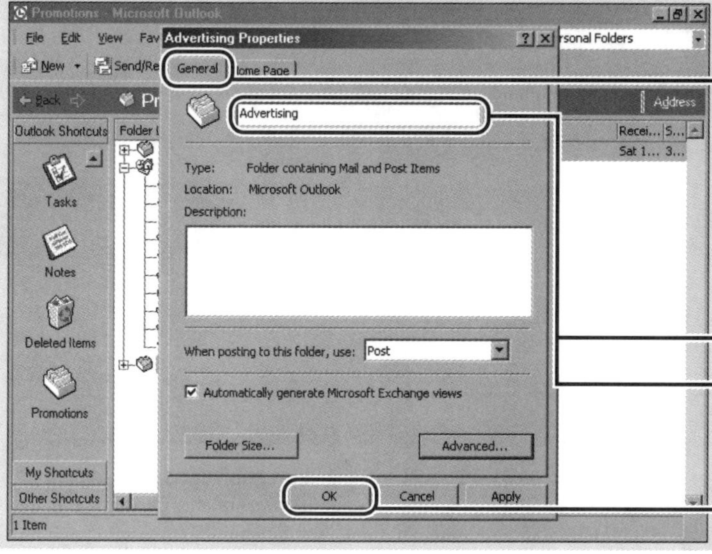

3 If not visible, click the **General** tab.

4 Click in the folder name field.

5 Type in the desired name changes.

6 Click **OK**.

- Outlook renames the folder.

CREATE A SHORTCUT TO A FOLDER

You can place shortcuts to Outlook folders and personal folders directly on an Outlook bar for easy access. You can add shortcuts to all three of the Outlook bars: Outlook Shortcuts, My Shortcuts, or Other Shortcuts.

ADD A SHORTCUT TO THE BOTTOM OF AN OUTLOOK BAR

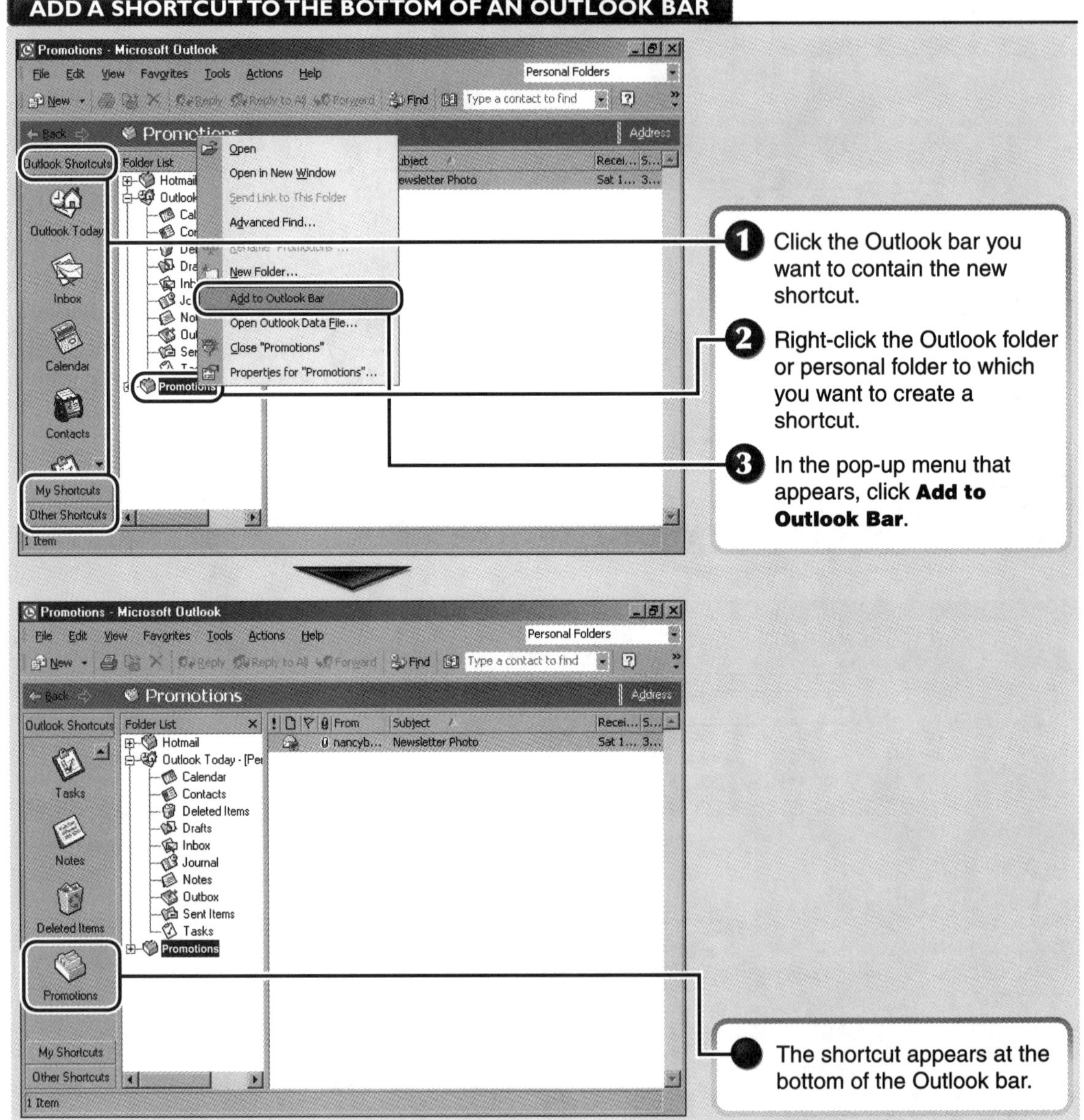

1 Click the Outlook bar you want to contain the new shortcut.

2 Right-click the Outlook folder or personal folder to which you want to create a shortcut.

3 In the pop-up menu that appears, click **Add to Outlook Bar**.

- The shortcut appears at the bottom of the Outlook bar.

in an instant

ADD A SHORTCUT TO A SPECIFIC PLACE IN AN OUTLOOK BAR

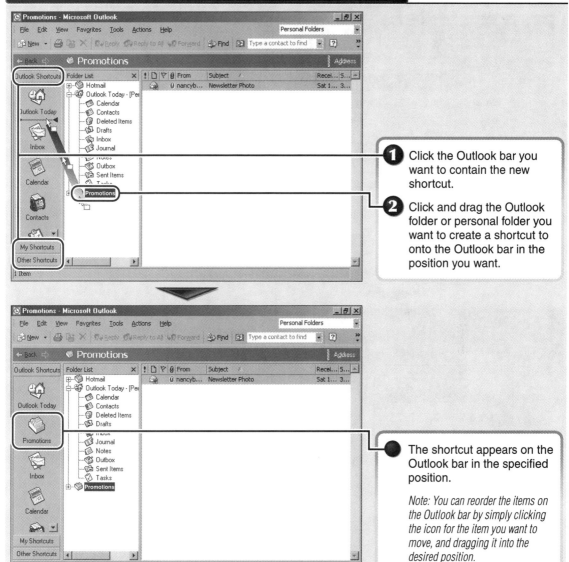

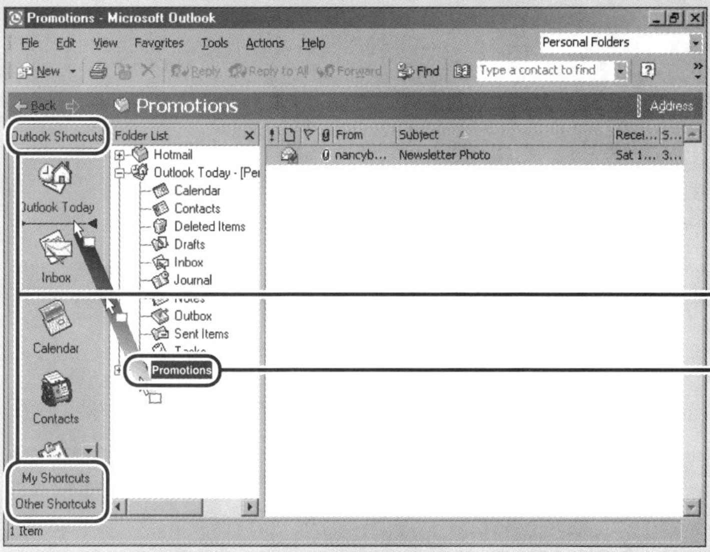

1 Click the Outlook bar you want to contain the new shortcut.

2 Click and drag the Outlook folder or personal folder you want to create a shortcut to onto the Outlook bar in the position you want.

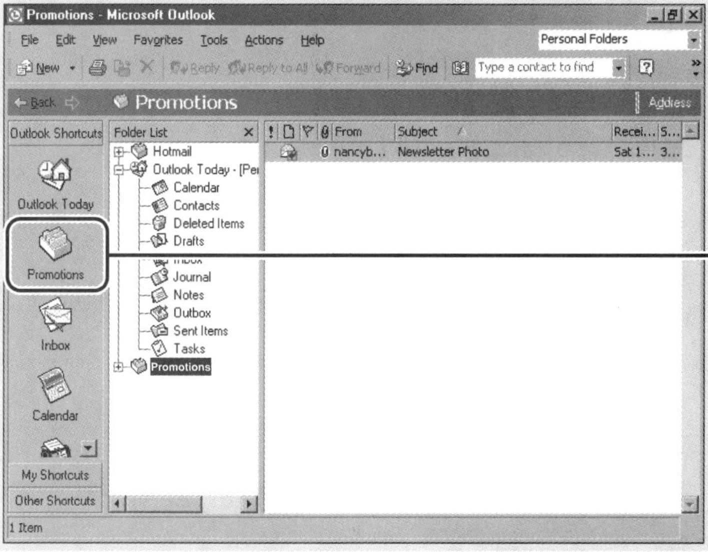

- The shortcut appears on the Outlook bar in the specified position.

Note: You can reorder the items on the Outlook bar by simply clicking the icon for the item you want to move, and dragging it into the desired position.

OPEN YOUR CALENDAR

You can open your calendar quickly from the Outlook bar. The Outlook Calendar allows you to track your schedule, set appointments, schedule meetings, and even print your calendar to take with you.

OPEN YOUR CALENDAR

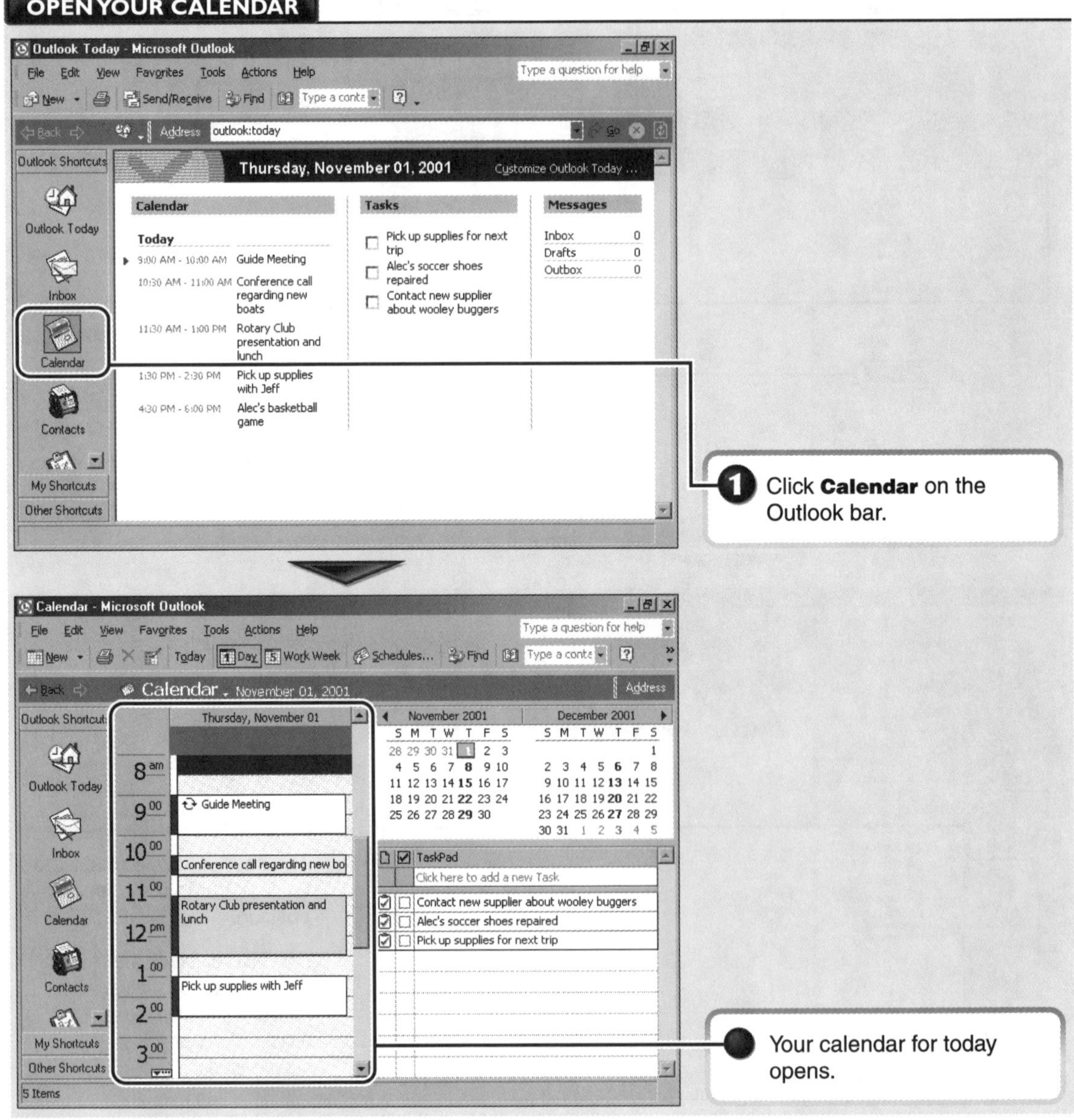

1 Click **Calendar** on the Outlook bar.

- Your calendar for today opens.

CHECK YOUR SCHEDULE

By default, the Outlook Calendar opens up to the current day. However, if you want to check appointments in the future or check days gone by to see when a meeting was held, you can open your calendar for any day in just a few clicks.

CHECK YOUR SCHEDULE

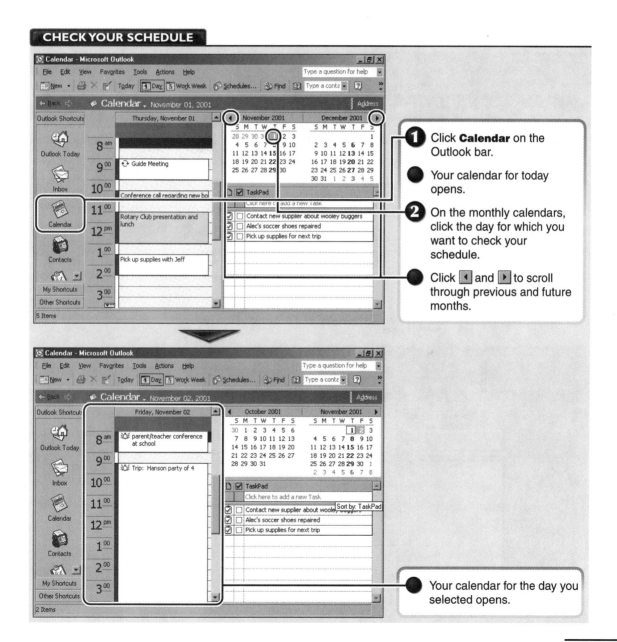

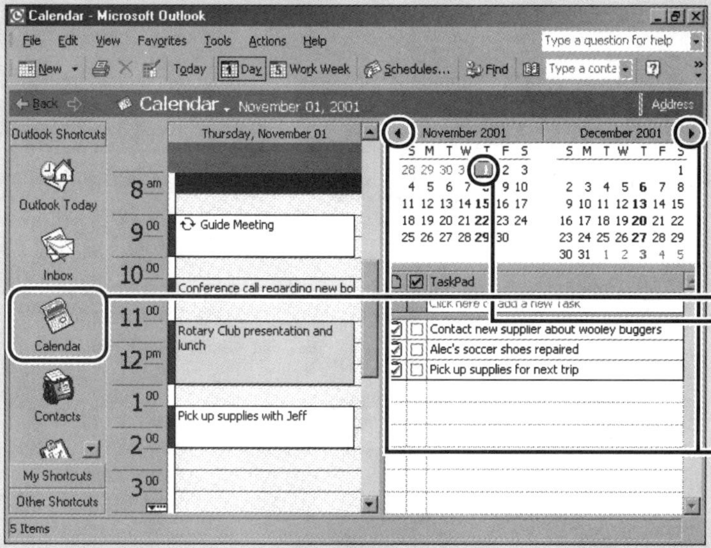

1. Click **Calendar** on the Outlook bar.

- Your calendar for today opens.

2. On the monthly calendars, click the day for which you want to check your schedule.

- Click ◀ and ▶ to scroll through previous and future months.

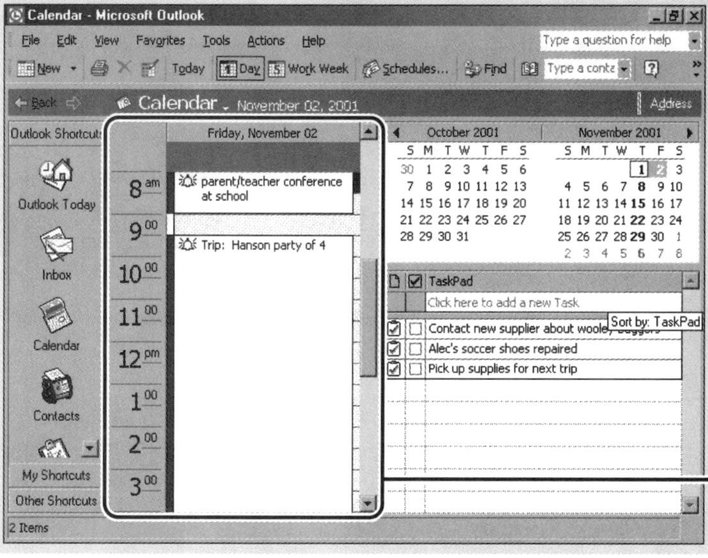

- Your calendar for the day you selected opens.

ADD AN APPOINTMENT

You can add appointments to your calendar by typing appointment descriptions directly into the desired date and time in your calendar. You can use the same process to specify a meeting location or even a conference call phone number. You can even specify how the time appears to others trying to schedule an appointment with you, and how the appointment is color coded and categorized on your own calendar.

ADD AN APPOINTMENT

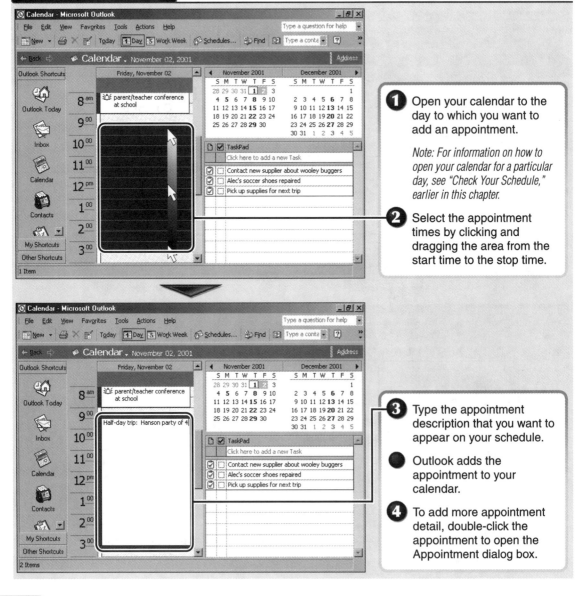

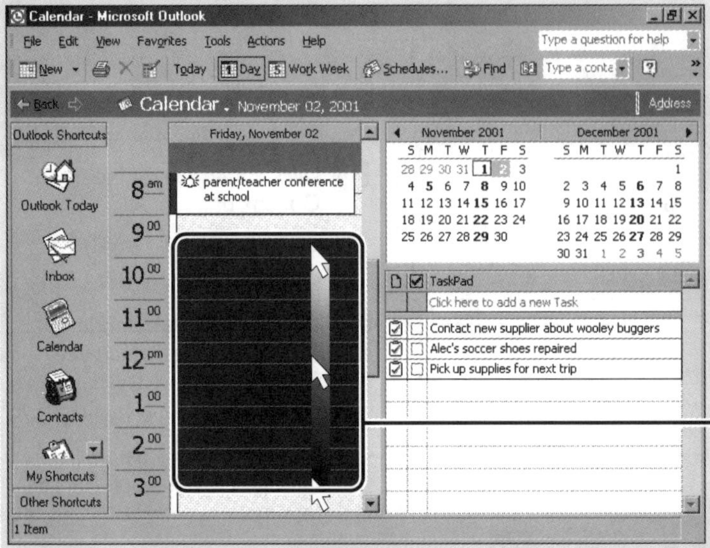

1. Open your calendar to the day to which you want to add an appointment.

   Note: For information on how to open your calendar for a particular day, see "Check Your Schedule," earlier in this chapter.

2. Select the appointment times by clicking and dragging the area from the start time to the stop time.

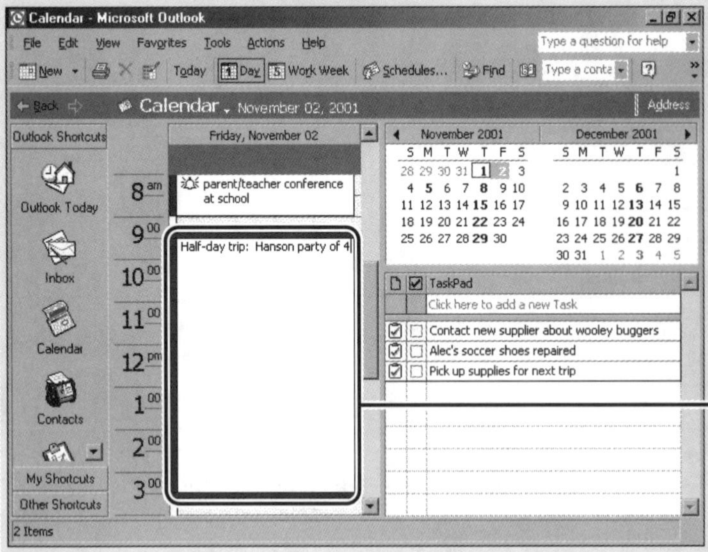

3. Type the appointment description that you want to appear on your schedule.

- Outlook adds the appointment to your calendar.

4. To add more appointment detail, double-click the appointment to open the Appointment dialog box.

in an instant

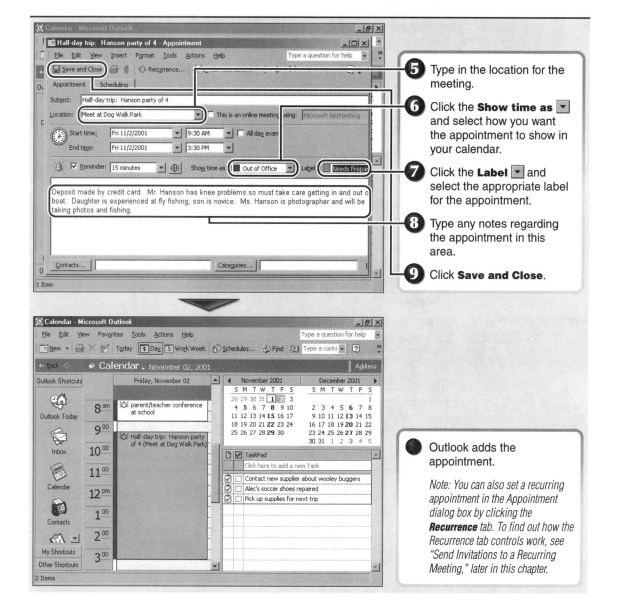

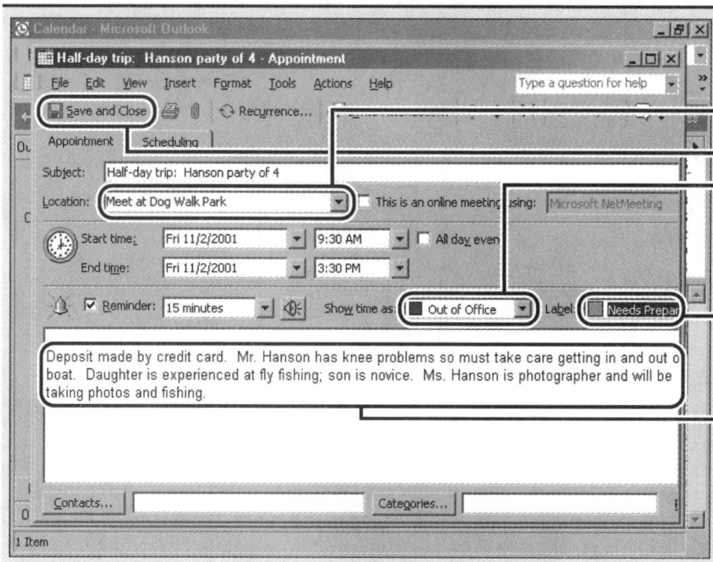

5 Type in the location for the meeting.

6 Click the **Show time as** ▼ and select how you want the appointment to show in your calendar.

7 Click the **Label** ▼ and select the appropriate label for the appointment.

8 Type any notes regarding the appointment in this area.

9 Click **Save and Close**.

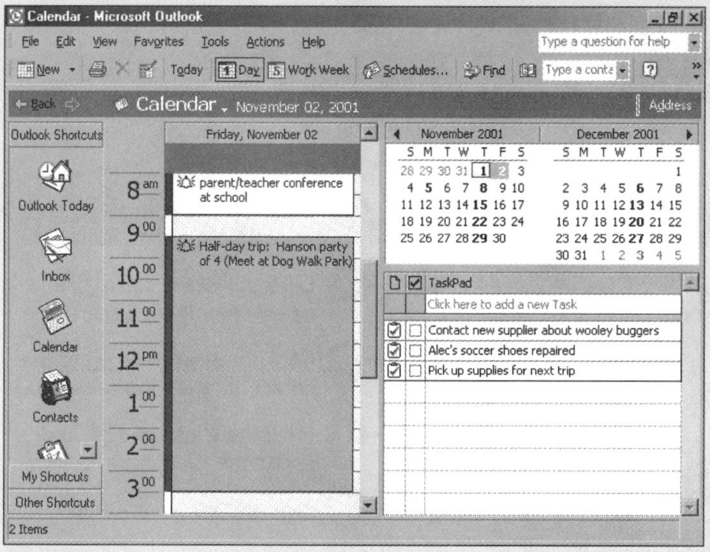

- Outlook adds the appointment.

Note: You can also set a recurring appointment in the Appointment dialog box by clicking the ***Recurrence*** *tab. To find out how the Recurrence tab controls work, see "Send Invitations to a Recurring Meeting," later in this chapter.*

SEND INVITATIONS TO A MEETING

You can easily schedule a meeting and invite others to attend using Outlook. For Outlook's purposes, a meeting is simply an appointment to which you invite other people or add other resources like a conference room. Outlook automatically sends meeting invitations when you finish scheduling the meeting.

SEND INVITATIONS TO A MEETING

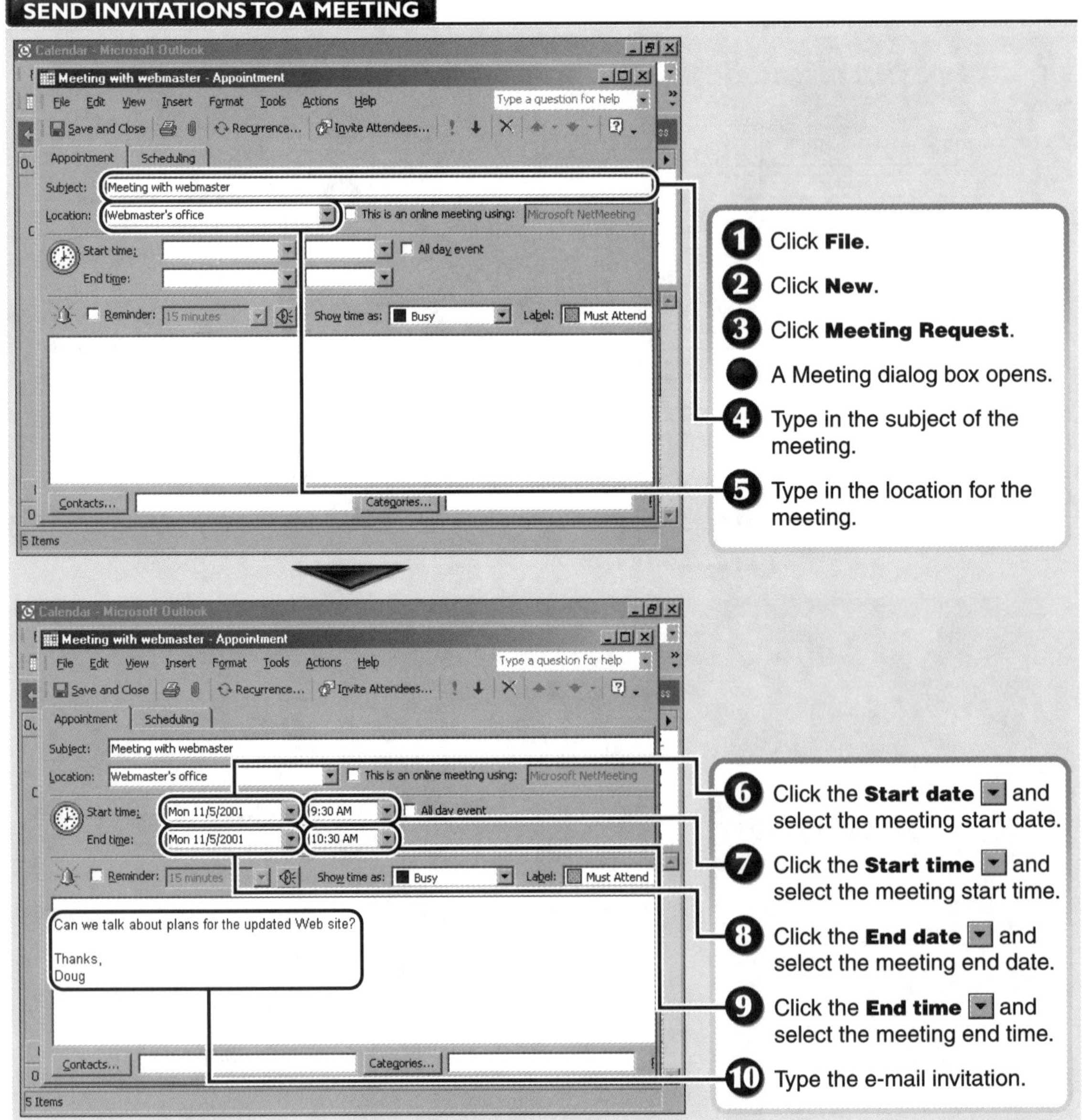

1. Click **File**.
2. Click **New**.
3. Click **Meeting Request**.

- A Meeting dialog box opens.

4. Type in the subject of the meeting.
5. Type in the location for the meeting.
6. Click the **Start date** ▾ and select the meeting start date.
7. Click the **Start time** ▾ and select the meeting start time.
8. Click the **End date** ▾ and select the meeting end date.
9. Click the **End time** ▾ and select the meeting end time.
10. Type the e-mail invitation.

in an instant

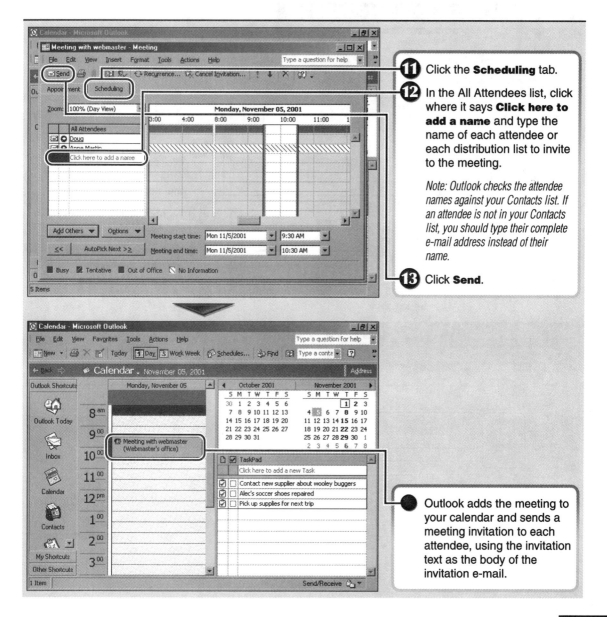

11 Click the **Scheduling** tab.

12 In the All Attendees list, click where it says **Click here to add a name** and type the name of each attendee or each distribution list to invite to the meeting.

Note: Outlook checks the attendee names against your Contacts list. If an attendee is not in your Contacts list, you should type their complete e-mail address instead of their name.

13 Click **Send**.

- Outlook adds the meeting to your calendar and sends a meeting invitation to each attendee, using the invitation text as the body of the invitation e-mail.

SEND INVITATIONS TO A RECURRING MEETING

You do not have to send separate meeting requests for a series of meetings; instead you can use Outlook to schedule a recurring meeting that occurs at a regular frequency that you specify.

SEND INVITATIONS TO A RECURRING MEETING

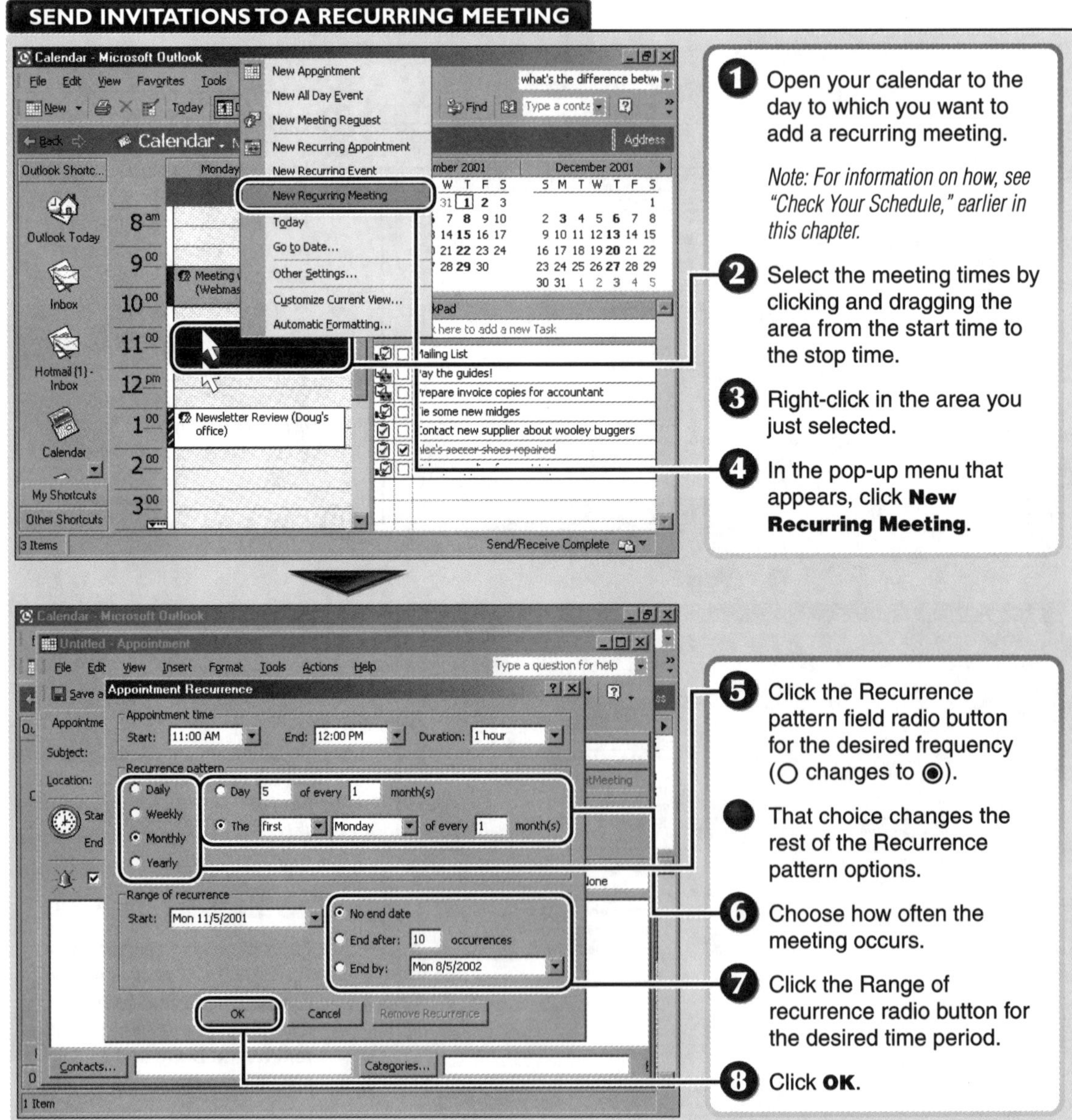

1. Open your calendar to the day to which you want to add a recurring meeting.

   Note: For information on how, see "Check Your Schedule," earlier in this chapter.

2. Select the meeting times by clicking and dragging the area from the start time to the stop time.
3. Right-click in the area you just selected.
4. In the pop-up menu that appears, click **New Recurring Meeting**.
5. Click the Recurrence pattern field radio button for the desired frequency (○ changes to ◉).

- That choice changes the rest of the Recurrence pattern options.

6. Choose how often the meeting occurs.
7. Click the Range of recurrence radio button for the desired time period.
8. Click **OK**.

in an instant

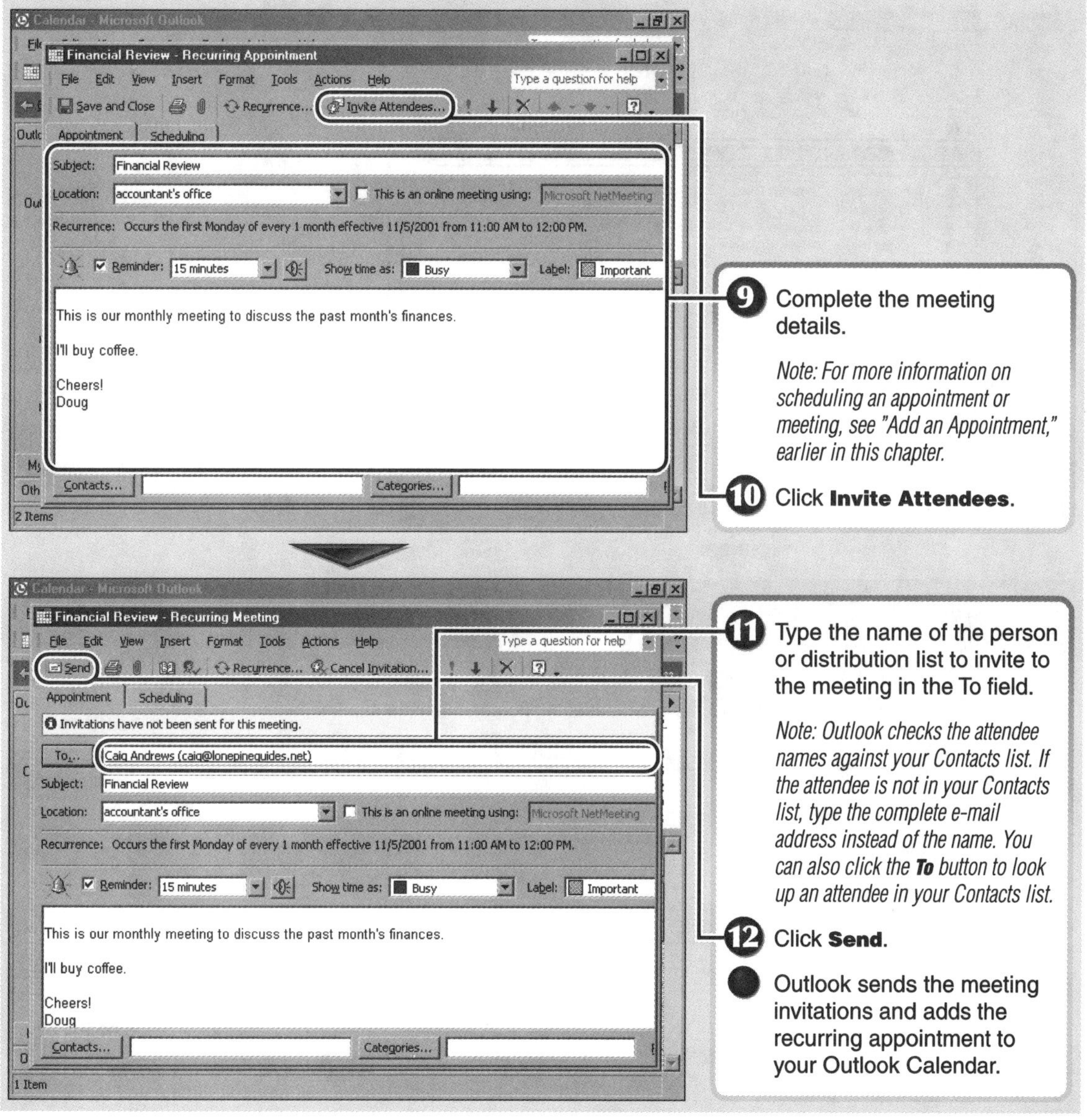

9 Complete the meeting details.

Note: For more information on scheduling an appointment or meeting, see "Add an Appointment," earlier in this chapter.

10 Click **Invite Attendees**.

11 Type the name of the person or distribution list to invite to the meeting in the To field.

*Note: Outlook checks the attendee names against your Contacts list. If the attendee is not in your Contacts list, type the complete e-mail address instead of the name. You can also click the **To** button to look up an attendee in your Contacts list.*

12 Click **Send**.

- Outlook sends the meeting invitations and adds the recurring appointment to your Outlook Calendar.

ACCEPT A MEETING REQUEST

When you receive an e-mail message with a meeting request, you can decide whether or not to accept it. If you accept the meeting request, Outlook adds the meeting to your calendar. Accepting a meeting request also informs the meeting organizer that you plan to attend.

ACCEPT A MEETING REQUEST

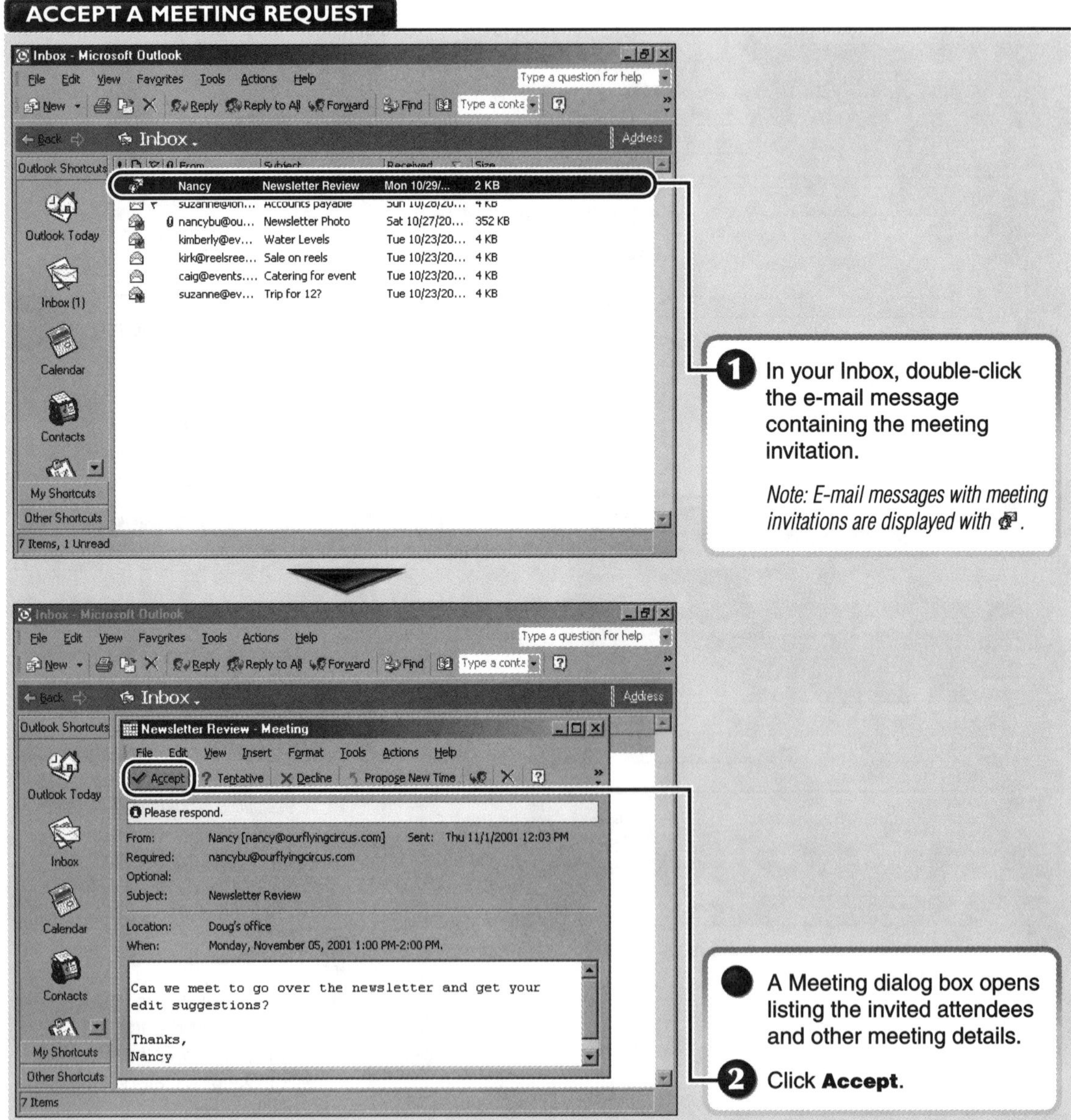

1 In your Inbox, double-click the e-mail message containing the meeting invitation.
Note: E-mail messages with meeting invitations are displayed with .
A Meeting dialog box opens listing the invited attendees and other meeting details.
2 Click Accept.

in an instant

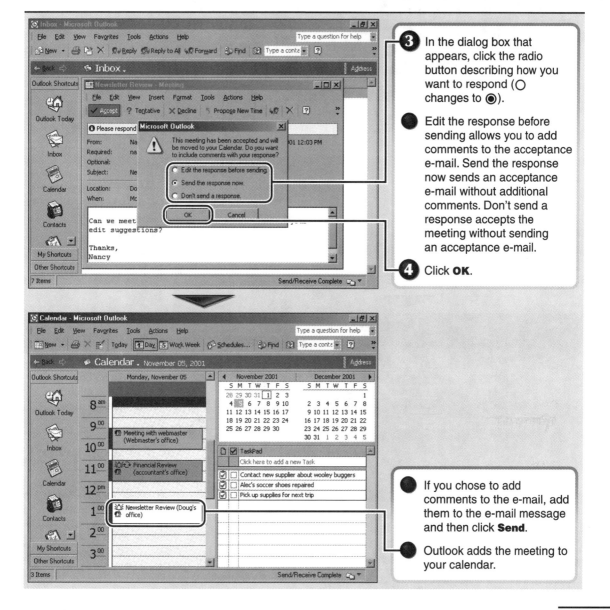

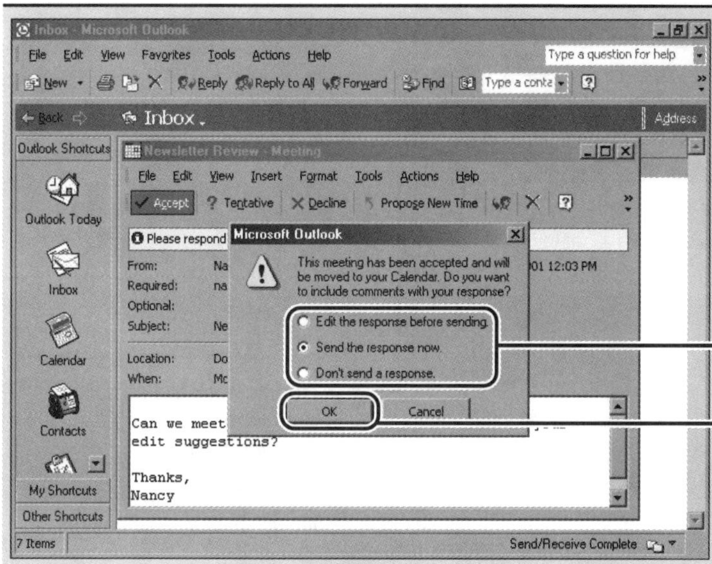

3 In the dialog box that appears, click the radio button describing how you want to respond (○ changes to ◉).

- Edit the response before sending allows you to add comments to the acceptance e-mail. Send the response now sends an acceptance e-mail without additional comments. Don't send a response accepts the meeting without sending an acceptance e-mail.

4 Click **OK**.

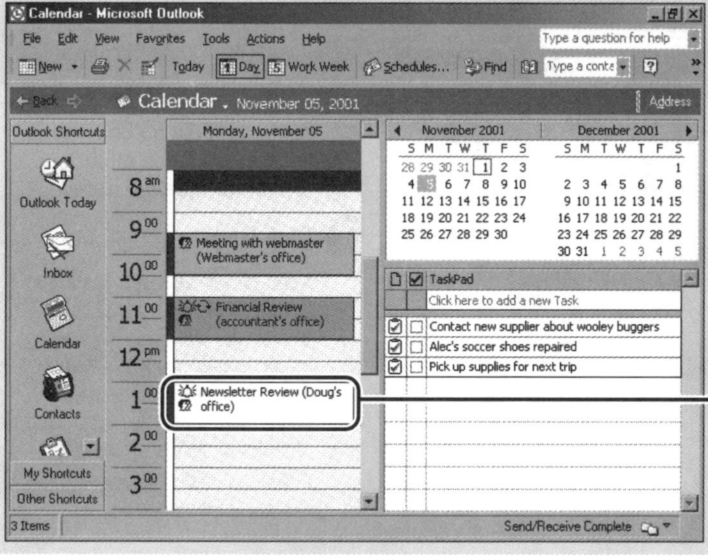

- If you chose to add comments to the e-mail, add them to the e-mail message and then click **Send**.
- Outlook adds the meeting to your calendar.

DECLINE A MEETING REQUEST

When you are not able to attend a meeting, you can decline the meeting request. Declining a meeting request removes the meeting from your calendar and moves the meeting request into the Deleted Items folder. You can also send an e-mail message declining the meeting in which you can add comments to inform the meeting organizer that you will not attend.

DECLINE A MEETING REQUEST

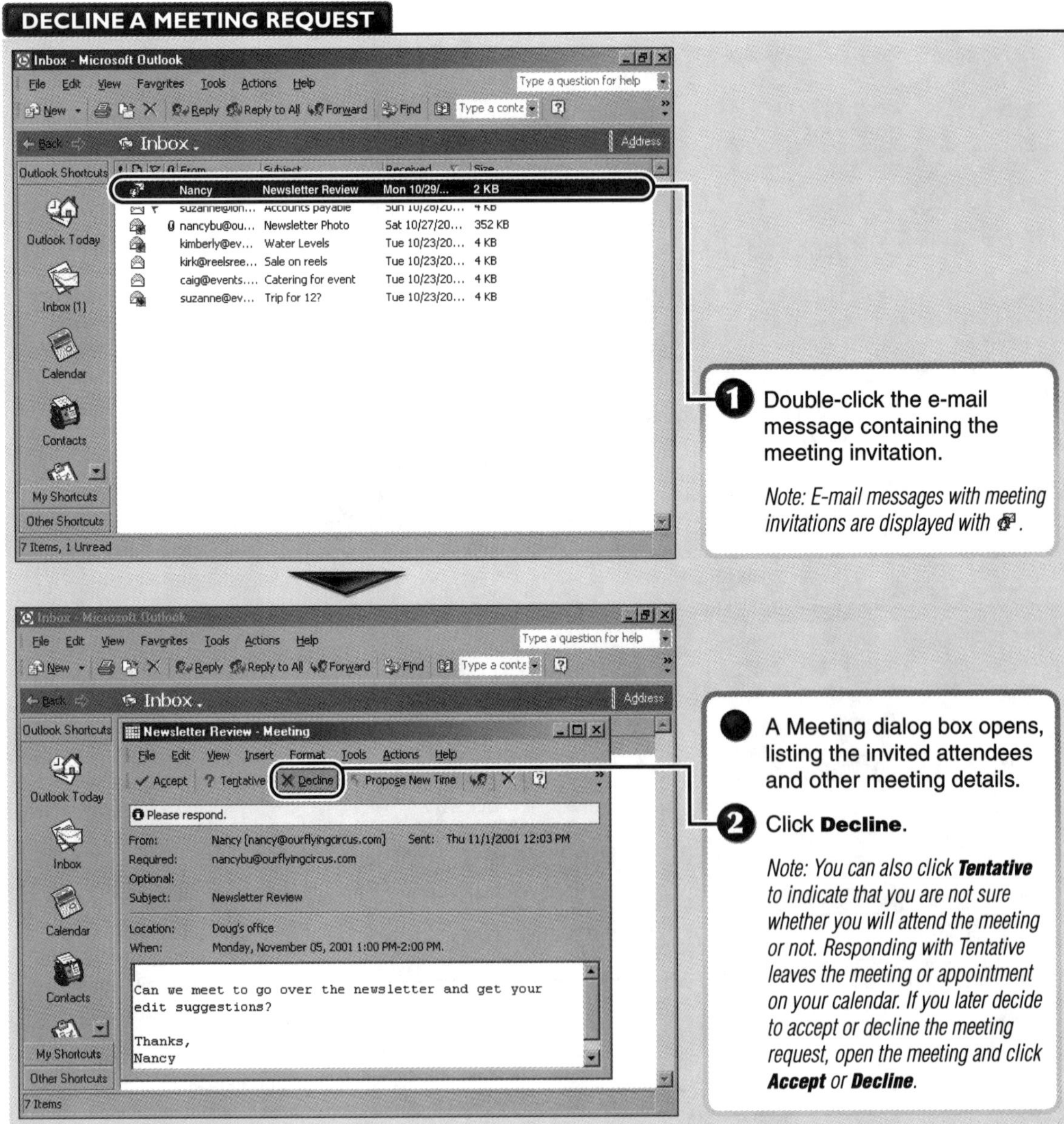

1. Double-click the e-mail message containing the meeting invitation.

Note: E-mail messages with meeting invitations are displayed with.

- A Meeting dialog box opens, listing the invited attendees and other meeting details.

2. Click **Decline**.

Note: You can also click ***Tentative*** *to indicate that you are not sure whether you will attend the meeting or not. Responding with Tentative leaves the meeting or appointment on your calendar. If you later decide to accept or decline the meeting request, open the meeting and click* ***Accept*** *or* ***Decline****.*

in an instant

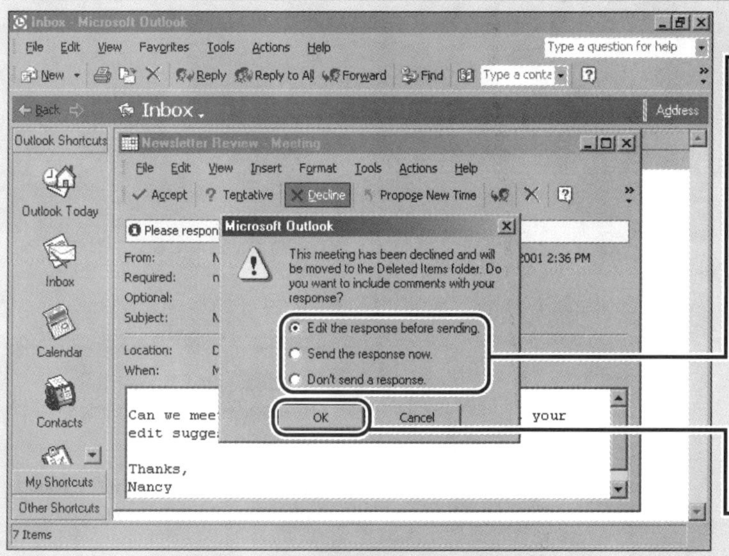

3 In the dialog box that appears, click the radio button describing how you want to respond (○ changes to ◉).

- Edit the response before sending allows you to add comments to your declining e-mail. Send the response now sends a declining e-mail without additional comments. Don't send a response declines the meeting without sending an e-mail.

4 Click **OK**.

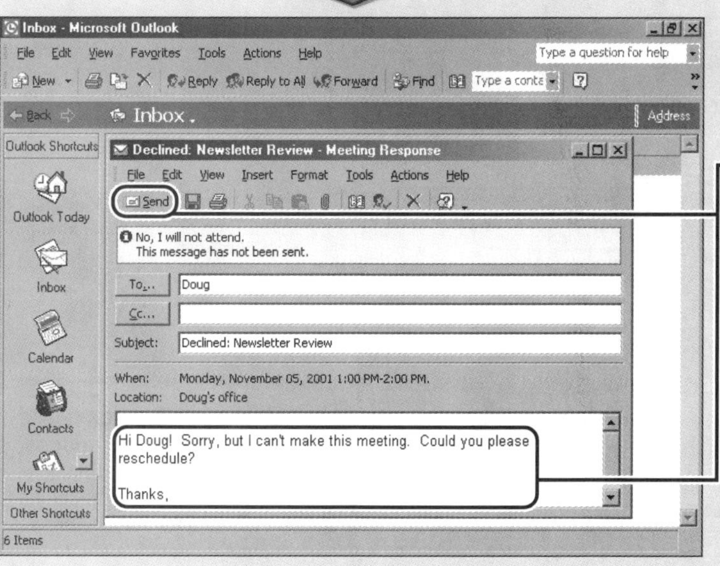

- If you chose to add comments to the declining e-mail, add them to the e-mail message. Optionally, you can copy or send this e-mail message to others by clicking the **To** or **Cc** or **Bcc** buttons. Click **Send** when you are ready for the message to be sent.
- Outlook removes the appointment from your calendar.

PROPOSE A NEW TIME FOR A MEETING

You can easily suggest a new time for a meeting. Proposing a new time sends an e-mail message to the meeting organizer requesting that they move the meeting date or time. If the meeting organizer agrees to move the meeting, you are sent an updated meeting request; if you accept the updated request, Outlook adds the meeting to your calendar.

PROPOSE A NEW TIME FOR A MEETING

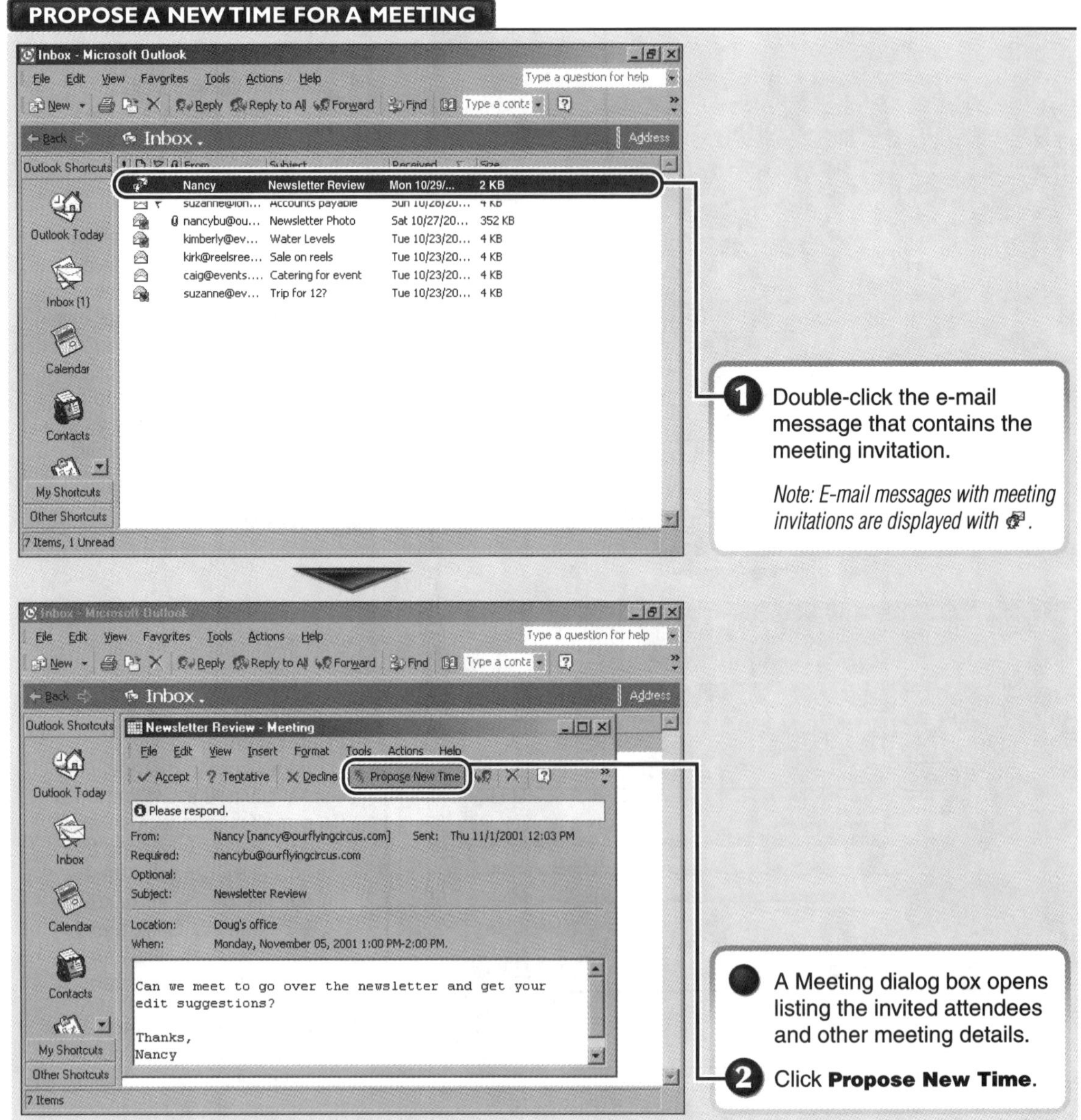

1. Double-click the e-mail message that contains the meeting invitation.

Note: E-mail messages with meeting invitations are displayed with ![icon].

- A Meeting dialog box opens listing the invited attendees and other meeting details.

2. Click **Propose New Time**.

in an instant

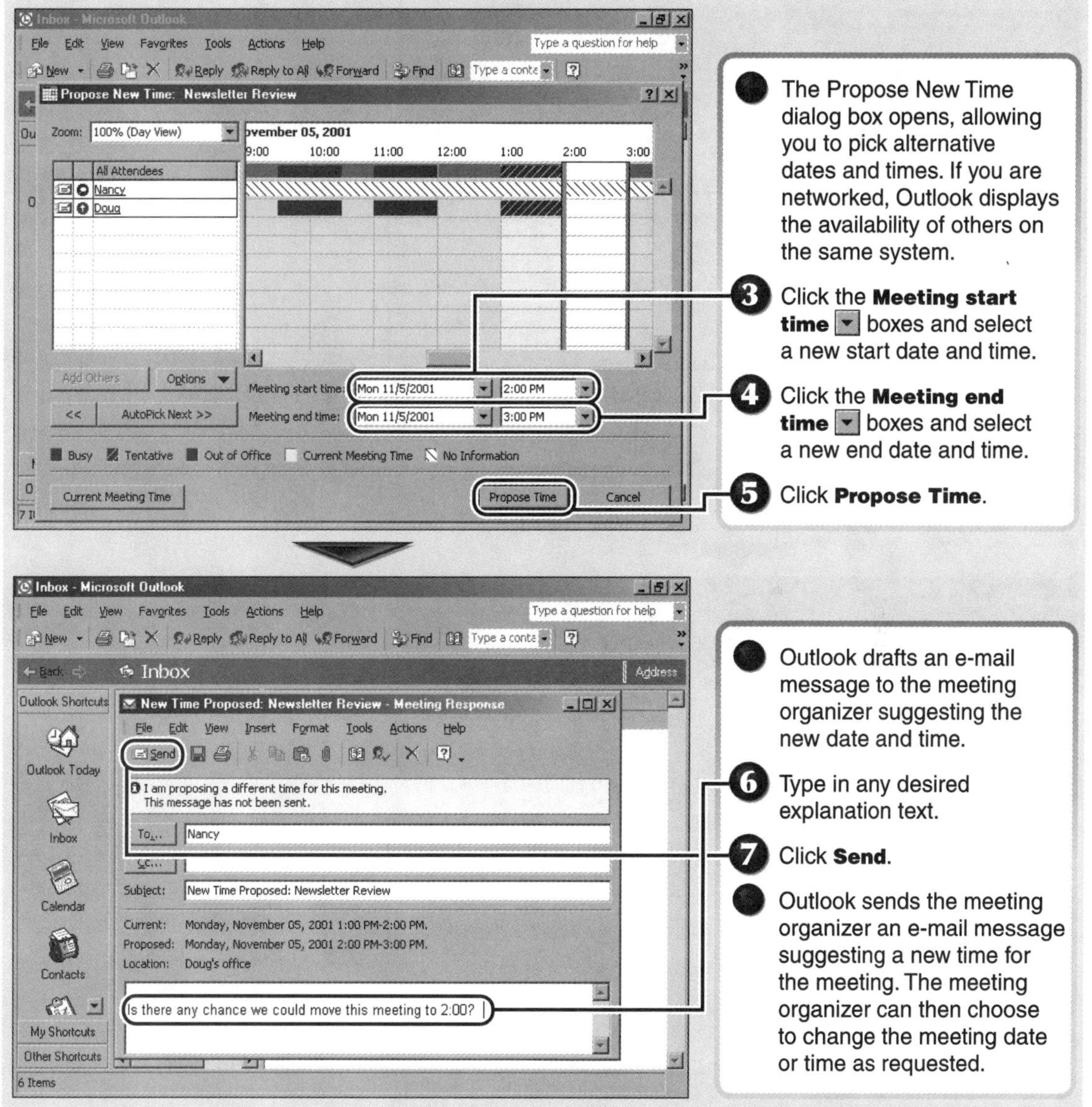

- The Propose New Time dialog box opens, allowing you to pick alternative dates and times. If you are networked, Outlook displays the availability of others on the same system.

3 Click the **Meeting start time** ▾ boxes and select a new start date and time.

4 Click the **Meeting end time** ▾ boxes and select a new end date and time.

5 Click **Propose Time**.

- Outlook drafts an e-mail message to the meeting organizer suggesting the new date and time.

6 Type in any desired explanation text.

7 Click **Send**.

- Outlook sends the meeting organizer an e-mail message suggesting a new time for the meeting. The meeting organizer can then choose to change the meeting date or time as requested.

MARK APPOINTMENT AS PRIVATE OR PERSONAL

You can mark appointments as private so that others who have privileges to access your calendar cannot see the appointment details. This functionality is available only to users who are on an e-mail network using Microsoft Exchange as the server, and only authorized delegates can open appointments marked as private. However, users with or without Microsoft Exchange can color code their appointments to show that they are personal.

MARK APPOINTMENT AS PRIVATE

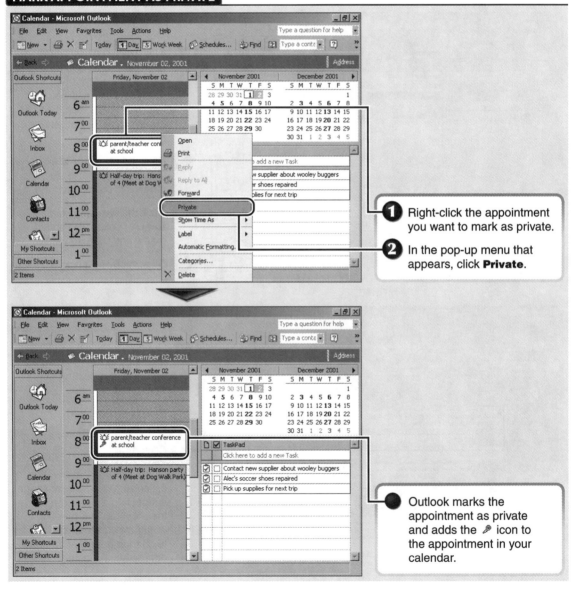

1. Right-click the appointment you want to mark as private.
2. In the pop-up menu that appears, click **Private**.

- Outlook marks the appointment as private and adds the 🔑 icon to the appointment in your calendar.

in an instant

MARK APPOINTMENT AS PERSONAL

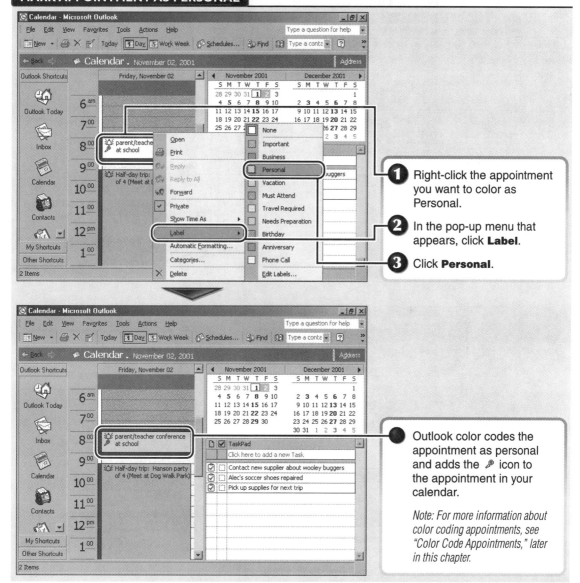

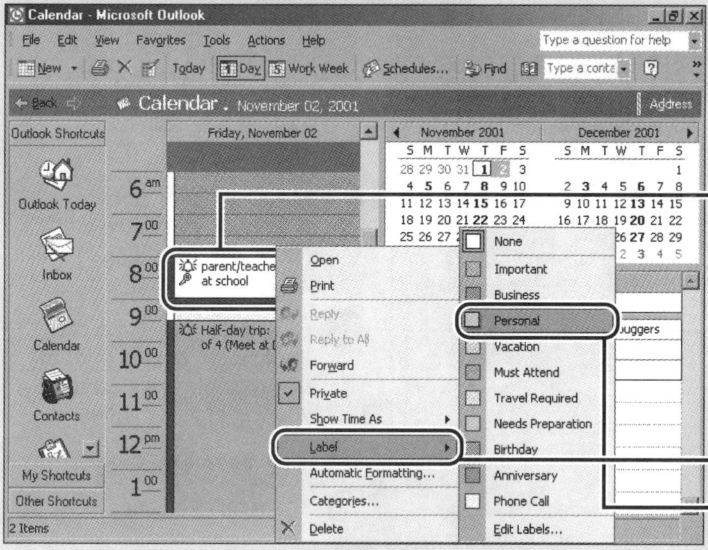

1. Right-click the appointment you want to color as Personal.
2. In the pop-up menu that appears, click **Label**.
3. Click **Personal**.

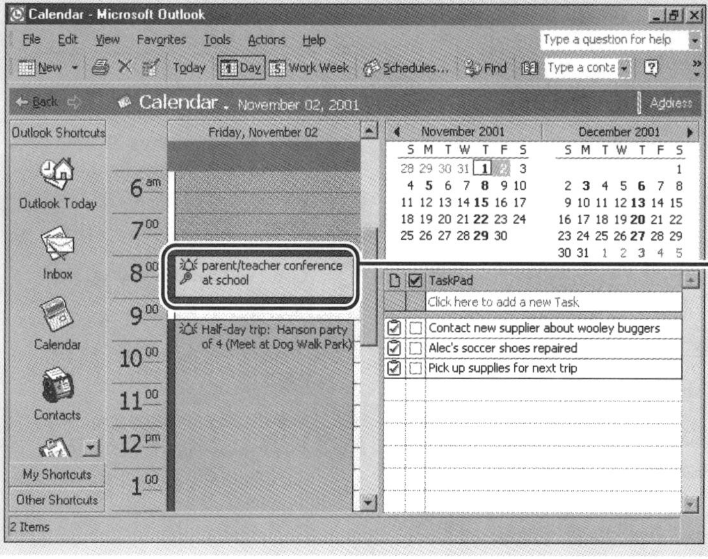

- Outlook color codes the appointment as personal and adds the icon to the appointment in your calendar.

Note: For more information about color coding appointments, see "Color Code Appointments," later in this chapter.

SET, POSTPONE, OR DISMISS MEETING REMINDERS

Reminders alert you and others that a meeting or appointment begins soon. You can choose the amount of time prior to a meeting or appointment for the reminder to notify you. You can also postpone the reminder for a set number of minutes or dismiss it. Tasks, covered in Chapter 11, and flags, covered in Chapter 9, can also trigger reminders.

SET, POSTPONE, OR DISMISS MEETING REMINDERS

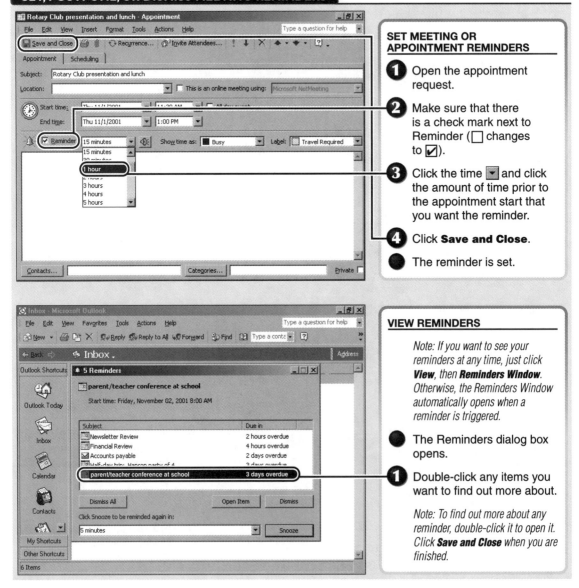

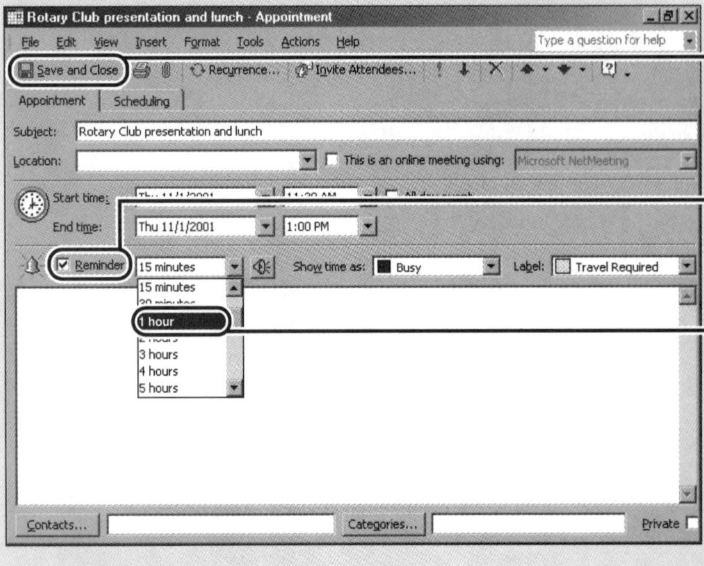

SET MEETING OR APPOINTMENT REMINDERS

1. Open the appointment request.
2. Make sure that there is a check mark next to Reminder (☐ changes to ☑).
3. Click the time ▾ and click the amount of time prior to the appointment start that you want the reminder.
4. Click **Save and Close**.

- The reminder is set.

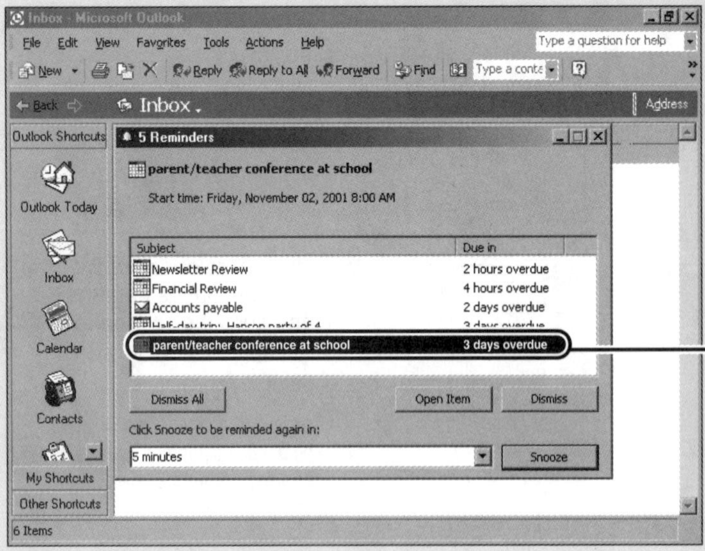

VIEW REMINDERS

*Note: If you want to see your reminders at any time, just click **View**, then **Reminders Window**. Otherwise, the Reminders Window automatically opens when a reminder is triggered.*

- The Reminders dialog box opens.

1. Double-click any items you want to find out more about.

*Note: To find out more about any reminder, double-click it to open it. Click **Save and Close** when you are finished.*

in an instant

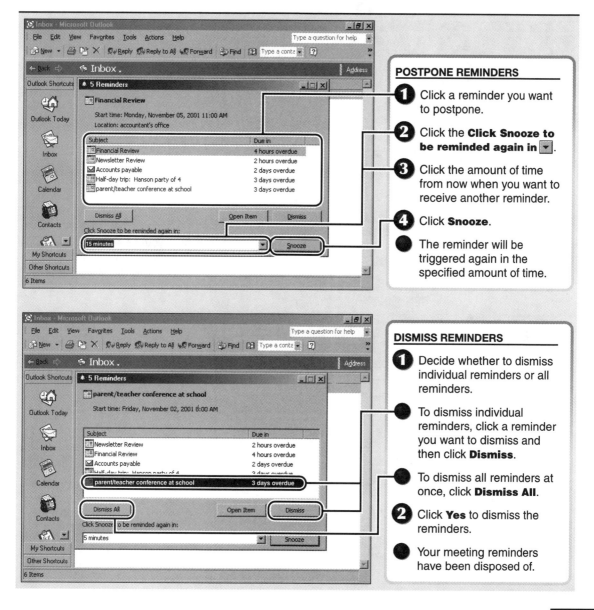

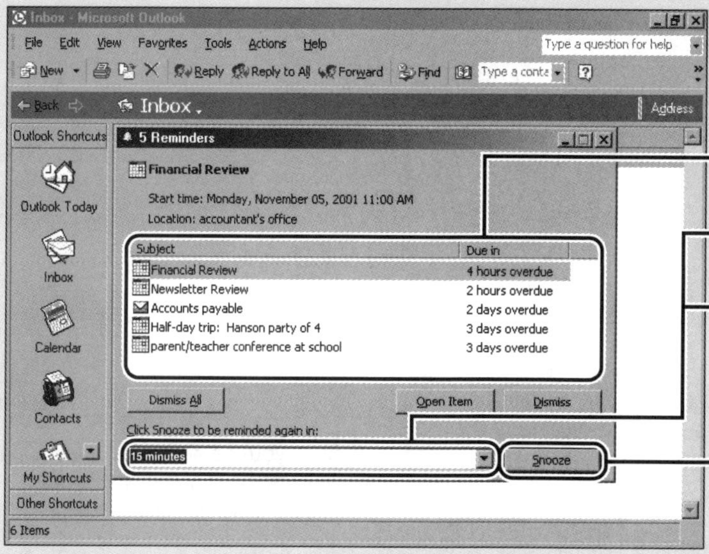

POSTPONE REMINDERS

1. Click a reminder you want to postpone.
2. Click the **Click Snooze to be reminded again in** ▾.
3. Click the amount of time from now when you want to receive another reminder.
4. Click **Snooze**.

- The reminder will be triggered again in the specified amount of time.

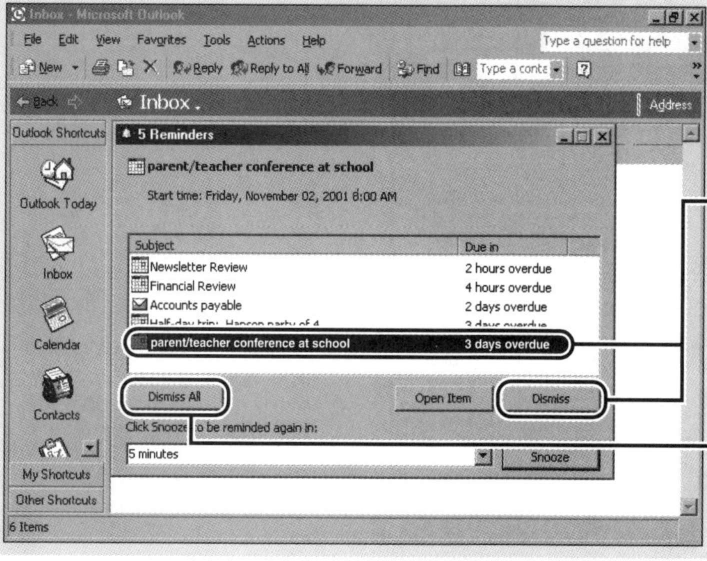

DISMISS REMINDERS

1. Decide whether to dismiss individual reminders or all reminders.

- To dismiss individual reminders, click a reminder you want to dismiss and then click **Dismiss**.
- To dismiss all reminders at once, click **Dismiss All**.

2. Click **Yes** to dismiss the reminders.

- Your meeting reminders have been disposed of.

CHECK RESPONSES TO A MEETING REQUEST

After you send invitations to a meeting and start getting responses, remembering who accepted the meeting and who declined is often difficult. You can let Outlook track who plans to attend and who does not.

CHECK RESPONSES TO A MEETING REQUEST

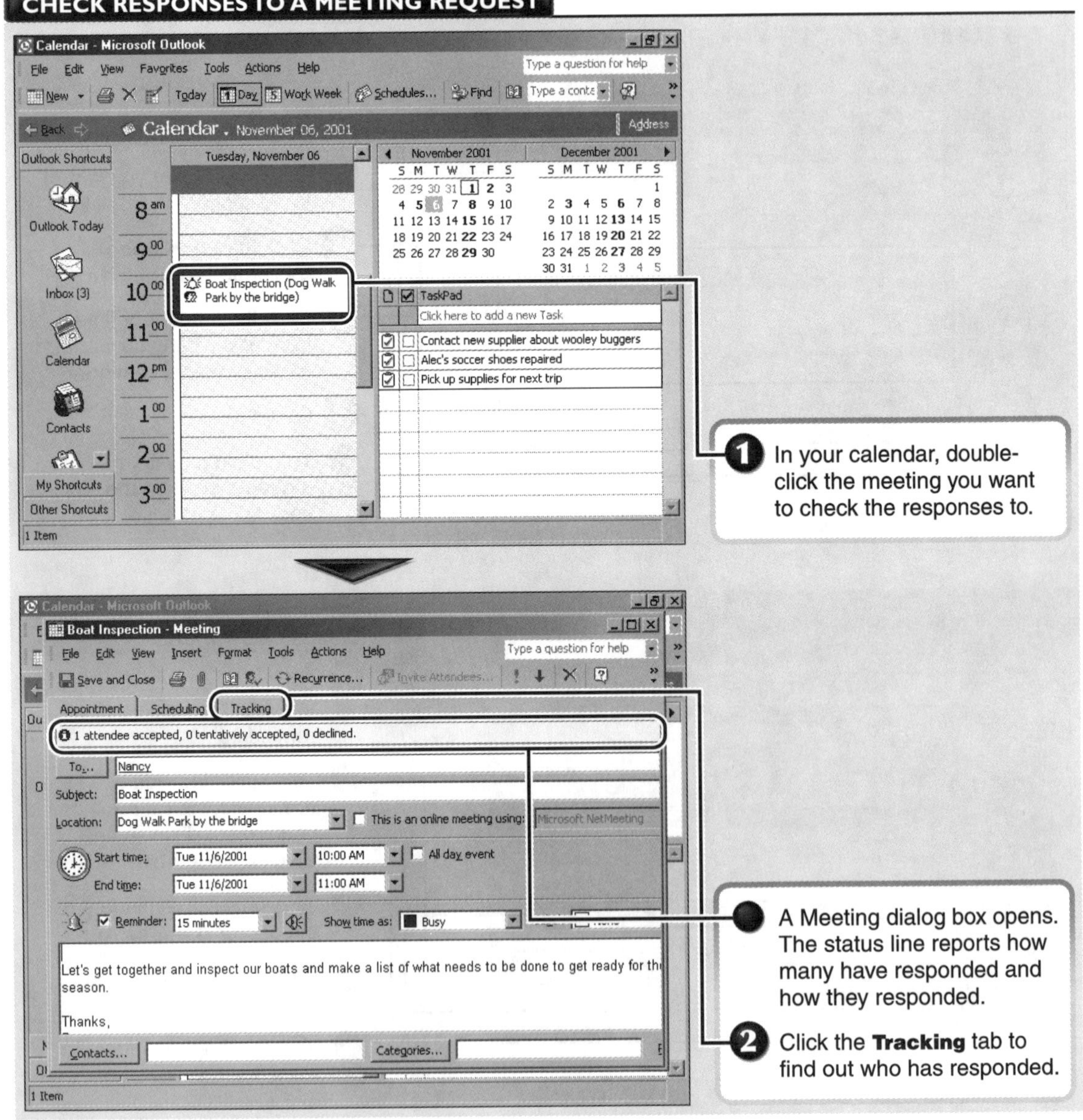

1. In your calendar, double-click the meeting you want to check the responses to.

- A Meeting dialog box opens. The status line reports how many have responded and how they responded.

2. Click the **Tracking** tab to find out who has responded.

in an instant

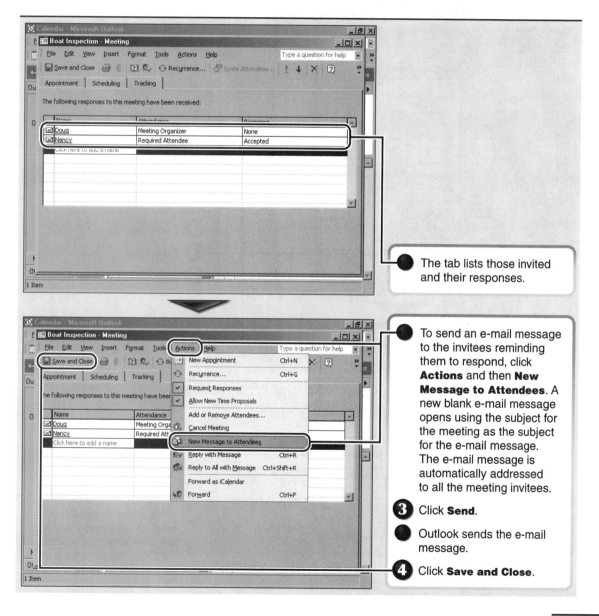

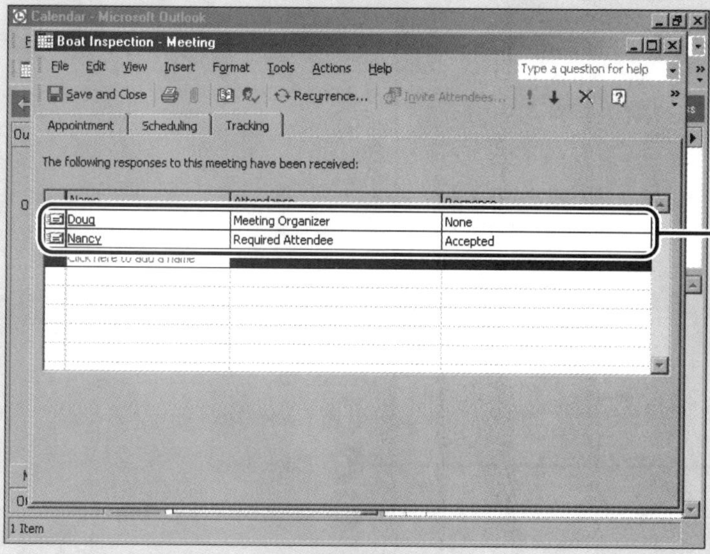

- The tab lists those invited and their responses.

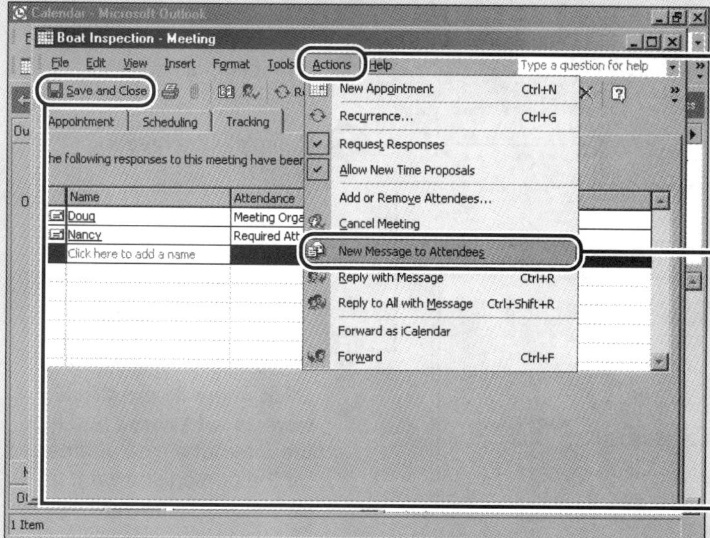

- To send an e-mail message to the invitees reminding them to respond, click **Actions** and then **New Message to Attendees**. A new blank e-mail message opens using the subject for the meeting as the subject for the e-mail message. The e-mail message is automatically addressed to all the meeting invitees.

3. Click **Send**.

- Outlook sends the e-mail message.

4. Click **Save and Close**.

SCHEDULE APPOINTMENTS OVER THE INTERNET

You do not have to be on the same network with people you want to schedule meetings with. You can schedule meetings with anyone as long as you have the complete e-mail address. You can also take advantage of the Microsoft Office/Internet Free/Busy Service to see availability of other service subscribers, even if they are not on your network. See http://freebusy.office.microsoft.com for subscription details.

SCHEDULE APPOINTMENTS OVER THE INTERNET

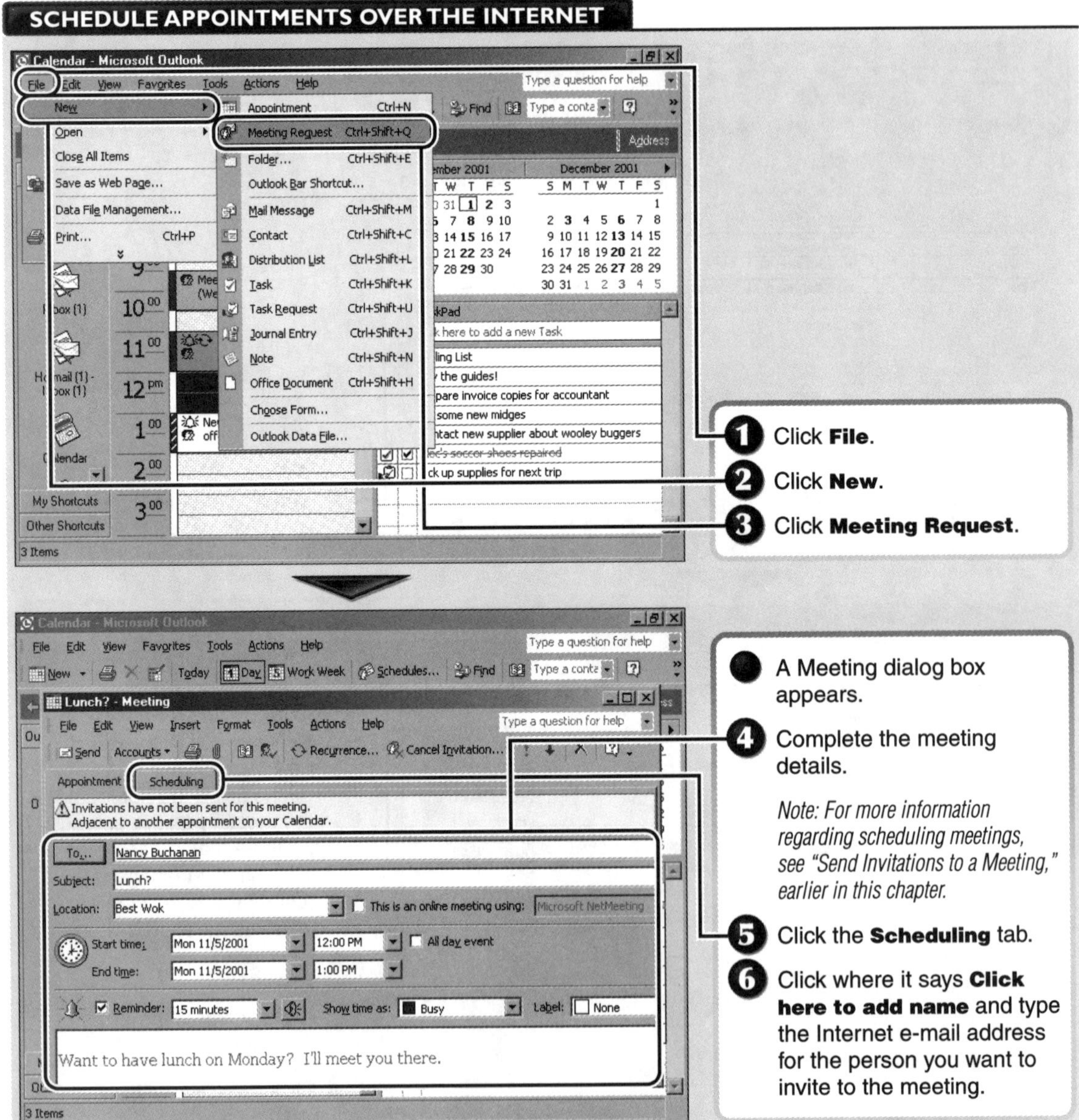

1. Click **File**.
2. Click **New**.
3. Click **Meeting Request**.

- A Meeting dialog box appears.

4. Complete the meeting details.

Note: For more information regarding scheduling meetings, see "Send Invitations to a Meeting," earlier in this chapter.

5. Click the **Scheduling** tab.
6. Click where it says **Click here to add name** and type the Internet e-mail address for the person you want to invite to the meeting.

in an instant

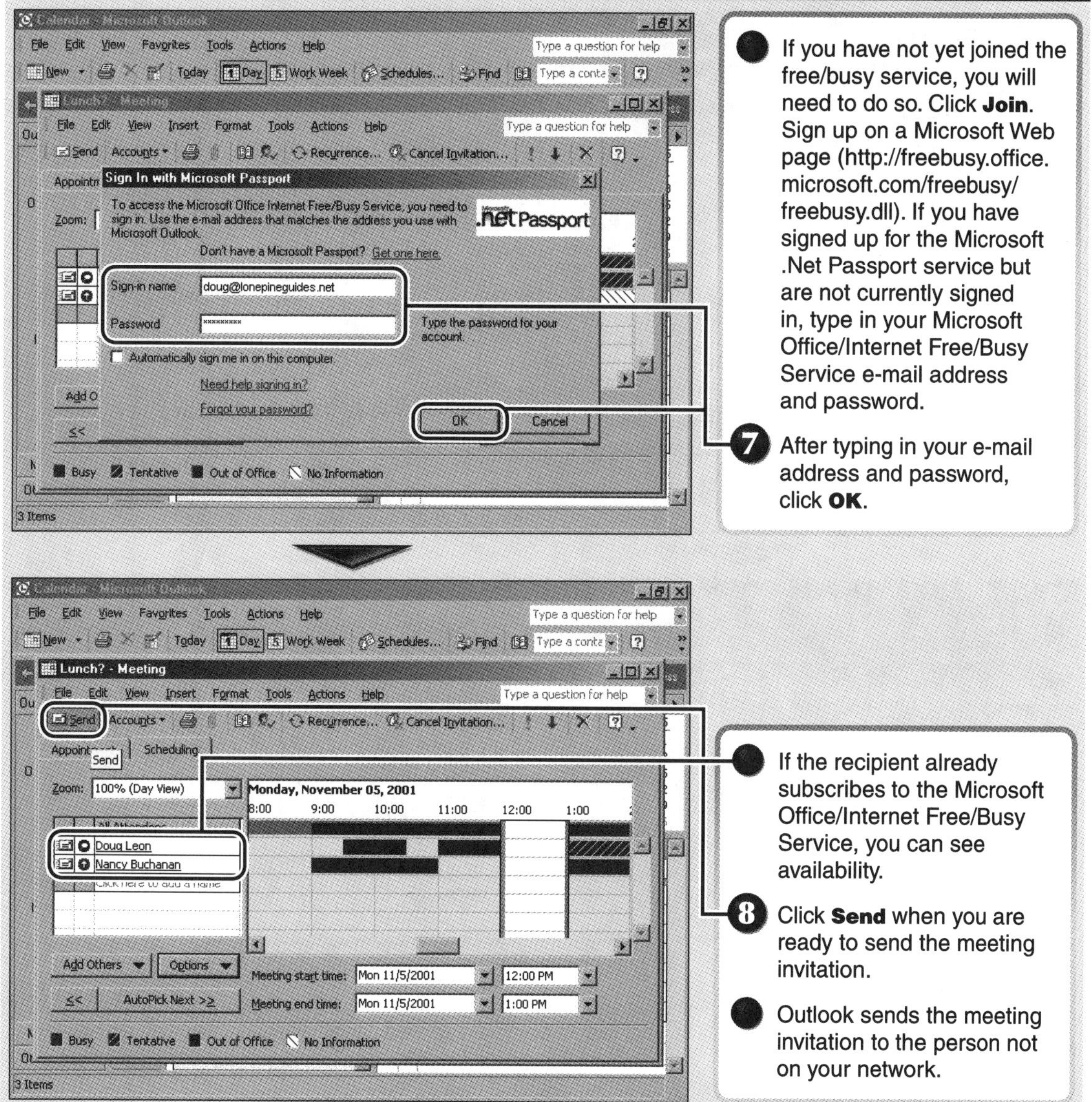

- If you have not yet joined the free/busy service, you will need to do so. Click **Join**. Sign up on a Microsoft Web page (http://freebusy.office.microsoft.com/freebusy/freebusy.dll). If you have signed up for the Microsoft .Net Passport service but are not currently signed in, type in your Microsoft Office/Internet Free/Busy Service e-mail address and password.

7 After typing in your e-mail address and password, click **OK**.

- If the recipient already subscribes to the Microsoft Office/Internet Free/Busy Service, you can see availability.

8 Click **Send** when you are ready to send the meeting invitation.

- Outlook sends the meeting invitation to the person not on your network.

COLOR CODE APPOINTMENTS

You can color code appointments so that you can identify appointments by type or urgency at a glance. You can even create your own color labels to suit your needs.

USING PRESET COLOR CODES

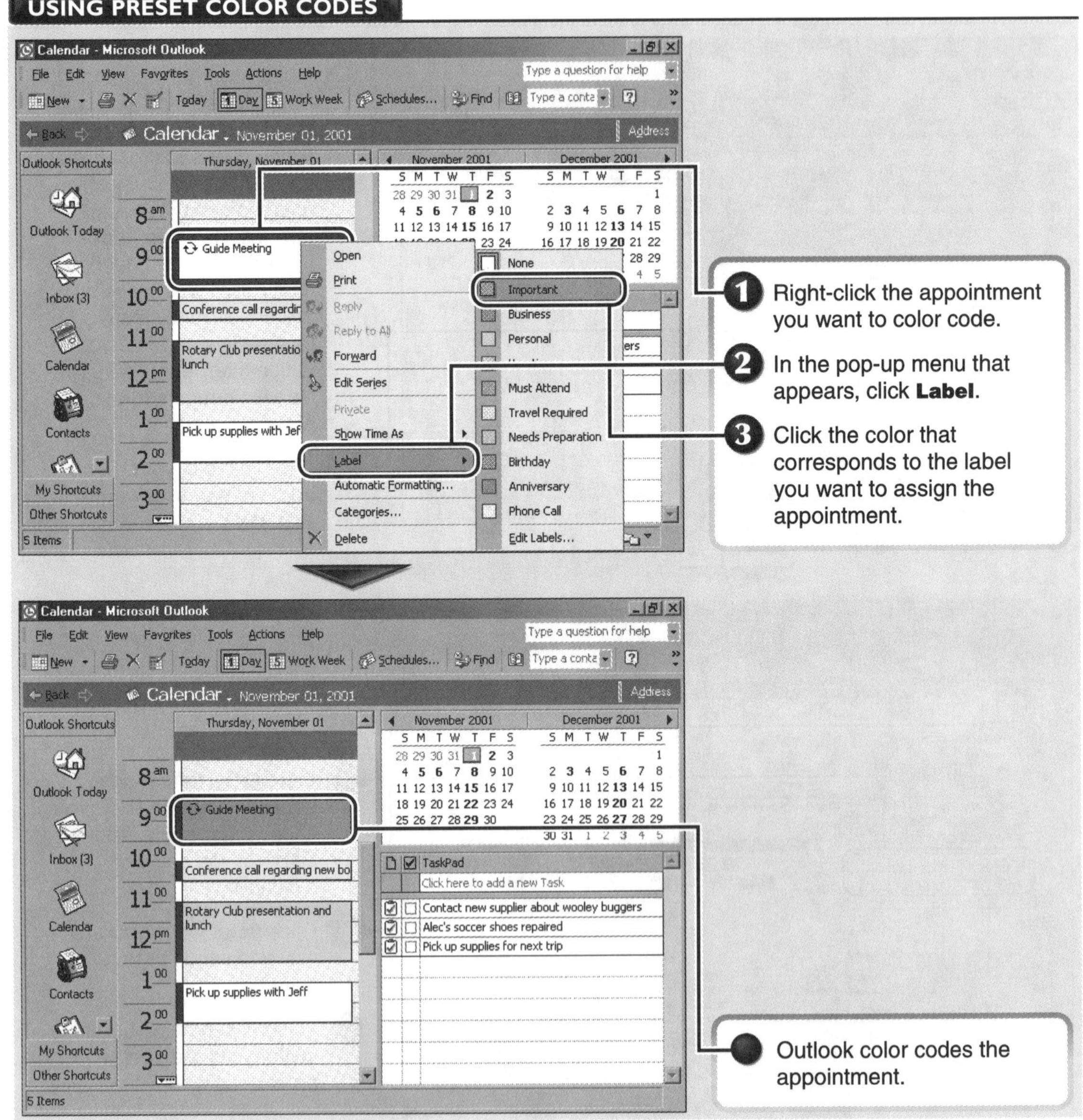

1. Right-click the appointment you want to color code.
2. In the pop-up menu that appears, click **Label**.
3. Click the color that corresponds to the label you want to assign the appointment.

- Outlook color codes the appointment.

in an instant

CUSTOMIZE COLOR CODES

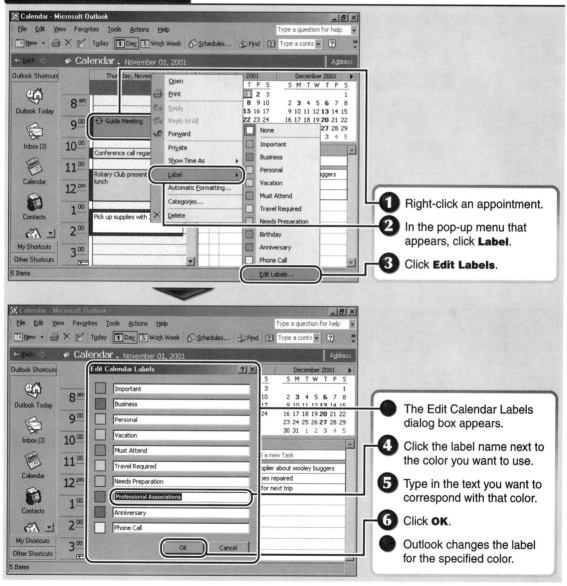

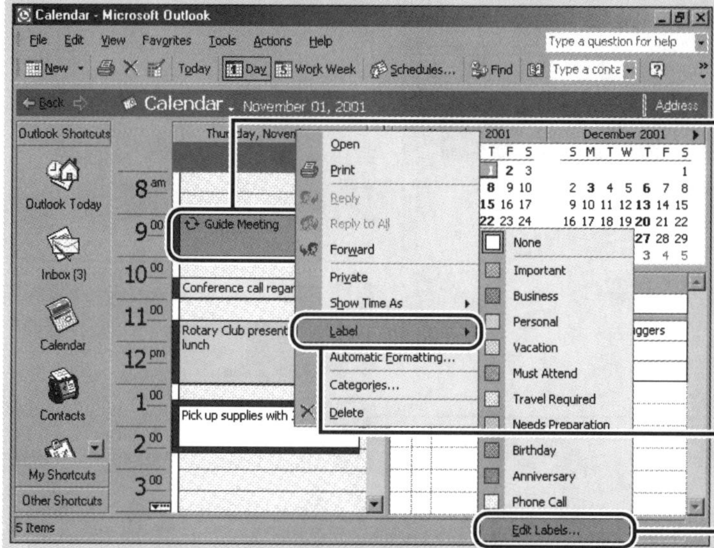

1 Right-click an appointment.

2 In the pop-up menu that appears, click **Label**.

3 Click **Edit Labels**.

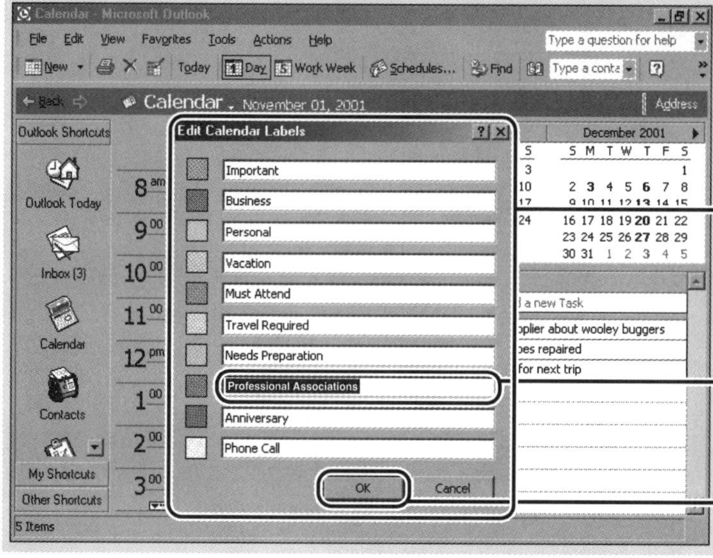

- The Edit Calendar Labels dialog box appears.

4 Click the label name next to the color you want to use.

5 Type in the text you want to correspond with that color.

6 Click **OK**.

- Outlook changes the label for the specified color.

PRINT YOUR CALENDAR

You can print your calendar to take with you in a variety of ways. Outlook Today gives you a quick snapshot of your entire day, including tasks and Inbox statistics. Printing from Outlook Calendar gives you flexibility and choice in how and how much to print.

PRINT YOUR CALENDAR

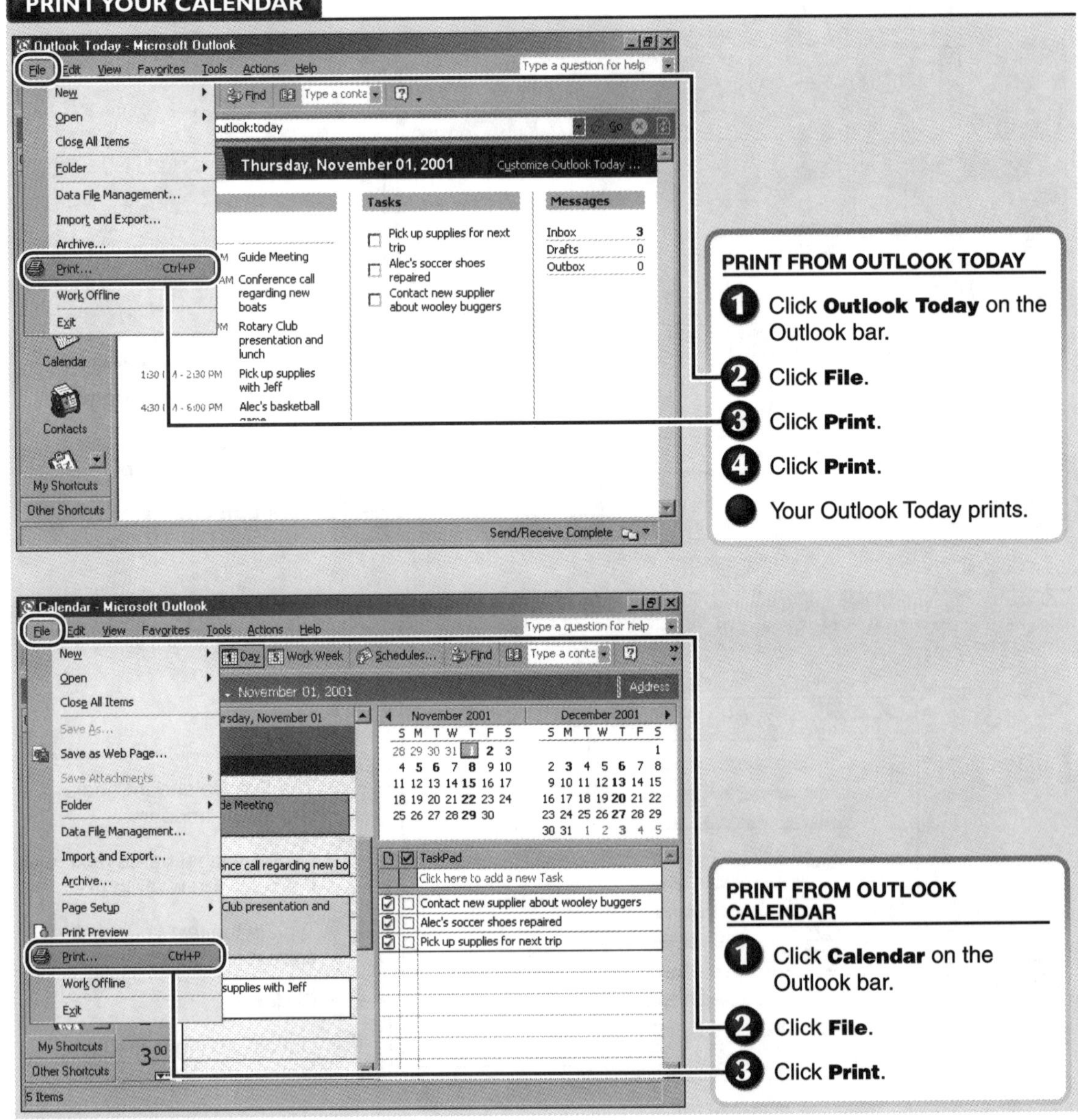

PRINT FROM OUTLOOK TODAY

1. Click **Outlook Today** on the Outlook bar.
2. Click **File**.
3. Click **Print**.
4. Click **Print**.

- Your Outlook Today prints.

PRINT FROM OUTLOOK CALENDAR

1. Click **Calendar** on the Outlook bar.
2. Click **File**.
3. Click **Print**.

in an instant

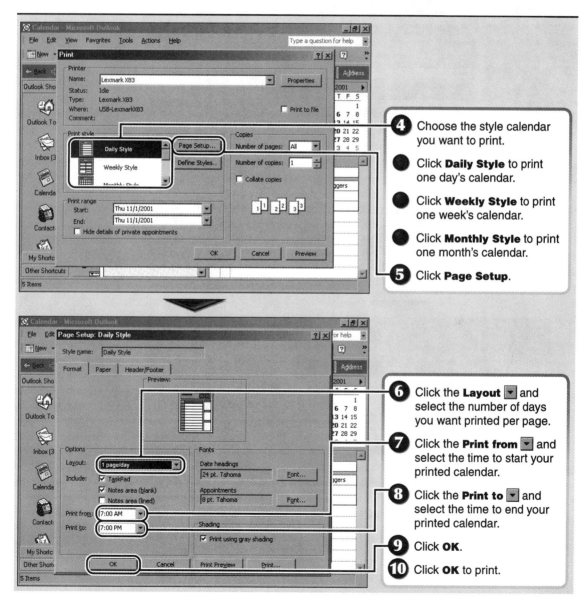

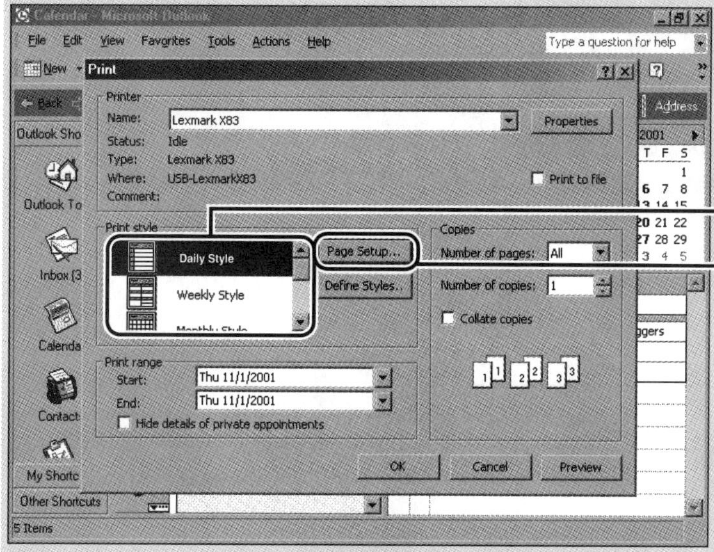

4 Choose the style calendar you want to print.

- Click **Daily Style** to print one day's calendar.
- Click **Weekly Style** to print one week's calendar.
- Click **Monthly Style** to print one month's calendar.

5 Click **Page Setup**.

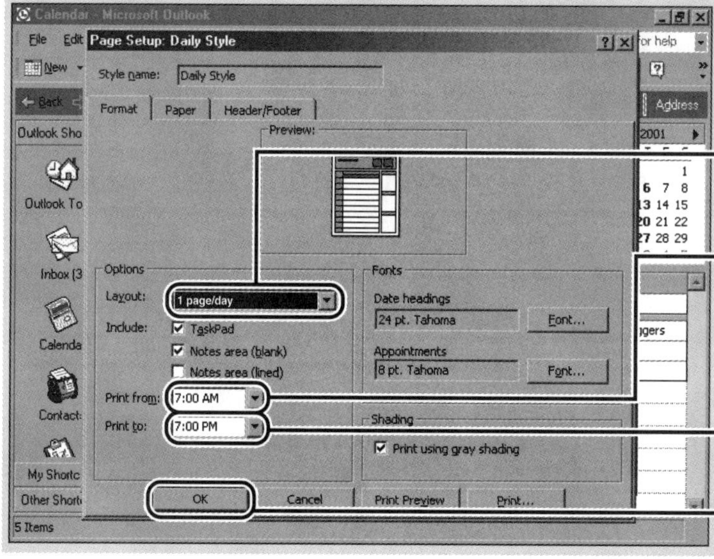

6 Click the **Layout** ▾ and select the number of days you want printed per page.

7 Click the **Print from** ▾ and select the time to start your printed calendar.

8 Click the **Print to** ▾ and select the time to end your printed calendar.

9 Click **OK**.

10 Click **OK** to print.

OPEN THE OUTLOOK CONTACTS LIST

Outlook allows you to store contact and distribution list information, and quickly and easily send e-mail messages to those listed in your Outlook Contacts list. Using the Outlook bar, your Outlook Contacts list is just a few clicks away from anywhere within Outlook.

OPEN THE OUTLOOK CONTACTS LIST

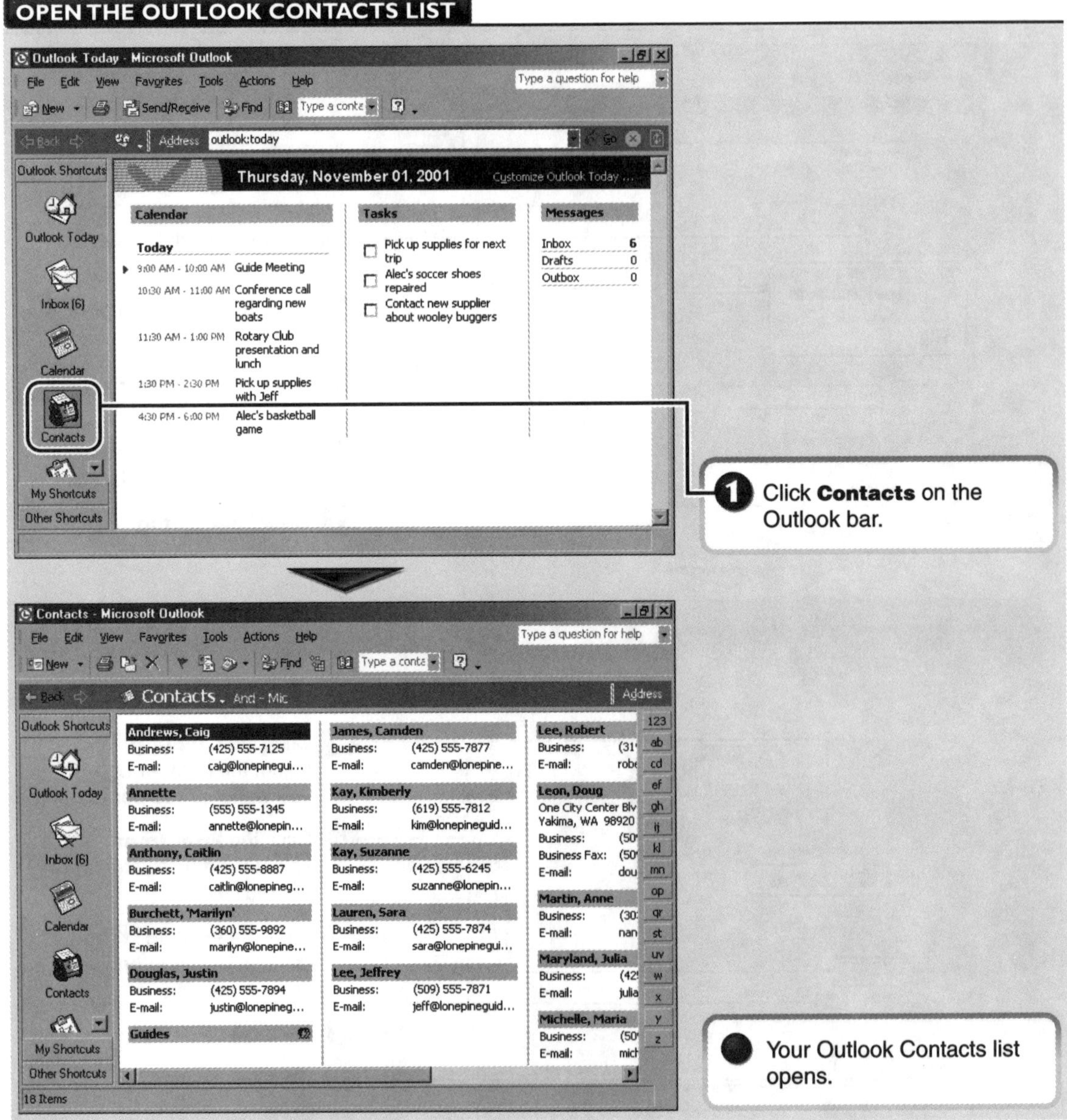

1 Click **Contacts** on the Outlook bar.

- Your Outlook Contacts list opens.

OPEN A CONTACT

Outlook Contacts cards contain key information for a specific person or distribution list. Opening an Outlook Contacts card is fast and easy.

OPEN A CONTACT

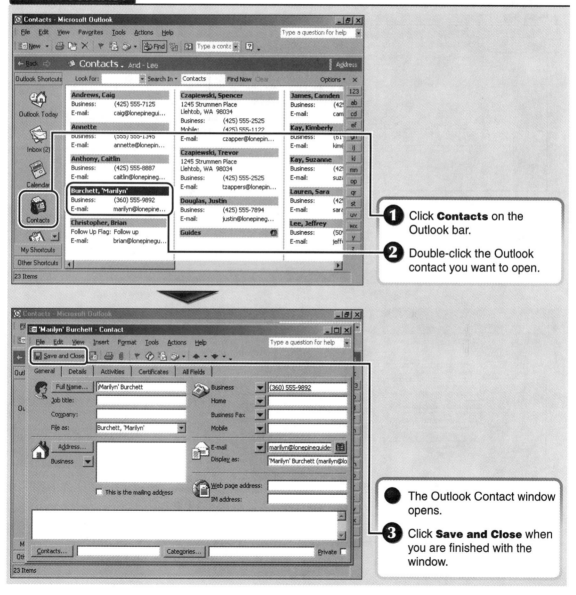

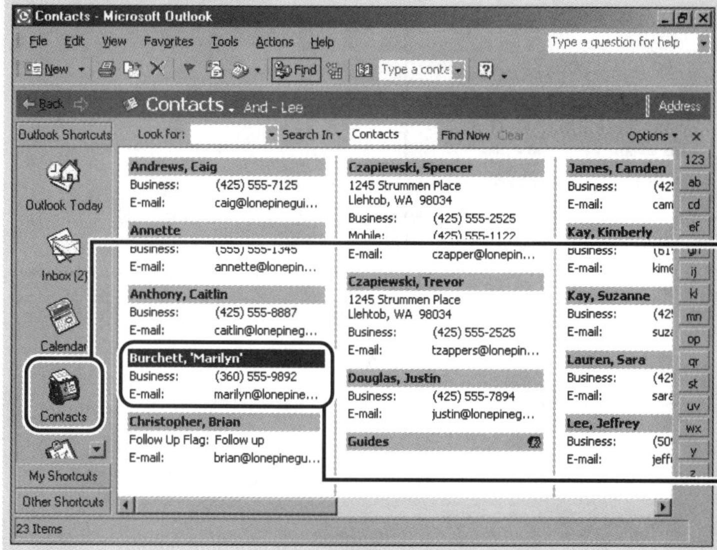

1. Click **Contacts** on the Outlook bar.
2. Double-click the Outlook contact you want to open.

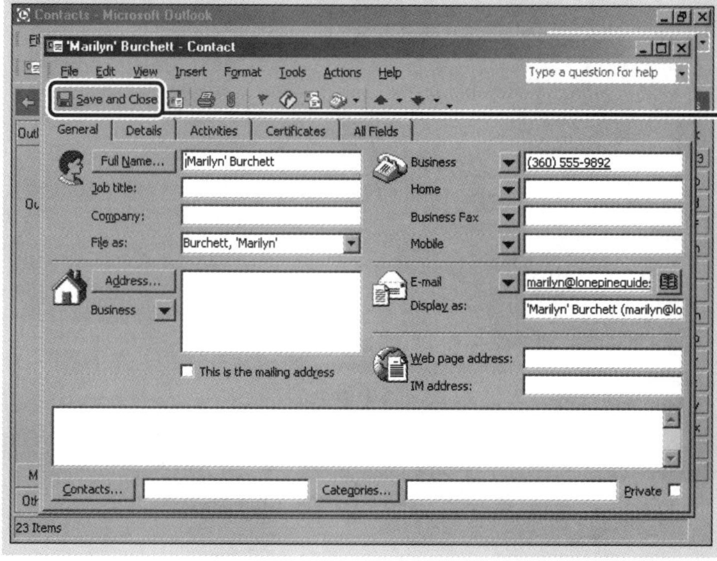

- The Outlook Contact window opens.

3. Click **Save and Close** when you are finished with the window.

ADD A NEW CONTACT

You can add a new Outlook contact easily. Using contacts is a great way to save e-mail messages, phone numbers, addresses, and more for clients, colleagues, friends, and family members.

ADD A NEW CONTACT

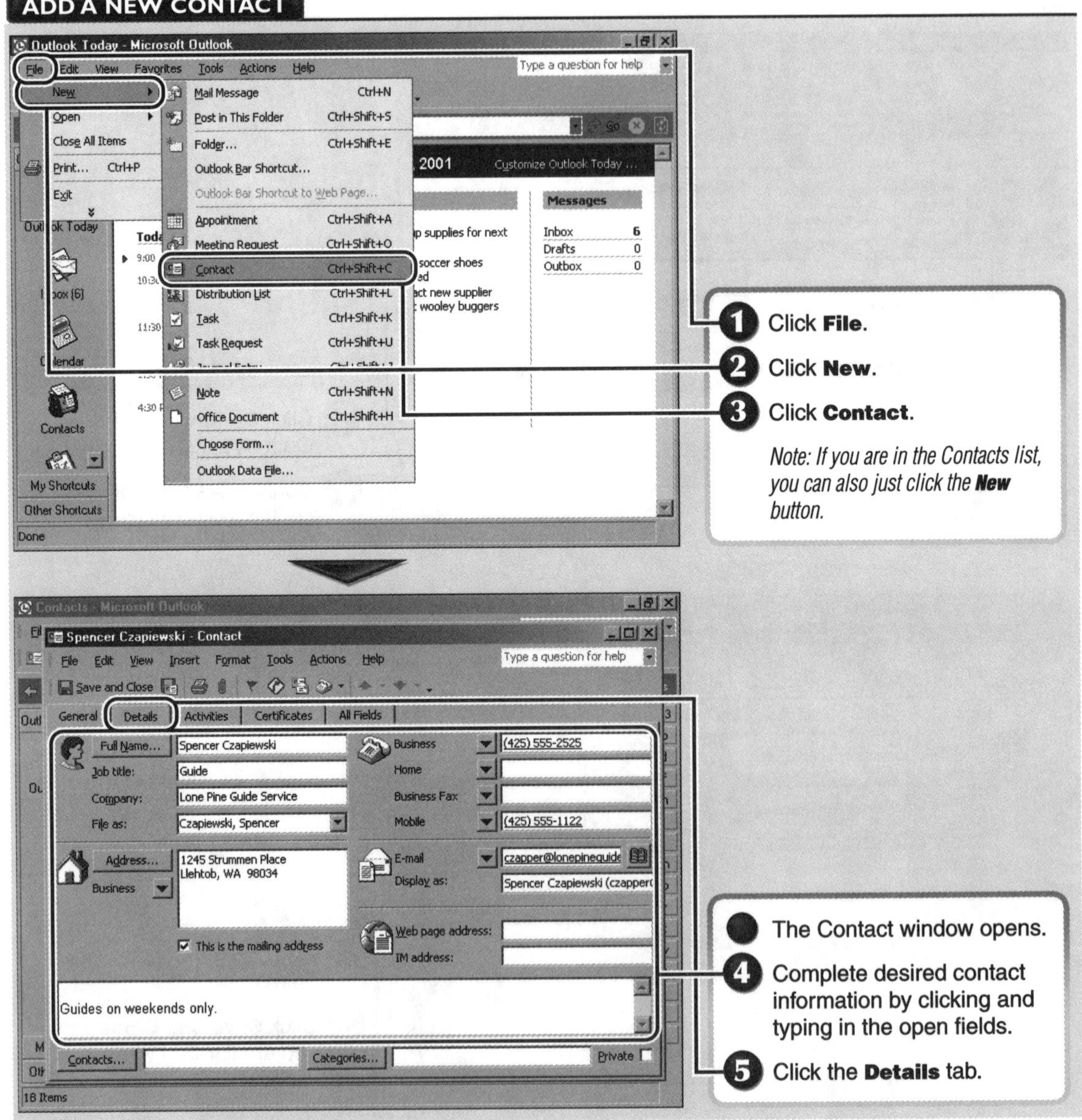

1. Click **File**.
2. Click **New**.
3. Click **Contact**.

*Note: If you are in the Contacts list, you can also just click the **New** button.*

- The Contact window opens.

4. Complete desired contact information by clicking and typing in the open fields.
5. Click the **Details** tab.

in an instant

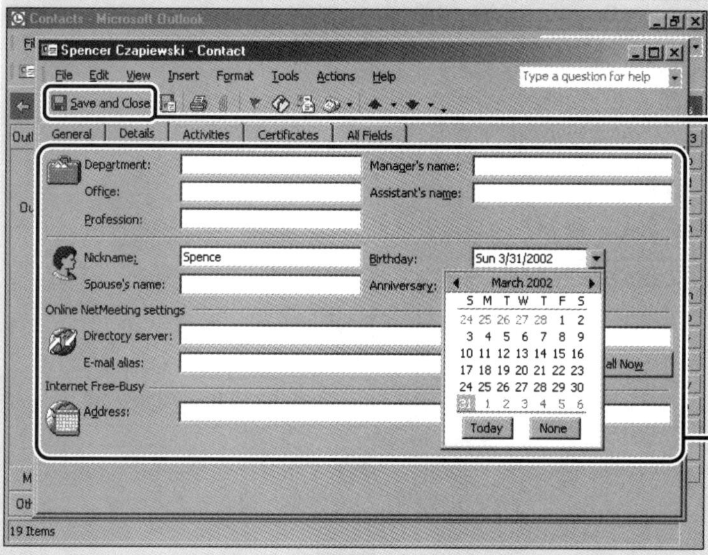

6 Complete desired details in the open fields.

7 Click **Save and Close**.

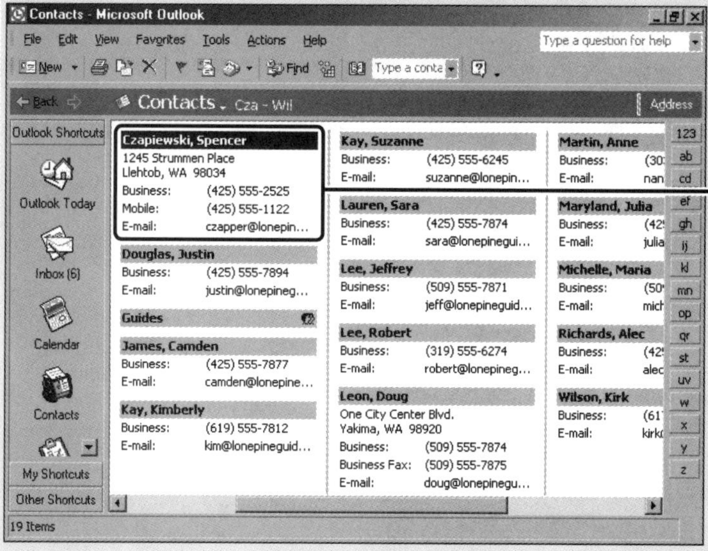

Outlook adds the contact to the Contacts list.

ADD A NEW CONTACT FROM AN E-MAIL MESSAGE

You can add a person to your Outlook Contacts list directly from an e-mail message you have received from that person.

ADD A NEW CONTACT FROM AN E-MAIL MESSAGE

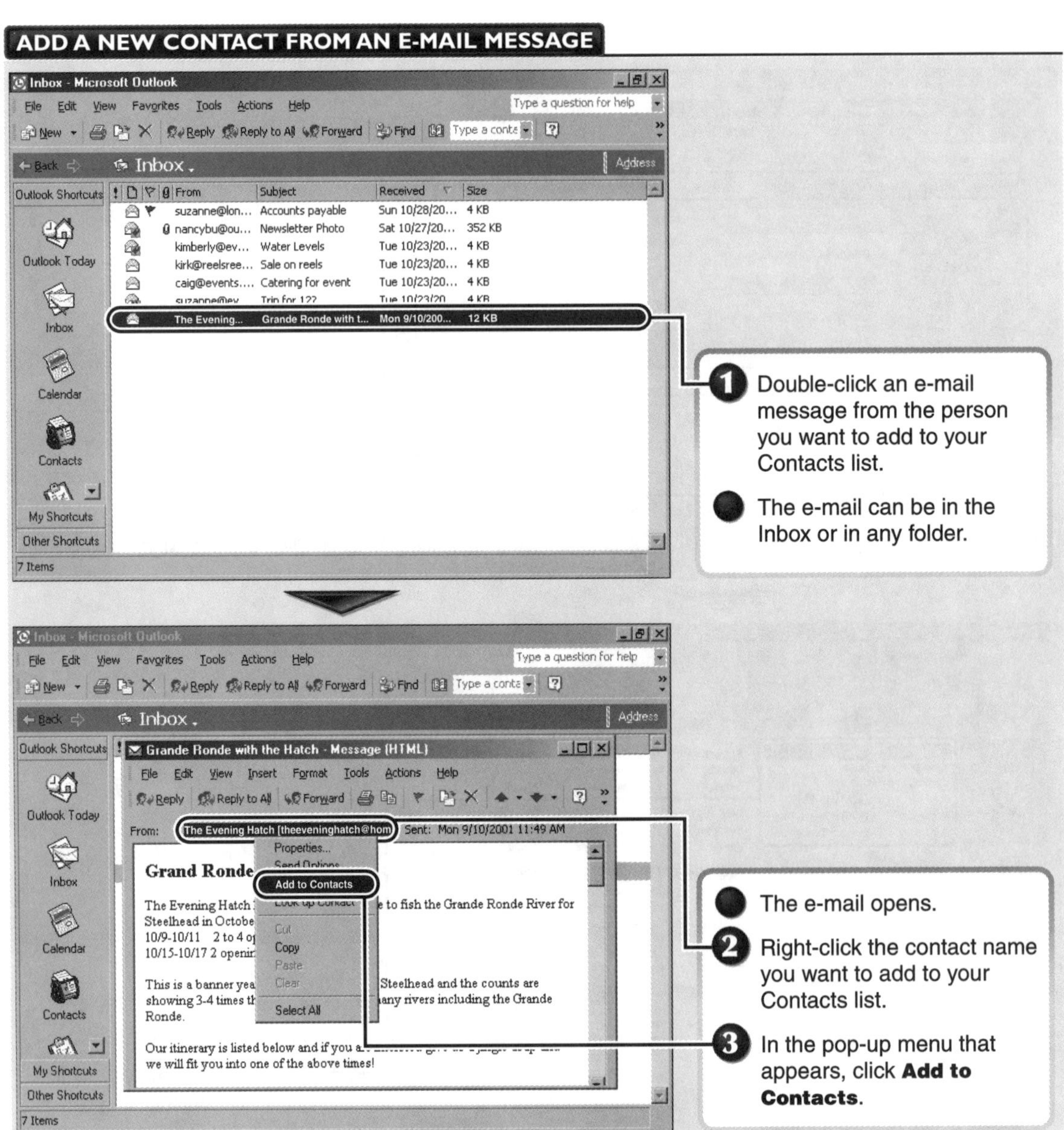

1. Double-click an e-mail message from the person you want to add to your Contacts list.

- The e-mail can be in the Inbox or in any folder.

- The e-mail opens.

2. Right-click the contact name you want to add to your Contacts list.

3. In the pop-up menu that appears, click **Add to Contacts**.

in an instant

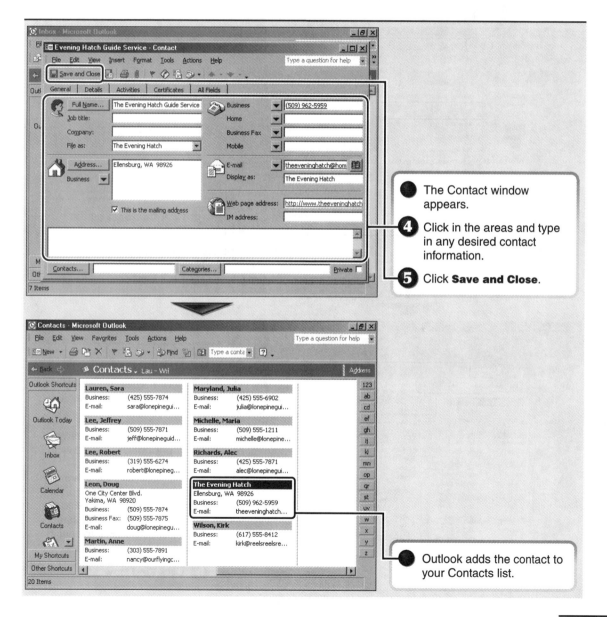

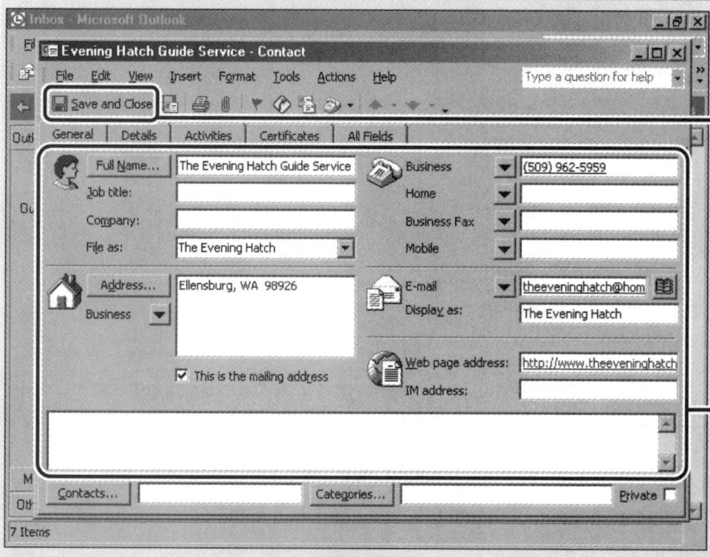

- The Contact window appears.
- **4** Click in the areas and type in any desired contact information.
- **5** Click **Save and Close**.

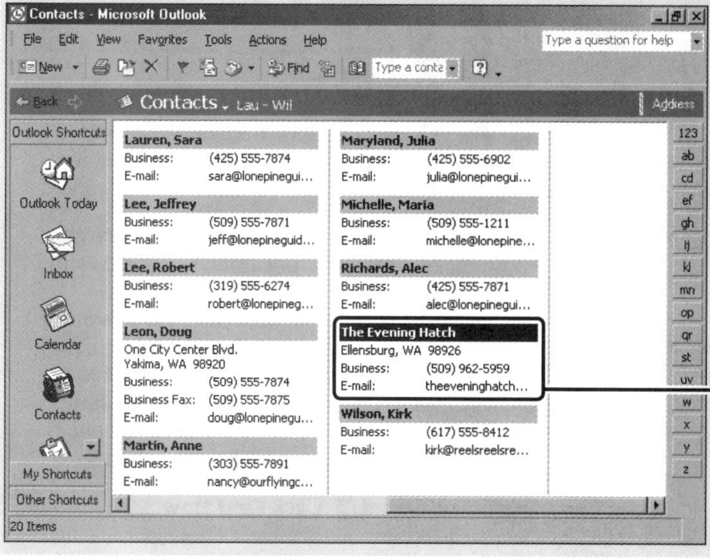

- Outlook adds the contact to your Contacts list.

FIND A CONTACT

When you have a lot of Outlook contacts, you may need some help finding the correct one. The Outlook Find and Advanced Find options on the Tools menu make finding contacts easy.

FIND A CONTACT

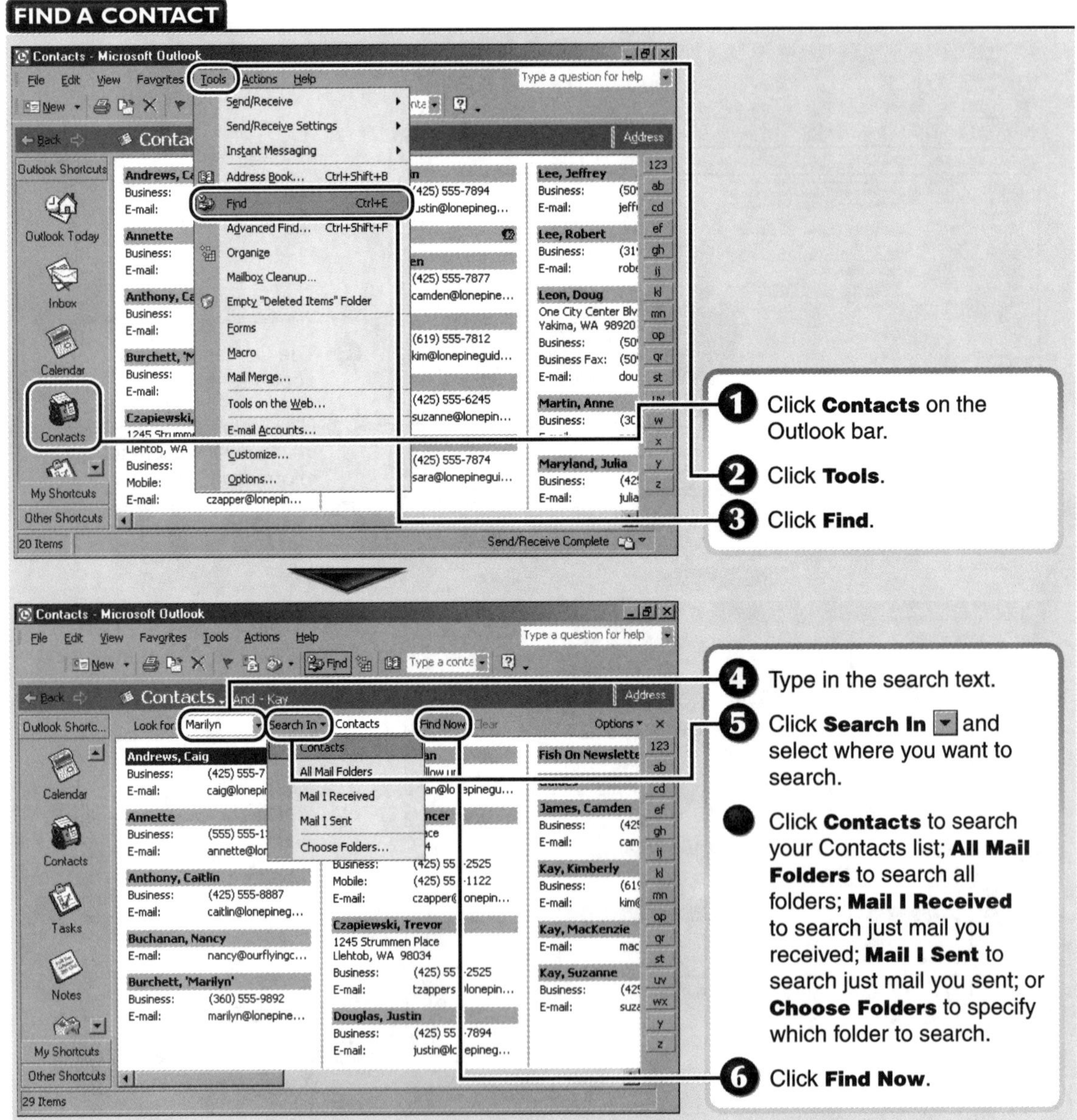

1. Click **Contacts** on the Outlook bar.
2. Click **Tools**.
3. Click **Find**.
4. Type in the search text.
5. Click **Search In** ▾ and select where you want to search.

- Click **Contacts** to search your Contacts list; **All Mail Folders** to search all folders; **Mail I Received** to search just mail you received; **Mail I Sent** to search just mail you sent; or **Choose Folders** to specify which folder to search.

6. Click **Find Now**.

in an instant

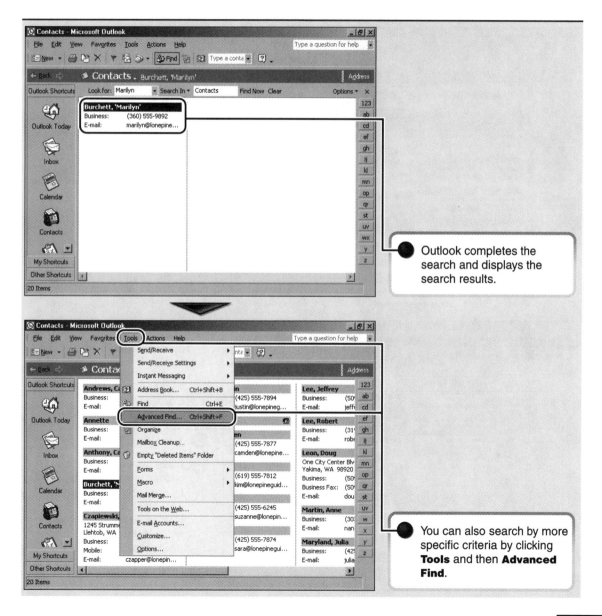

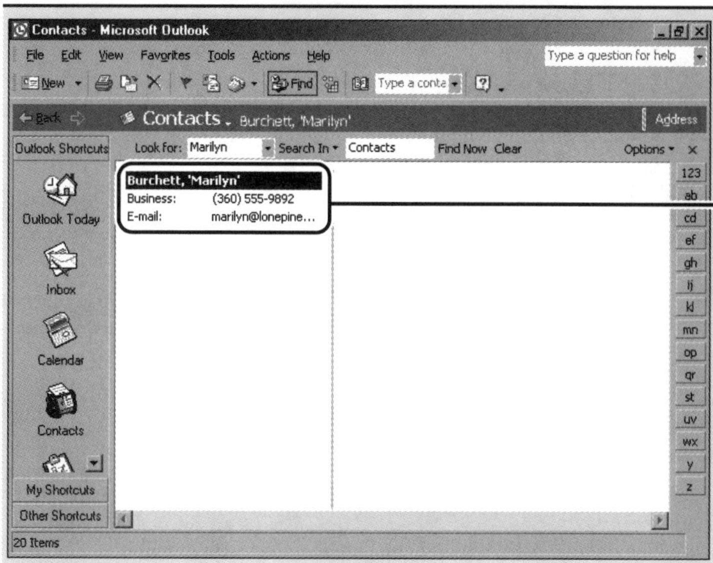

- Outlook completes the search and displays the search results.

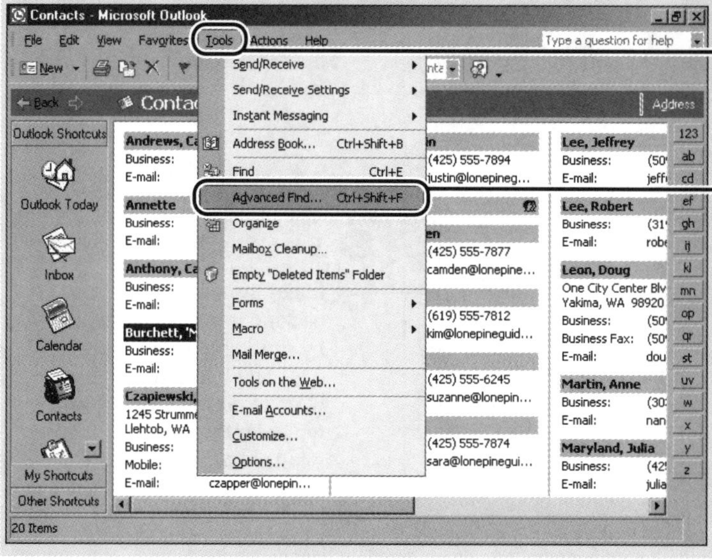

- You can also search by more specific criteria by clicking **Tools** and then **Advanced Find**.

EDIT A CONTACT

You can edit contact information at any time. This allows you to stay up-to-date when, for example, a key client receives a promotion or a friend switches e-mail addresses.

EDIT A CONTACT

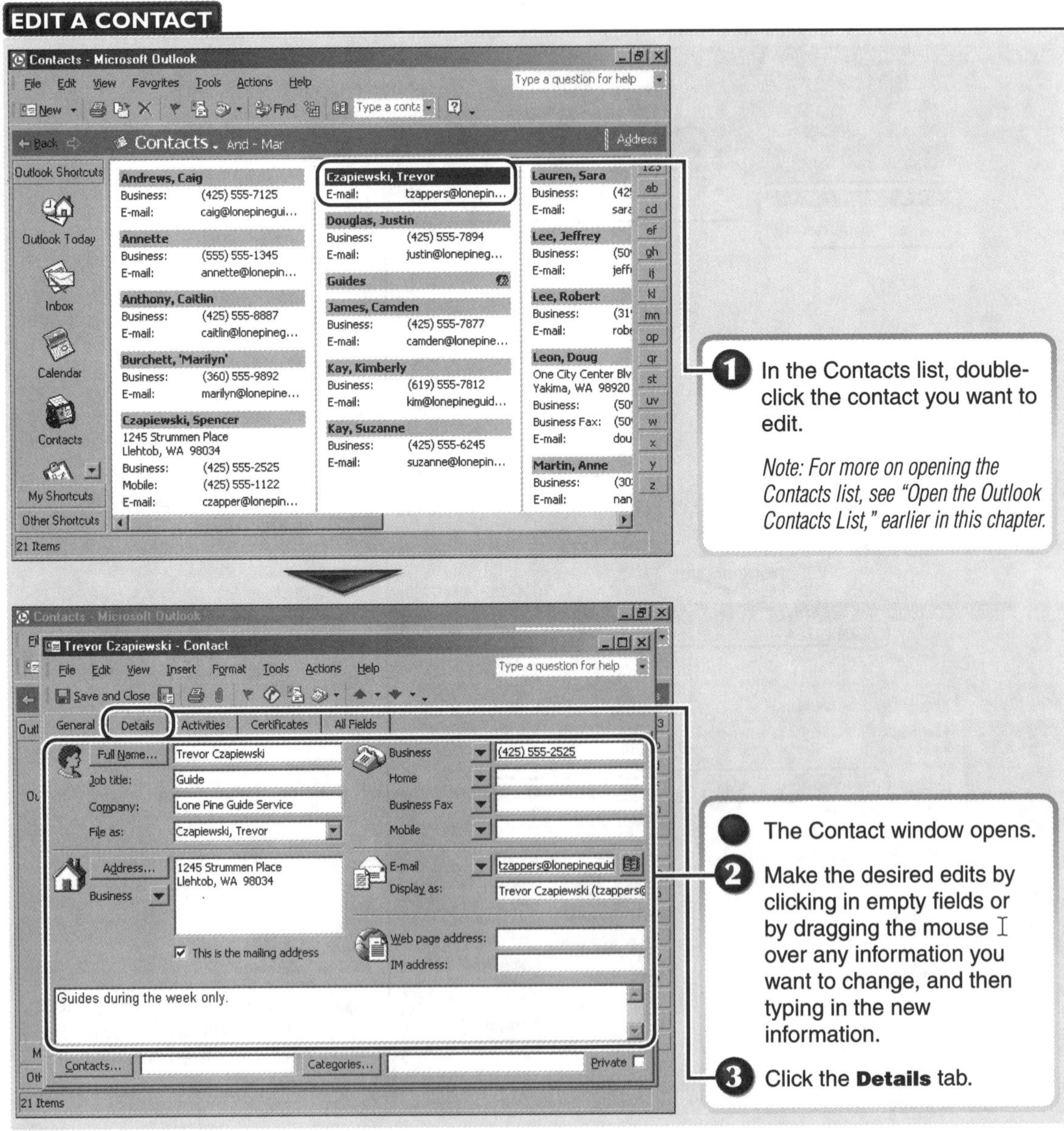

1 In the Contacts list, double-click the contact you want to edit.

Note: For more on opening the Contacts list, see "Open the Outlook Contacts List," earlier in this chapter.

- The Contact window opens.

2 Make the desired edits by clicking in empty fields or by dragging the mouse I over any information you want to change, and then typing in the new information.

3 Click the **Details** tab.

in an instant

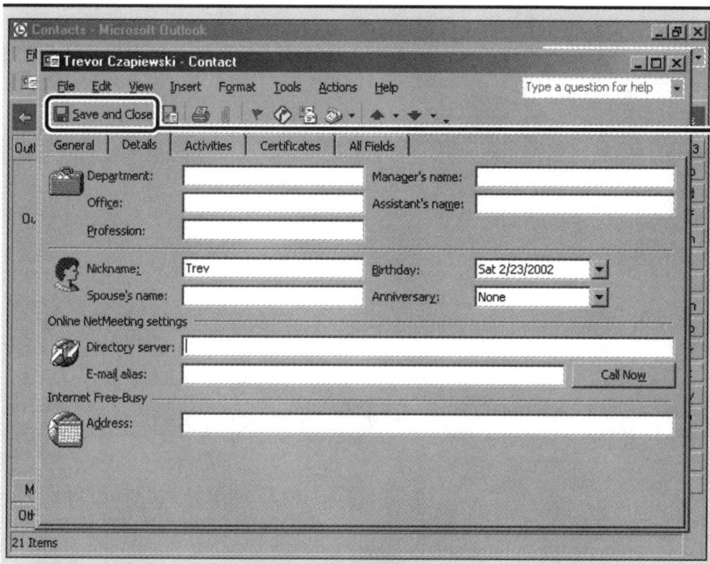

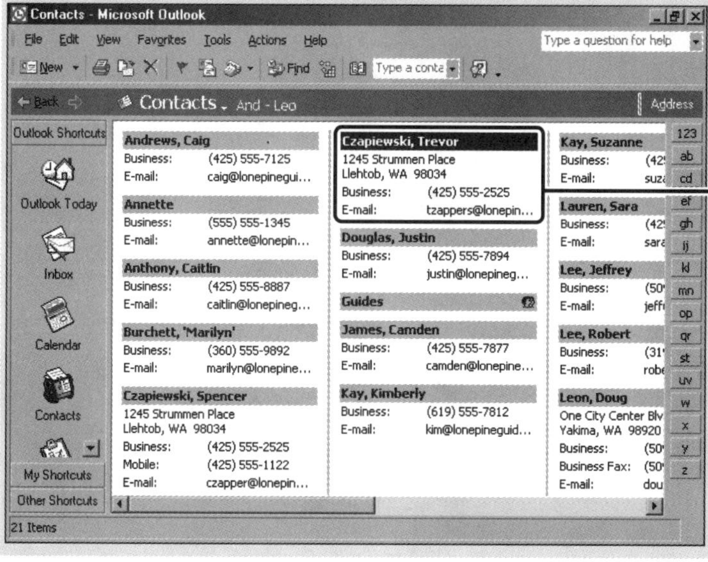

4 Make any desired edits to the contact details.

5 Click **Save and Close**.

● Outlook updates the contact information.

CHANGE HOW YOU VIEW CONTACTS

You can change how you view your Outlook Contacts list depending on what types of contacts you are looking for. Among the choices that Outlook offers is to view contacts by basic address card, detailed address card, phone list, category, company, and location. Most users find a view that they like and return to frequently.

IDENTIFY THE CURRENT VIEW

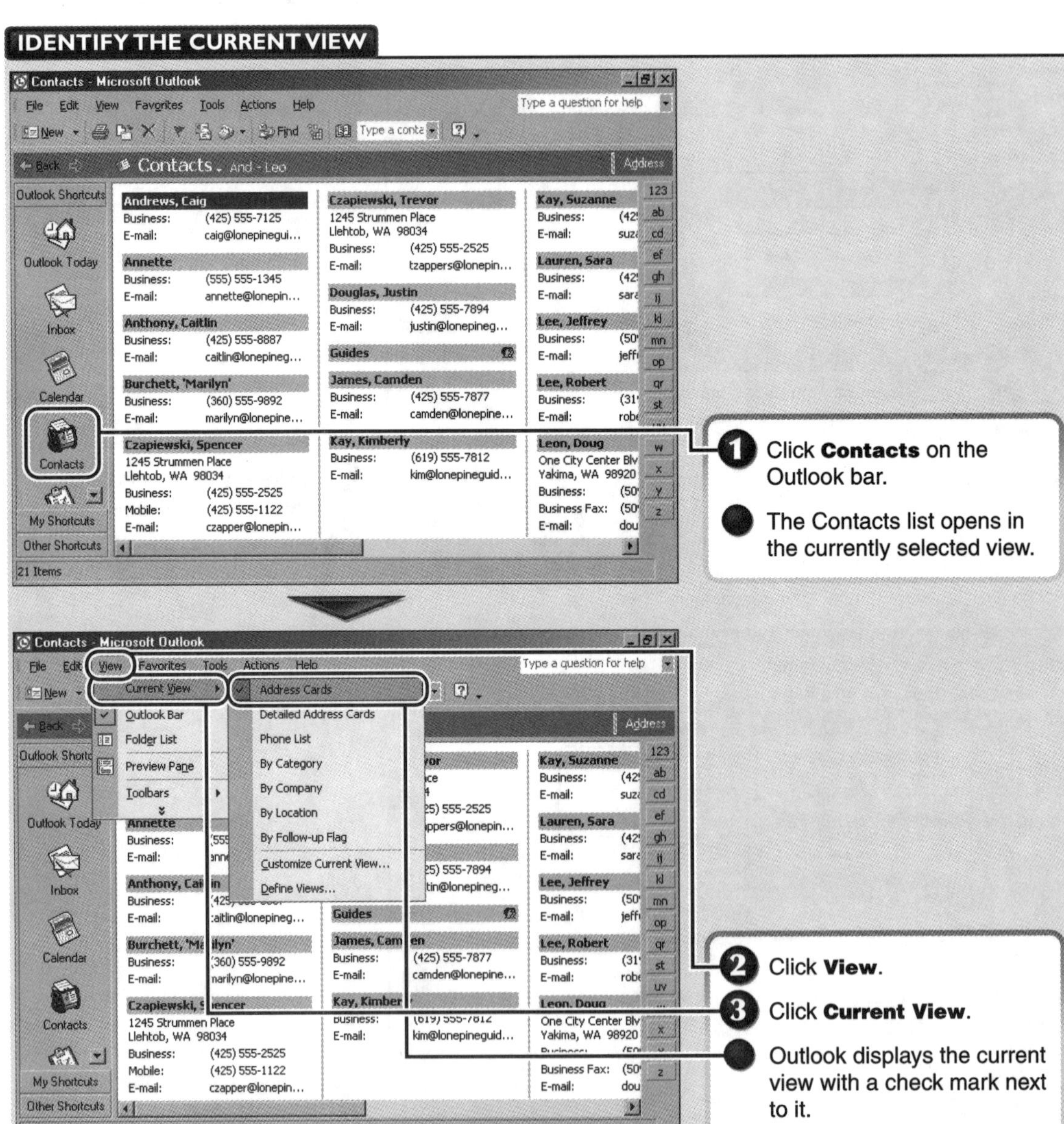

1. Click **Contacts** on the Outlook bar.

- The Contacts list opens in the currently selected view.

2. Click **View**.
3. Click **Current View**.

- Outlook displays the current view with a check mark next to it.

in an instant

CHANGE THE CURRENT VIEW

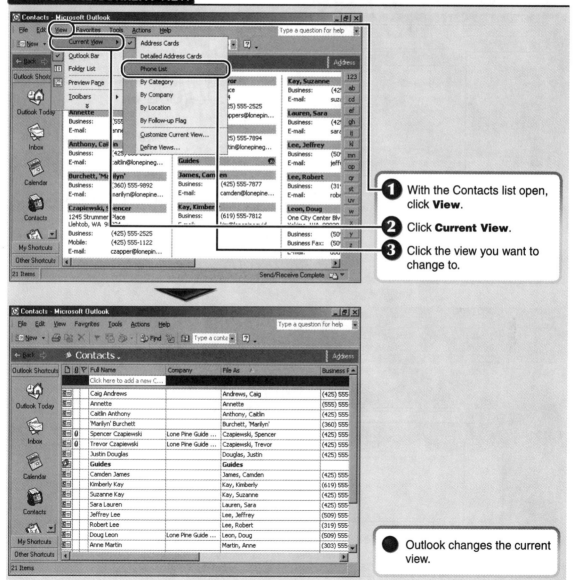

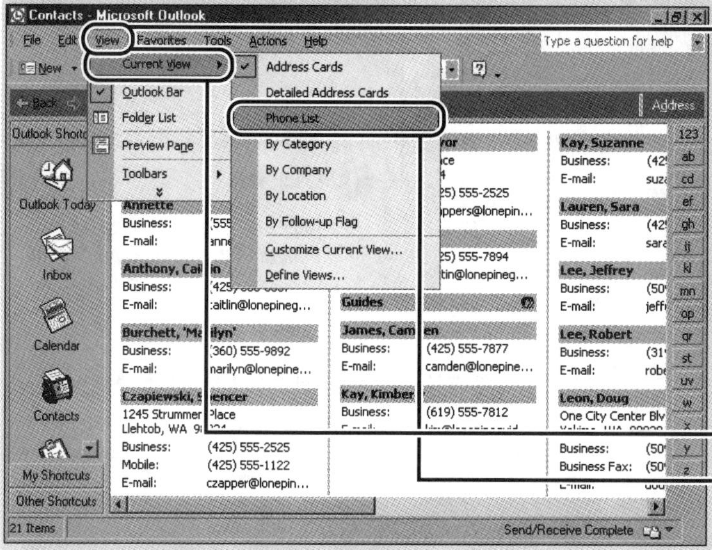

1. With the Contacts list open, click **View**.
2. Click **Current View**.
3. Click the view you want to change to.

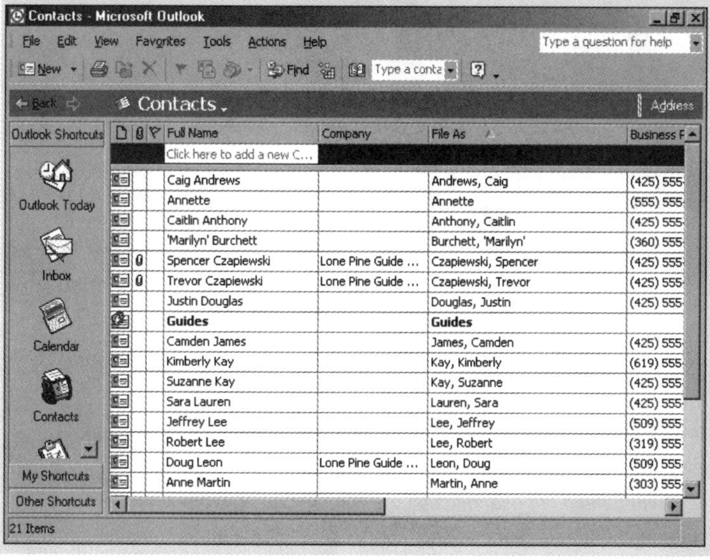

- Outlook changes the current view.

CREATE YOUR OWN DISTRIBUTION LIST

You can create a distribution list so that you can send e-mails to multiple people (or even to multiple distribution lists) at one time. For example, if you are working in a sales position, you might want to create a distribution list with all your buyers on it. Creating your own distribution list is easy.

CREATE YOUR OWN DISTRIBUTION LIST

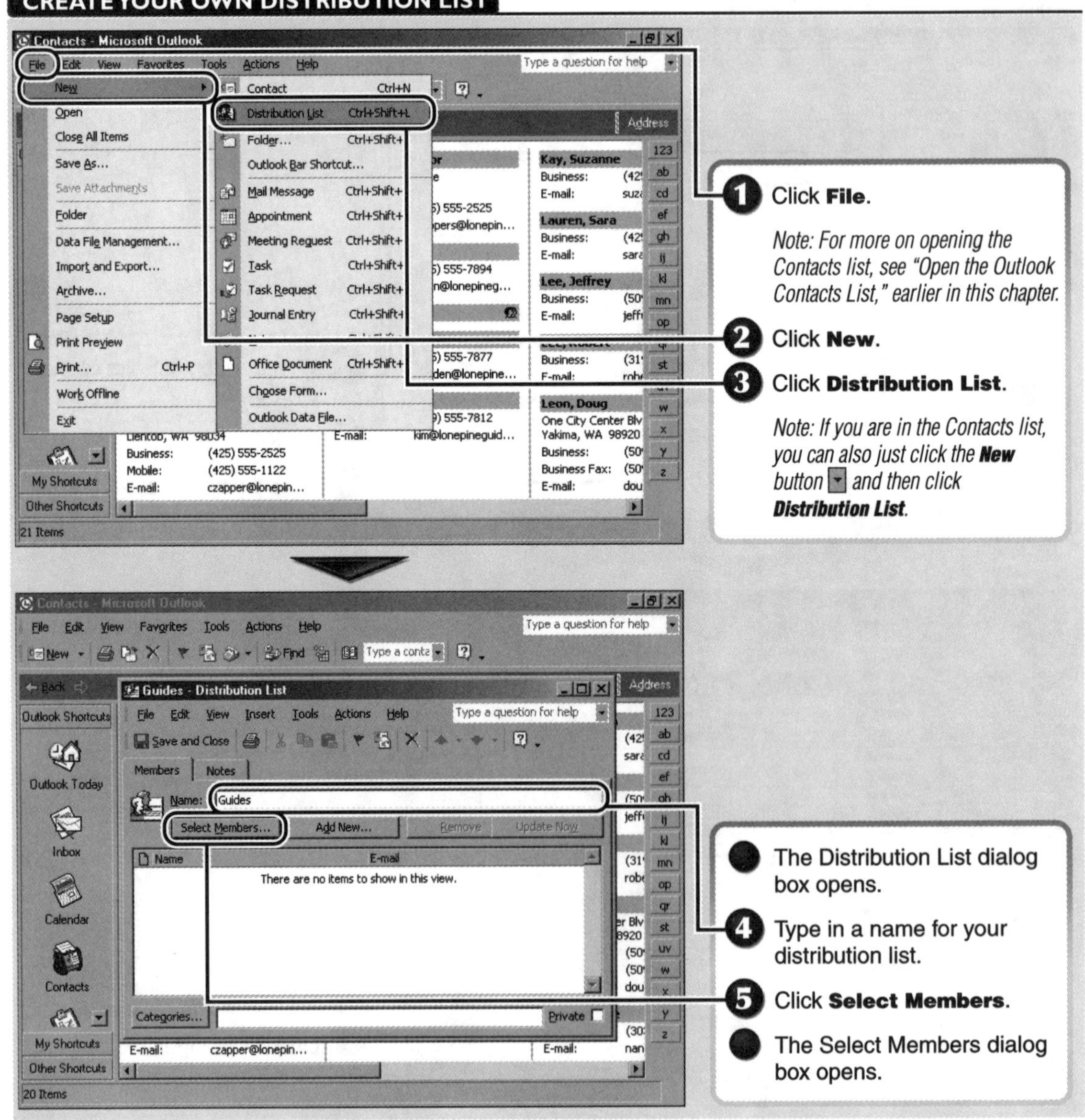

1 Click **File**.
Note: For more on opening the Contacts list, see "Open the Outlook Contacts List," earlier in this chapter.
2 Click **New**.
3 Click **Distribution List**.
*Note: If you are in the Contacts list, you can also just click the **New** button and then click **Distribution List**.*
■ The Distribution List dialog box opens.
4 Type in a name for your distribution list.
5 Click **Select Members**.
■ The Select Members dialog box opens.

in an instant

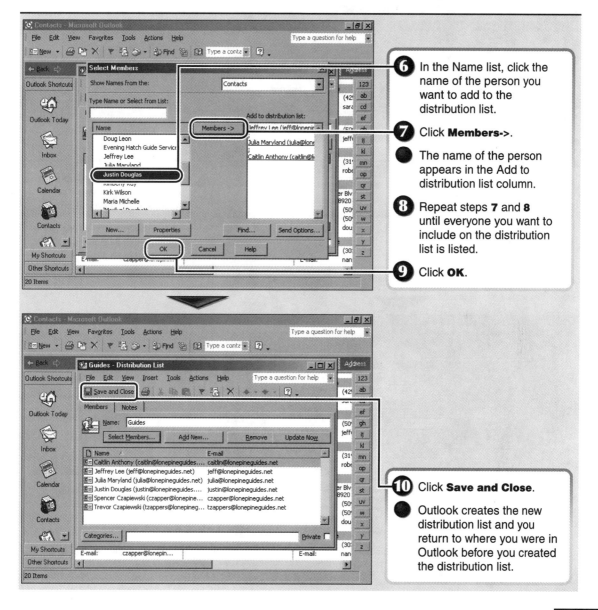

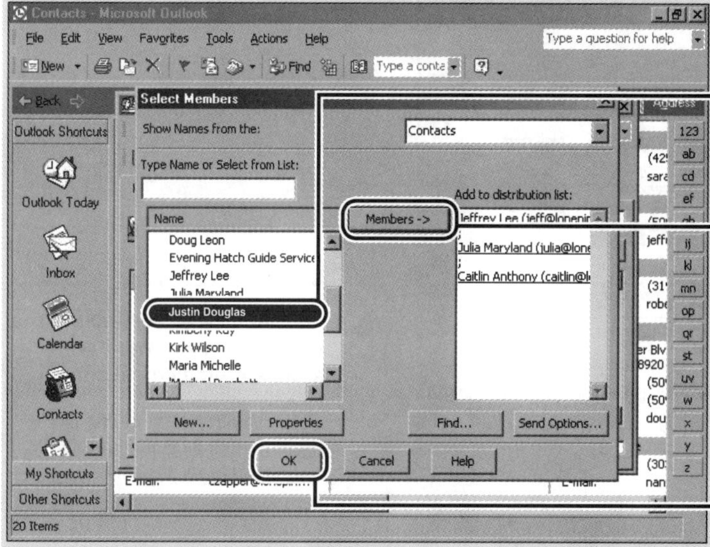

6 In the Name list, click the name of the person you want to add to the distribution list.

7 Click **Members->**.

- The name of the person appears in the Add to distribution list column.

8 Repeat steps **7** and **8** until everyone you want to include on the distribution list is listed.

9 Click **OK**.

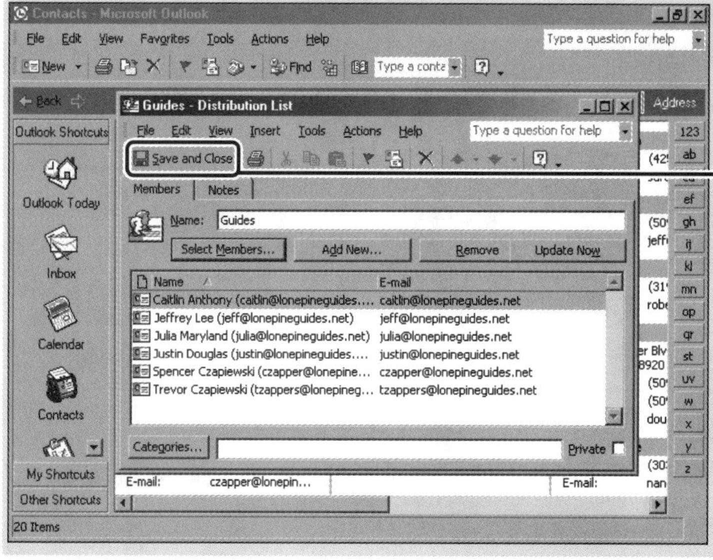

10 Click **Save and Close**.

- Outlook creates the new distribution list and you return to where you were in Outlook before you created the distribution list.

SEND E-MAIL TO A DISTRIBUTION LIST

You can send an e-mail message to a distribution list as easily as you can send an e-mail message to a single person.

SEND E-MAIL TO A DISTRIBUTION LIST

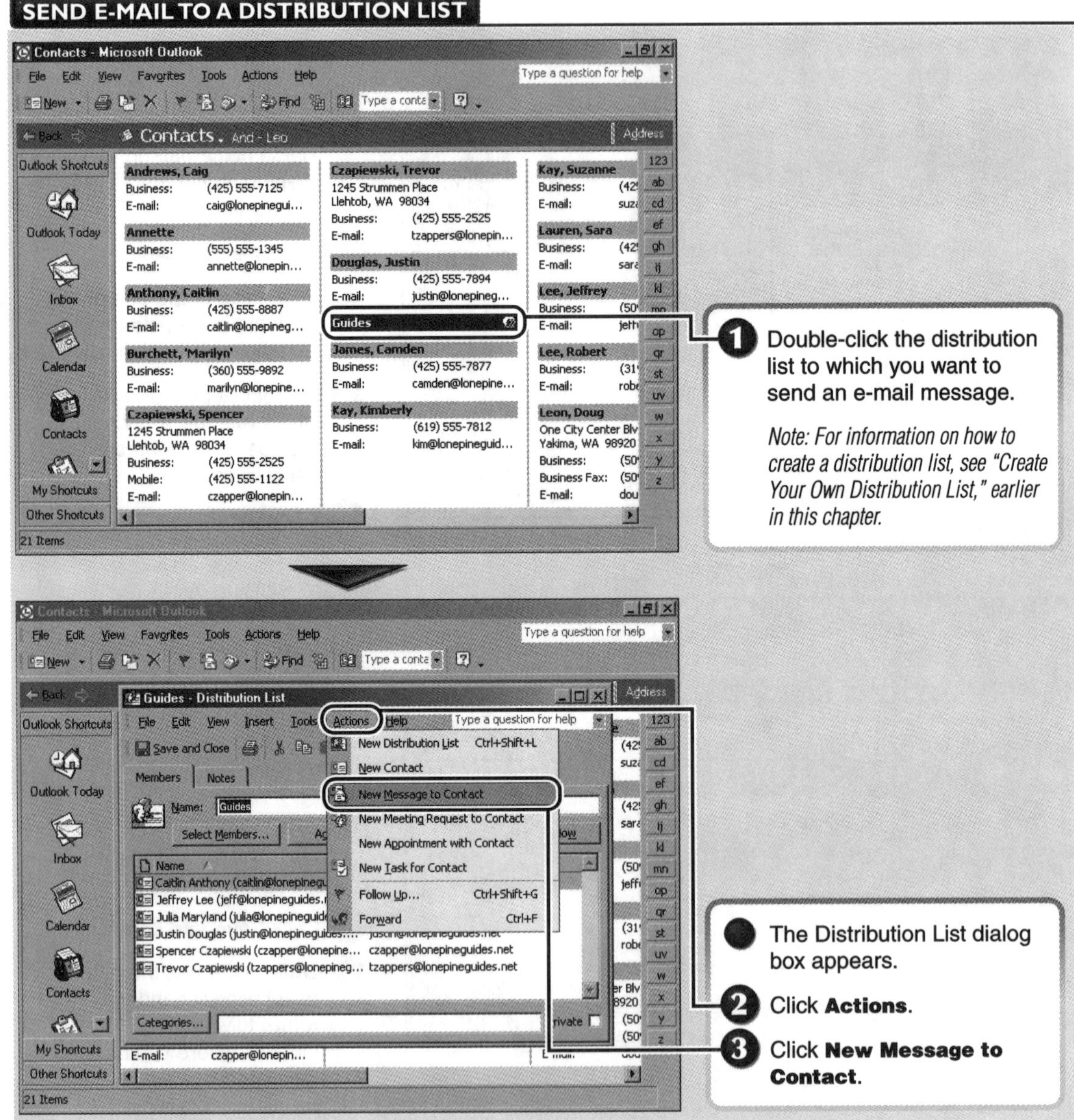

1 Double-click the distribution list to which you want to send an e-mail message.

Note: For information on how to create a distribution list, see "Create Your Own Distribution List," earlier in this chapter.

- The Distribution List dialog box appears.

2 Click **Actions**.

3 Click **New Message to Contact**.

in an instant

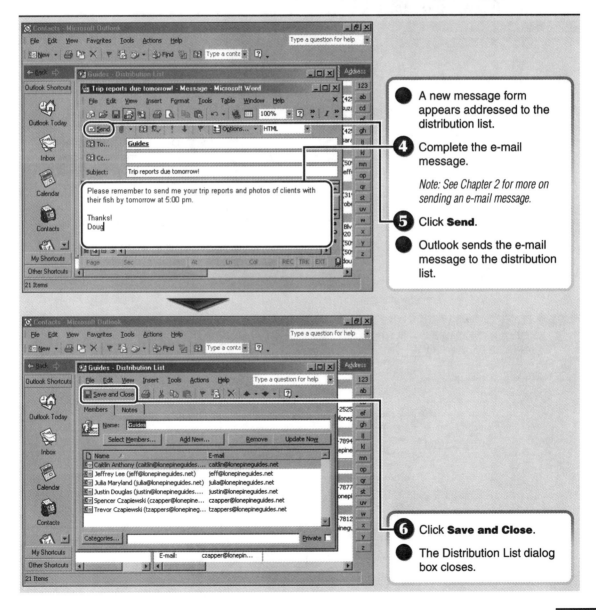

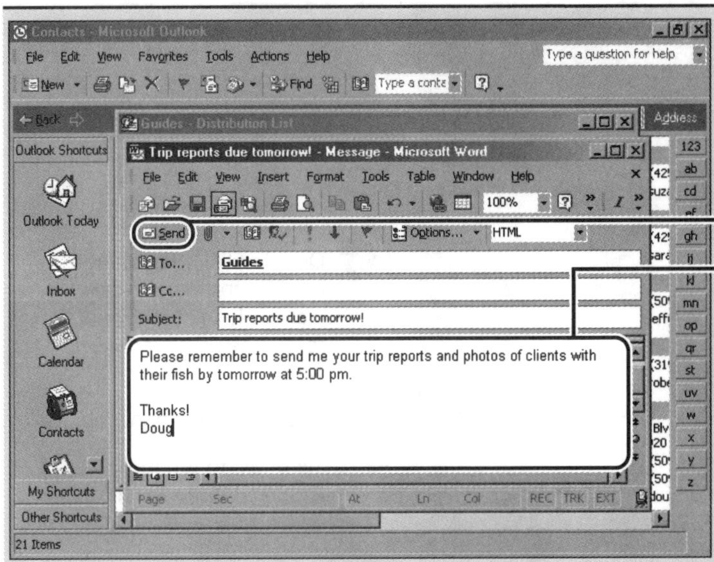

- A new message form appears addressed to the distribution list.

4 Complete the e-mail message.

Note: See Chapter 2 for more on sending an e-mail message.

5 Click **Send**.

- Outlook sends the e-mail message to the distribution list.

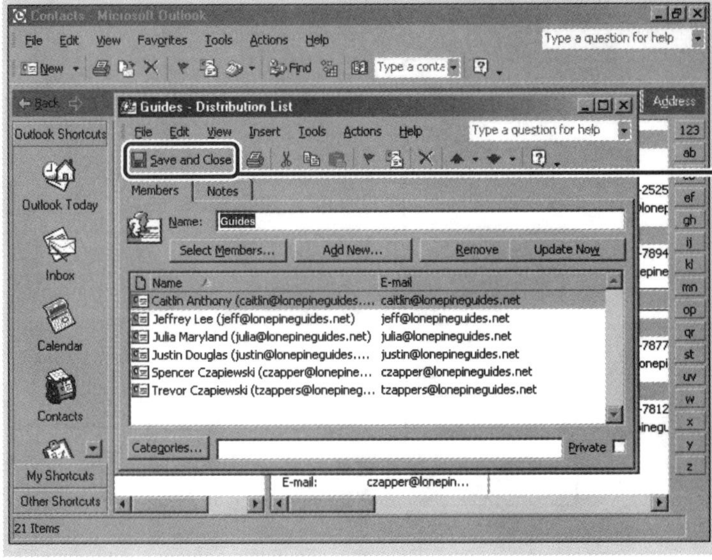

6 Click **Save and Close**.

- The Distribution List dialog box closes.

REMIND YOURSELF TO FOLLOW UP

You can assign a flag to a contact to remind yourself to take some action by a specific date and time. The flag you set comes up with your other Outlook reminders at the specified date and time. For more information about Outlook reminders, see Chapter 8.

REMIND YOURSELF TO FOLLOW UP

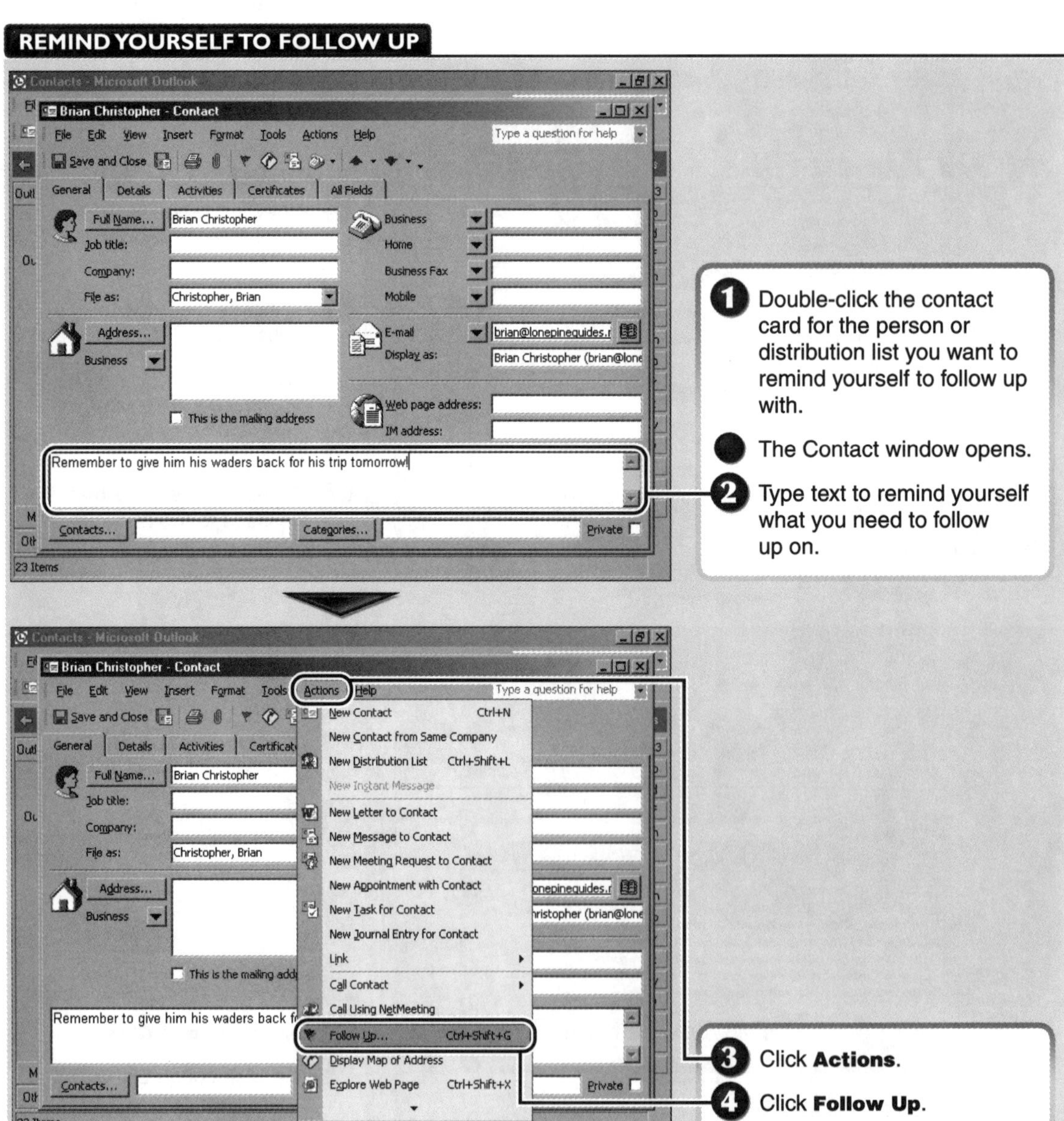

1. Double-click the contact card for the person or distribution list you want to remind yourself to follow up with.

- The Contact window opens.

2. Type text to remind yourself what you need to follow up on.

3. Click **Actions**.

4. Click **Follow Up**.

in an instant

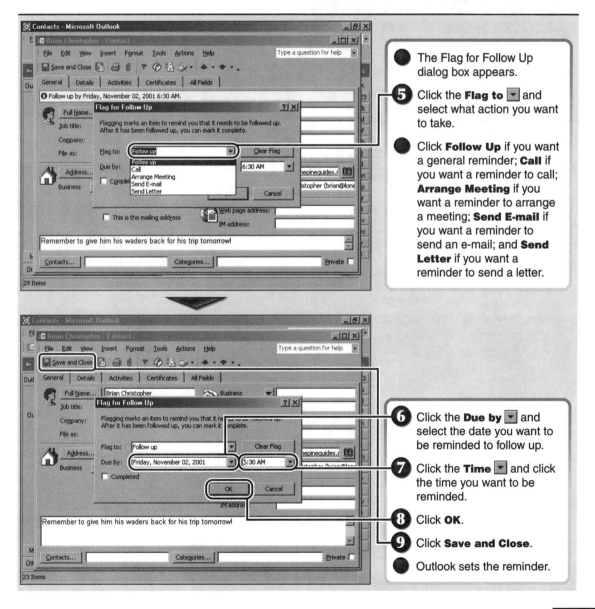

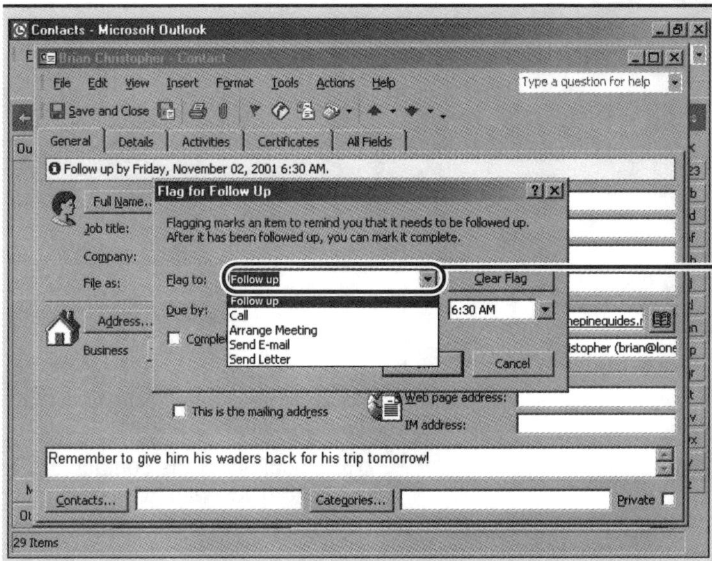

- The Flag for Follow Up dialog box appears.

5. Click the **Flag to** ▾ and select what action you want to take.

- Click **Follow Up** if you want a general reminder; **Call** if you want a reminder to call; **Arrange Meeting** if you want a reminder to arrange a meeting; **Send E-mail** if you want a reminder to send an e-mail; and **Send Letter** if you want a reminder to send a letter.

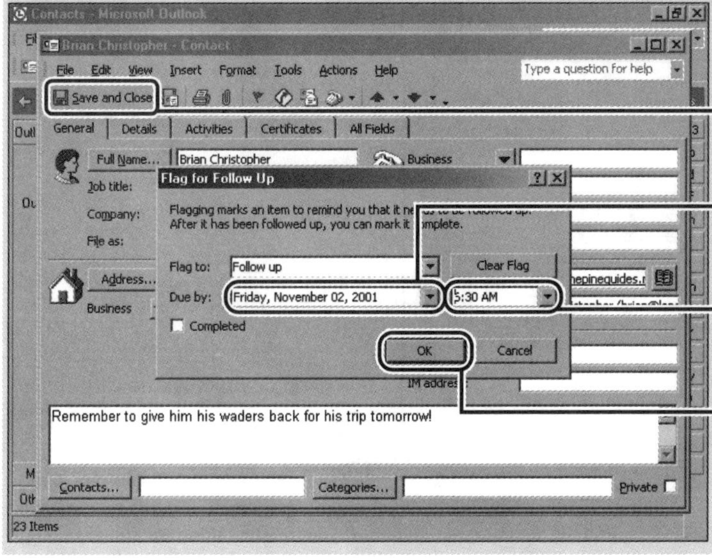

6. Click the **Due by** ▾ and select the date you want to be reminded to follow up.

7. Click the **Time** ▾ and click the time you want to be reminded.

8. Click **OK**.

9. Click **Save and Close**.

- Outlook sets the reminder.

SEND AN E-MAIL MESSAGE TO A CONTACT

You can send an e-mail message to someone listed in your contacts list without leaving the Outlook Contacts list.

SEND AN E-MAIL MESSAGE TO A CONTACT

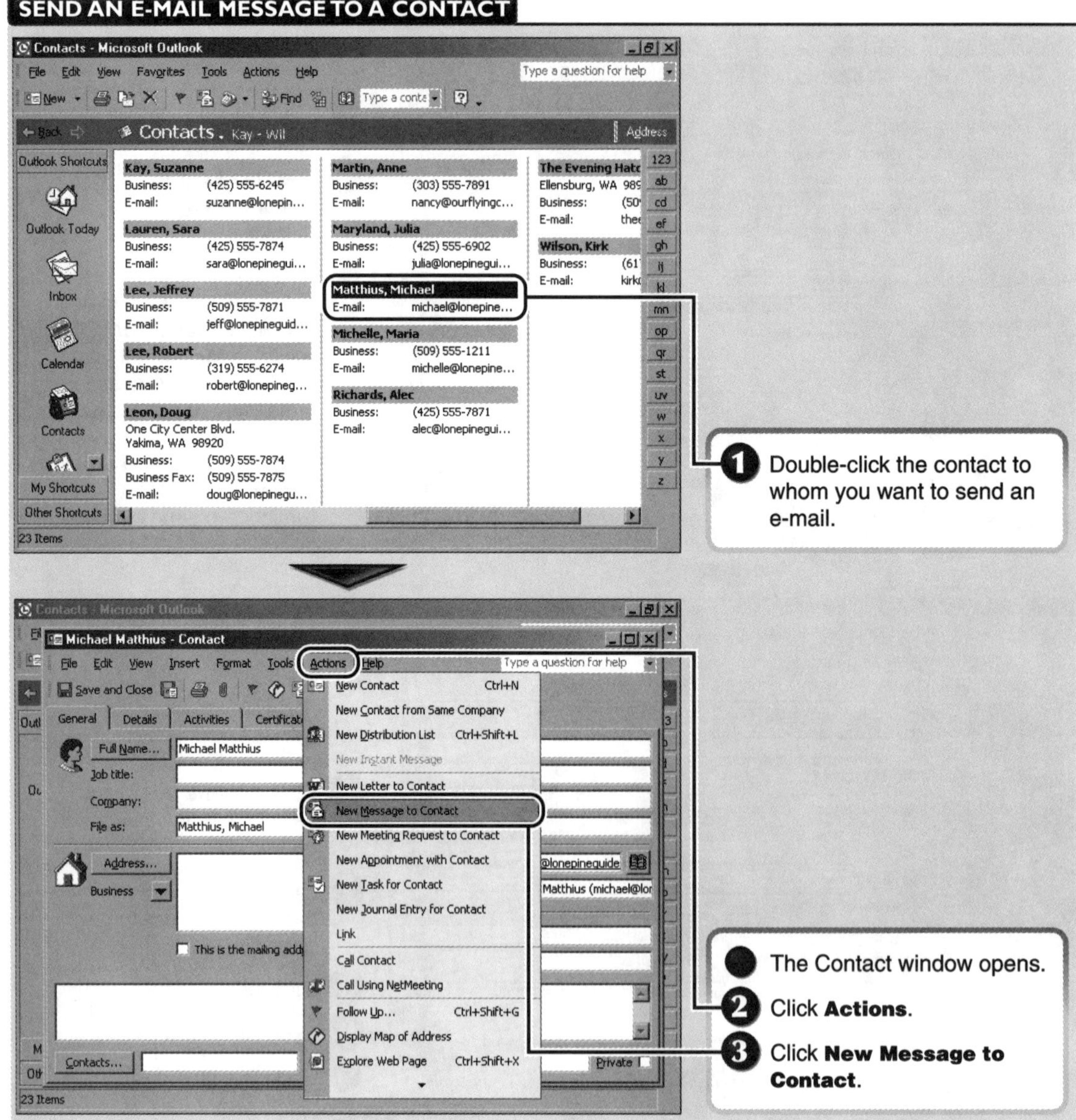

1. Double-click the contact to whom you want to send an e-mail.

- The Contact window opens.

2. Click **Actions**.
3. Click **New Message to Contact**.

in an instant

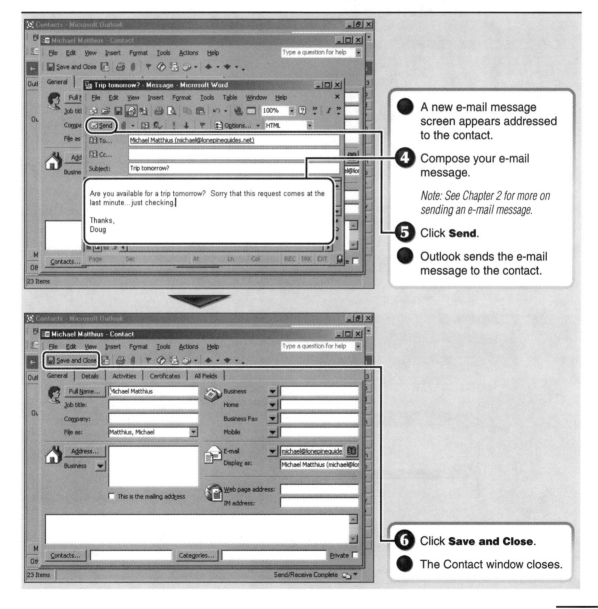

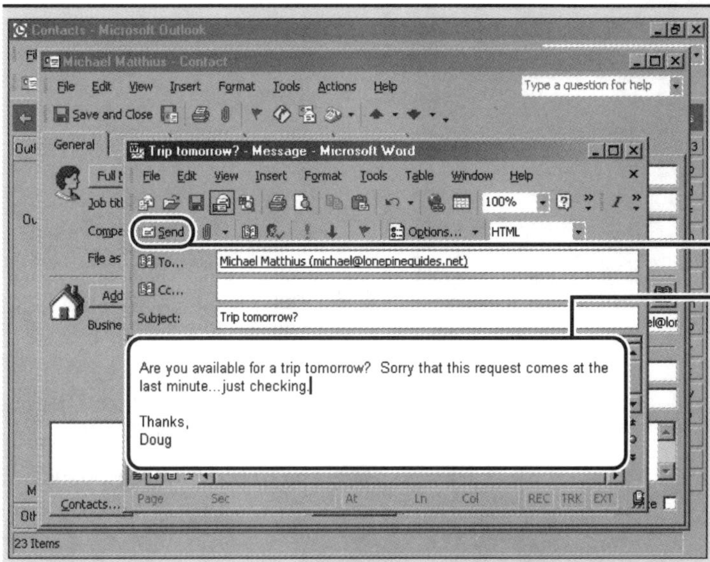

- A new e-mail message screen appears addressed to the contact.

4. Compose your e-mail message.

Note: See Chapter 2 for more on sending an e-mail message.

5. Click **Send**.

- Outlook sends the e-mail message to the contact.

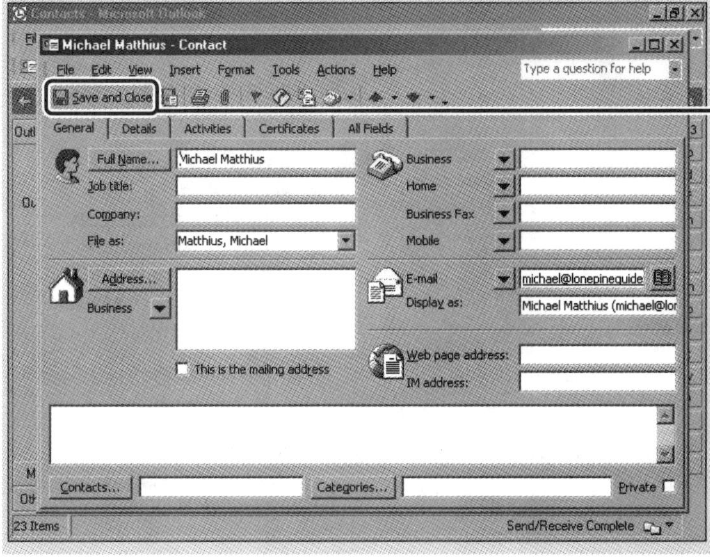

6. Click **Save and Close**.

- The Contact window closes.

ASSIGN CONTACTS TO CATEGORIES

You can assign your contacts to categories so that you can find them easily. For example, you can assign contacts to a Holiday Cards category, and when it comes time to send holiday cards, you can easily get a list of everyone who should be sent a card. You can also create your own categories.

ASSIGN CONTACTS TO CATEGORIES

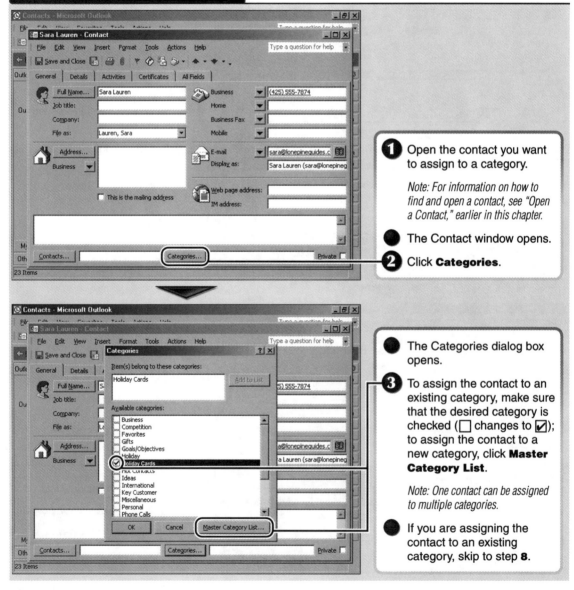

1. Open the contact you want to assign to a category.

   Note: For information on how to find and open a contact, see "Open a Contact," earlier in this chapter.

- The Contact window opens.

2. Click **Categories**.

- The Categories dialog box opens.

3. To assign the contact to an existing category, make sure that the desired category is checked (☐ changes to ☑); to assign the contact to a new category, click **Master Category List**.

   Note: One contact can be assigned to multiple categories.

- If you are assigning the contact to an existing category, skip to step **8**.

in an instant

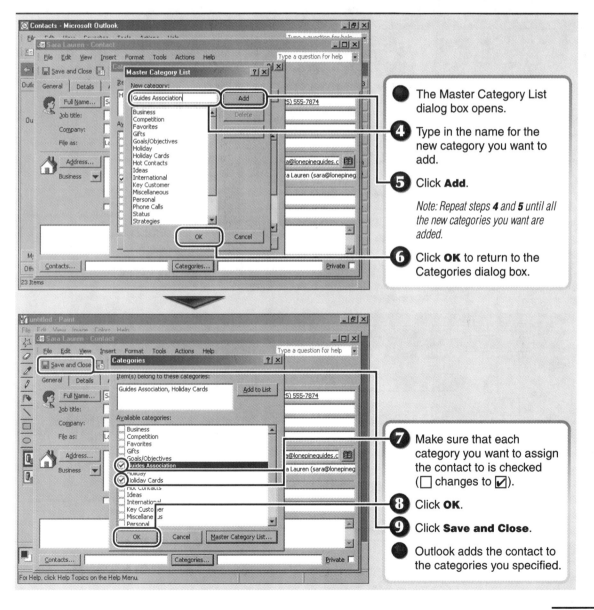

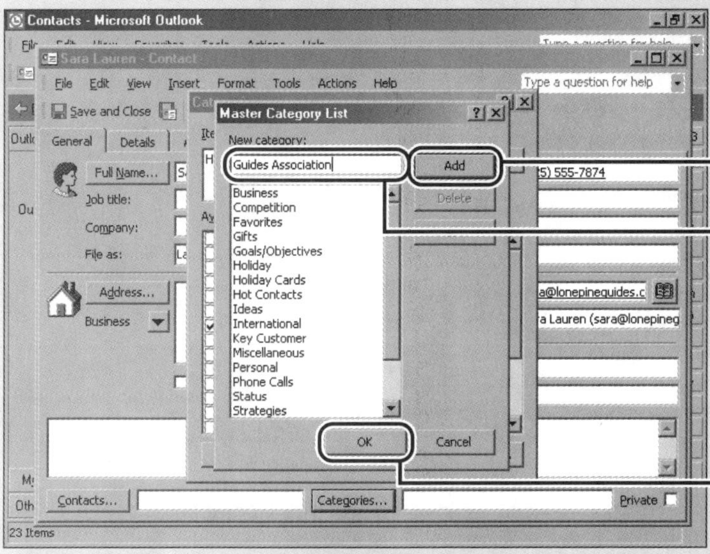

- The Master Category List dialog box opens.

4 Type in the name for the new category you want to add.

5 Click **Add**.

*Note: Repeat steps **4** and **5** until all the new categories you want are added.*

6 Click **OK** to return to the Categories dialog box.

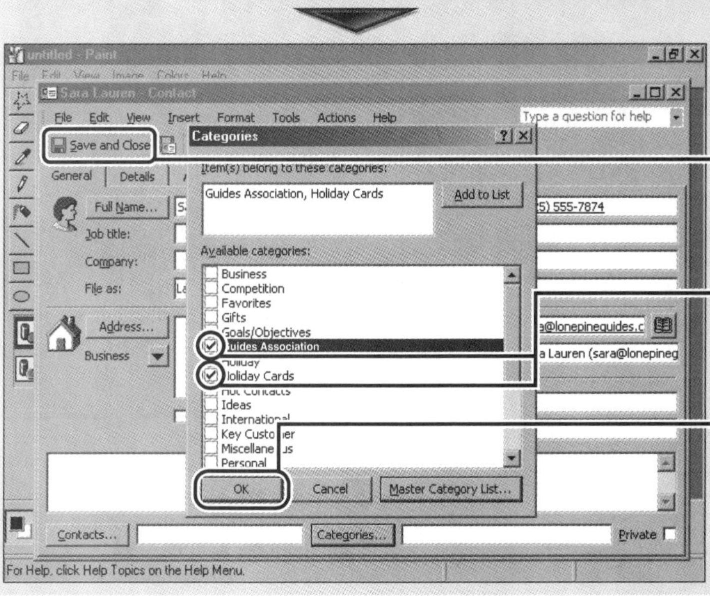

7 Make sure that each category you want to assign the contact to is checked (☐ changes to ☑).

8 Click **OK**.

9 Click **Save and Close**.

- Outlook adds the contact to the categories you specified.

VIEW ALL CONTACTS IN A CATEGORY

You can find all the contacts assigned to categories very easily. This is particularly convenient if you want to take some action for each contact in a category. As an example, if you are a sales professional, you can use categories to find all customers you have categorized as "VIP" and then make phone calls to them.

VIEW ALL CONTACTS IN A CATEGORY

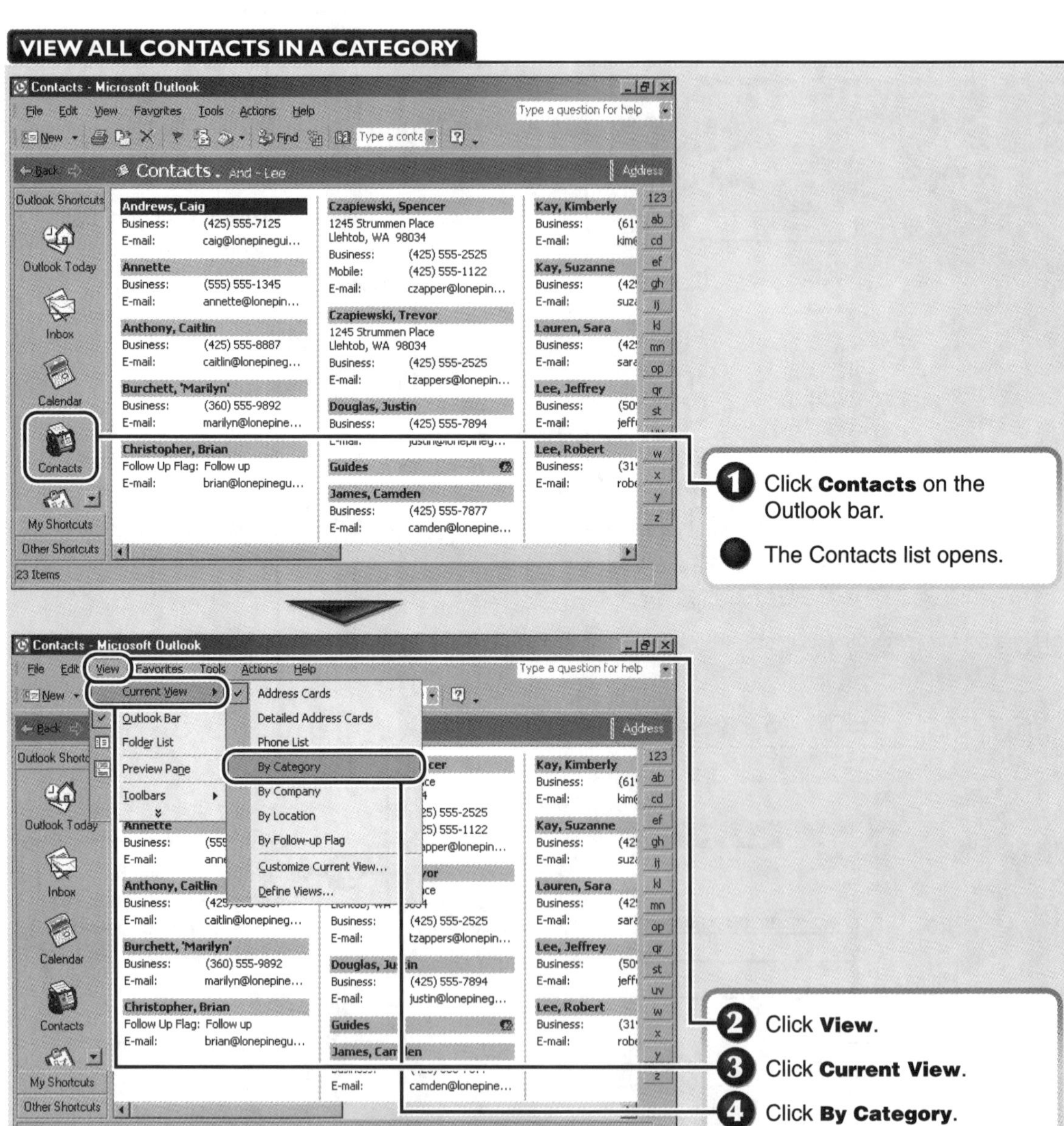

1 Click **Contacts** on the Outlook bar.
● The Contacts list opens.
2 Click **View**.
3 Click **Current View**.
4 Click **By Category**.

in an instant

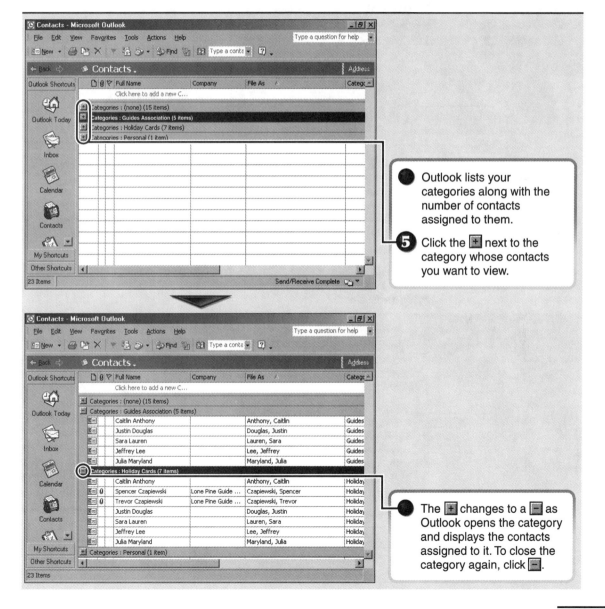

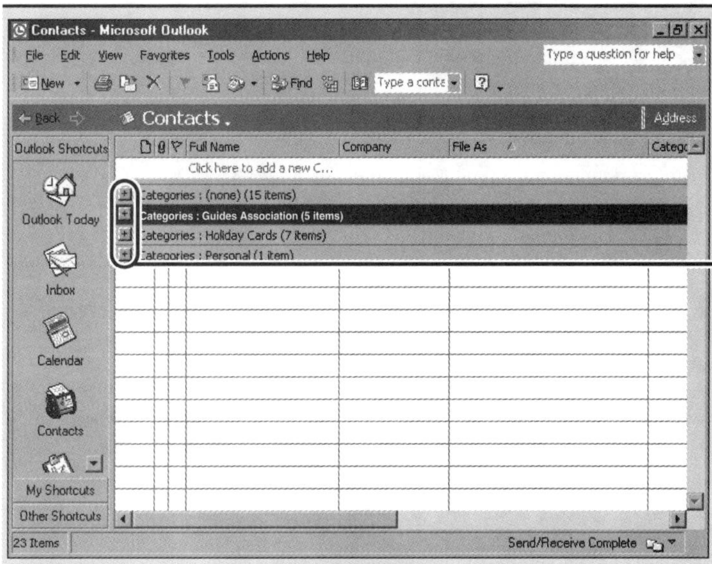

- Outlook lists your categories along with the number of contacts assigned to them.

5. Click the [+] next to the category whose contacts you want to view.

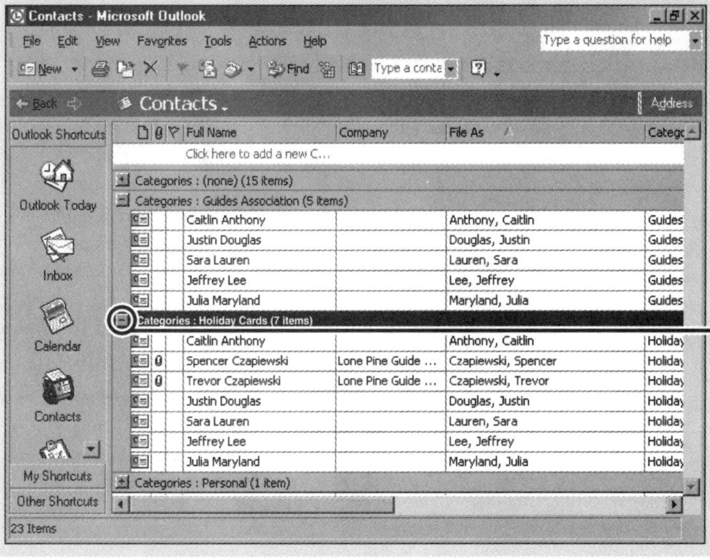

- The [+] changes to a [−] as Outlook opens the category and displays the contacts assigned to it. To close the category again, click [−].

MAP DIRECTIONS TO A CONTACT

You can open a contact and quickly get an Expedia.com map to the address listed on the Outlook Contacts card. For example, if you are preparing to visit a customer, you can quickly find their address and get an Expedia-based map you can print and take with you.

MAP DIRECTIONS TO A CONTACT

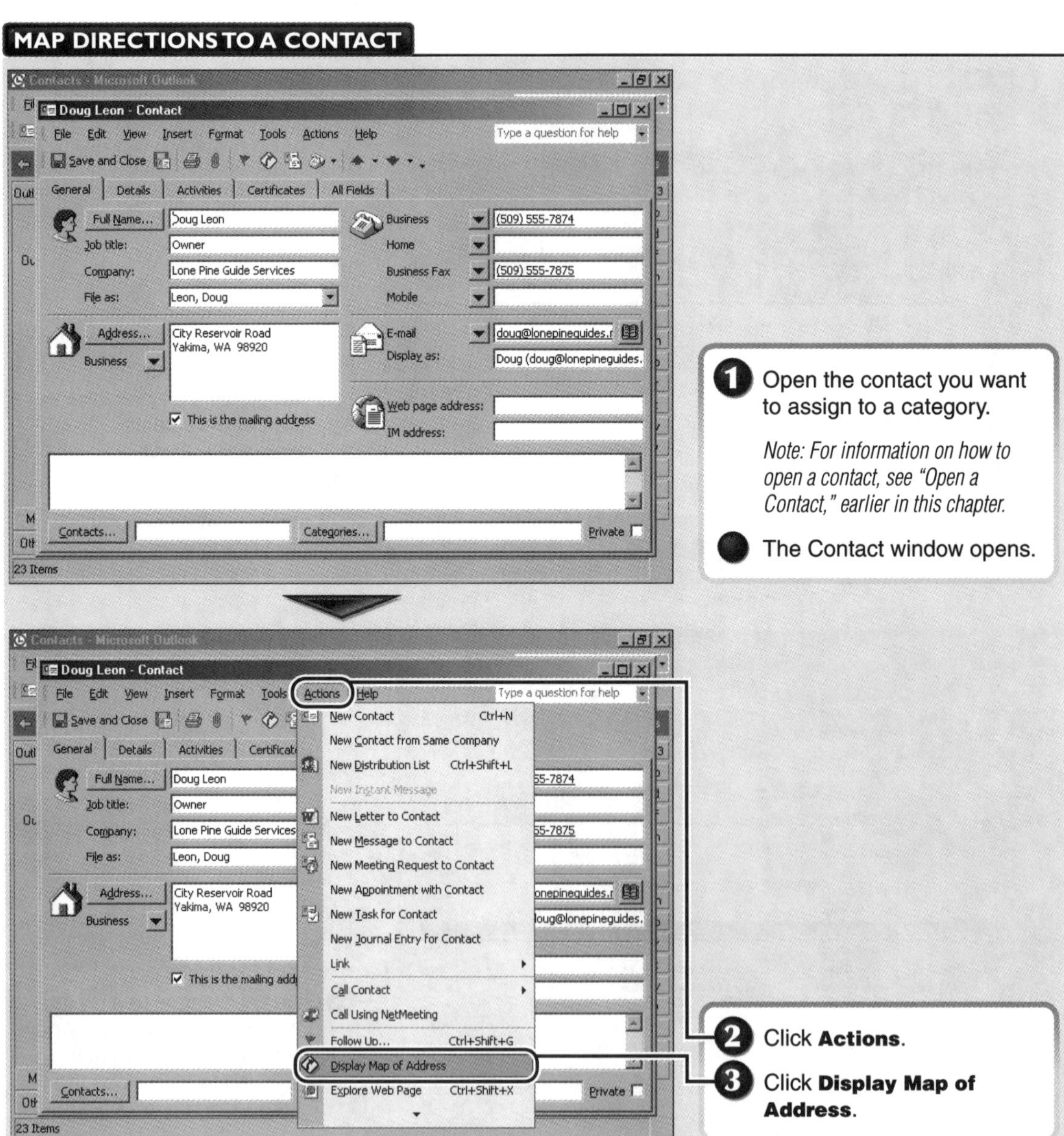

1. Open the contact you want to assign to a category.

   Note: For information on how to open a contact, see "Open a Contact," earlier in this chapter.

   - The Contact window opens.

2. Click **Actions**.
3. Click **Display Map of Address**.

in an instant

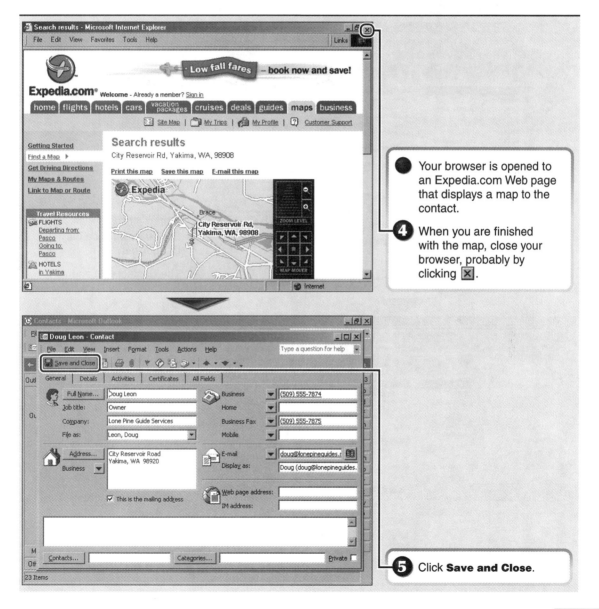

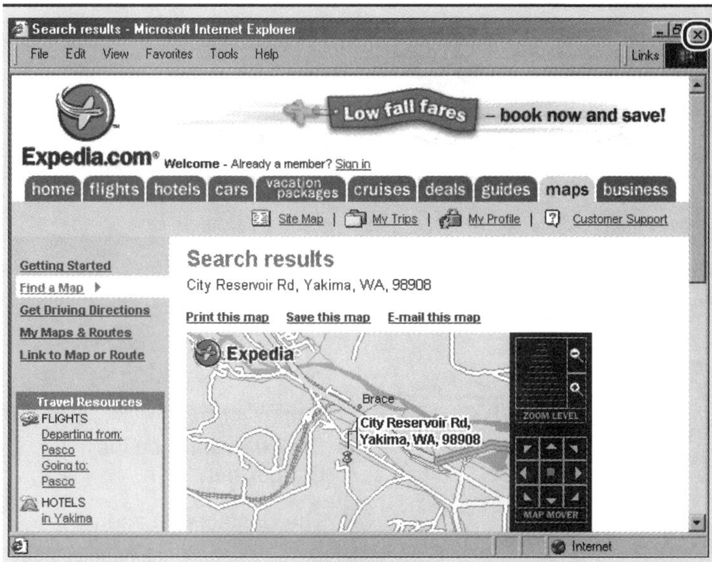

- Your browser is opened to an Expedia.com Web page that displays a map to the contact.

4. When you are finished with the map, close your browser, probably by clicking ☒.

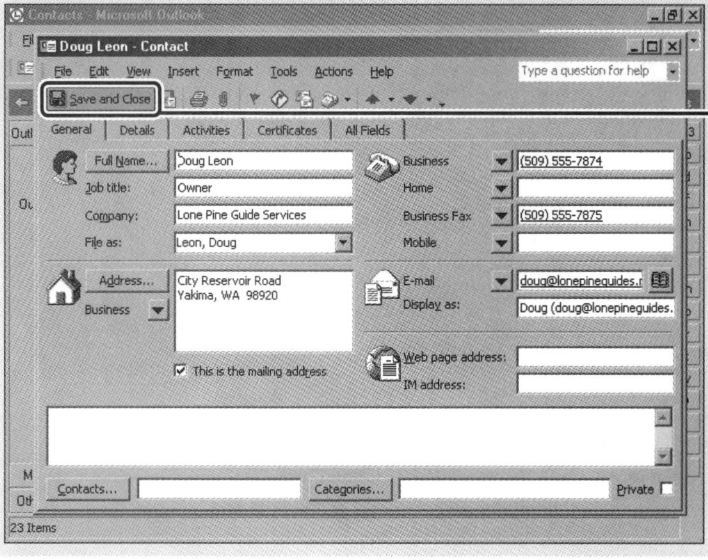

5. Click **Save and Close**.

PRINT A CONTACT LIST

You can print your Outlook Contacts list using any of the printing options available to your system. When you print the Contacts list, remember that the current view is what will be printed. If you want to change the current view, see "Change How You View Contacts," earlier in this chapter.

PRINT A CONTACT LIST

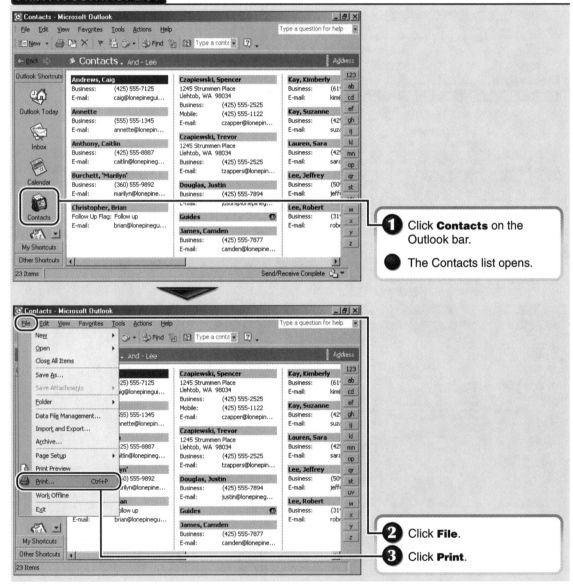

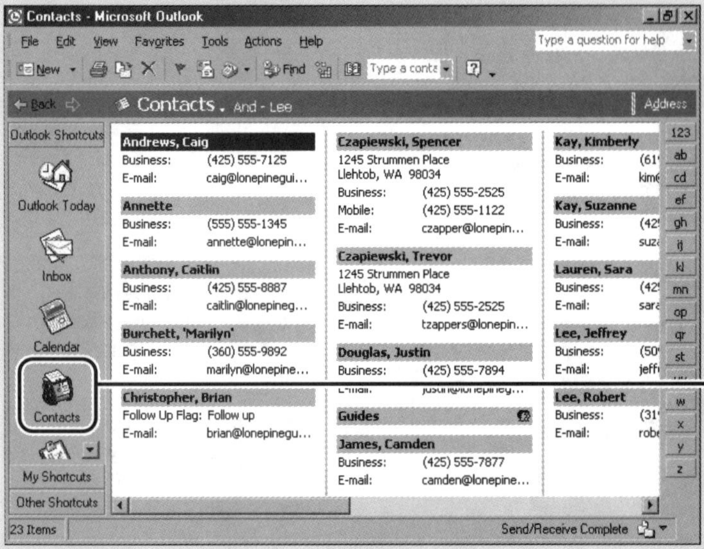

1. Click **Contacts** on the Outlook bar.

- The Contacts list opens.

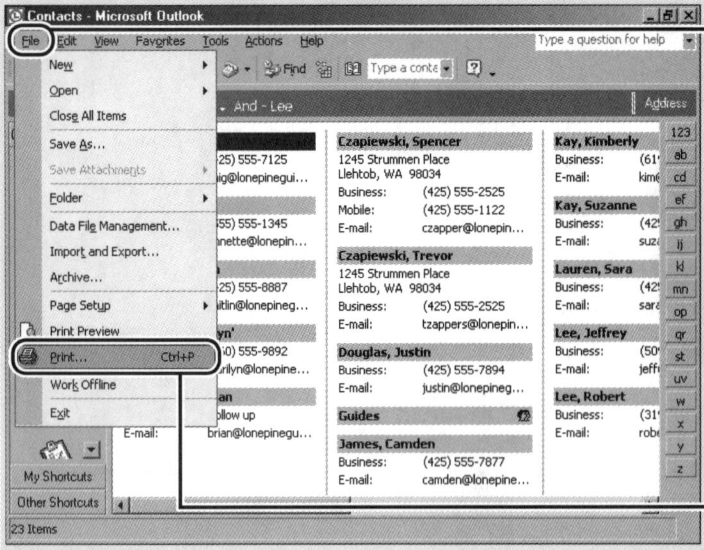

2. Click **File**.
3. Click **Print**.

in an instant

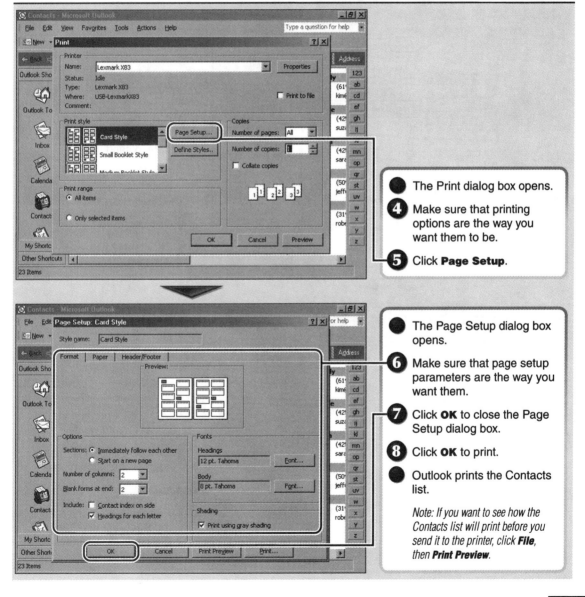

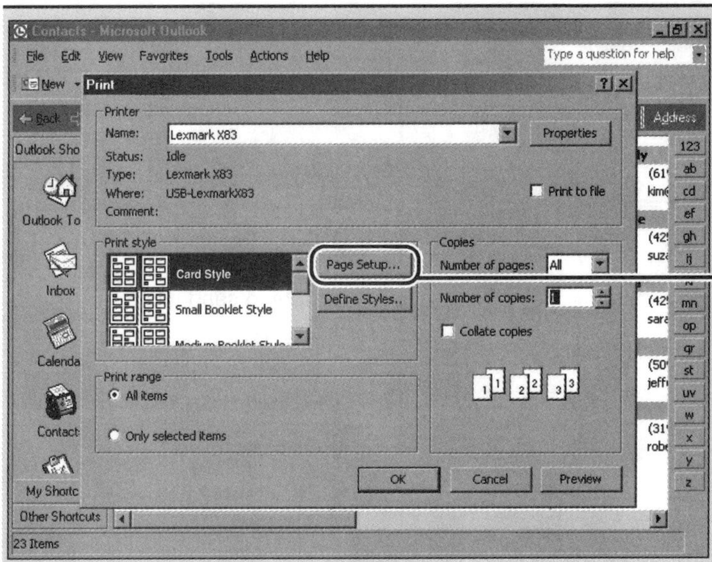

- The Print dialog box opens.

4 Make sure that printing options are the way you want them to be.

5 Click **Page Setup**.

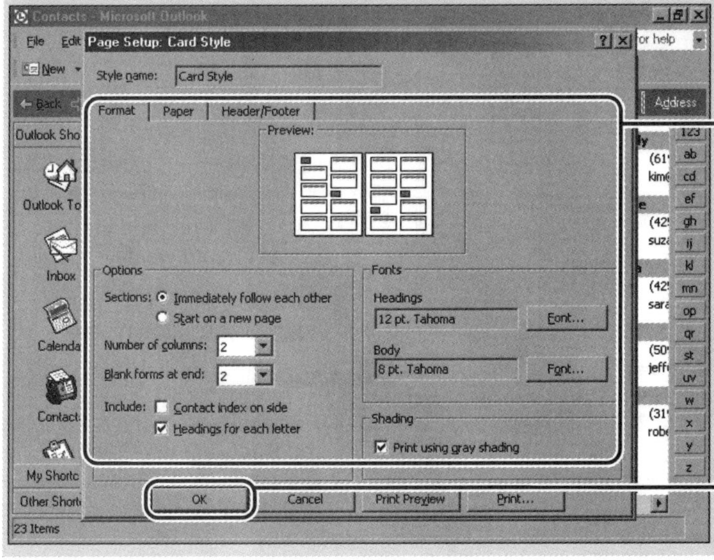

- The Page Setup dialog box opens.

6 Make sure that page setup parameters are the way you want them.

7 Click **OK** to close the Page Setup dialog box.

8 Click **OK** to print.

- Outlook prints the Contacts list.

*Note: If you want to see how the Contacts list will print before you send it to the printer, click **File**, then **Print Preview**.*

SEND A LETTER TO A CONTACT

You can easily look up a contact and then start a Microsoft Word letter to that contact with the contact's information already included. The Word Letter Wizard allows you to specify the style for the letter and what additional information to include.

SEND A LETTER TO A CONTACT

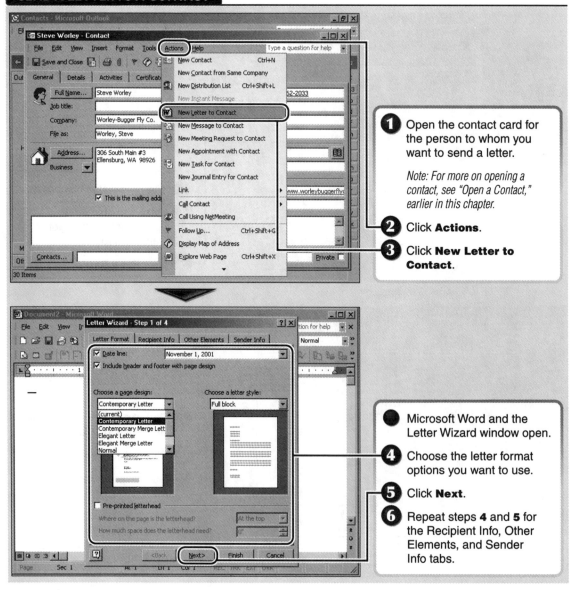

1. Open the contact card for the person to whom you want to send a letter.

   Note: For more on opening a contact, see "Open a Contact," earlier in this chapter.

2. Click **Actions**.
3. Click **New Letter to Contact**.

- Microsoft Word and the Letter Wizard window open.

4. Choose the letter format options you want to use.
5. Click **Next**.
6. Repeat steps **4** and **5** for the Recipient Info, Other Elements, and Sender Info tabs.

in an instant

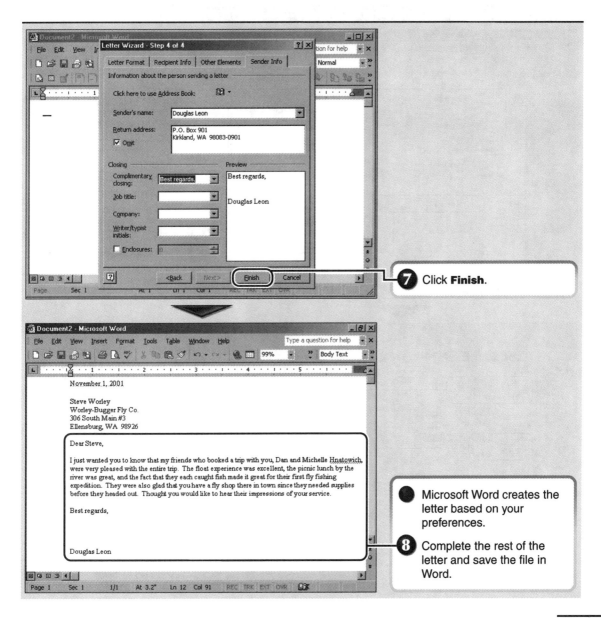

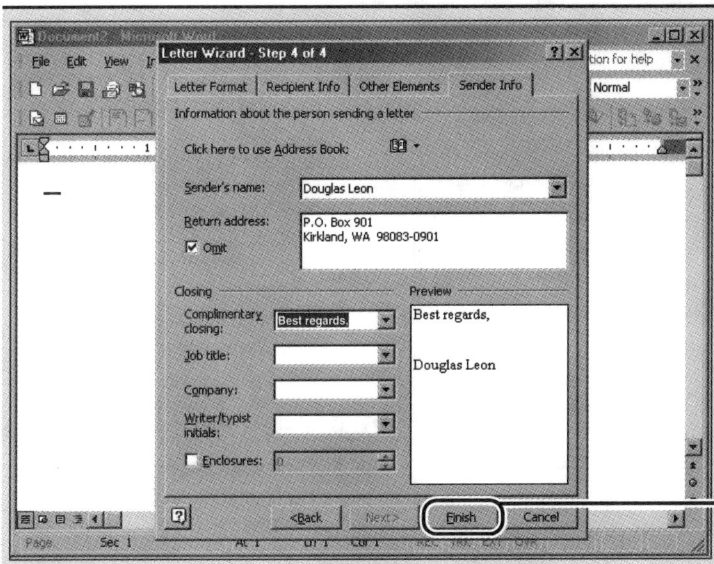

7 Click **Finish**.

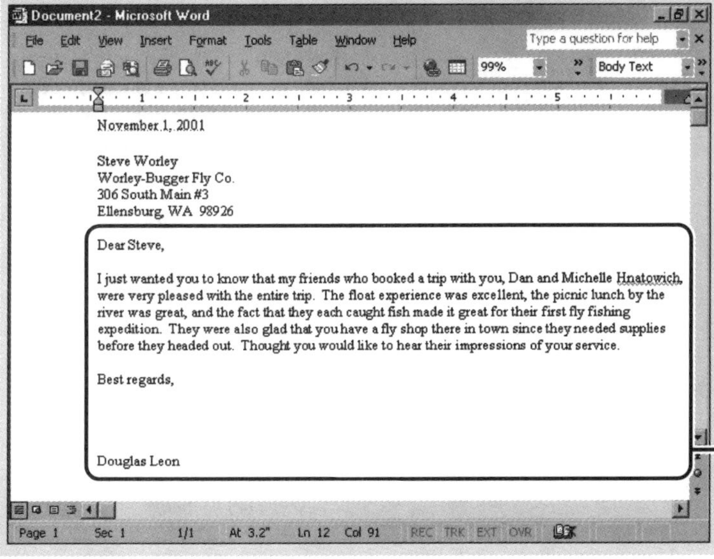

- Microsoft Word creates the letter based on your preferences.

8 Complete the rest of the letter and save the file in Word.

SEND A LETTER TO MULTIPLE CONTACTS USING MAIL MERGE

You can use the Microsoft Word mail merge feature to generate a mass mailing directly from your Outlook Contacts list. This is particularly convenient because you do not need to maintain a separate mailing list just for generating letters with Word. You can use your Outlook Contacts list as the address list for mail merges.

SEND A LETTER TO MULTIPLE CONTACTS USING MAIL MERGE

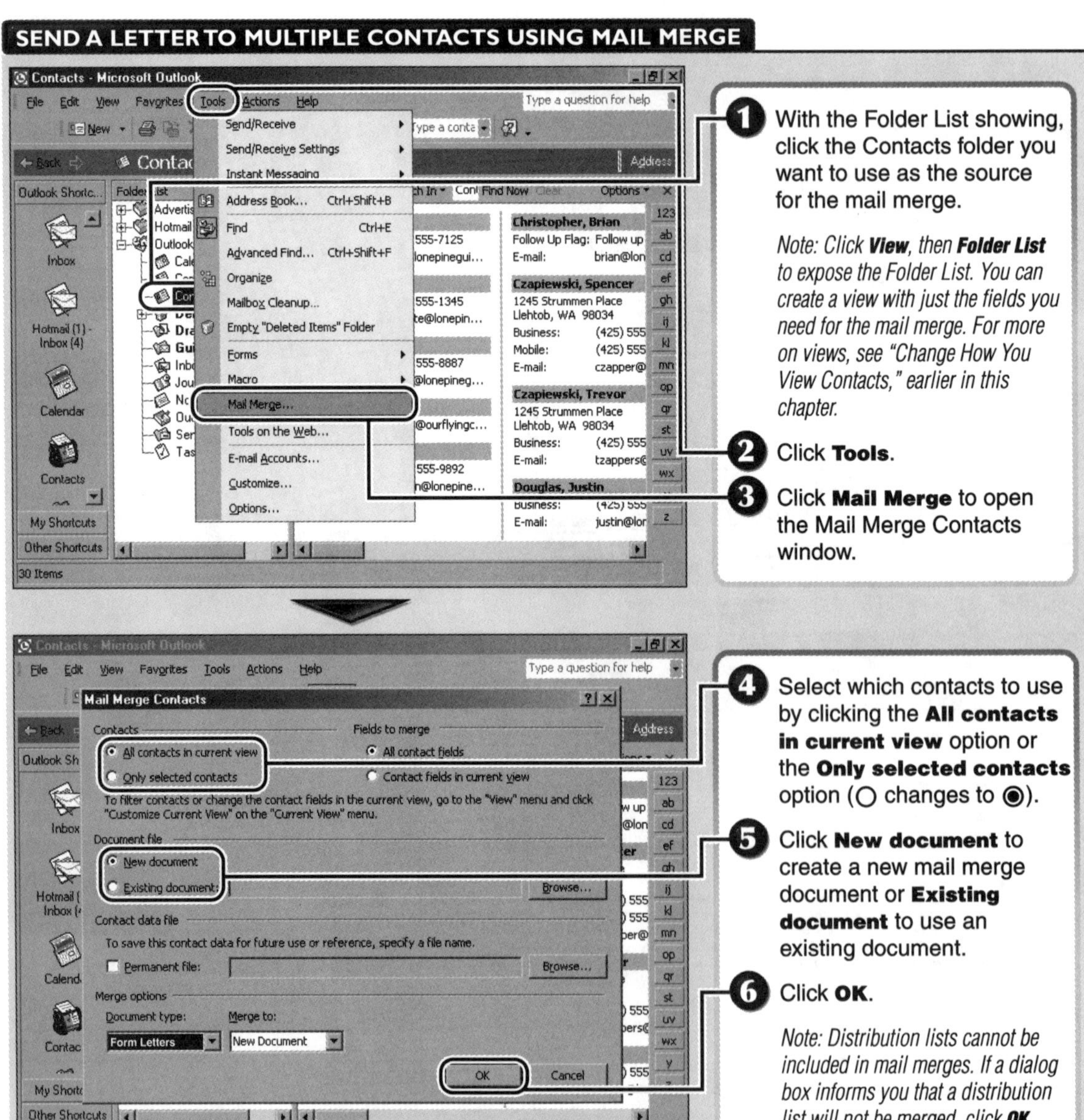

1. With the Folder List showing, click the Contacts folder you want to use as the source for the mail merge.

   *Note: Click **View**, then **Folder List** to expose the Folder List. You can create a view with just the fields you need for the mail merge. For more on views, see "Change How You View Contacts," earlier in this chapter.*

2. Click **Tools**.
3. Click **Mail Merge** to open the Mail Merge Contacts window.
4. Select which contacts to use by clicking the **All contacts in current view** option or the **Only selected contacts** option (○ changes to ◉).
5. Click **New document** to create a new mail merge document or **Existing document** to use an existing document.
6. Click **OK**.

   *Note: Distribution lists cannot be included in mail merges. If a dialog box informs you that a distribution list will not be merged, click **OK**.*

in an instant

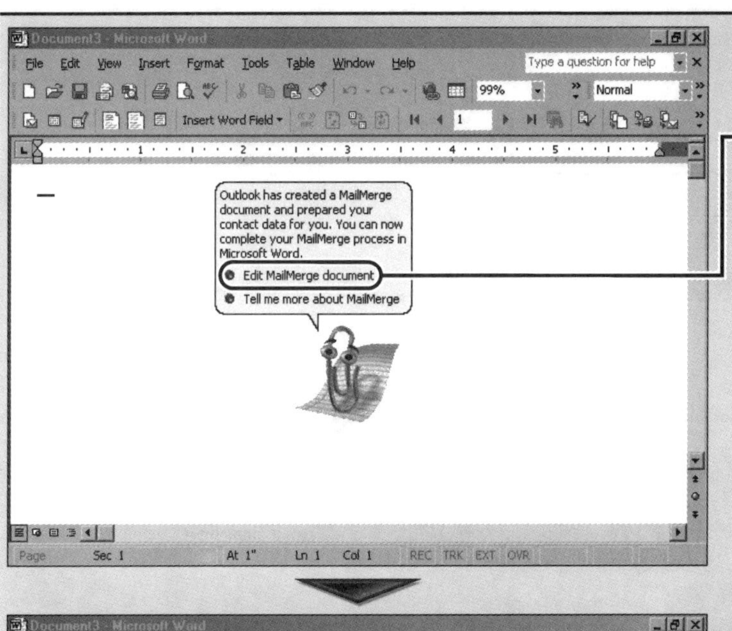

- Microsoft Word opens.

7. Click **Edit MailMerge document** to start editing the document (○ changes to ◉).

   *Note: You can find out more about Mail Merge if you click **Tell me more about MailMerge** (○ changes to ◉).*

- A blank Word document opens and the Mail Merge toolbar appears.

8. Compose the letter as desired.

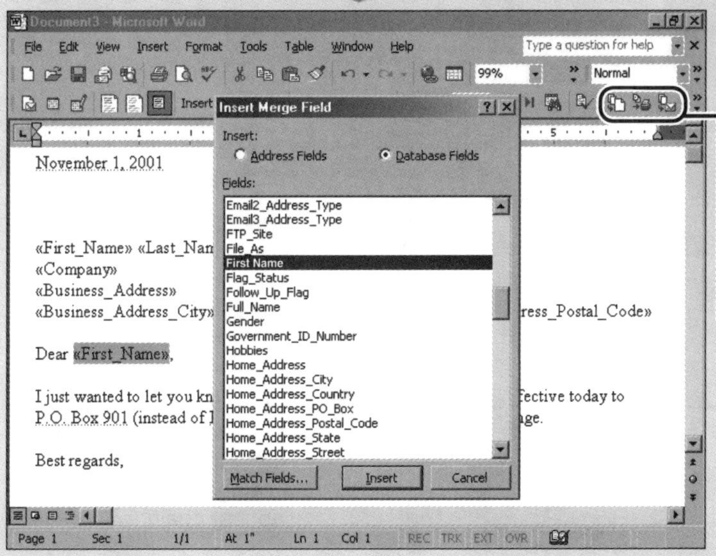

9. Insert the desired fields.

- Click in the Word document and then click ▤. Click the name of the field you want to insert and then click **Insert**. Repeat until all desired fields have been added. Then click **Cancel**.

10. Click the desired merge button to complete the merge. ▤ sends the finished letters to a new Word file. ▤ sends the finished letters directly to your printer. ▤ sends the finished letters to new e-mail messages.

JOURNAL OVERVIEW

You can reference all the items that pertain to a specific contact in one place: the Outlook Journal. The Journal allows you to see all the e-mail messages, meeting requests, meeting responses, and even documents you created regarding this contact on a convenient timeline.

JOURNAL OVERVIEW

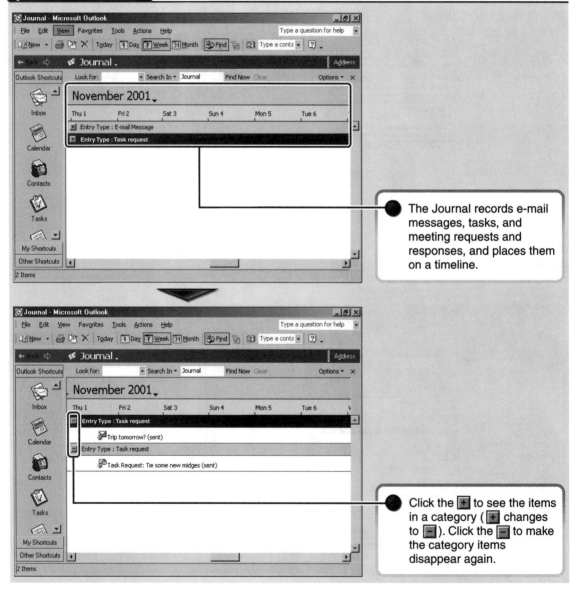

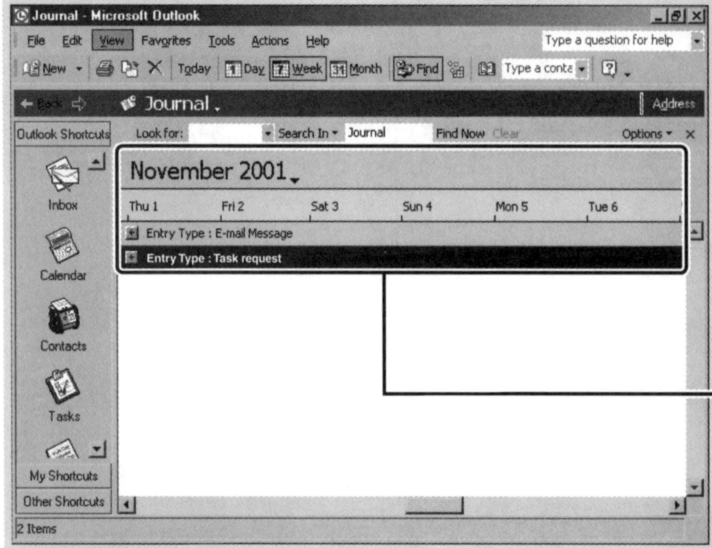

- The Journal records e-mail messages, tasks, and meeting requests and responses, and places them on a timeline.

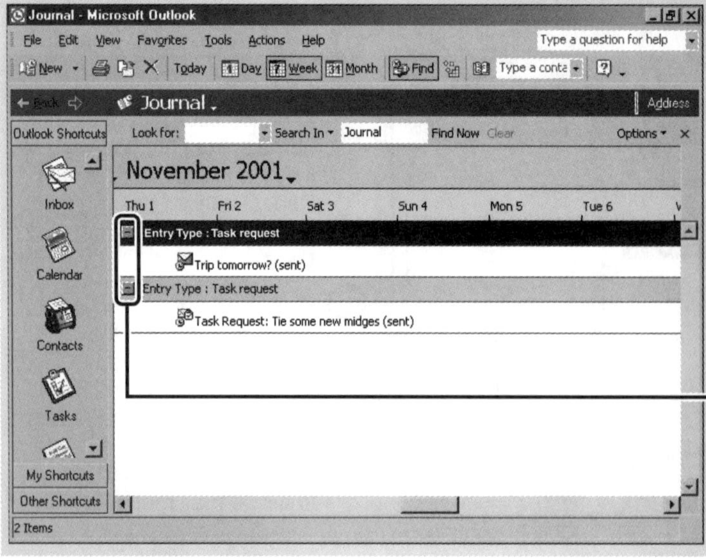

- Click the + to see the items in a category (+ changes to −). Click the − to make the category items disappear again.

OPEN THE JOURNAL

You can open the Journal from the Folder List in just a few clicks of the mouse. The Journal is a convenient place to find the work you have done by date, by contact, and by category.

OPEN THE JOURNAL

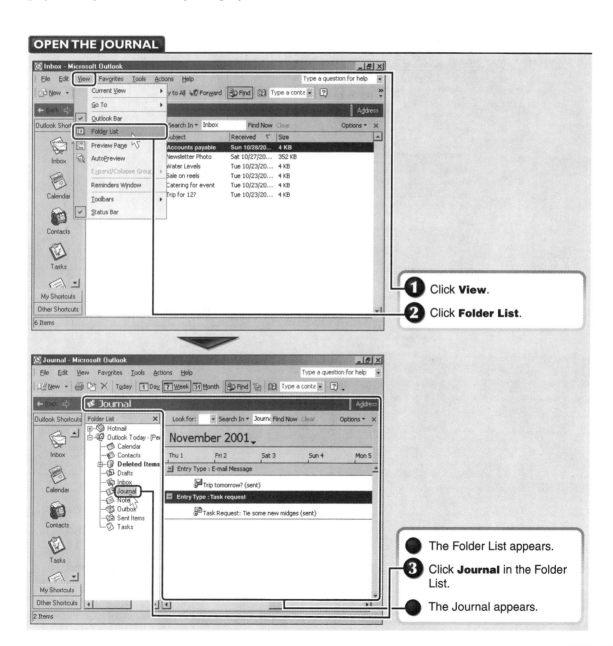

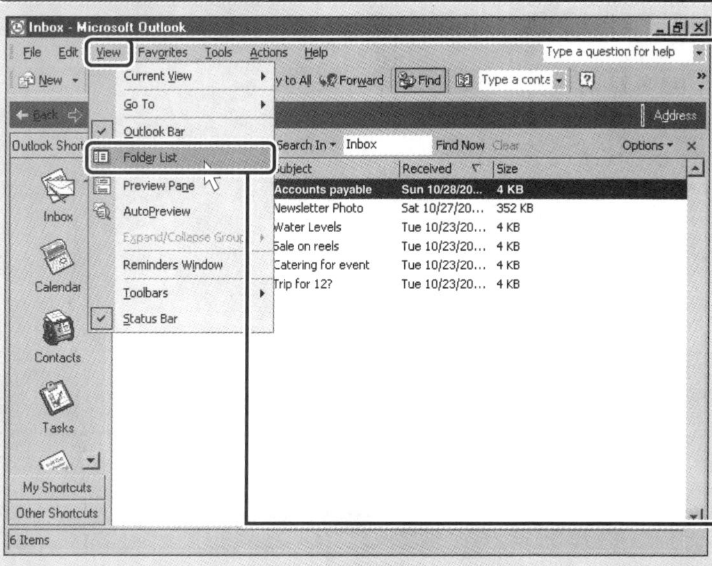

1. Click **View**.
2. Click **Folder List**.

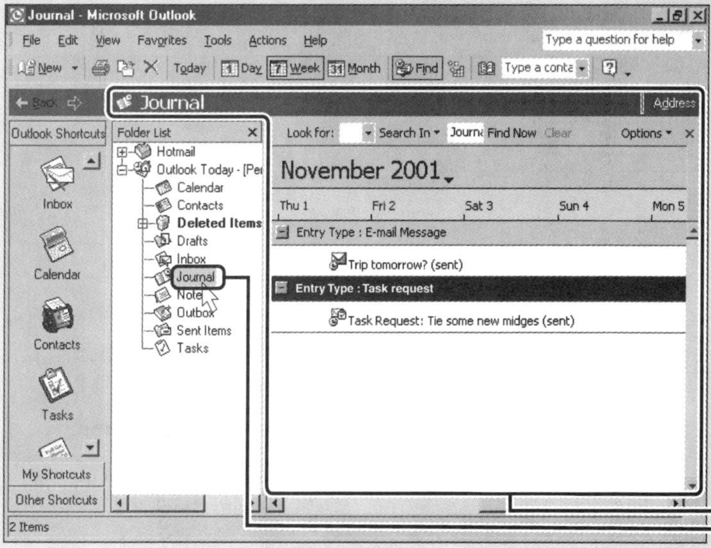

- The Folder List appears.

3. Click **Journal** in the Folder List.

- The Journal appears.

AUTOMATICALLY RECORD JOURNAL ENTRIES

You can automatically track all the e-mail messages, meetings, conversations, and more with a contact when you allow Outlook to automatically record Journal entries.

AUTOMATICALLY RECORD JOURNAL ENTRIES

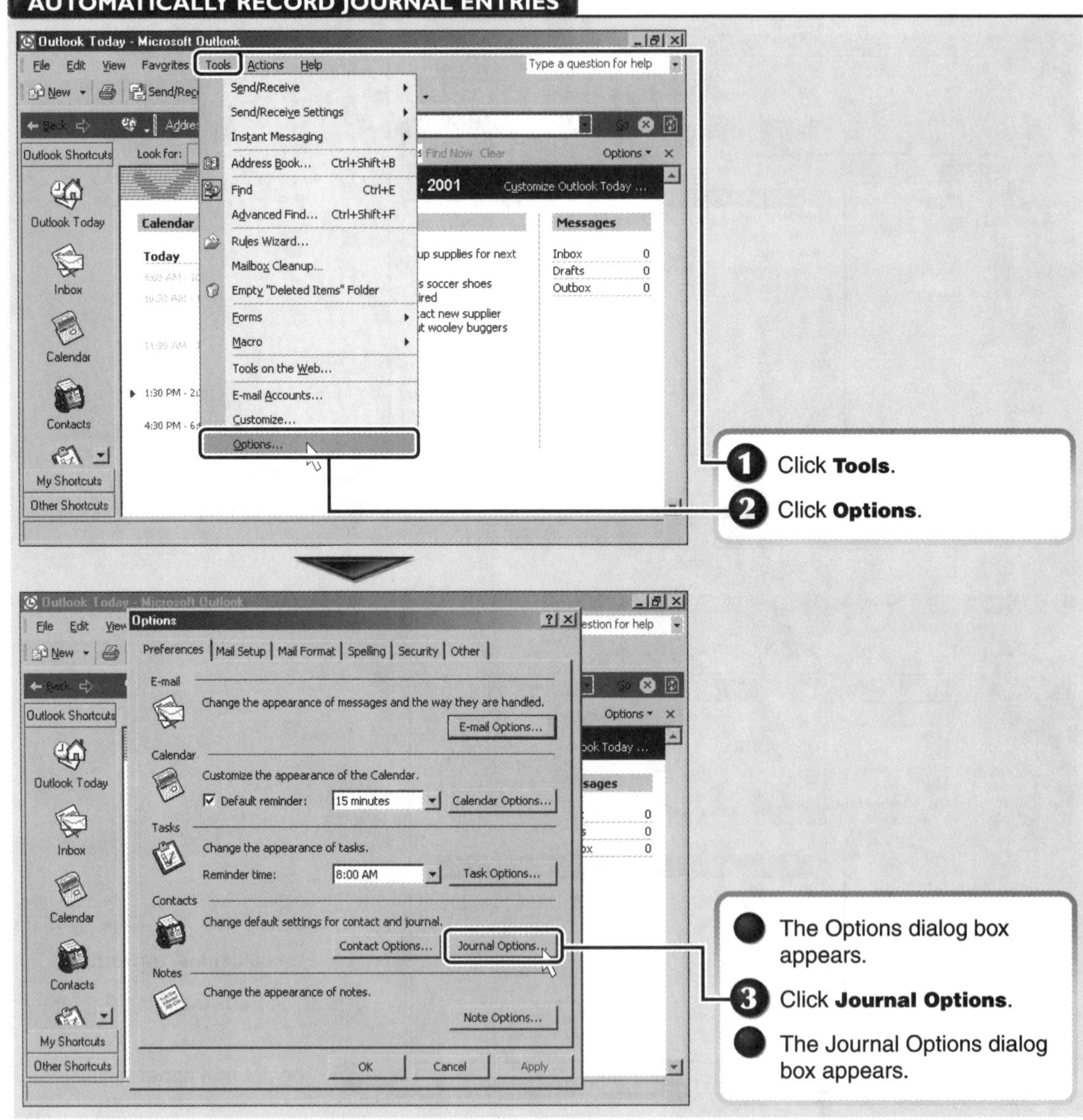

1. Click **Tools**.
2. Click **Options**.

- The Options dialog box appears.

3. Click **Journal Options**.

- The Journal Options dialog box appears.

in an instant

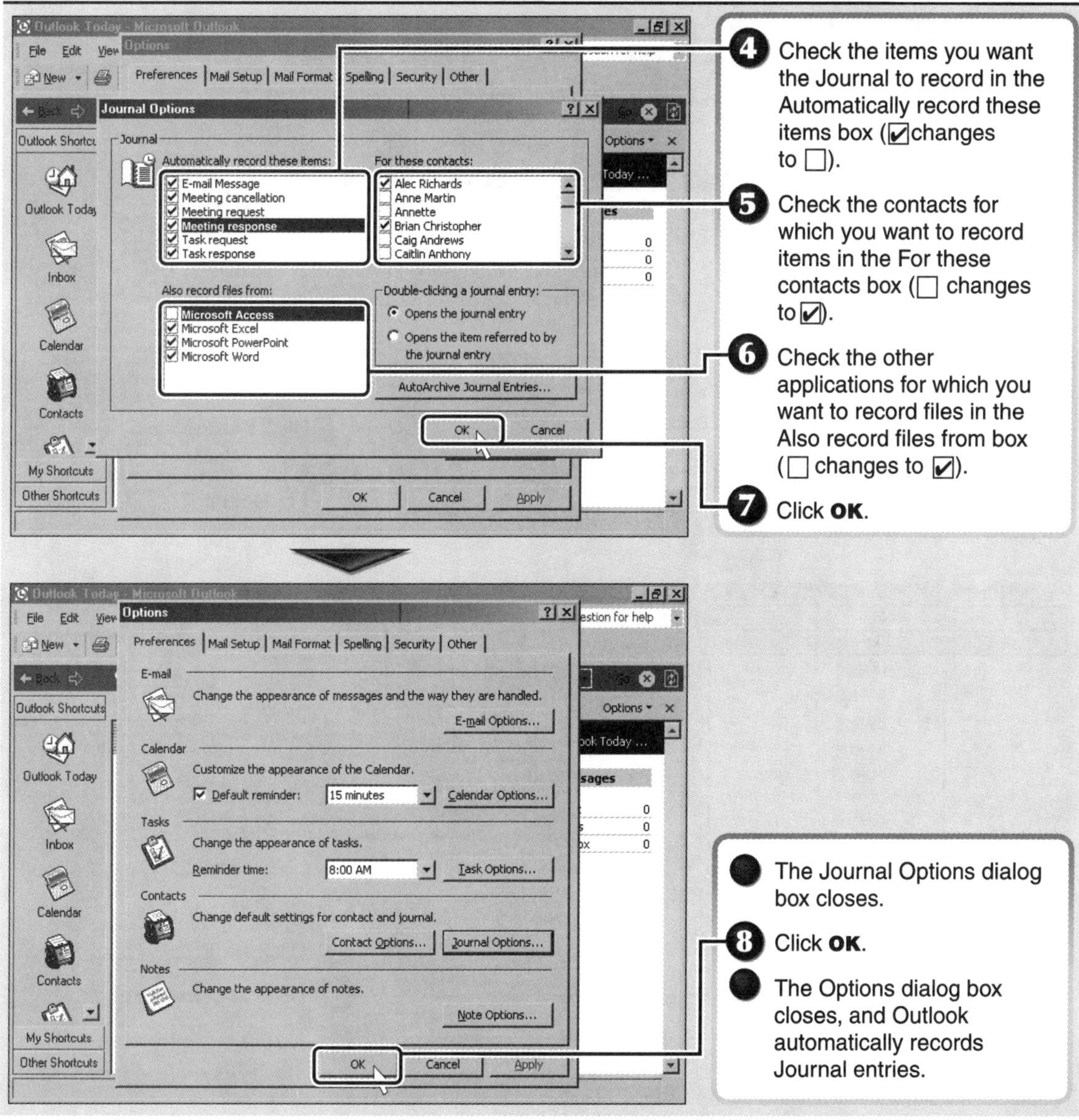

4 Check the items you want the Journal to record in the Automatically record these items box (☑ changes to ☐).
5 Check the contacts for which you want to record items in the For these contacts box (☐ changes to ☑).
6 Check the other applications for which you want to record files in the Also record files from box (☐ changes to ☑).
7 Click **OK**.
• The Journal Options dialog box closes.
8 Click **OK**.
• The Options dialog box closes, and Outlook automatically records Journal entries.

MANUALLY RECORD A JOURNAL ENTRY

You can manually record a Journal entry any time you want. You might want to manually record activities that occur outside Outlook, such as phone calls, faxes, and face-to-face meetings.

MANUALLY RECORD A JOURNAL ENTRY

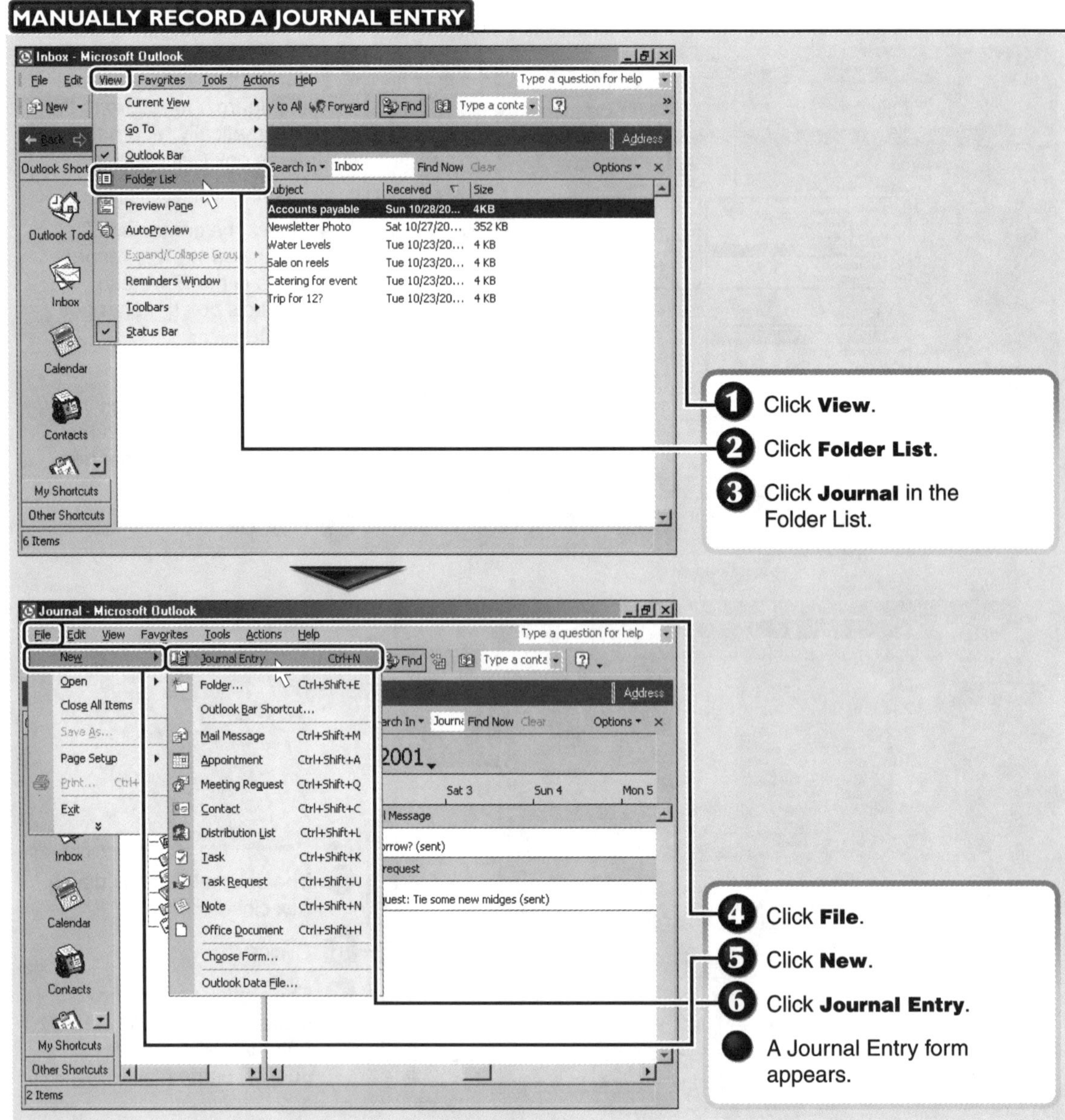

1. Click **View**.
2. Click **Folder List**.
3. Click **Journal** in the Folder List.
4. Click **File**.
5. Click **New**.
6. Click **Journal Entry**.

- A Journal Entry form appears.

in an instant

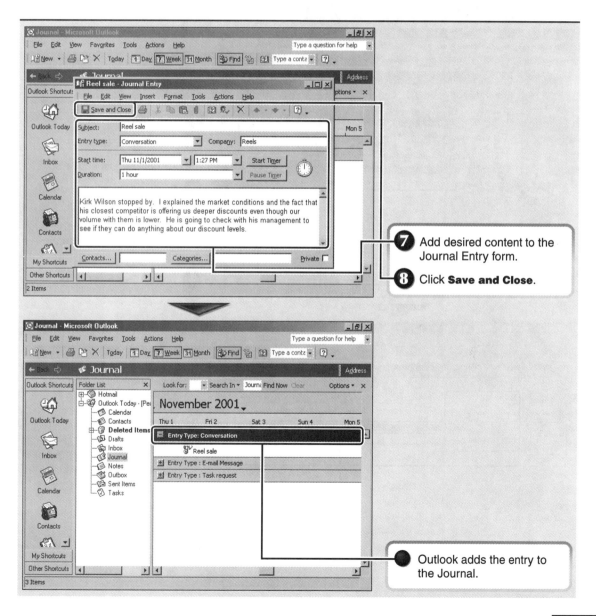

7. Add desired content to the Journal Entry form.
8. Click **Save and Close**.

- Outlook adds the entry to the Journal.

RECORD A FILE FROM OUTSIDE OUTLOOK

You can record any file to the Journal, even if the file is not a Microsoft Outlook or Microsoft Office document. For example, you can add a file to your Journal entry that was created with a graphics application or drawing program.

RECORD A FILE FROM OUTSIDE OUTLOOK

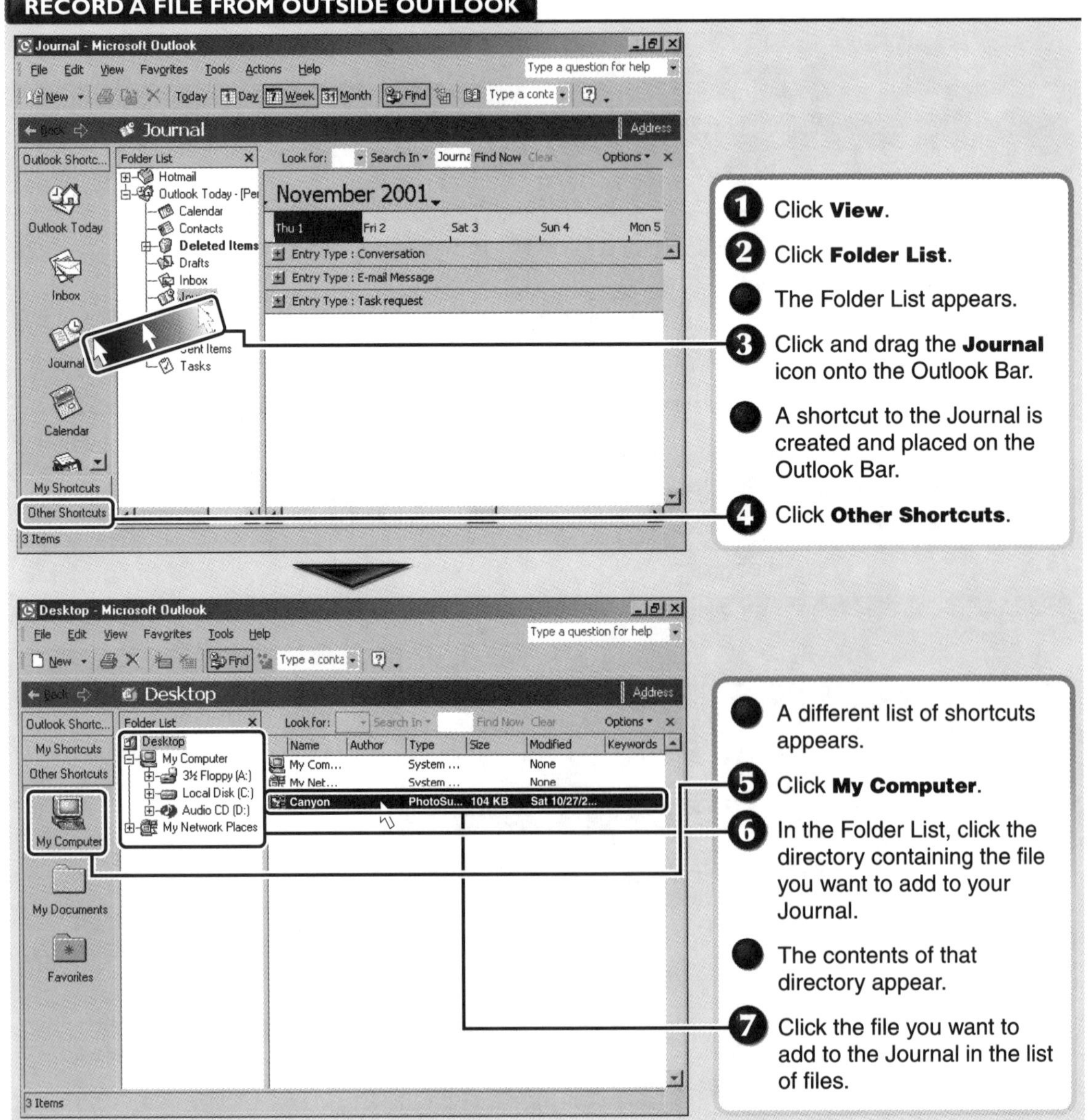

Journal - Microsoft Outlook
November 2001
Entry Type : Conversation
Entry Type : E-mail Message
Entry Type : Task request
1 Click **View**.
2 Click **Folder List**.
● The Folder List appears.
3 Click and drag the **Journal** icon onto the Outlook Bar.
● A shortcut to the Journal is created and placed on the Outlook Bar.
4 Click **Other Shortcuts**.
Desktop - Microsoft Outlook
● A different list of shortcuts appears.
5 Click **My Computer**.
6 In the Folder List, click the directory containing the file you want to add to your Journal.
● The contents of that directory appear.
7 Click the file you want to add to the Journal in the list of files.

in an instant

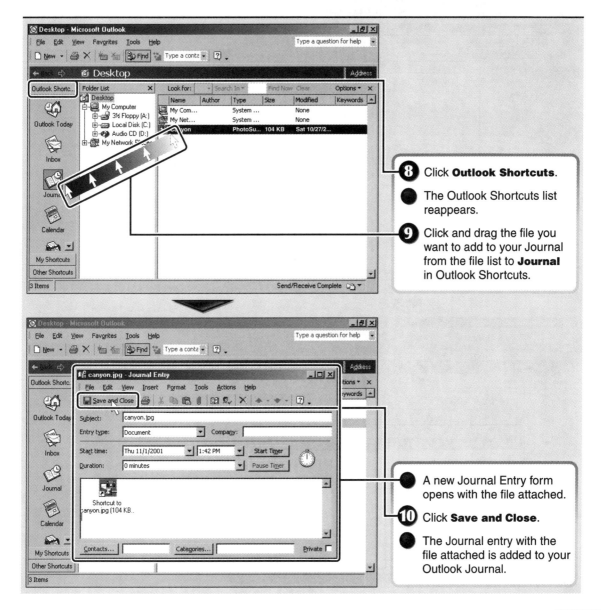

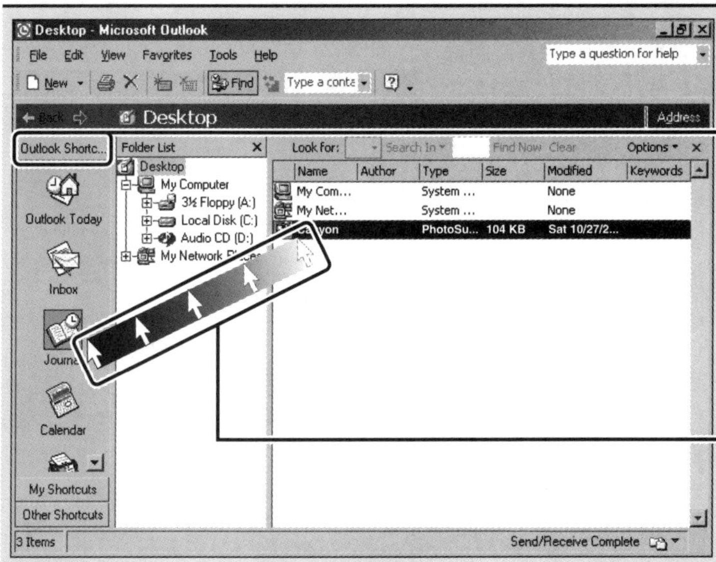

8 Click **Outlook Shortcuts**.

- The Outlook Shortcuts list reappears.

9 Click and drag the file you want to add to your Journal from the file list to **Journal** in Outlook Shortcuts.

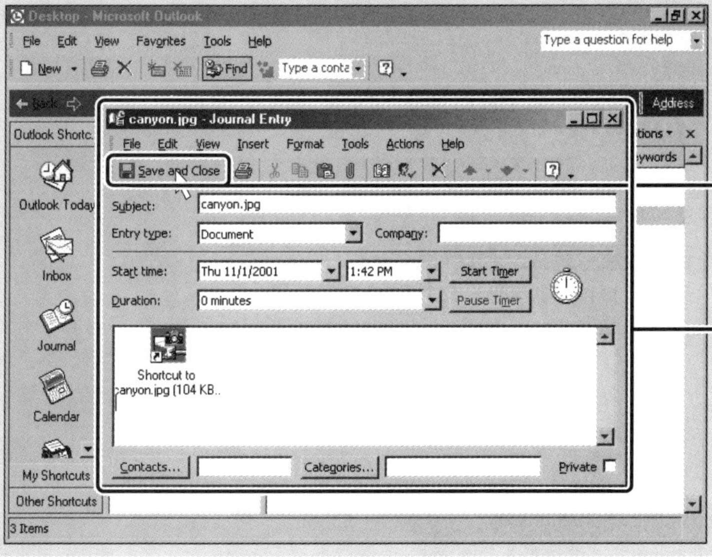

- A new Journal Entry form opens with the file attached.

10 Click **Save and Close**.

- The Journal entry with the file attached is added to your Outlook Journal.

CHANGE THE CURRENT JOURNAL VIEW

You can change the way your Journal displays Journal entries by changing the view. You can view Journal entries by the application in which the files were created, by contact, by category, in a flat list, by entries made in the last seven days, and by phone call entries. The last view used is the one you will see the next time you access your Journal.

CHANGE THE CURRENT JOURNAL VIEW

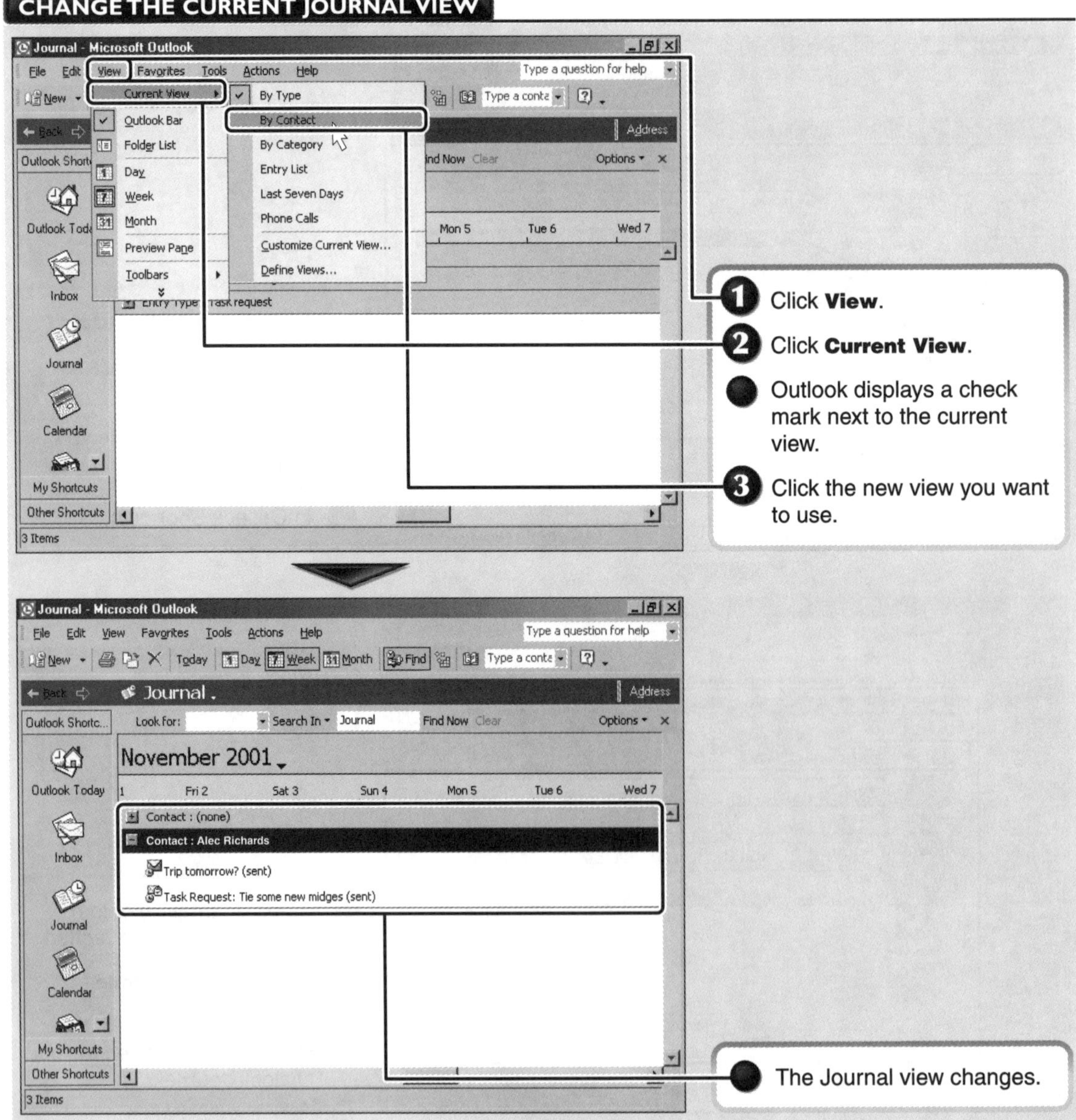

1. Click **View**.
2. Click **Current View**.
- Outlook displays a check mark next to the current view.
3. Click the new view you want to use.

- The Journal view changes.

PRINT JOURNAL ENTRIES

You can easily print the current view of Journal entries to keep a hard copy record of your activities. You can print Journal entries by the application in which the files were created, by contact, by category, in a flat list, by entries made in the last seven days, and by phone call entries. The ability to print these views gives you a great way to summarize activities for a particular matter or contact for hard copy files.

PRINT JOURNAL ENTRIES

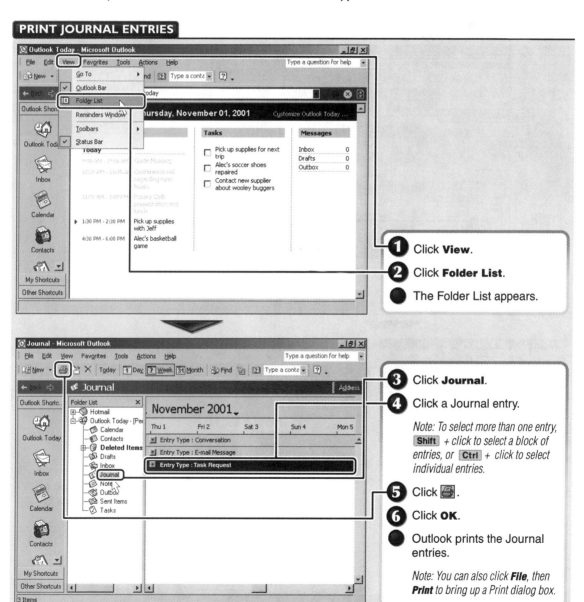

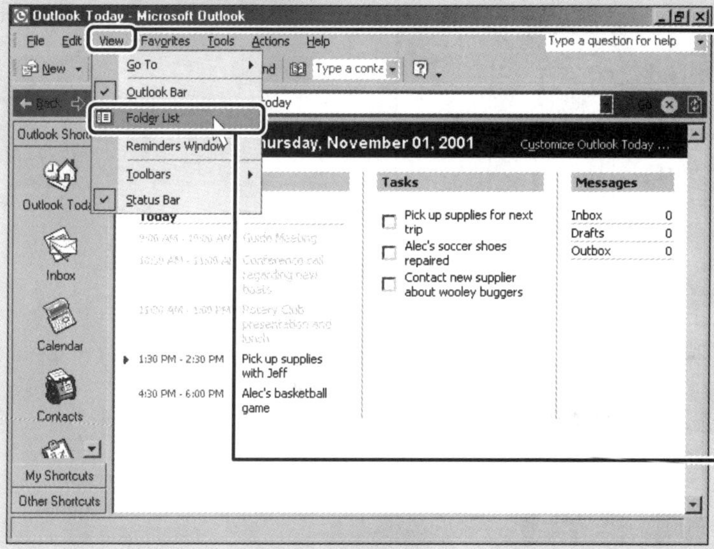

1. Click **View**.
2. Click **Folder List**.

- The Folder List appears.

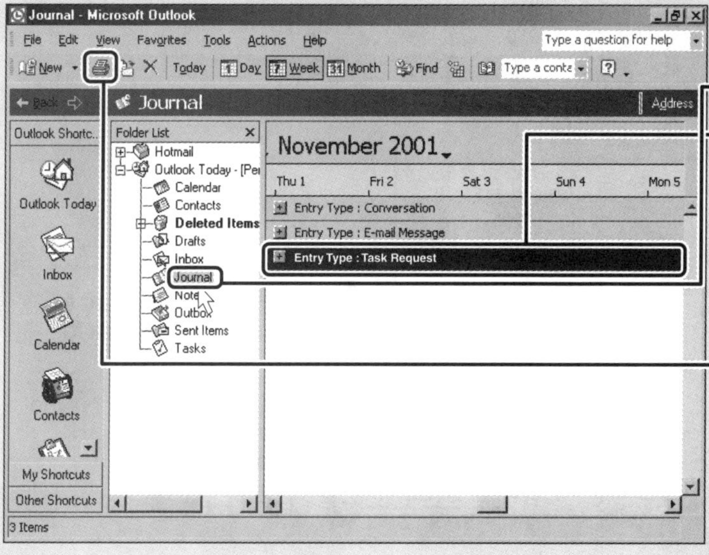

3. Click **Journal**.
4. Click a Journal entry.

Note: To select more than one entry, Shift *+ click to select a block of entries, or* Ctrl *+ click to select individual entries.*

5. Click the print button.
6. Click **OK**.

- Outlook prints the Journal entries.

*Note: You can also click **File**, then **Print** to bring up a Print dialog box.*

FIND A JOURNAL ENTRY

You can search your Journal to find entries that include specific text, and then open the found Journal entries for review. The Journal is a great place to search for items and documents related to a specific contact because it will find e-mail messages, tasks, notes, phone call records, meeting requests, and even files created in any application.

FIND A JOURNAL ENTRY

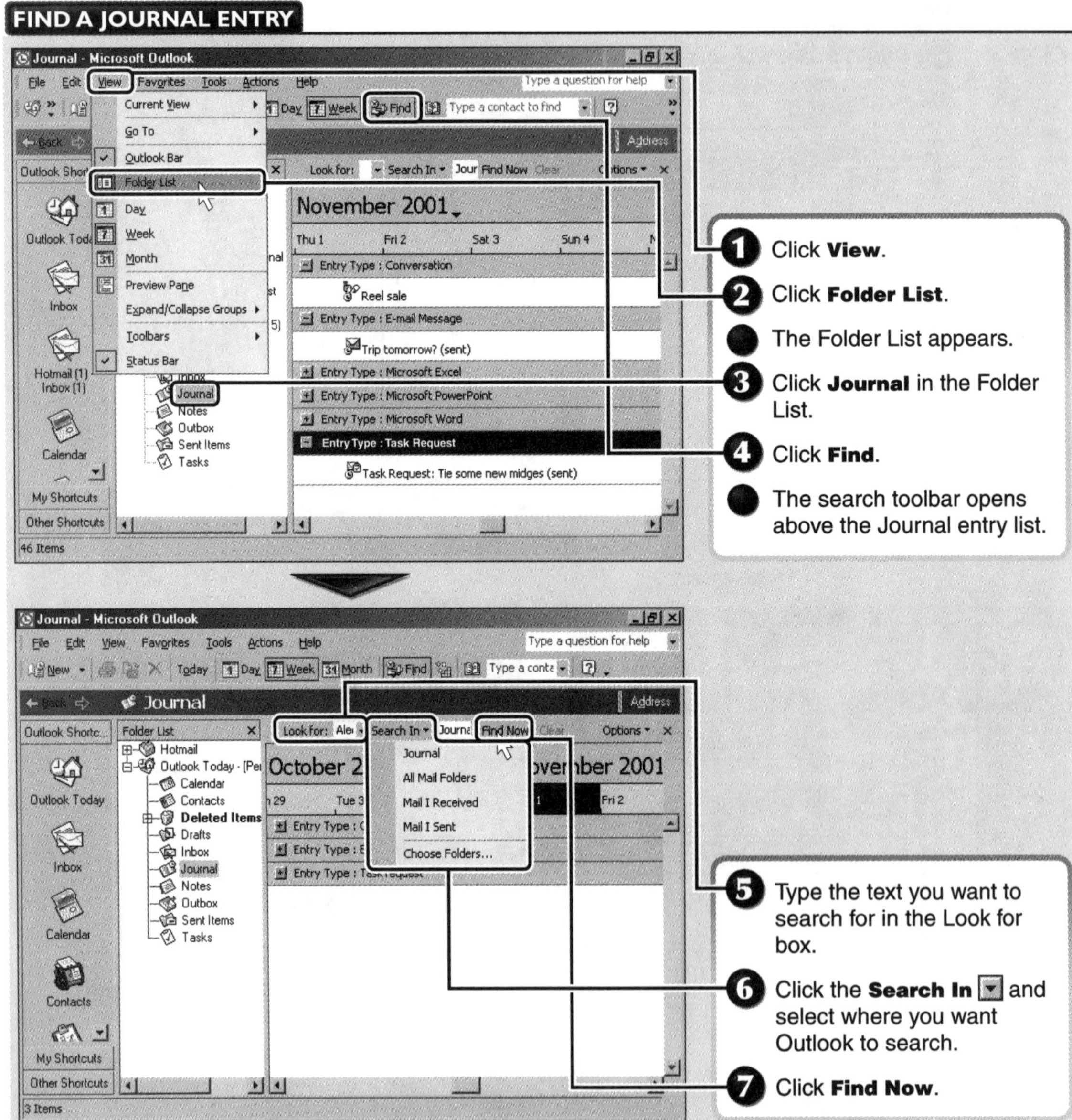

1. Click **View**.
2. Click **Folder List**.
   - The Folder List appears.
3. Click **Journal** in the Folder List.
4. Click **Find**.
   - The search toolbar opens above the Journal entry list.
5. Type the text you want to search for in the Look for box.
6. Click the **Search In** ▾ and select where you want Outlook to search.
7. Click **Find Now**.

in an instant

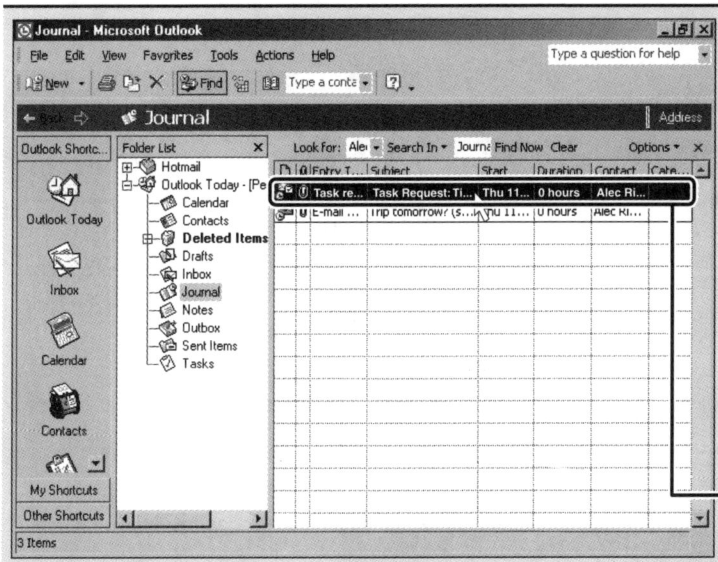

- Outlook displays the search results.

8. Double-click any Journal entry you want to review.

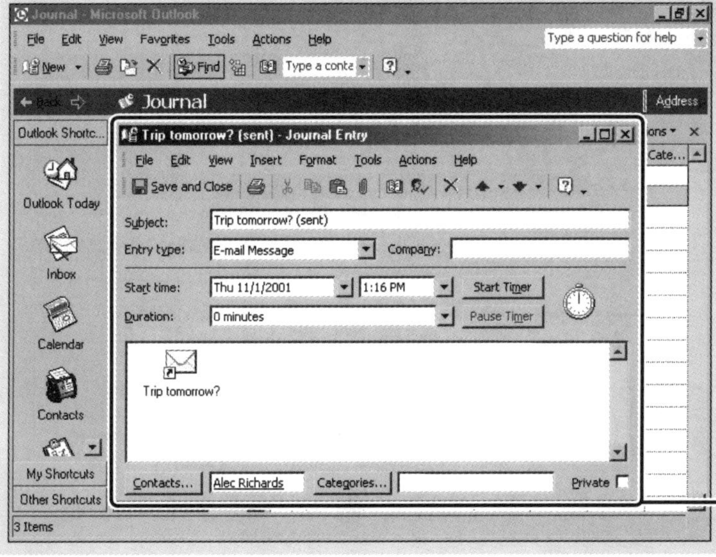

- The Journal entry opens.

OPEN TASKS

You can use the Outlook Tasks list to keep track of your to-do list, to remind you of tasks that are due, and to give you a record of completed tasks. You can access your Outlook Tasks list from a variety of places in Outlook, including Outlook Today, the Outlook bar, Outlook Calendar, and the Folder List.

OPEN TASKS

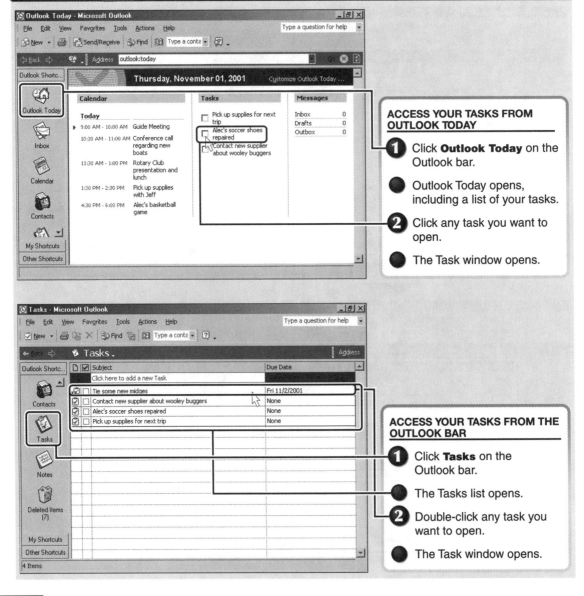

ACCESS YOUR TASKS FROM OUTLOOK TODAY

1. Click **Outlook Today** on the Outlook bar.
   - Outlook Today opens, including a list of your tasks.
2. Click any task you want to open.
   - The Task window opens.

ACCESS YOUR TASKS FROM THE OUTLOOK BAR

1. Click **Tasks** on the Outlook bar.
   - The Tasks list opens.
2. Double-click any task you want to open.
   - The Task window opens.

in an instant

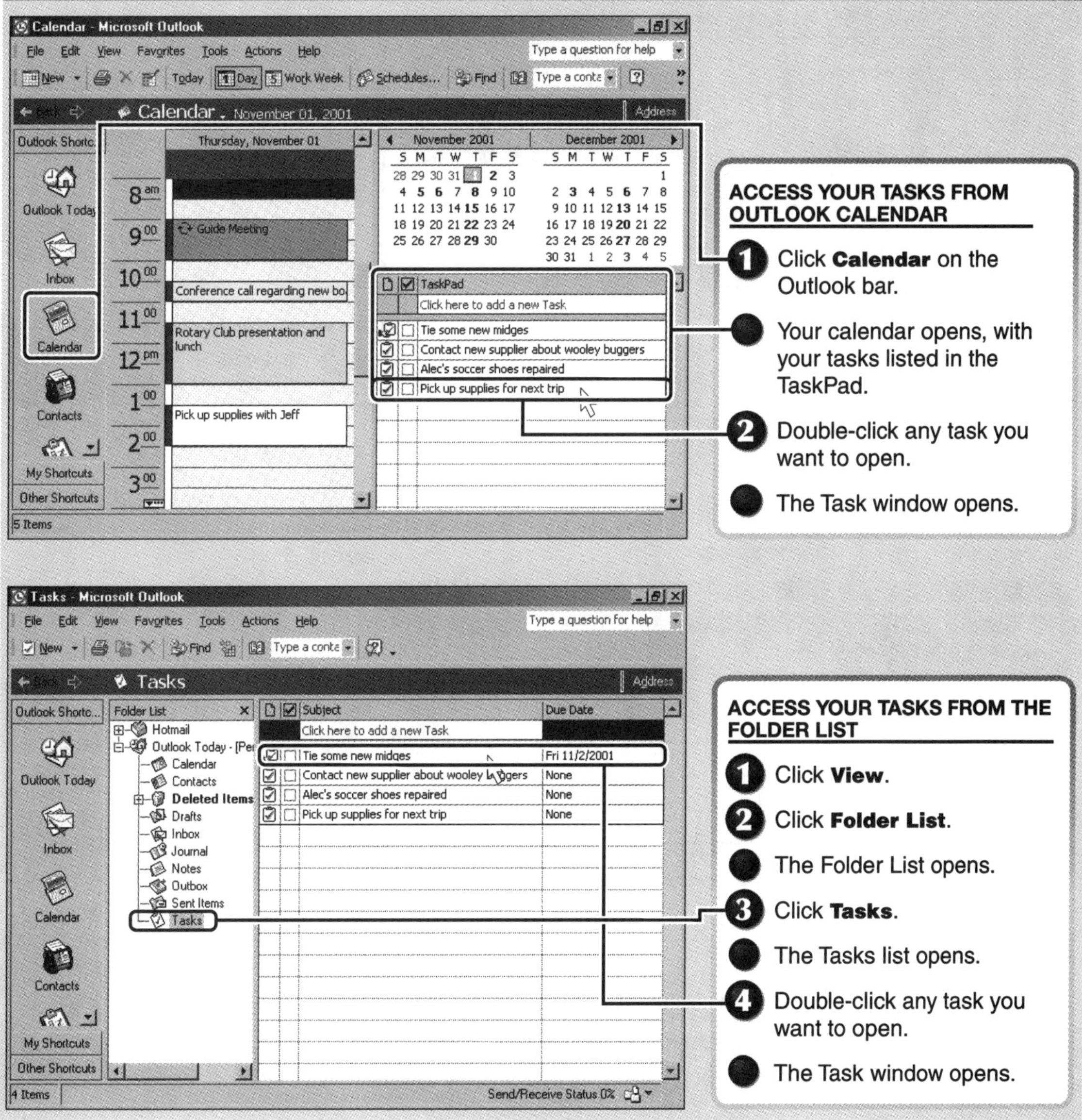

ACCESS YOUR TASKS FROM OUTLOOK CALENDAR

1. Click **Calendar** on the Outlook bar.

- Your calendar opens, with your tasks listed in the TaskPad.

2. Double-click any task you want to open.

- The Task window opens.

ACCESS YOUR TASKS FROM THE FOLDER LIST

1. Click **View**.
2. Click **Folder List**.

- The Folder List opens.

3. Click **Tasks**.

- The Tasks list opens.

4. Double-click any task you want to open.

- The Task window opens.

CREATE A TASK

You can easily add new tasks for new work items you want to track. You can also use tasks as reminders of personal items or personal goals.

CREATE A TASK

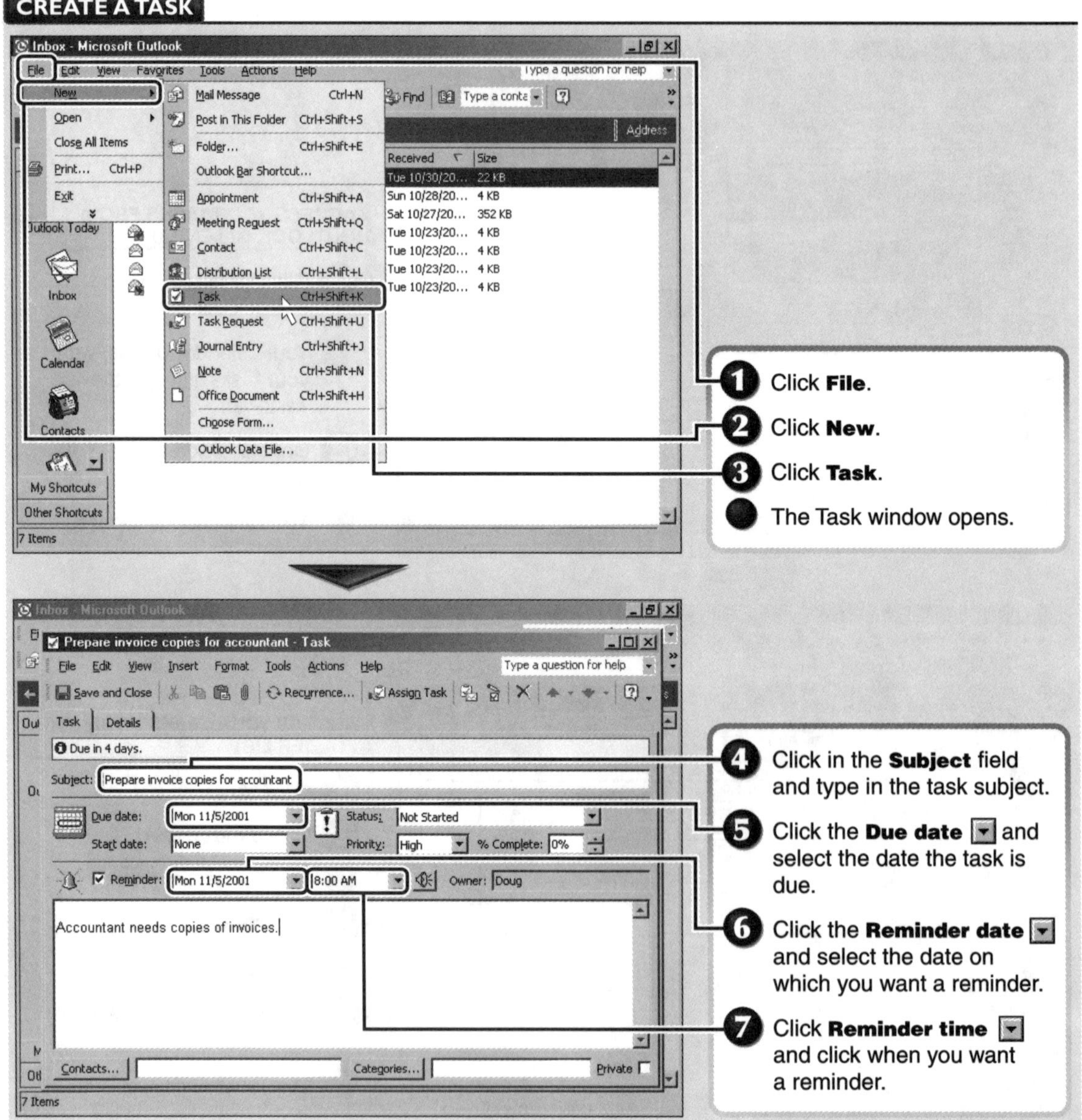

1. Click **File**.
2. Click **New**.
3. Click **Task**.

- The Task window opens.

4. Click in the **Subject** field and type in the task subject.
5. Click the **Due date** ▾ and select the date the task is due.
6. Click the **Reminder date** ▾ and select the date on which you want a reminder.
7. Click **Reminder time** ▾ and click when you want a reminder.

in an instant

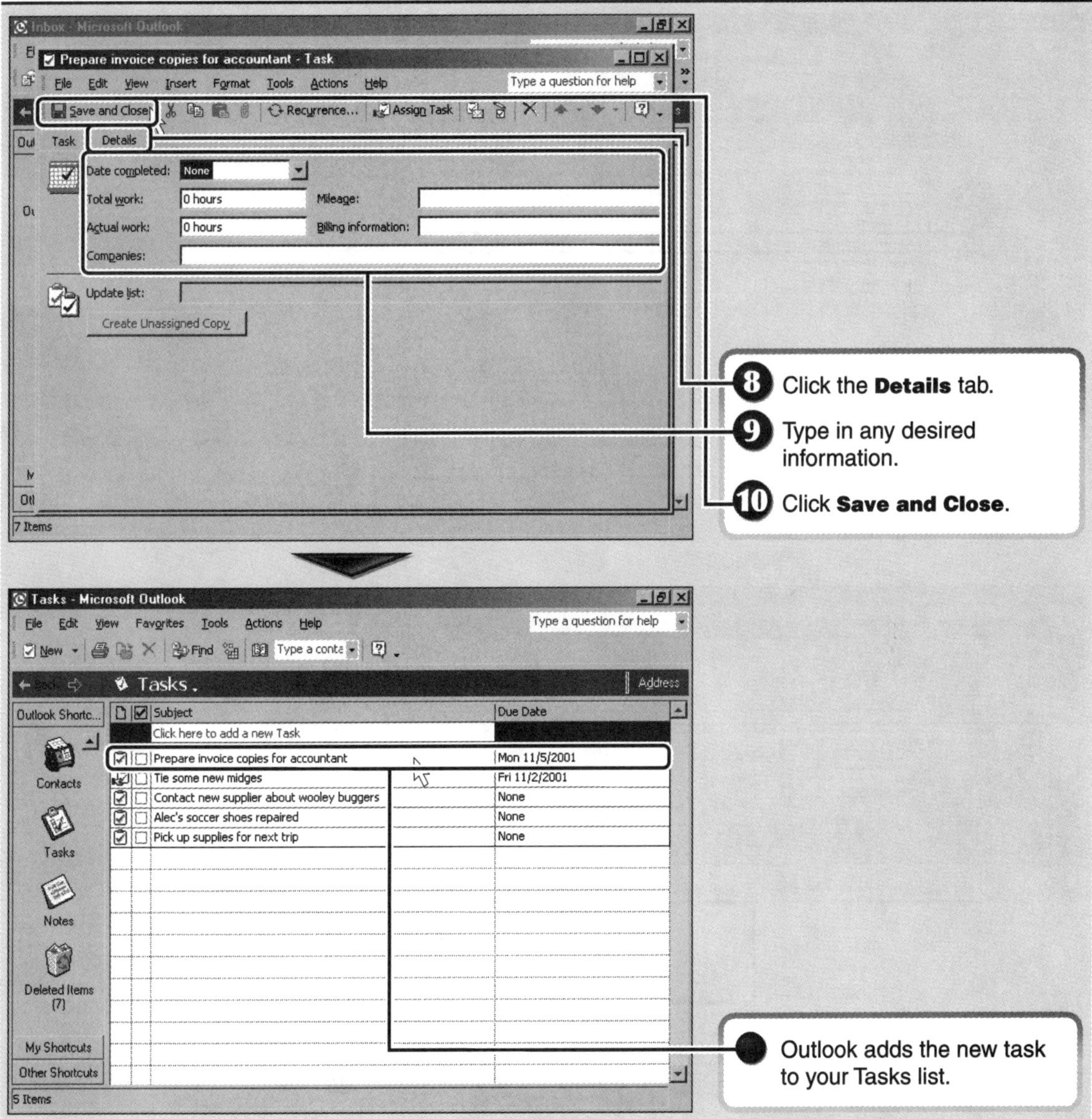

MODIFY A TASK

You can easily change task content or update your progress on the task. Reminders pop up if a task is not completed by the due date, so keep your tasks updated. See Chapter 8 for more information about Reminders.

MODIFY A TASK

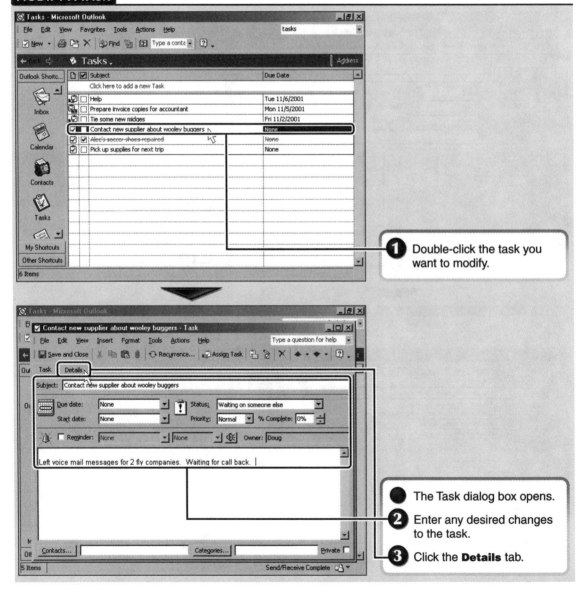

1. Double-click the task you want to modify.

- The Task dialog box opens.

2. Enter any desired changes to the task.

3. Click the **Details** tab.

in an instant

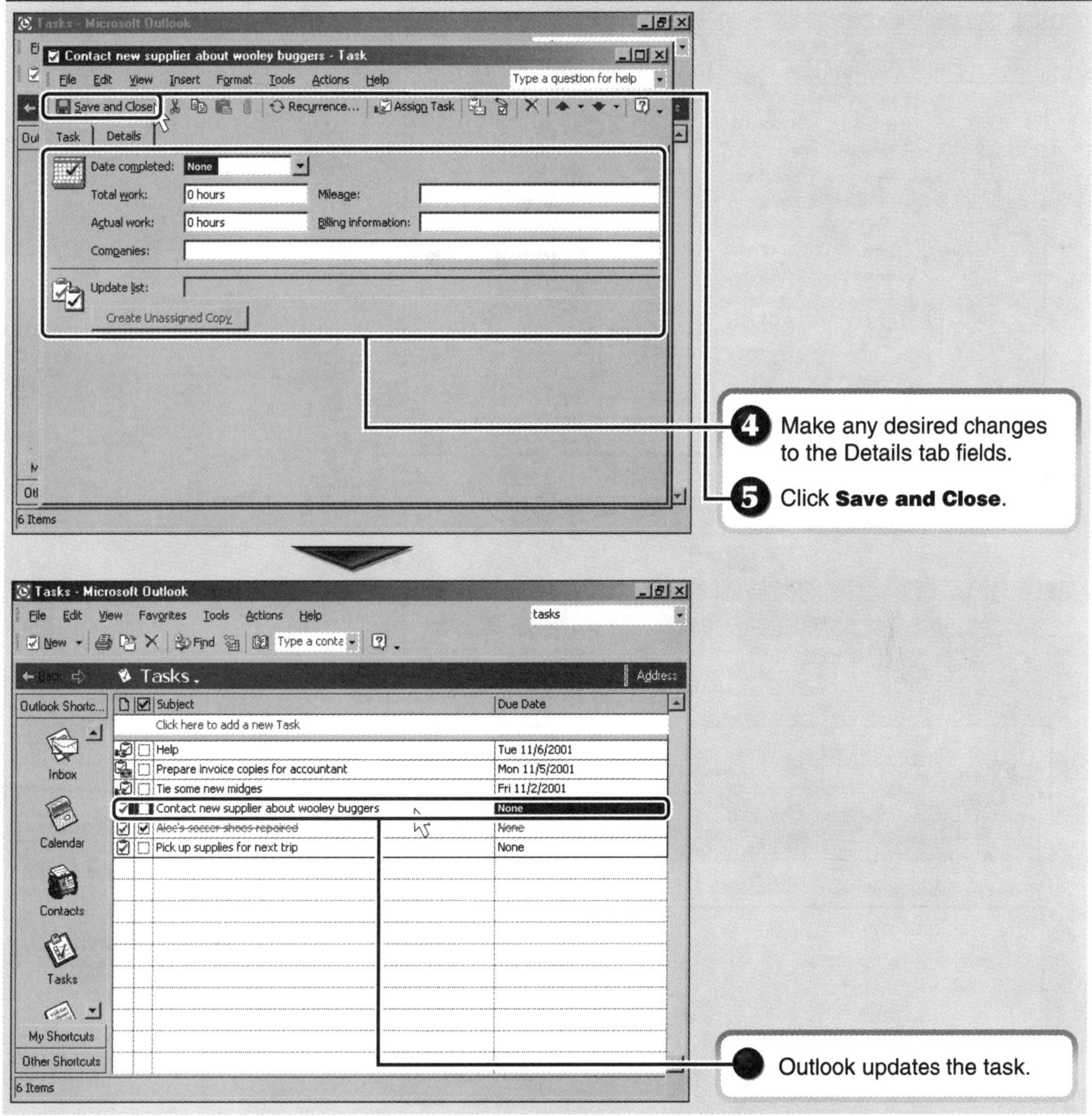

CREATE A RECURRING TASK

If you have tasks that occur regularly, you can set them up as recurring tasks so that you do not have re-enter them. As examples, you can add tasks to remind yourself to check the smoke detector battery every two months, send invoices monthly, or send holiday or birthday cards annually.

CREATE A RECURRING TASK

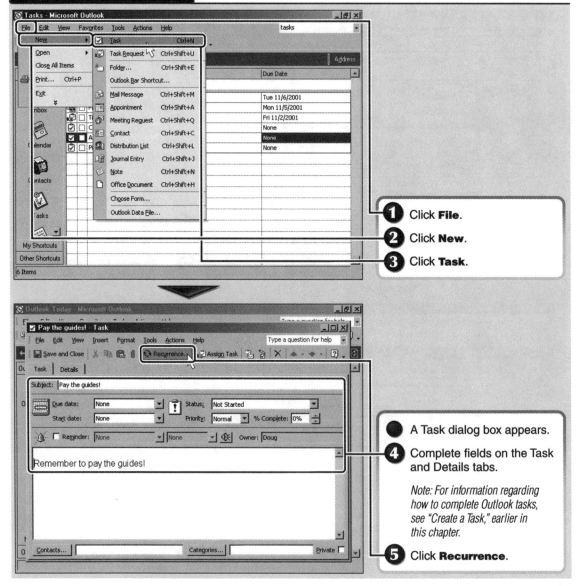

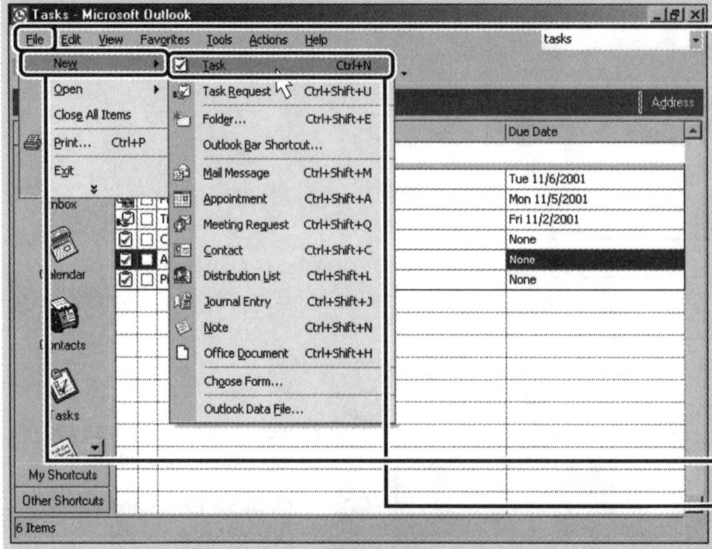

1. Click **File**.
2. Click **New**.
3. Click **Task**.

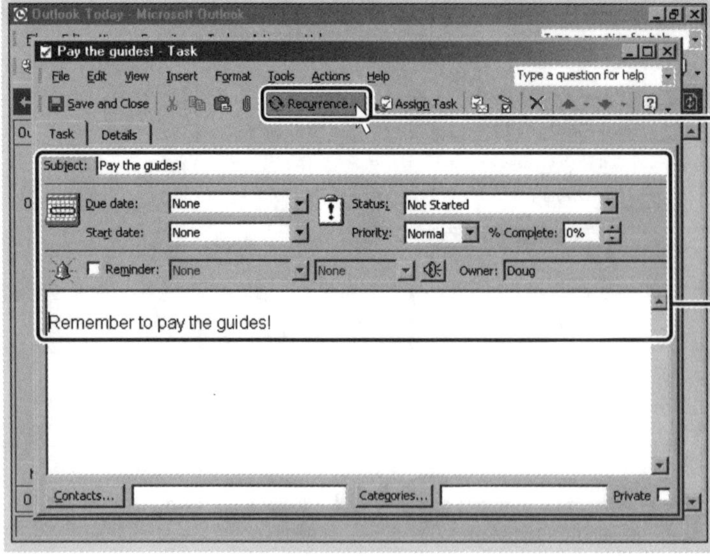

- A Task dialog box appears.

4. Complete fields on the Task and Details tabs.

Note: For information regarding how to complete Outlook tasks, see "Create a Task," earlier in this chapter.

5. Click **Recurrence**.

in an instant

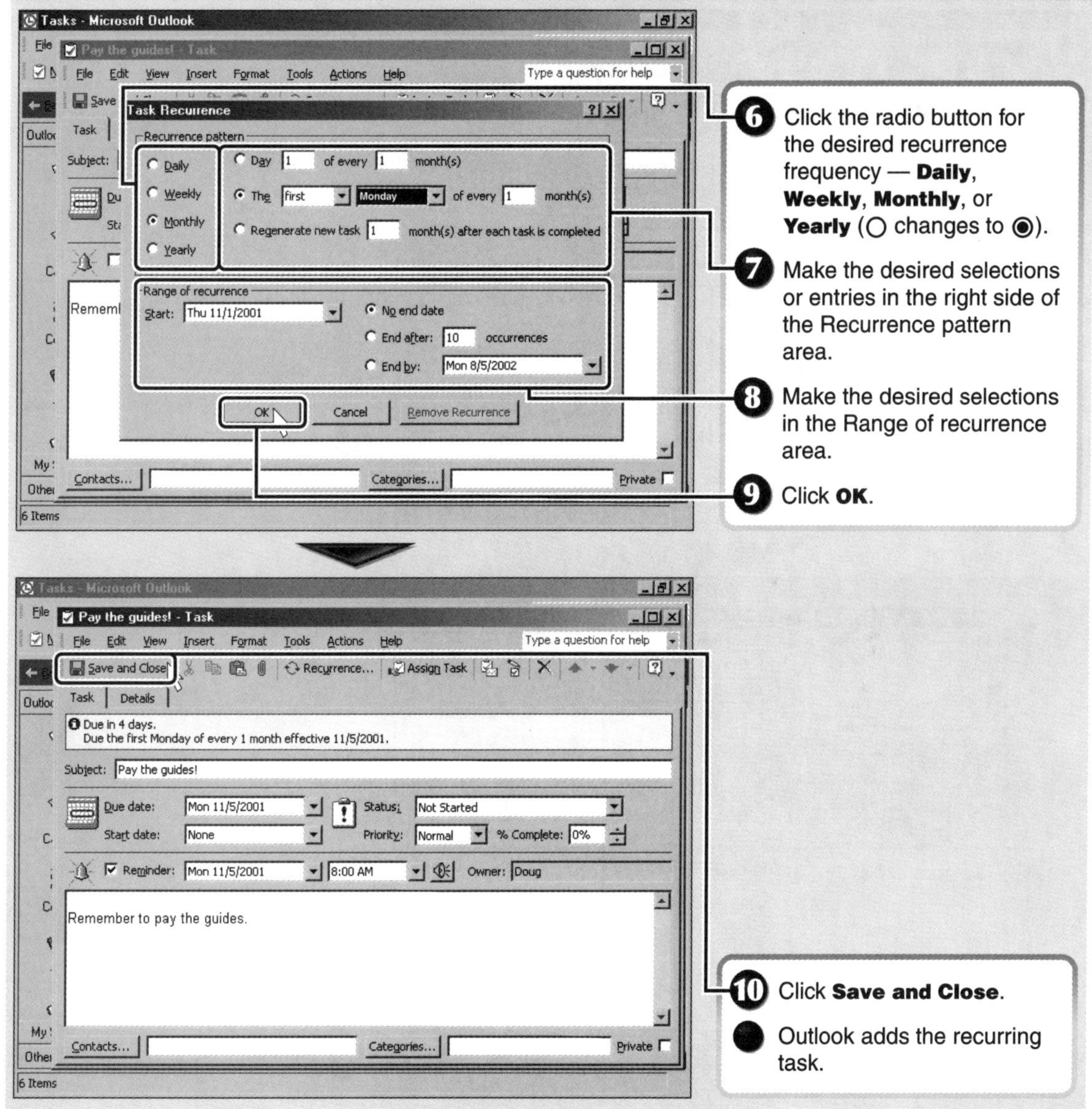

6. Click the radio button for the desired recurrence frequency — **Daily**, **Weekly**, **Monthly**, or **Yearly** (○ changes to ◉).
7. Make the desired selections or entries in the right side of the Recurrence pattern area.
8. Make the desired selections in the Range of recurrence area.
9. Click **OK**.
10. Click **Save and Close**.

- Outlook adds the recurring task.

SEND A STATUS REPORT ON A TASK

You can easily send others a status report to update them on the progress you are making on a task.

SEND A STATUS REPORT ON A TASK

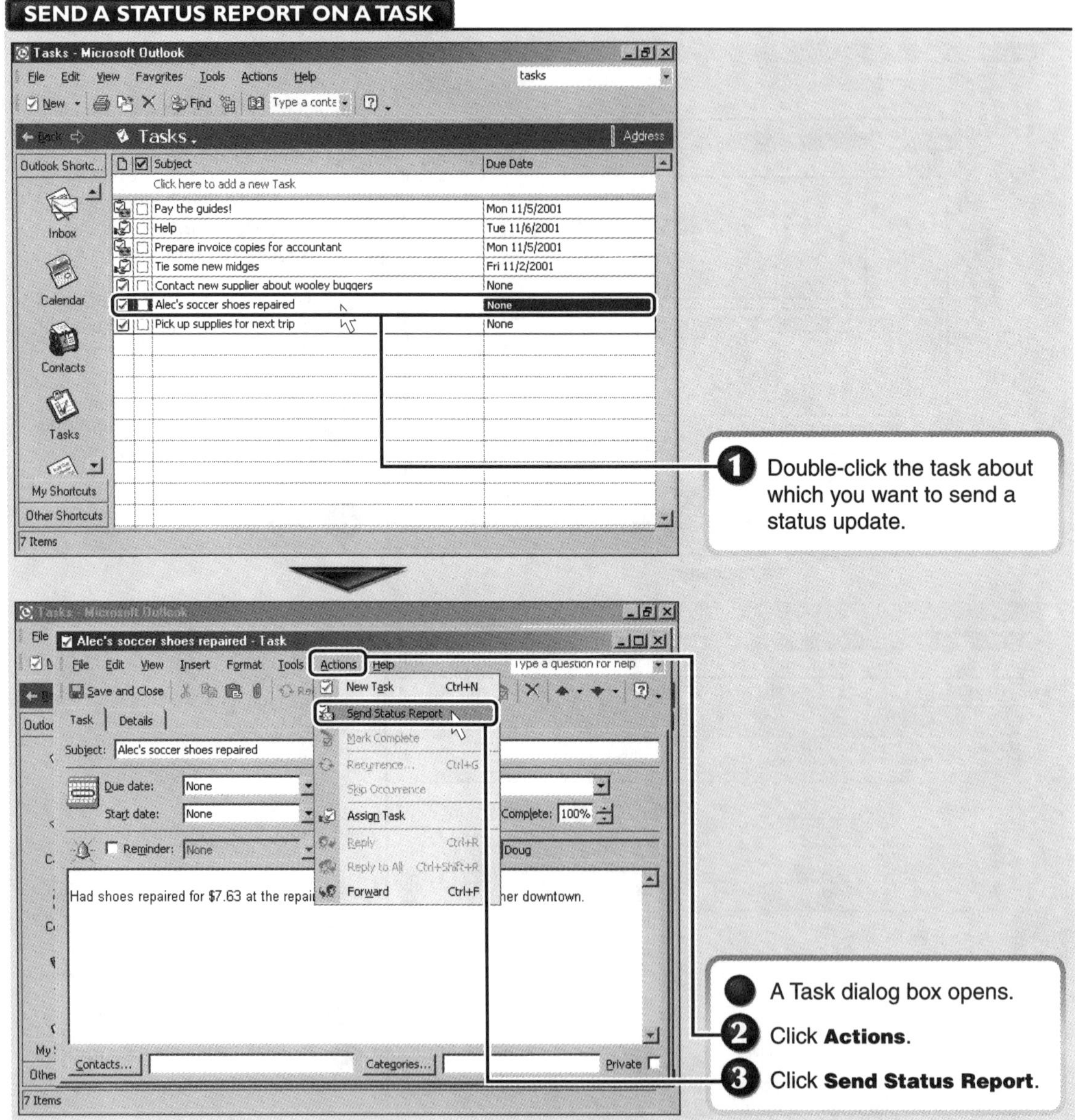

1 Double-click the task about which you want to send a status update.

- A Task dialog box opens.

2 Click **Actions**.

3 Click **Send Status Report**.

in an instant

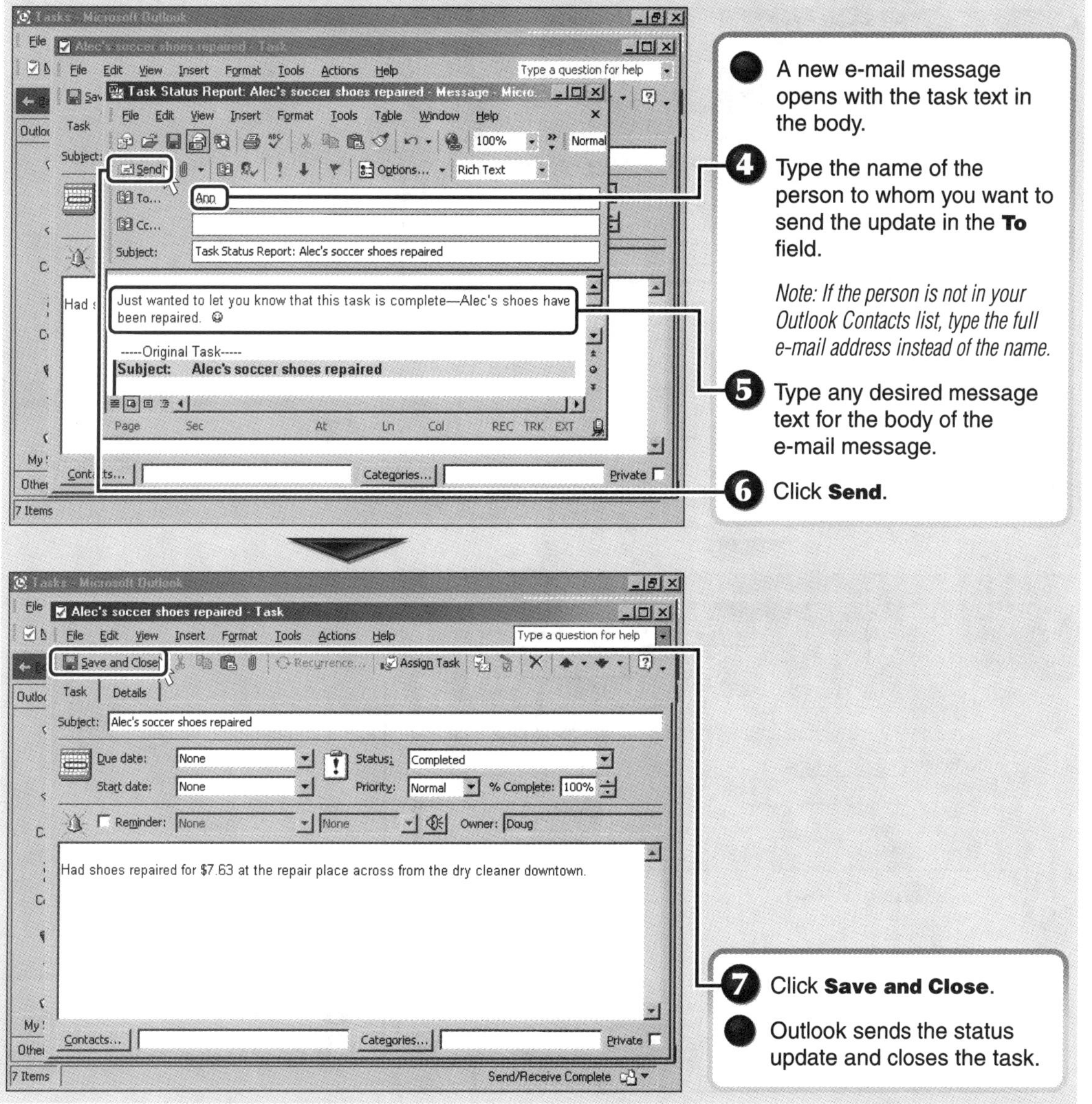

- A new e-mail message opens with the task text in the body.

4. Type the name of the person to whom you want to send the update in the **To** field.

   Note: If the person is not in your Outlook Contacts list, type the full e-mail address instead of the name.

5. Type any desired message text for the body of the e-mail message.

6. Click **Send**.

7. Click **Save and Close**.

- Outlook sends the status update and closes the task.

ASSIGN A TASK TO SOMEONE ELSE

You can create an Outlook task and then assign it to someone else to track and take responsibility for.

ASSIGN A TASK TO SOMEONE ELSE

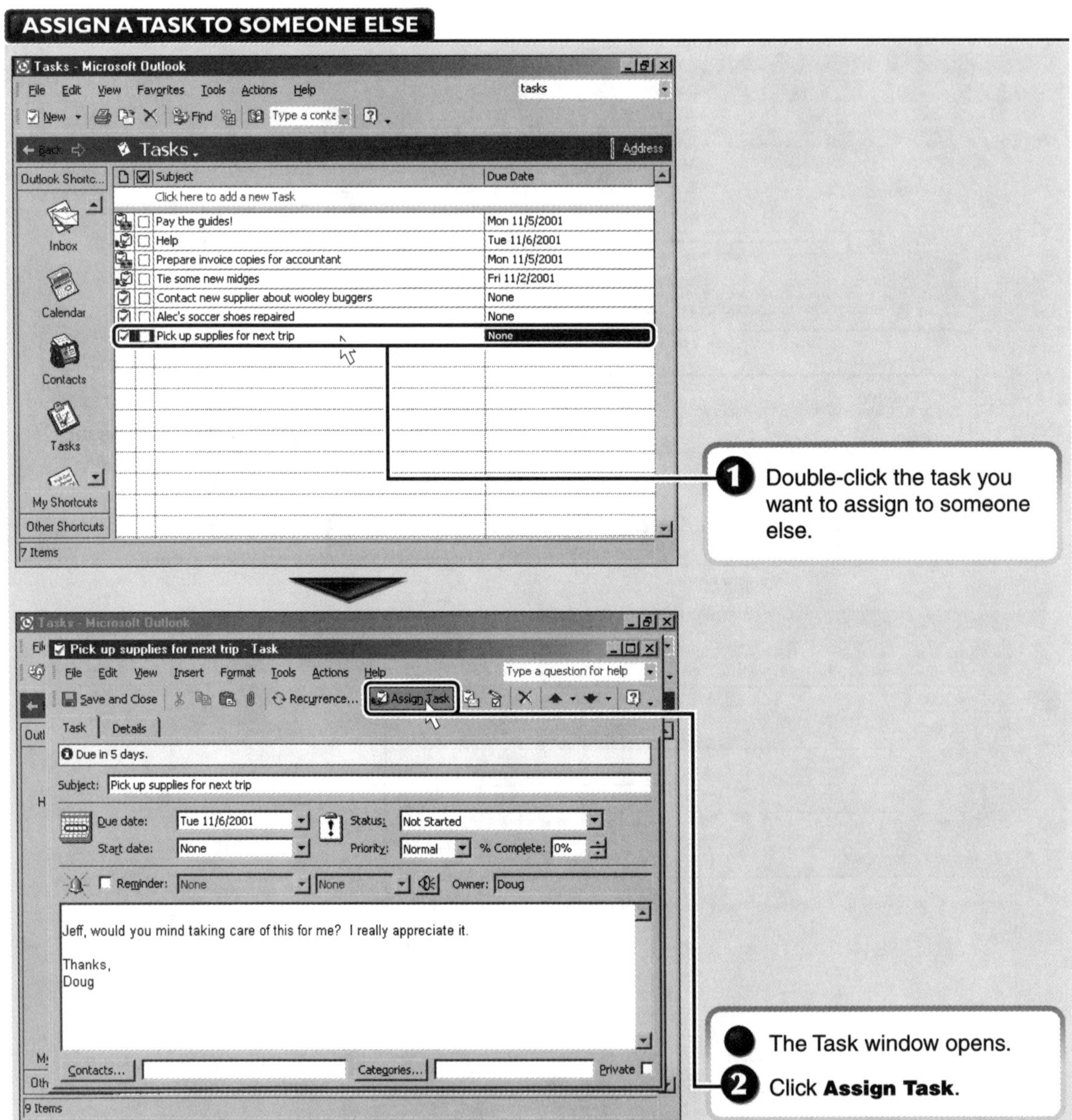

1. Double-click the task you want to assign to someone else.

- The Task window opens.

2. Click **Assign Task**.

in an instant

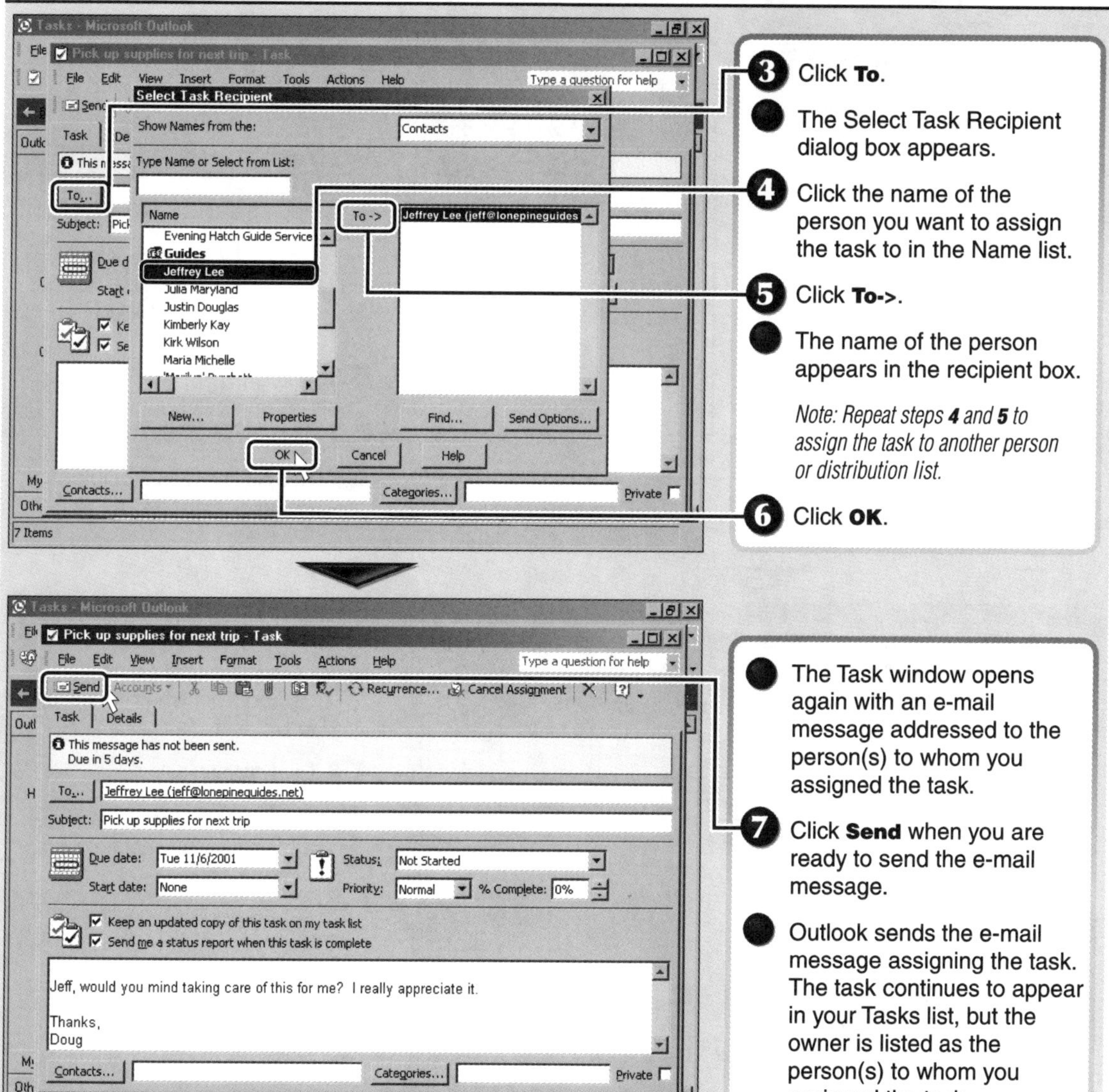

3. Click **To**.
- The Select Task Recipient dialog box appears.

4. Click the name of the person you want to assign the task to in the Name list.

5. Click **To->**.
- The name of the person appears in the recipient box.

*Note: Repeat steps **4** and **5** to assign the task to another person or distribution list.*

6. Click **OK**.

- The Task window opens again with an e-mail message addressed to the person(s) to whom you assigned the task.

7. Click **Send** when you are ready to send the e-mail message.
- Outlook sends the e-mail message assigning the task. The task continues to appear in your Tasks list, but the owner is listed as the person(s) to whom you assigned the task.

REQUEST A TASK FROM SOMEONE ELSE

You can use Outlook to ask someone else to create a task and even to report back with the status in the future.

REQUEST A TASK FROM SOMEONE ELSE

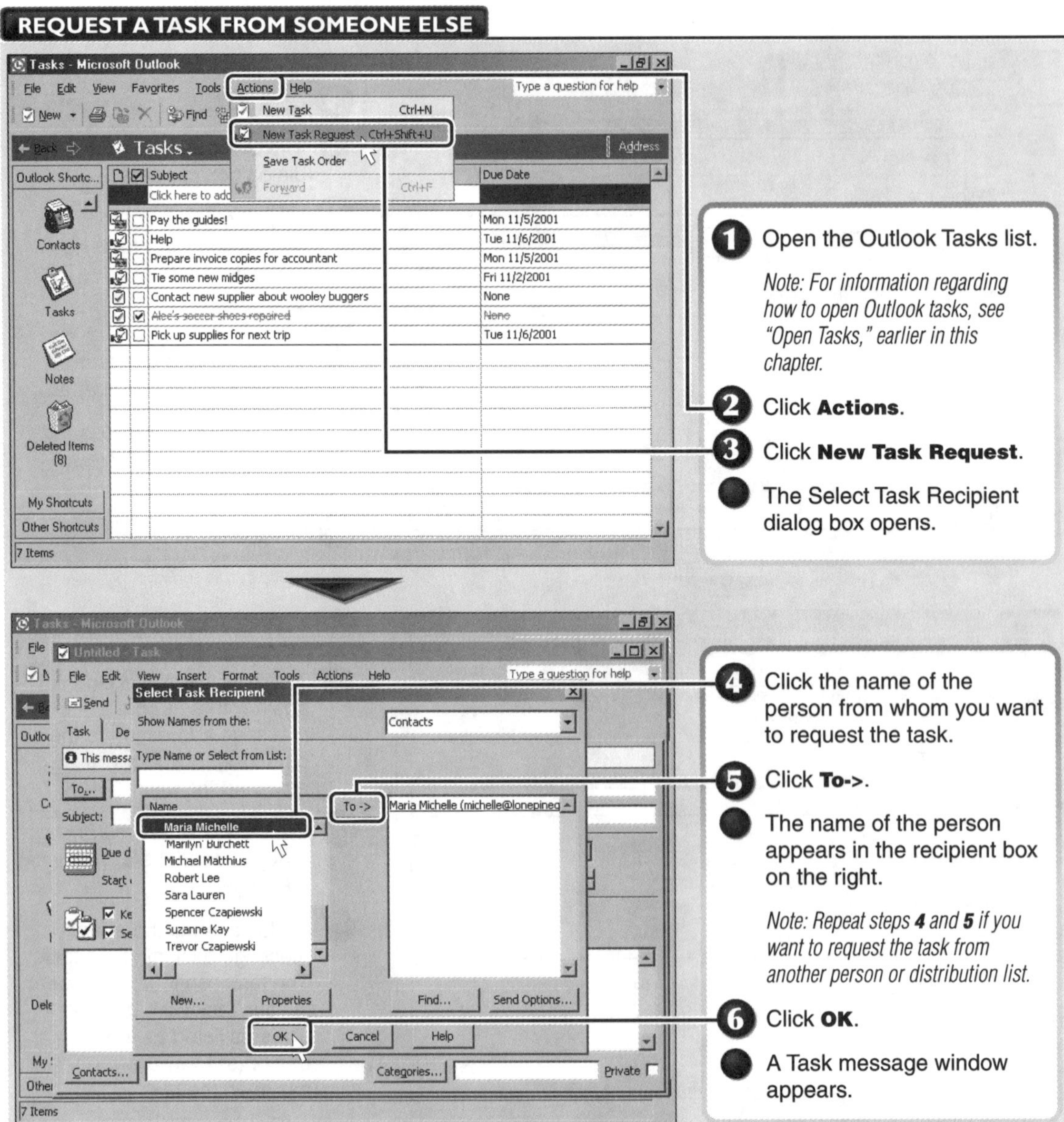

1. Open the Outlook Tasks list.

   Note: For information regarding how to open Outlook tasks, see "Open Tasks," earlier in this chapter.

2. Click **Actions**.
3. Click **New Task Request**.

- The Select Task Recipient dialog box opens.

4. Click the name of the person from whom you want to request the task.
5. Click **To->**.

- The name of the person appears in the recipient box on the right.

   *Note: Repeat steps **4** and **5** if you want to request the task from another person or distribution list.*

6. Click **OK**.

- A Task message window appears.

in an instant

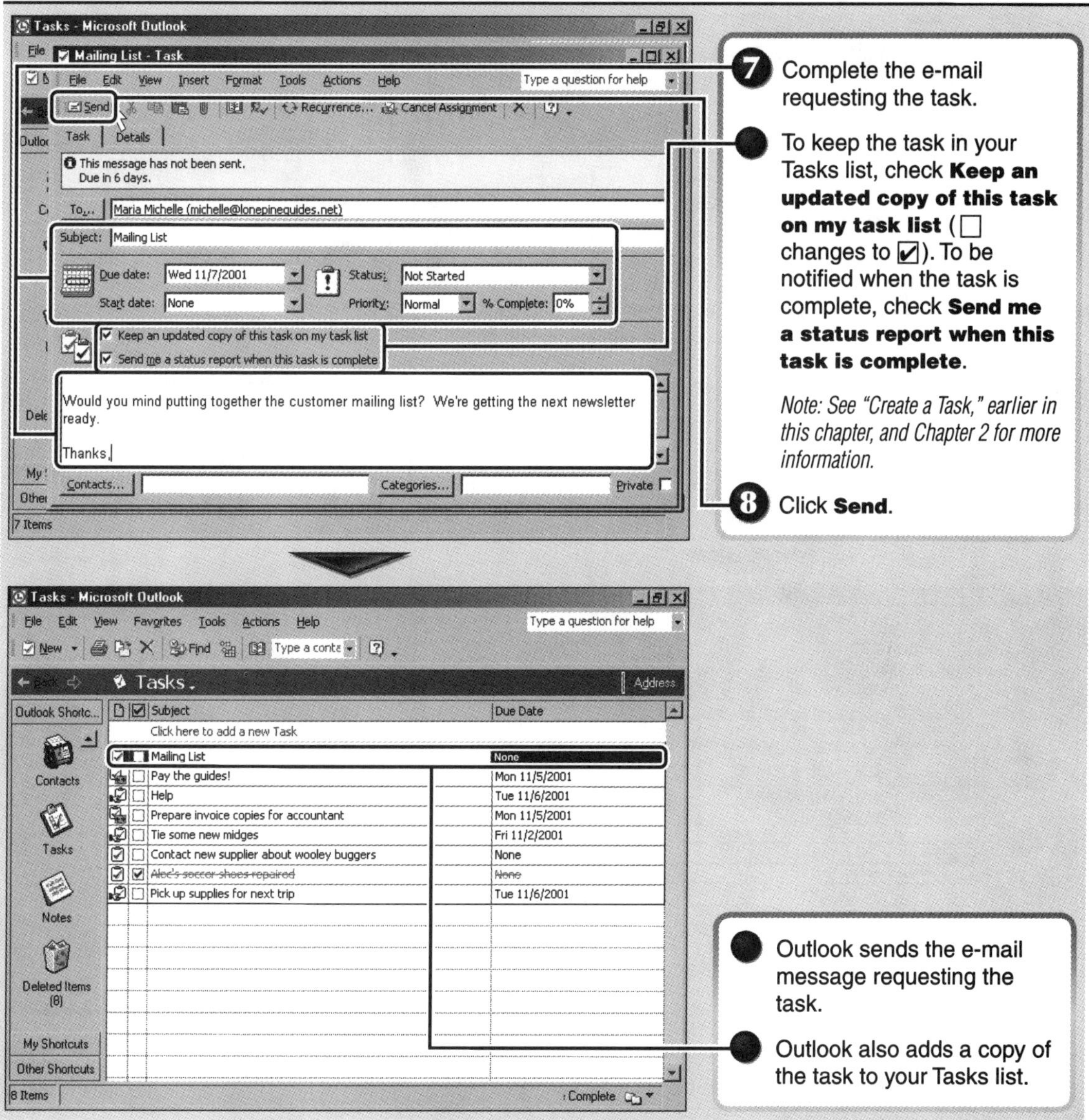

7 Complete the e-mail requesting the task.

- To keep the task in your Tasks list, check **Keep an updated copy of this task on my task list** (☐ changes to ☑). To be notified when the task is complete, check **Send me a status report when this task is complete**.

Note: See "Create a Task," earlier in this chapter, and Chapter 2 for more information.

8 Click **Send**.

- Outlook sends the e-mail message requesting the task.
- Outlook also adds a copy of the task to your Tasks list.

MARK A TASK AS COMPLETE

You can mark tasks as complete. Marking tasks as complete turns off the reminder for that task but keeps the task in your Outlook Tasks as a record of what you have accomplished.

MARK A TASK AS COMPLETE

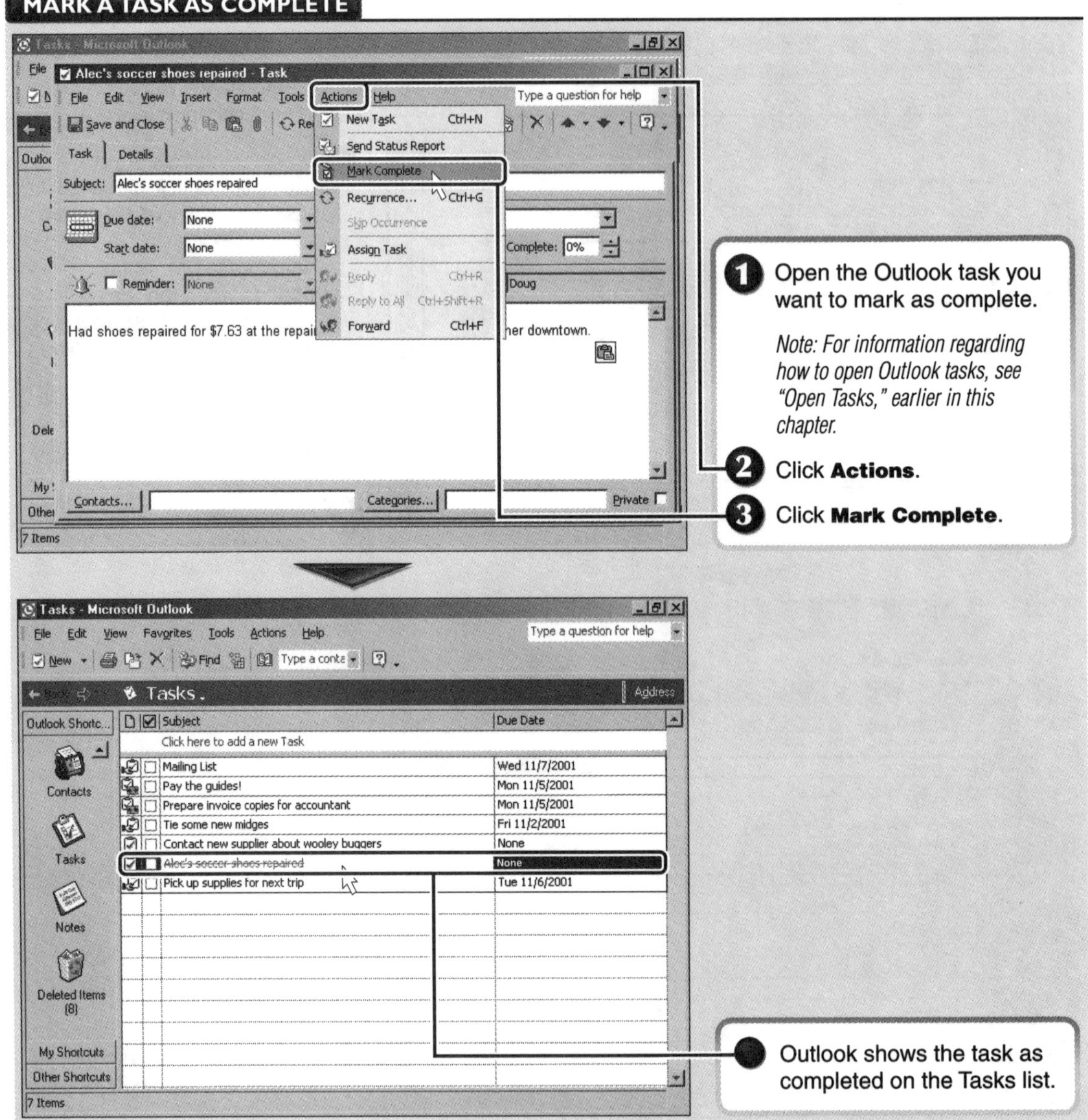

1. Open the Outlook task you want to mark as complete.

   Note: For information regarding how to open Outlook tasks, see "Open Tasks," earlier in this chapter.

2. Click **Actions**.

3. Click **Mark Complete**.

- Outlook shows the task as completed on the Tasks list.

DELETE A TASK

You can delete a task and remove it from your Outlook Tasks list. If you want to keep the task in your Outlook Tasks list as a record of your work, you should mark the task as complete instead of deleting it. For more on how, see "Mark a Task as Complete," earlier in this chapter.

DELETE A TASK

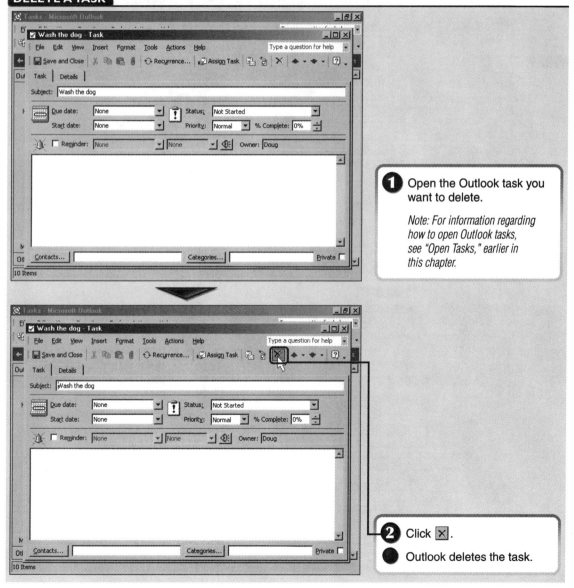

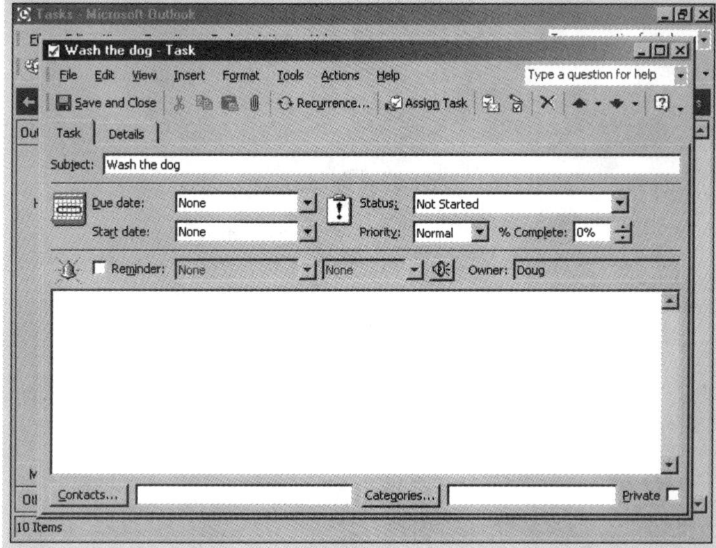

1. Open the Outlook task you want to delete.

   Note: For information regarding how to open Outlook tasks, see "Open Tasks," earlier in this chapter.

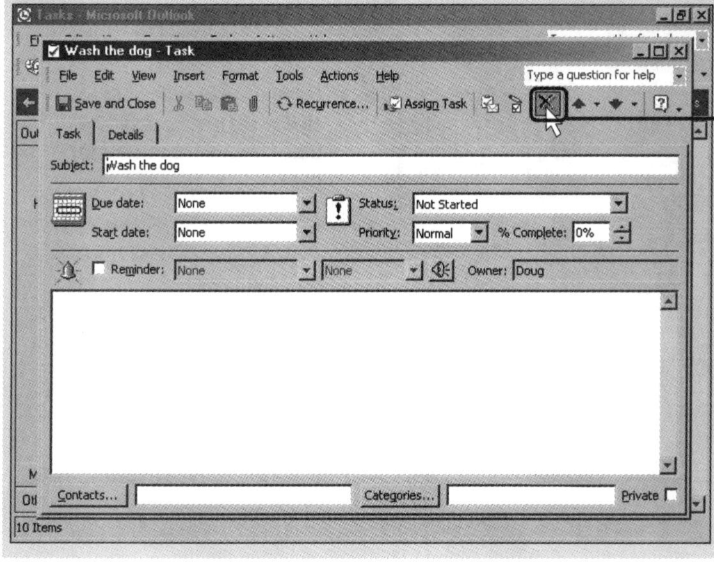

2. Click ✕.

- Outlook deletes the task.

CHANGE DEFAULT COLORS FOR OVERDUE AND COMPLETED TASKS

You can easily change the default font colors Outlook uses to mark overdue and completed tasks. By default, overdue tasks are red and completed tasks are grey.

CHANGE DEFAULT COLORS FOR OVERDUE AND COMPLETED TASKS

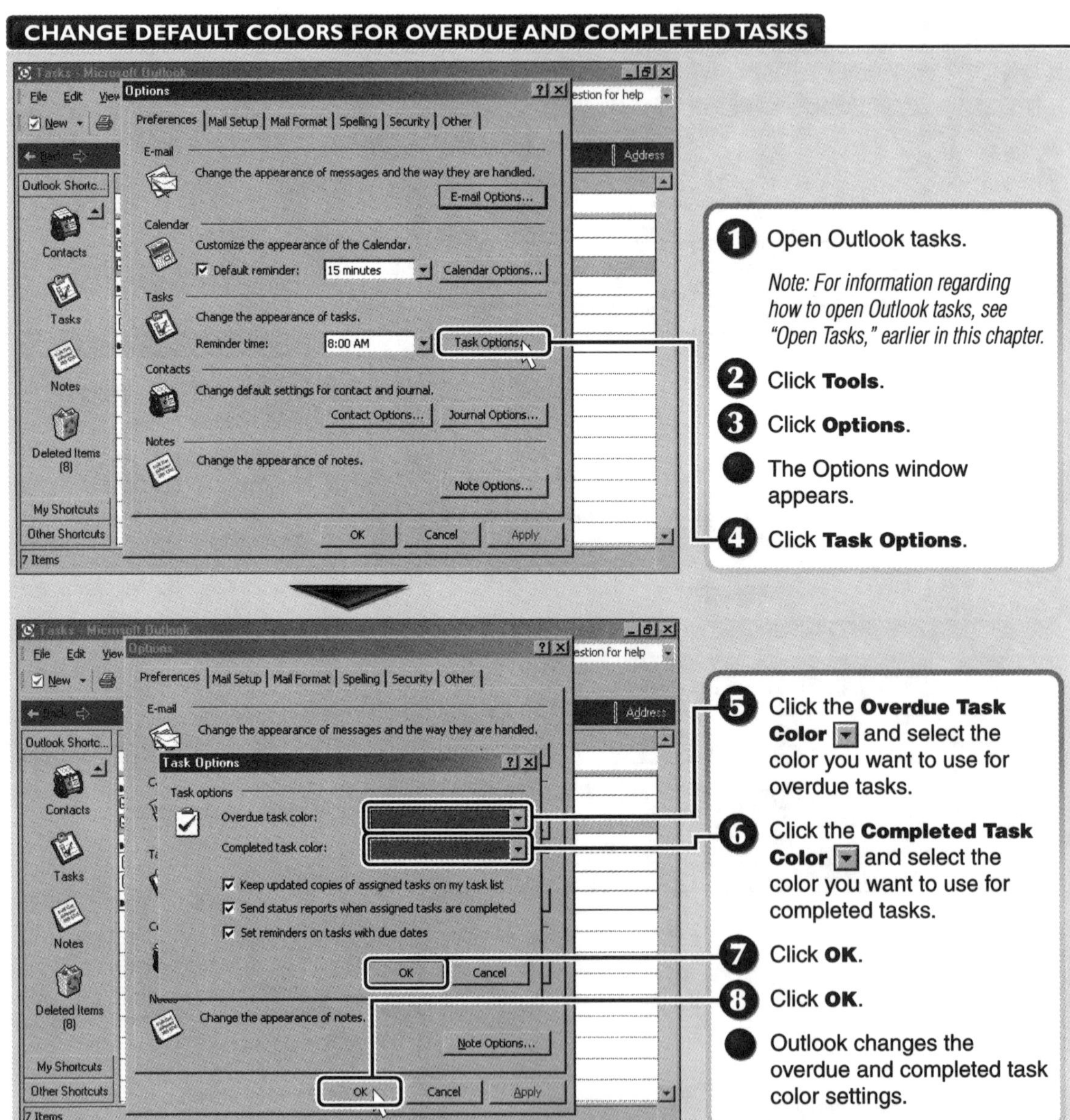

1. Open Outlook tasks.

   Note: For information regarding how to open Outlook tasks, see "Open Tasks," earlier in this chapter.

2. Click **Tools**.
3. Click **Options**.

- The Options window appears.

4. Click **Task Options**.
5. Click the **Overdue Task Color** ▼ and select the color you want to use for overdue tasks.
6. Click the **Completed Task Color** ▼ and select the color you want to use for completed tasks.
7. Click **OK**.
8. Click **OK**.

- Outlook changes the overdue and completed task color settings.

PRINT TASKS

You can quickly and easily print any task from your Outlook Tasks list. A printed task includes key information about the item, including due date, priority, status, percent complete, number of work hours expected and actually spent on the task, and the task owner.

PRINT TASKS

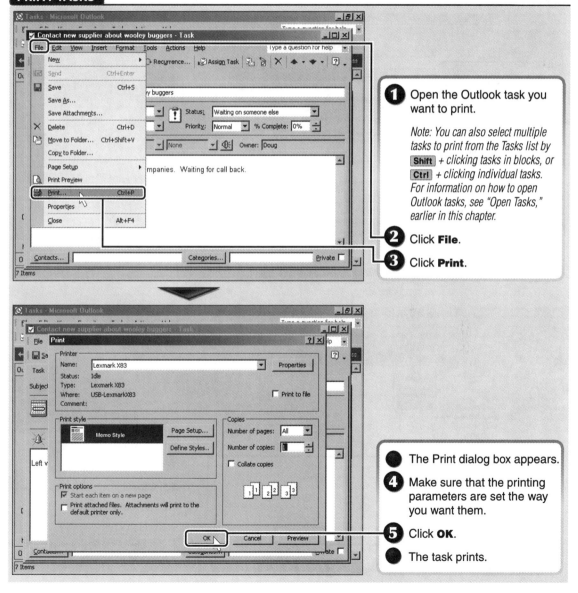

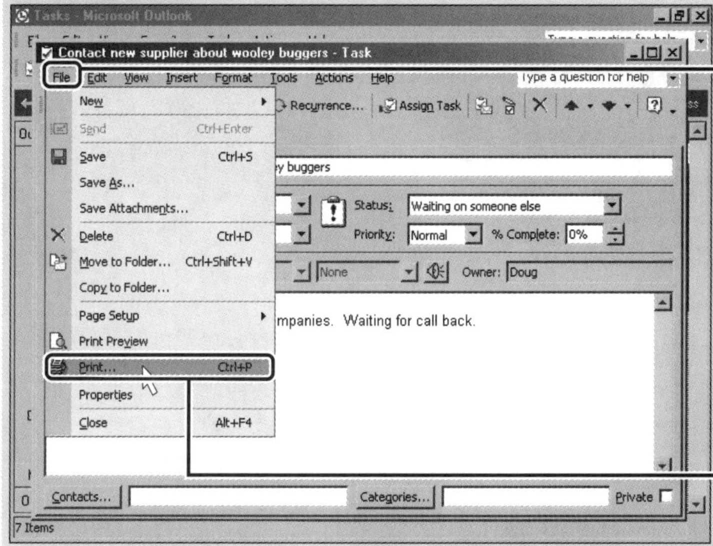

1. Open the Outlook task you want to print.

   Note: You can also select multiple tasks to print from the Tasks list by **Shift** *+ clicking tasks in blocks, or* **Ctrl** *+ clicking individual tasks. For information on how to open Outlook tasks, see "Open Tasks," earlier in this chapter.*

2. Click **File**.
3. Click **Print**.

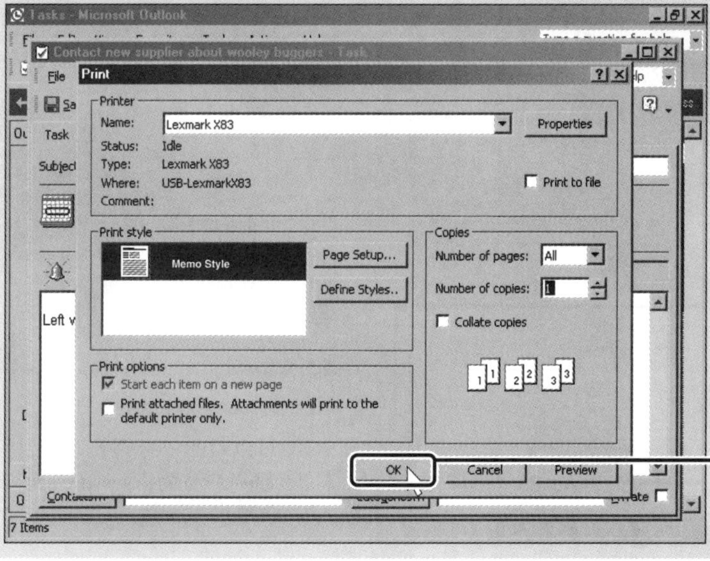

- The Print dialog box appears.

4. Make sure that the printing parameters are set the way you want them.
5. Click **OK**.

- The task prints.

OPEN NOTES

You can use notes like a note on your desk to jot down information you want to refer to or file later. Notes are a convenient way to store and find miscellaneous pieces of information.

OPEN NOTES

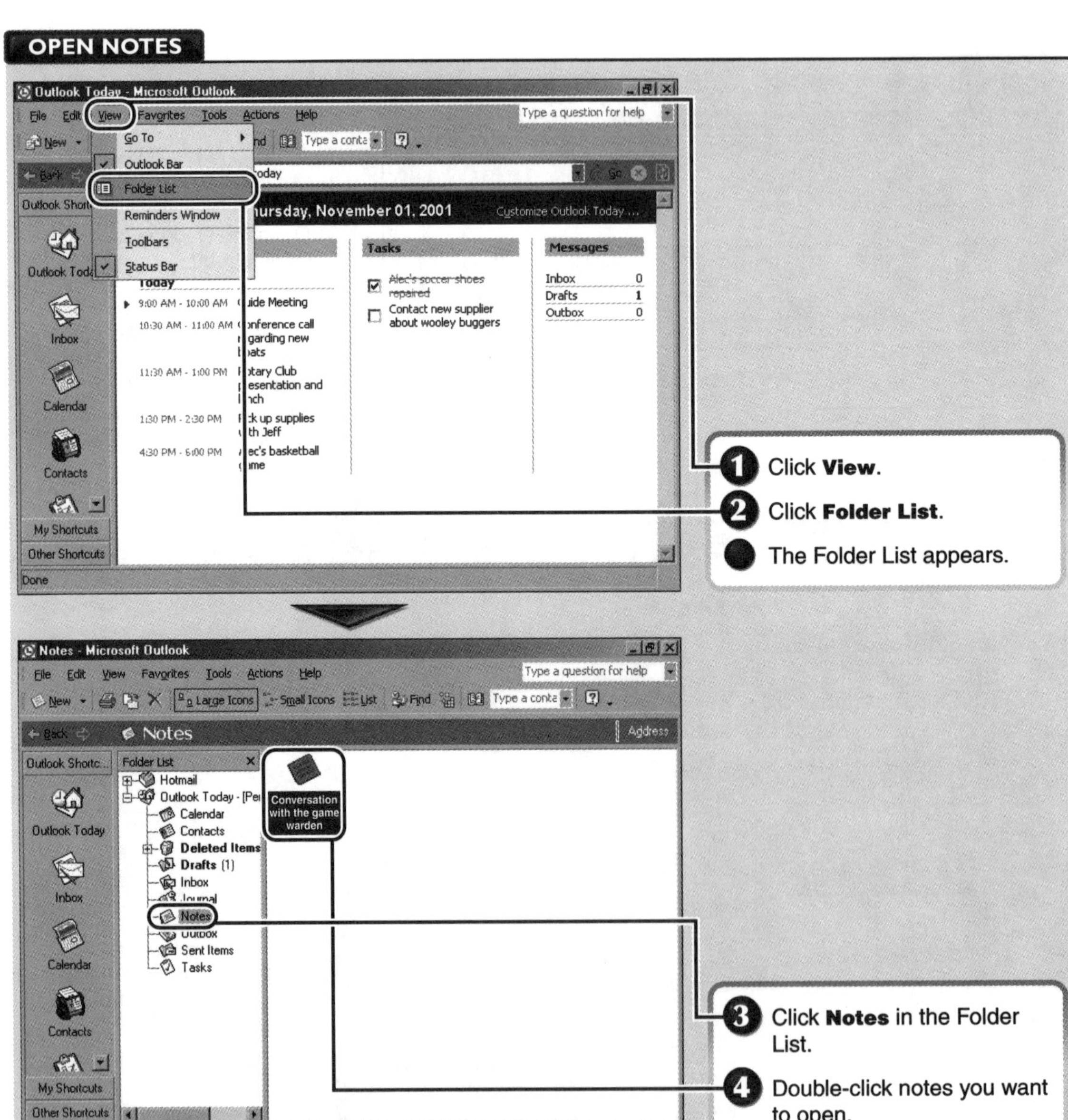

1. Click **View**.
2. Click **Folder List**.

- The Folder List appears.

3. Click **Notes** in the Folder List.
4. Double-click notes you want to open.

in an instant

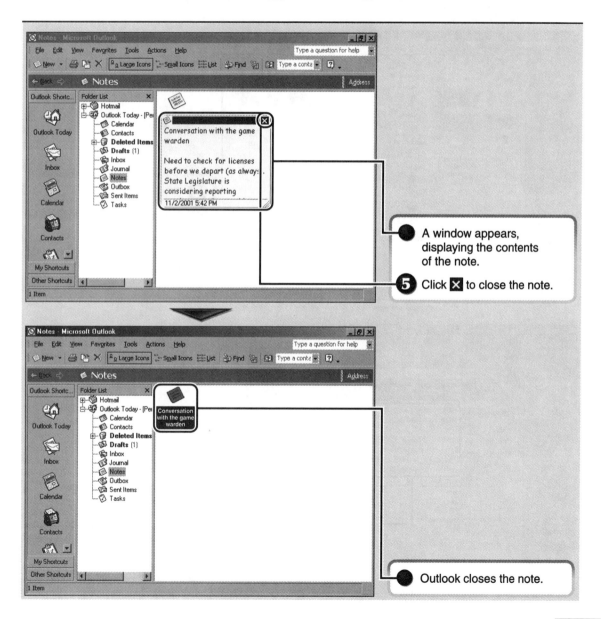

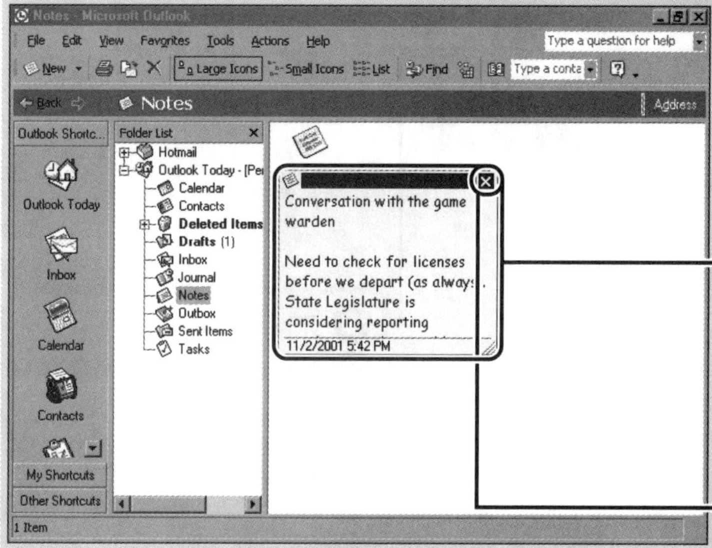

- A window appears, displaying the contents of the note.

5 Click ☒ to close the note.

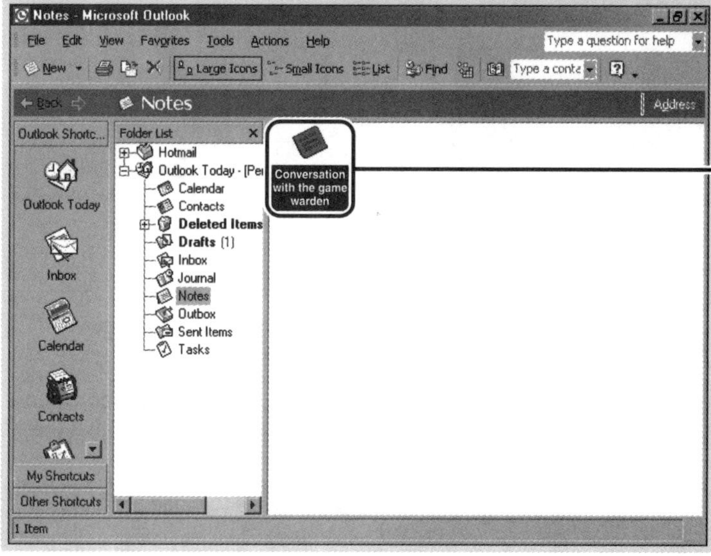

- Outlook closes the note.

WRITE A NOTE

You can write a note in a matter of seconds because notes are accessible from just about anywhere in Outlook. You do not have to leave your Inbox or Calendar to write a Note.

WRITE A NOTE

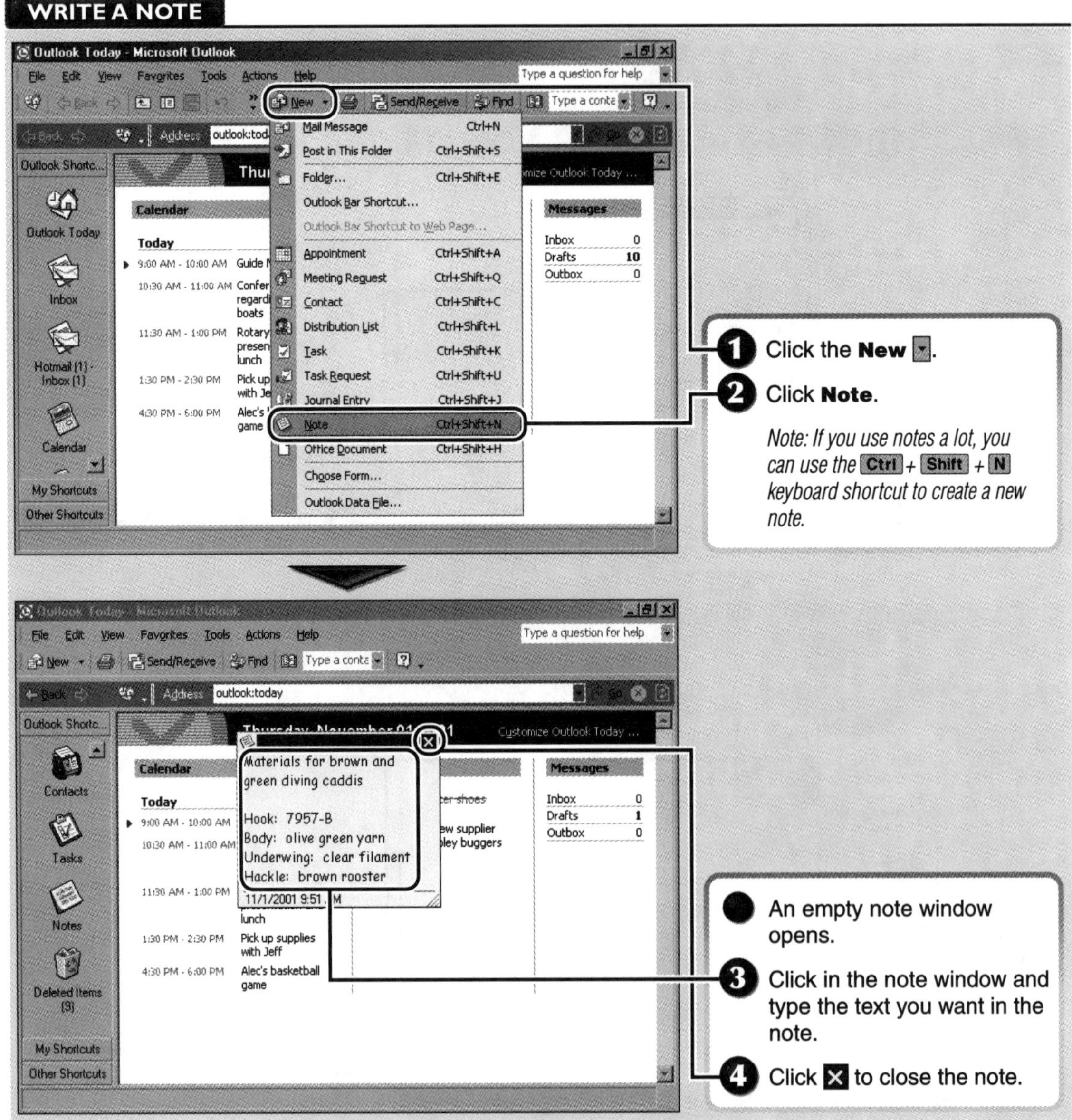

1. Click the **New** ▾.
2. Click **Note**.

Note: If you use notes a lot, you can use the Ctrl + Shift + N keyboard shortcut to create a new note.

- An empty note window opens.

3. Click in the note window and type the text you want in the note.
4. Click ☒ to close the note.

in an instant

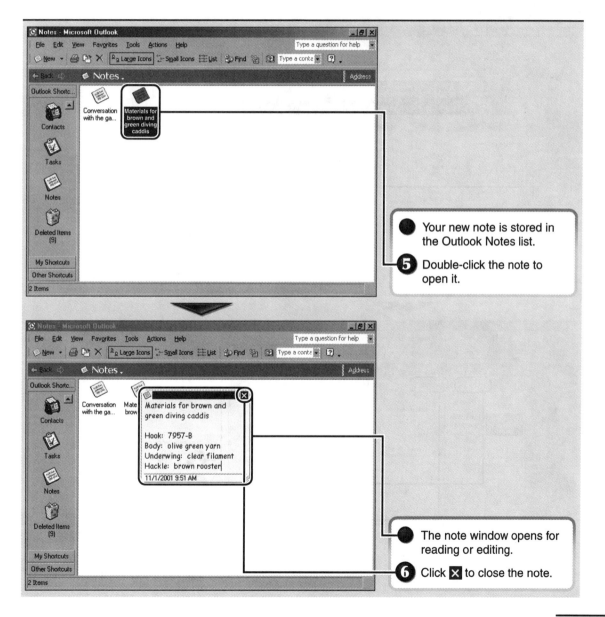

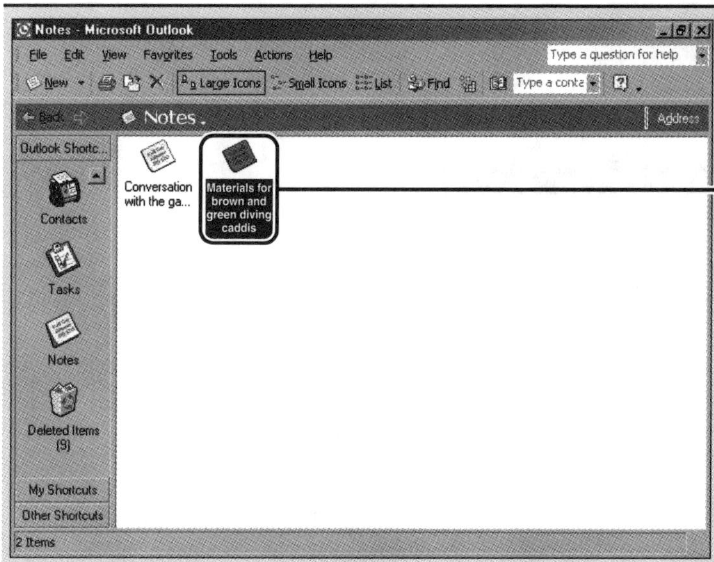

- Your new note is stored in the Outlook Notes list.

5 Double-click the note to open it.

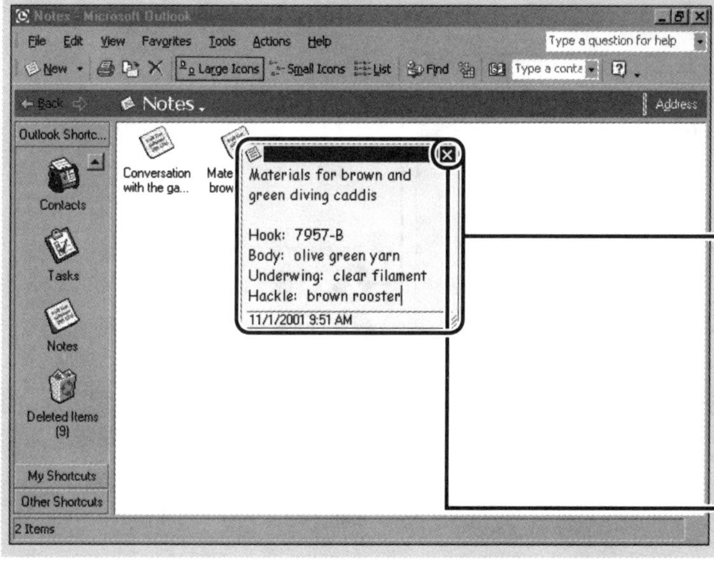

- The note window opens for reading or editing.

6 Click ☒ to close the note.

FIND A NOTE

You can find Outlook notes by searching for any of the text that they contain. If you use the Outlook journal or manually add notes to the journal, your notes will also be found when you search the Journal. See Chapter 10 for more information about searching for items in the Journal.

FIND A NOTE

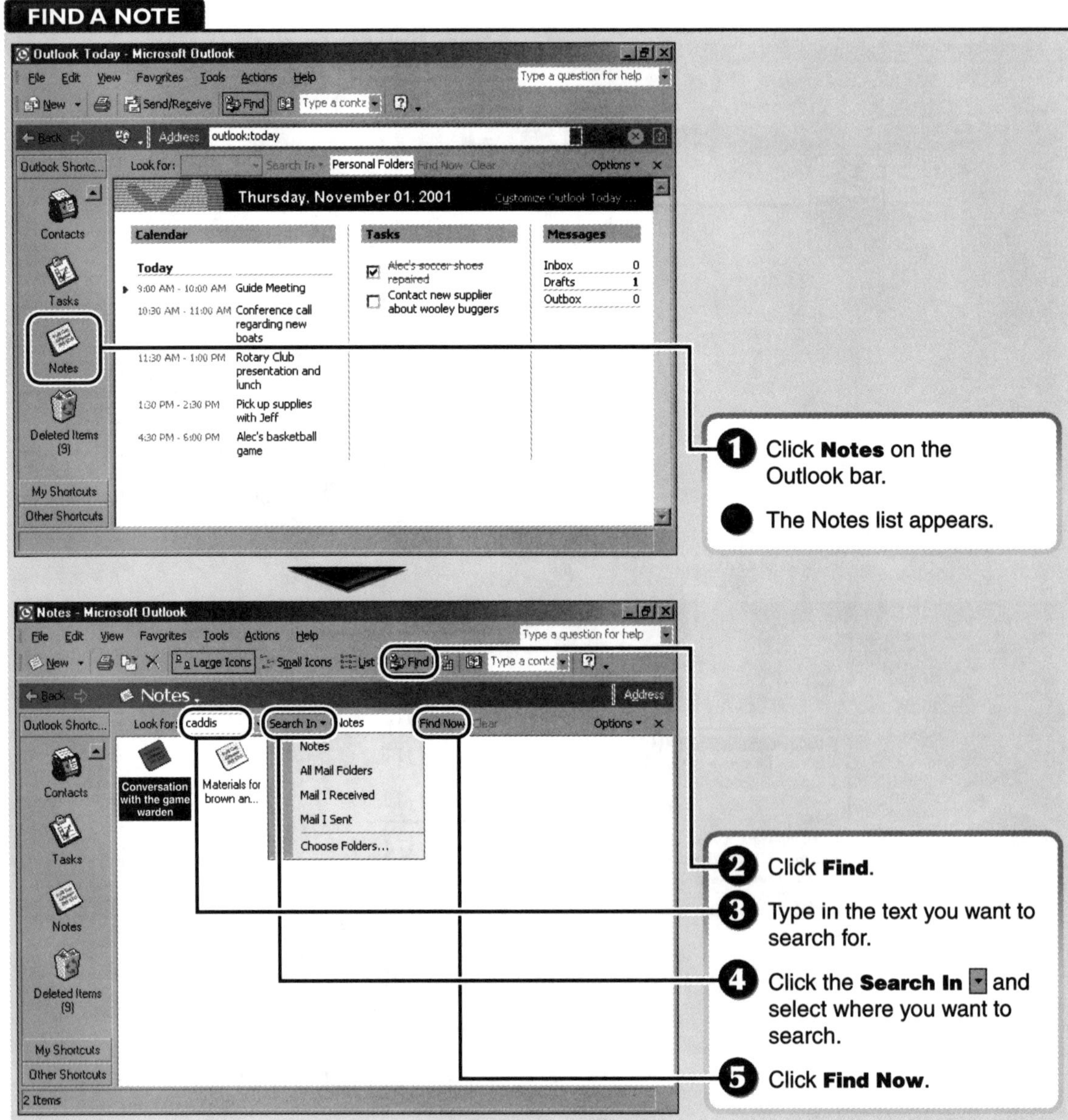

1 Click **Notes** on the Outlook bar.

- The Notes list appears.

2 Click **Find**.

3 Type in the text you want to search for.

4 Click the **Search In** ▾ and select where you want to search.

5 Click **Find Now**.

in an instant

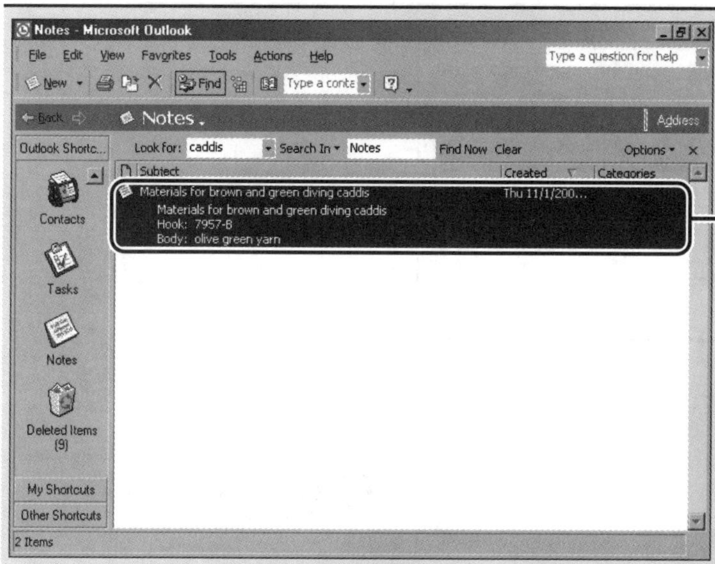

- Outlook displays the search results.
6. Double-click the note you want to open.

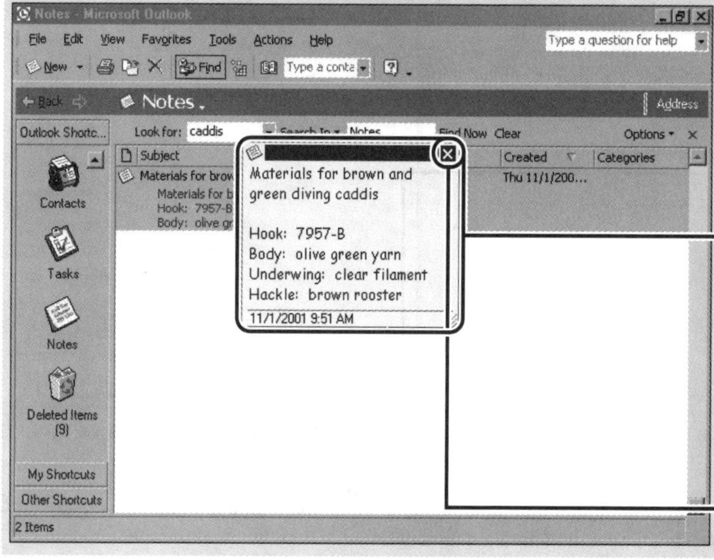

- The note opens.
7. Click ☒ to close the note.

EDIT A NOTE

You can easily edit an Outlook note. Because you can find and open notes so quickly and easily, they can be a good permanent location for important tidbits of information that you want to refer back to quickly. Editing notes is easy, so you can keep them current with very little effort.

EDIT A NOTE

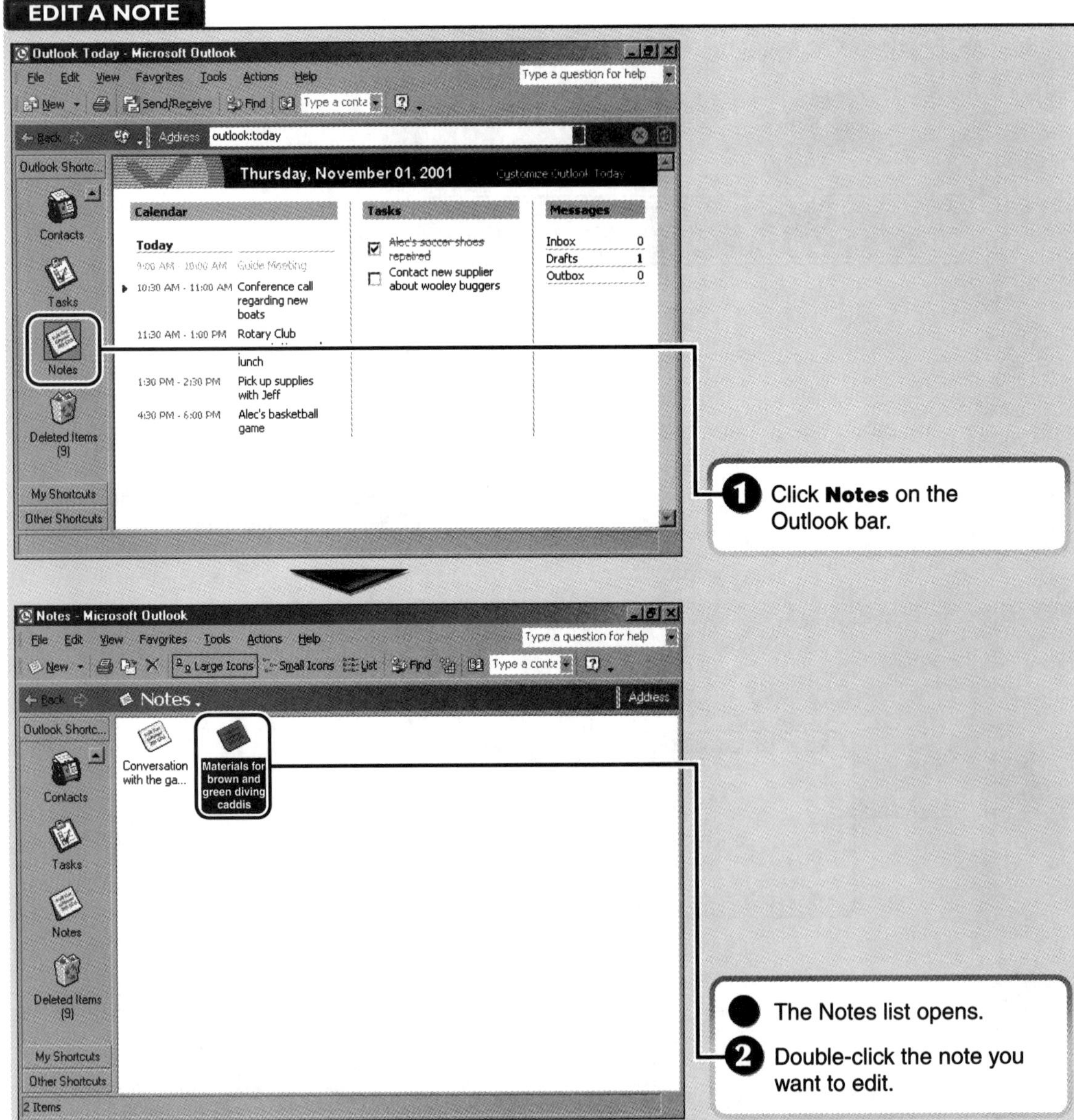

1 Click **Notes** on the Outlook bar.

- The Notes list opens.

2 Double-click the note you want to edit.

in an instant

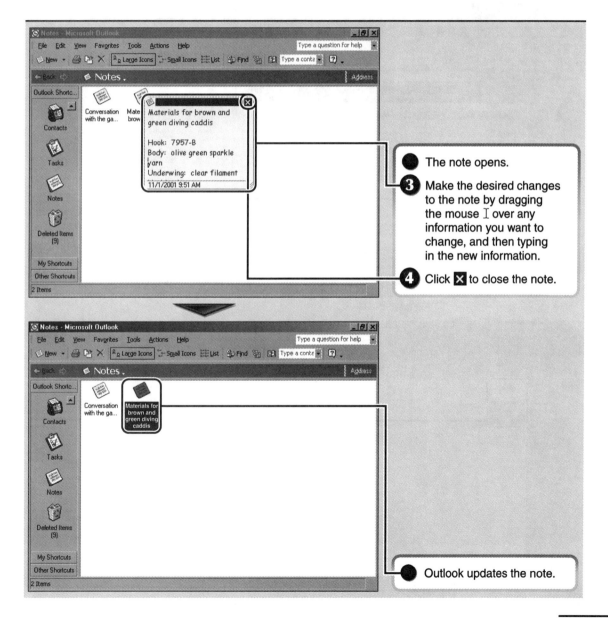

- The note opens.

3. Make the desired changes to the note by dragging the mouse I over any information you want to change, and then typing in the new information.

4. Click ☒ to close the note.

- Outlook updates the note.

DELETE A NOTE

You can quickly delete an Outlook note. Deleted notes are moved to your Deleted Items folder if you change your mind and want to be able to get them back. For more information on deleting items, see Chapter 5.

DELETE A NOTE

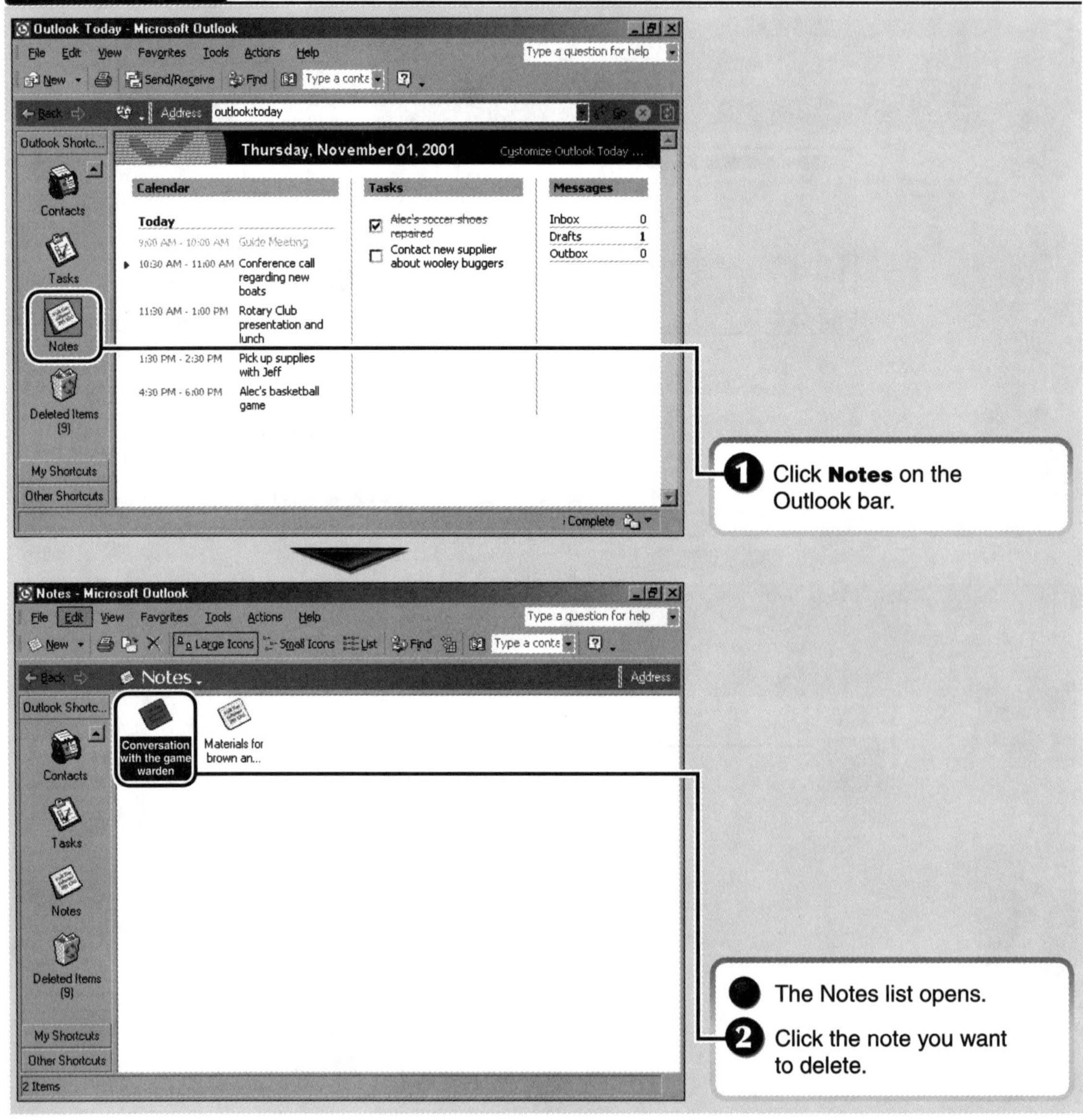

in an instant

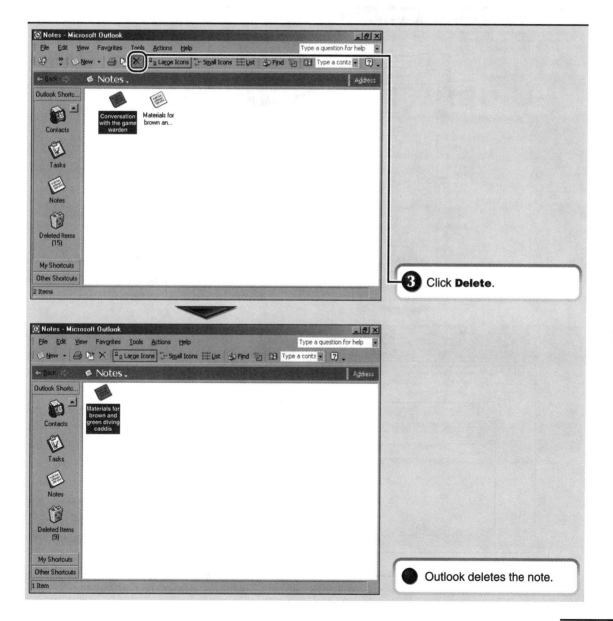

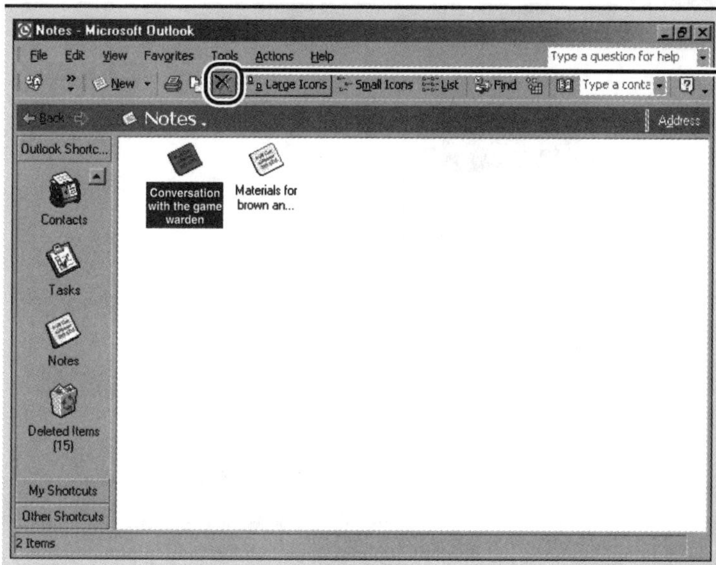

3 Click **Delete**.

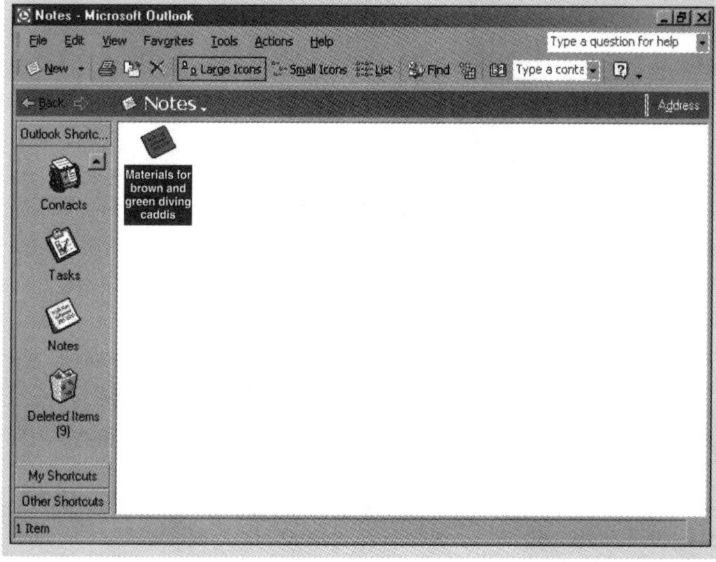

- Outlook deletes the note.

SEND A NOTE IN AN E-MAIL MESSAGE

You can send Outlook notes you have created to others as e-mail attachments. Sending notes as attachments allows you to send more than one note at one time, and also gives you the flexibility to include other files and items in the same e-mail message.

SEND A NOTE IN AN E-MAIL MESSAGE

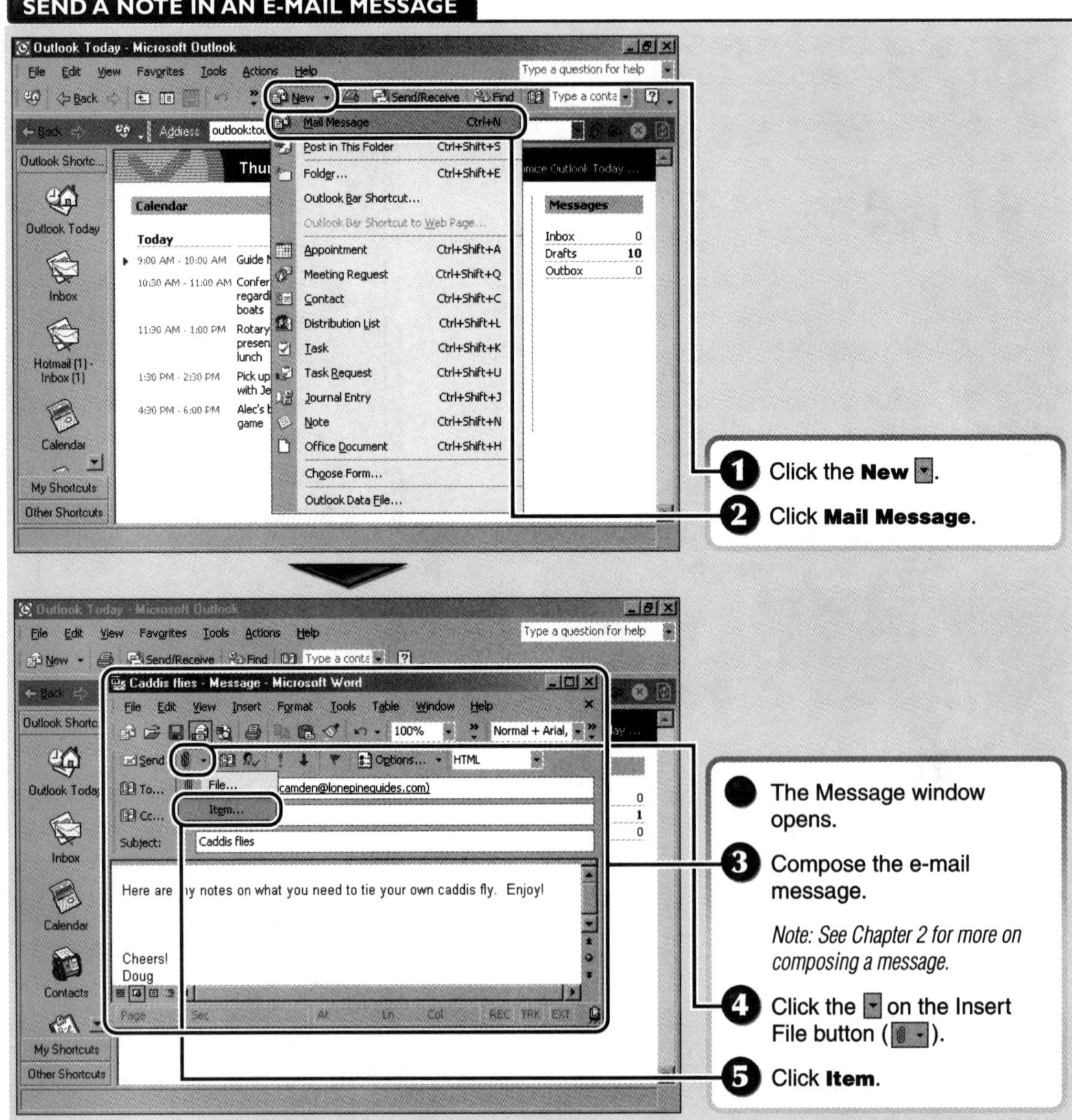

1. Click the **New** ▾.
2. Click **Mail Message**.

- The Message window opens.

3. Compose the e-mail message.

Note: See Chapter 2 for more on composing a message.

4. Click the ▾ on the Insert File button (📎 ▾).
5. Click **Item**.

in an instant

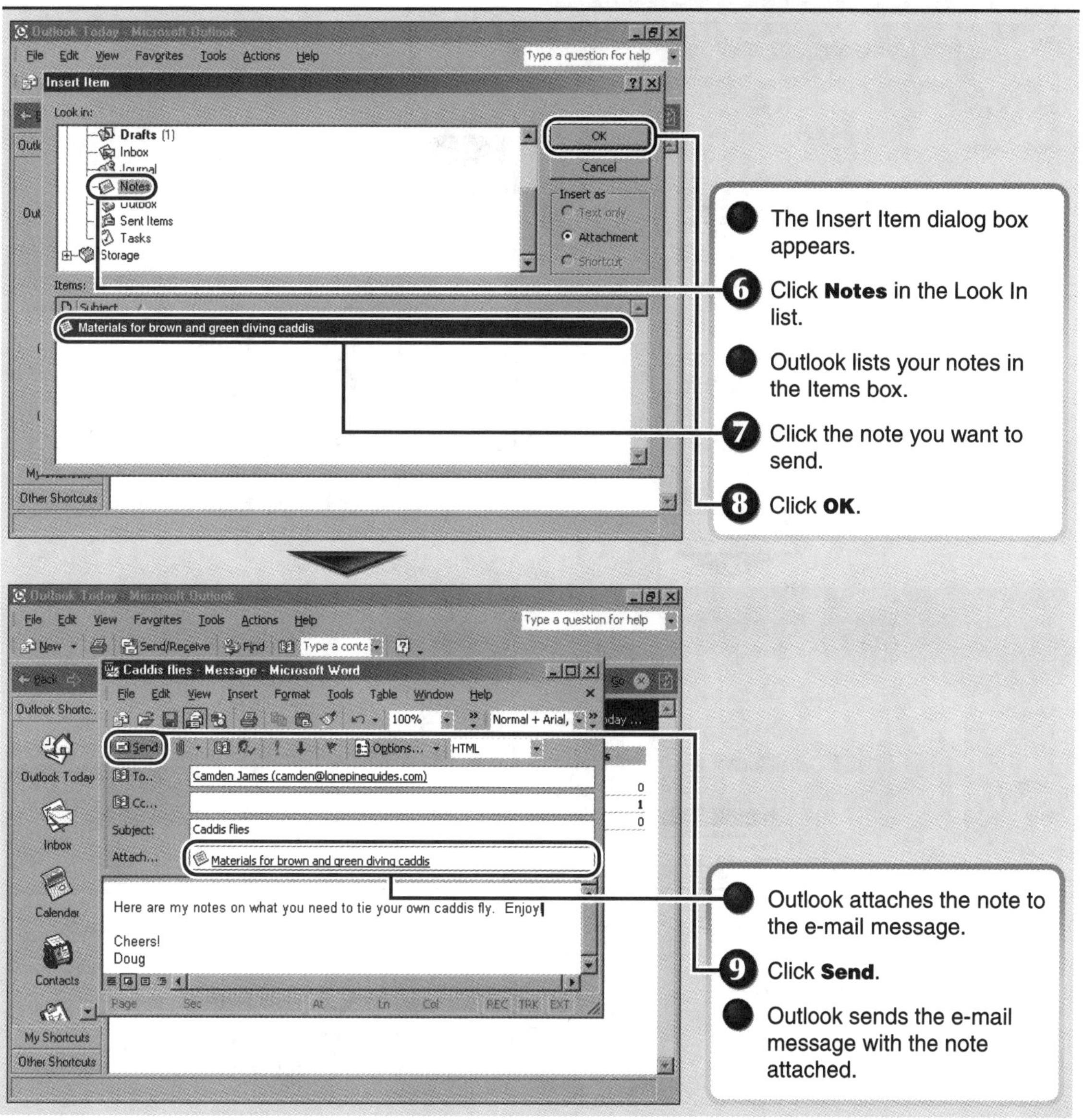

- The Insert Item dialog box appears.
- 6 Click **Notes** in the Look In list.
- Outlook lists your notes in the Items box.
- 7 Click the note you want to send.
- 8 Click **OK**.

- Outlook attaches the note to the e-mail message.
- 9 Click **Send**.
- Outlook sends the e-mail message with the note attached.

CHANGE THE DEFAULT FONT FOR NOTES

You can specify what font to use for Outlook notes. The default font for notes is 10 point Comic Sans MS, but you can change it to whatever fonts you have installed on your system.

CHANGE THE DEFAULT FONT FOR NOTES

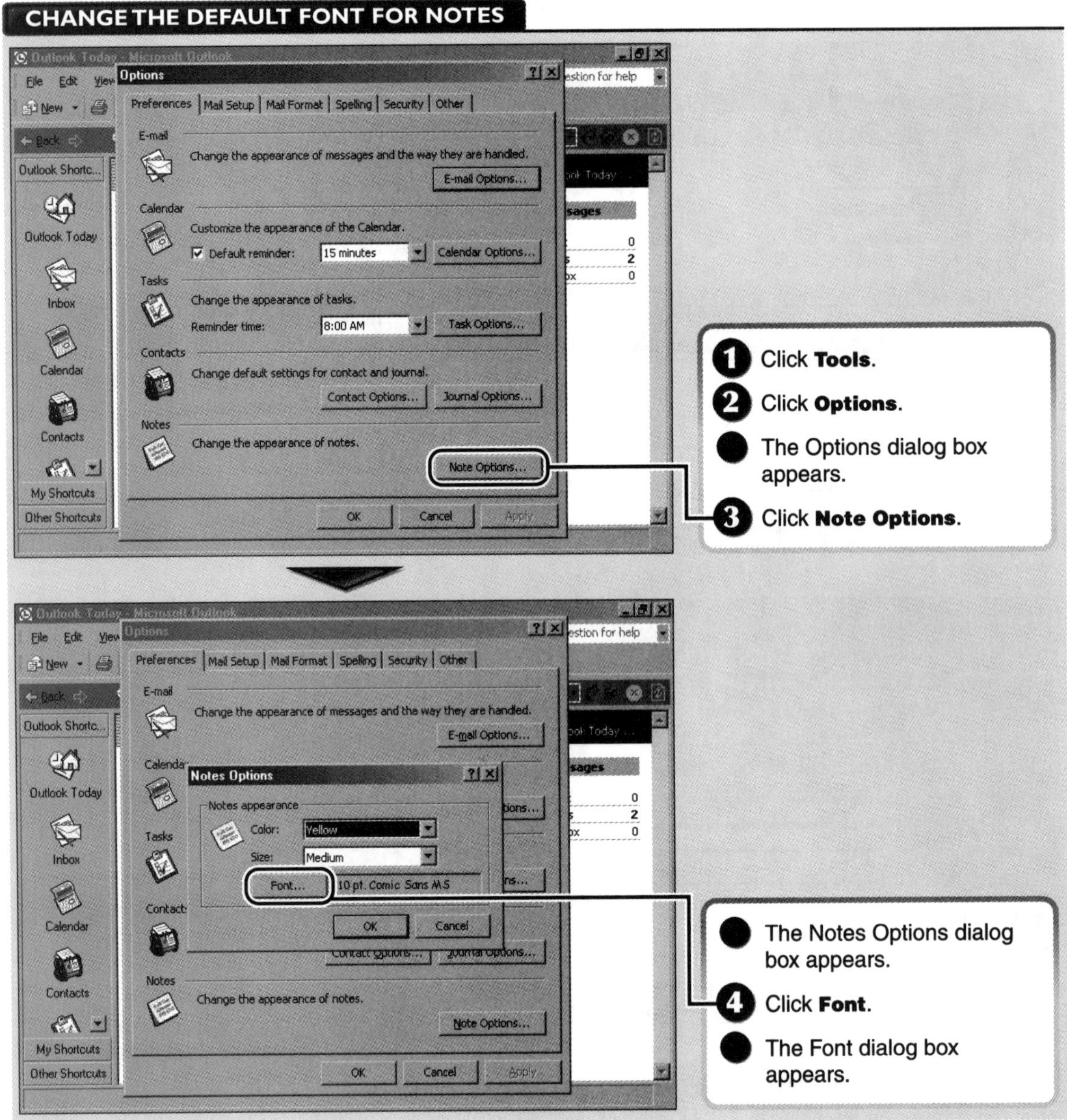

1 Click **Tools**.
2 Click **Options**.
The Options dialog box appears.
3 Click **Note Options**.
The Notes Options dialog box appears.
4 Click **Font**.
The Font dialog box appears.

in an instant

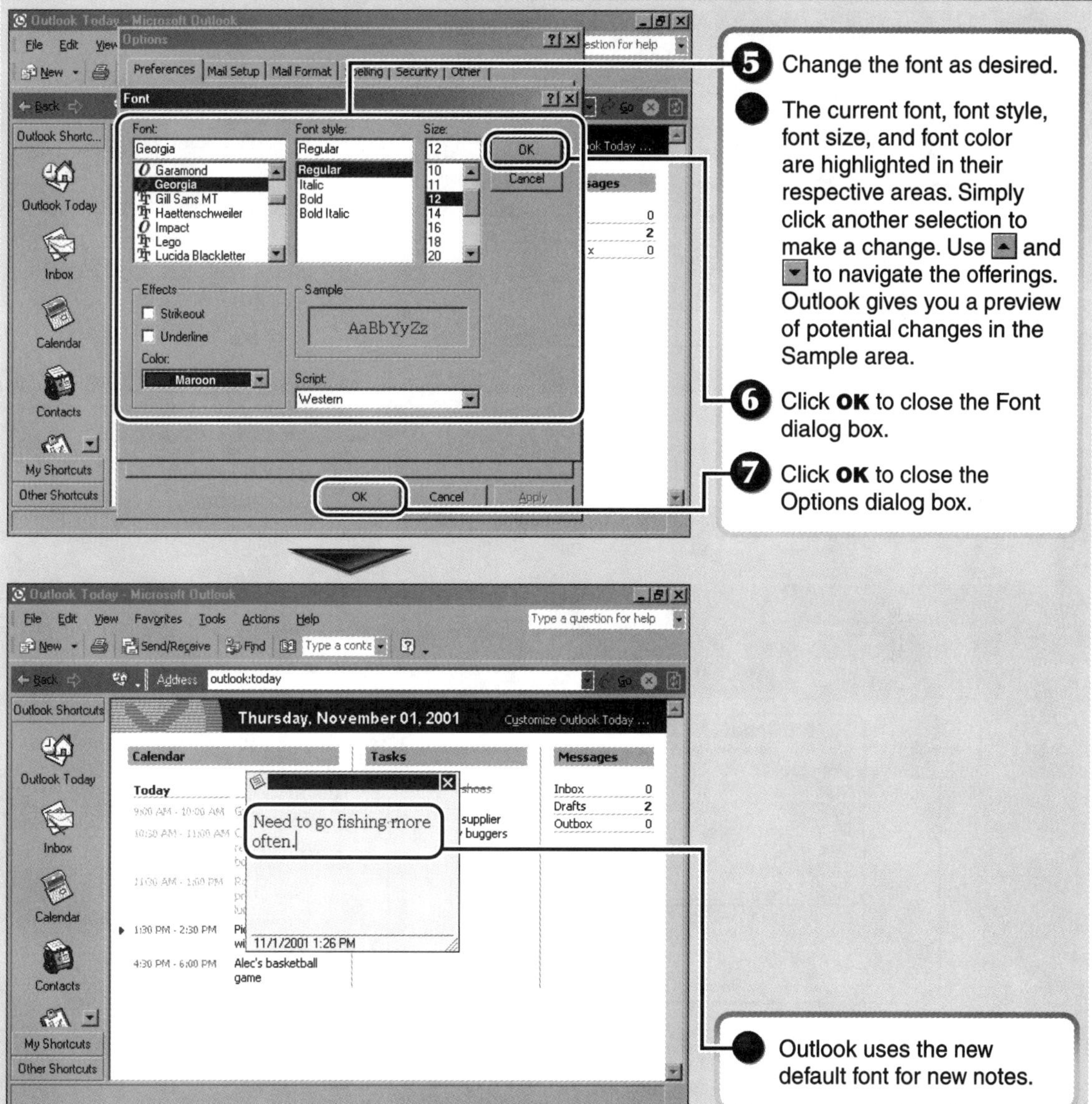

5. Change the font as desired.

- The current font, font style, font size, and font color are highlighted in their respective areas. Simply click another selection to make a change. Use ▲ and ▼ to navigate the offerings. Outlook gives you a preview of potential changes in the Sample area.

6. Click **OK** to close the Font dialog box.

7. Click **OK** to close the Options dialog box.

- Outlook uses the new default font for new notes.

CHANGE THE SIZE OF A NOTE

You can resize Outlook notes by clicking on the corner of the note and dragging the note until it is the desired size.

CHANGE THE SIZE OF A NOTE

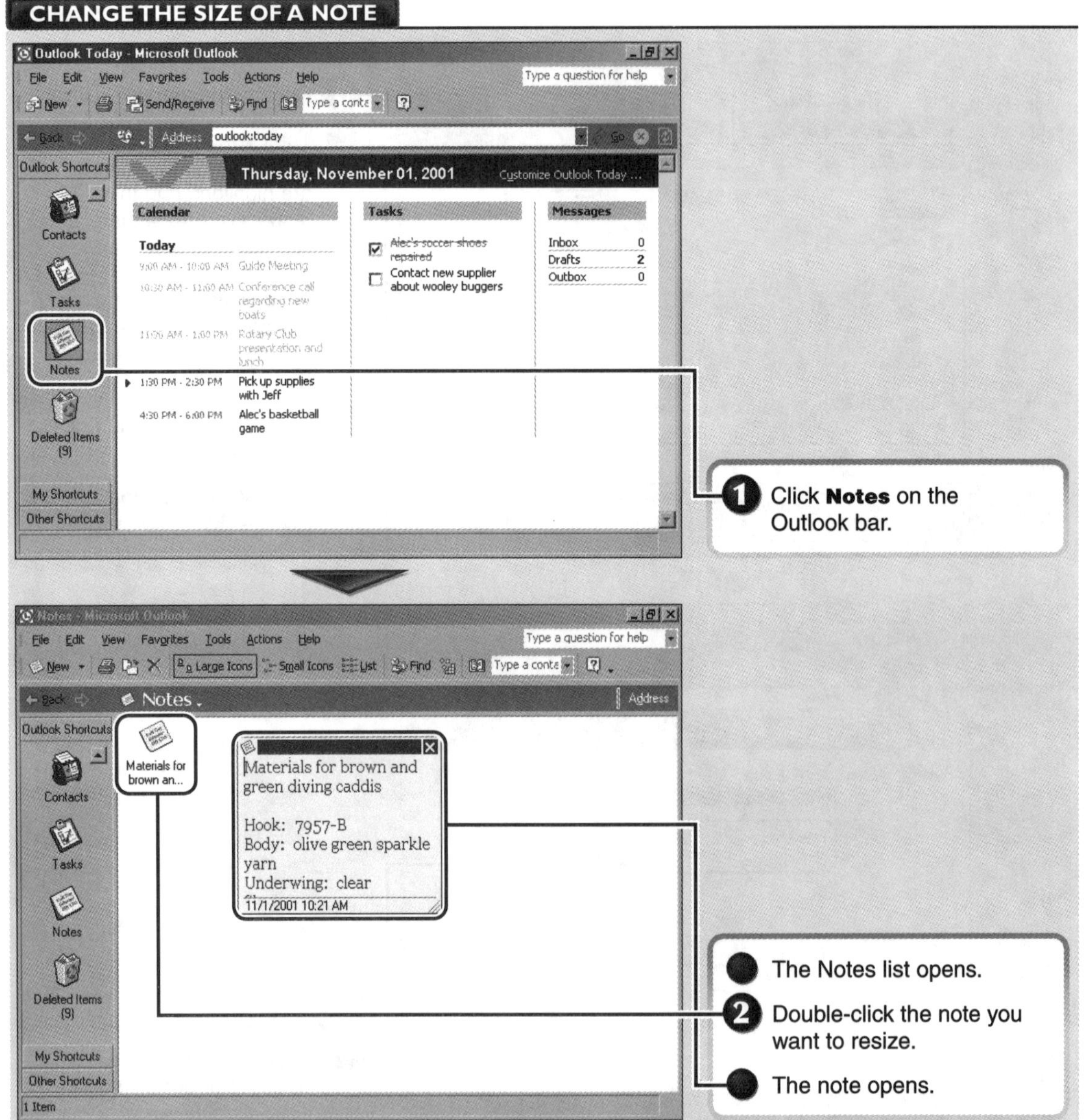

in an instant

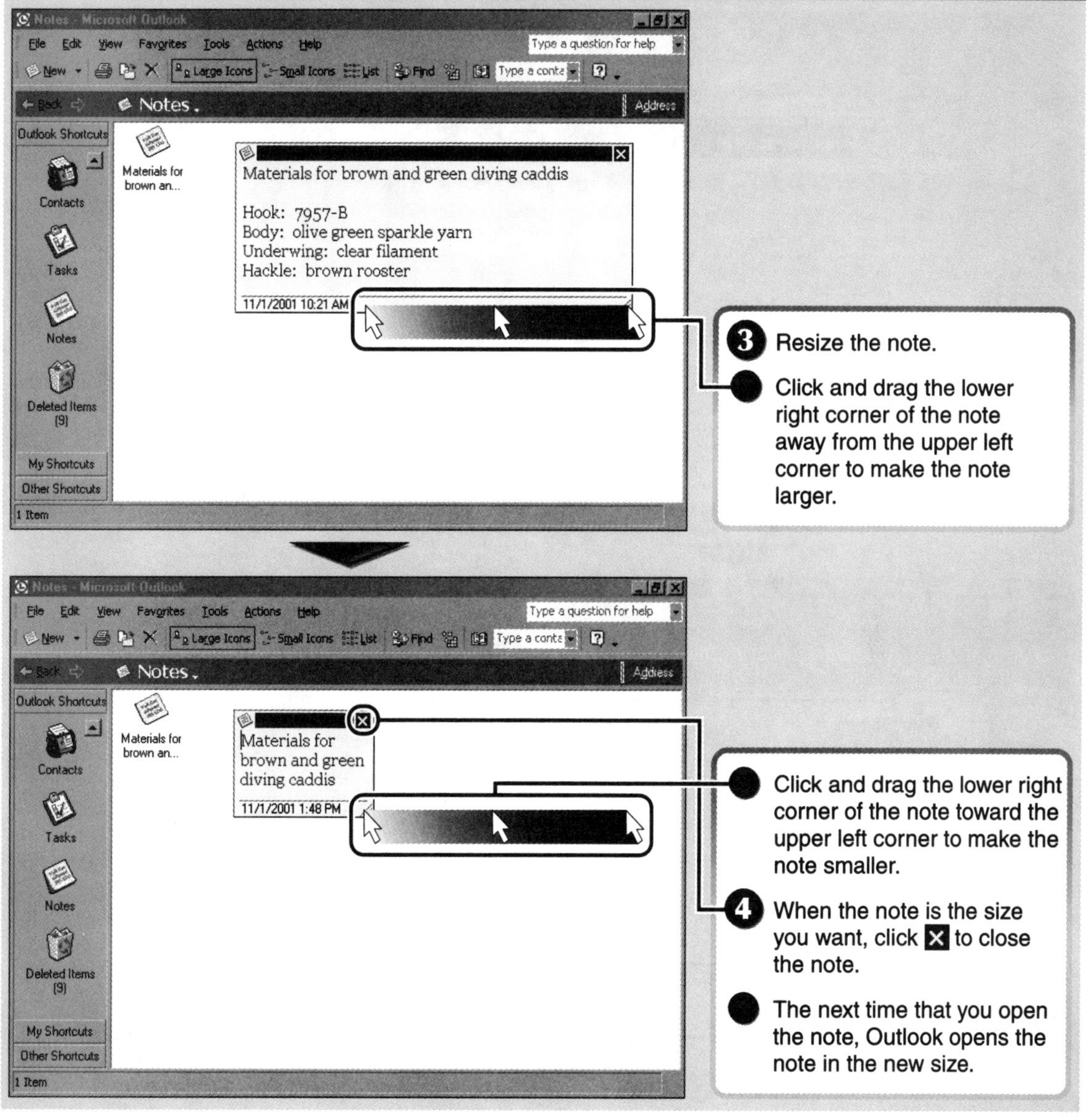

3 Resize the note.

- Click and drag the lower right corner of the note away from the upper left corner to make the note larger.

- Click and drag the lower right corner of the note toward the upper left corner to make the note smaller.

4 When the note is the size you want, click ☒ to close the note.

- The next time that you open the note, Outlook opens the note in the new size.

CHANGE THE COLOR OF A NOTE

You can easily change the color of any Outlook note. This is a convenient way to easily recognize similar notes. For example, you could color all urgent notes with pink, all personal notes with white, and all routine notes with green.

CHANGE THE COLOR OF A NOTE

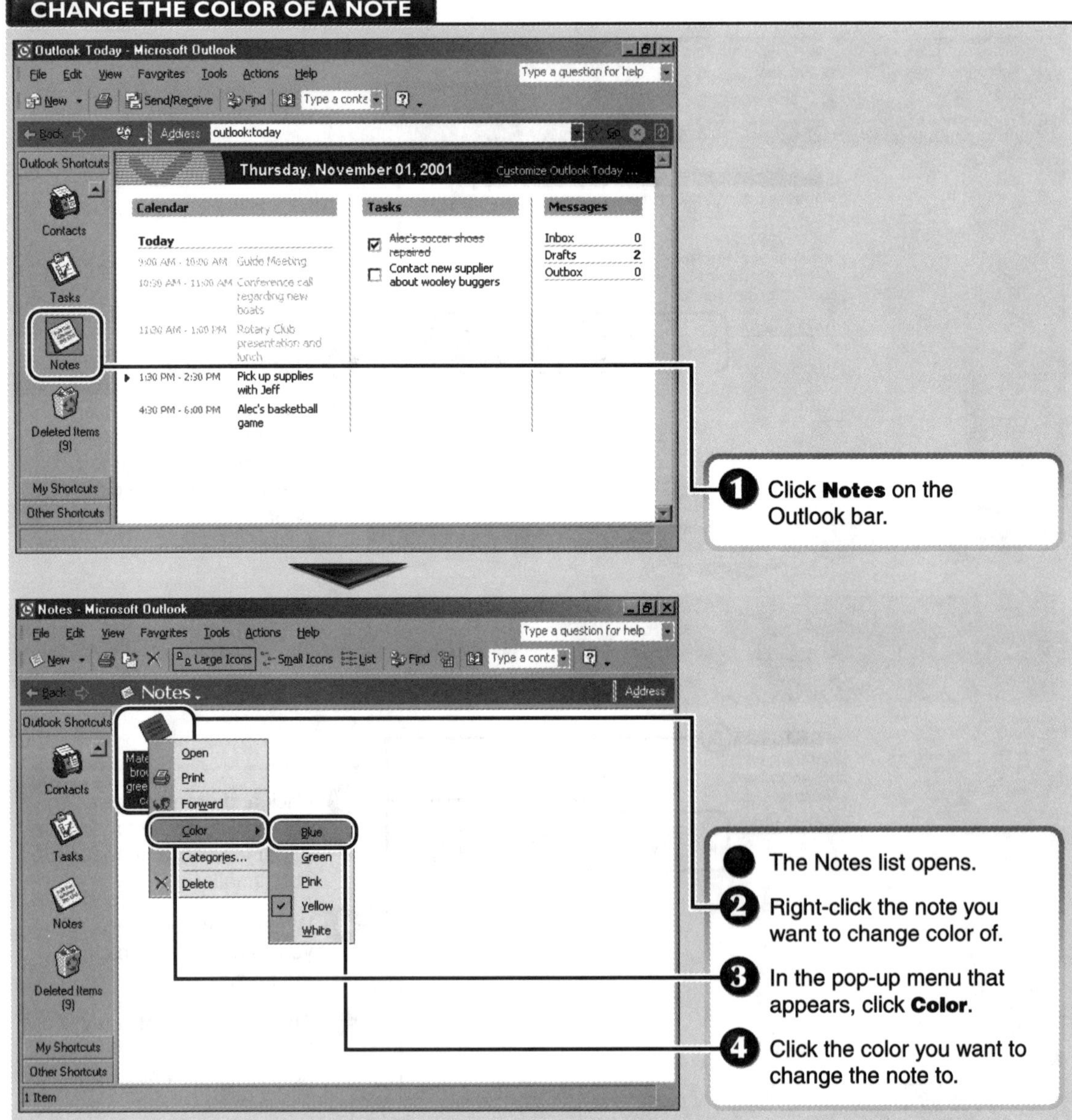

Outlook Today - Microsoft Outlook
Thursday, November 01, 2001
Calendar
Tasks
Messages
Notes
1 Click **Notes** on the Outlook bar.
Notes - Microsoft Outlook
Open
Print
Forward
Color
Categories...
Delete
Blue
Green
Pink
Yellow
White
• The Notes list opens.
2 Right-click the note you want to change color of.
3 In the pop-up menu that appears, click **Color**.
4 Click the color you want to change the note to.

in an instant

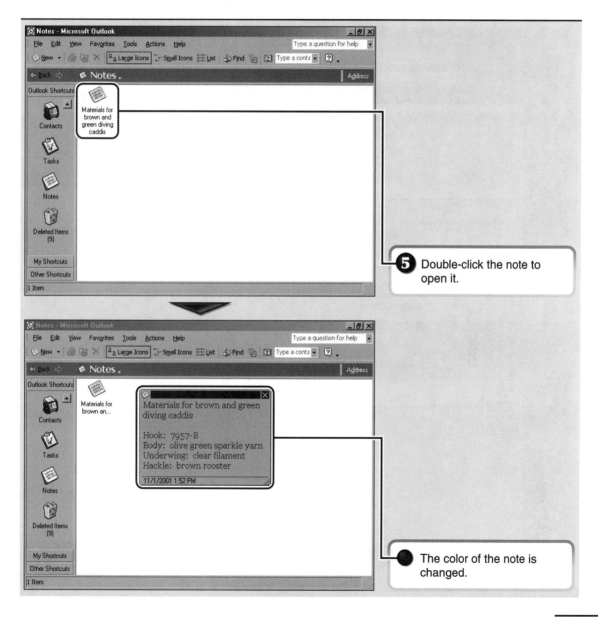

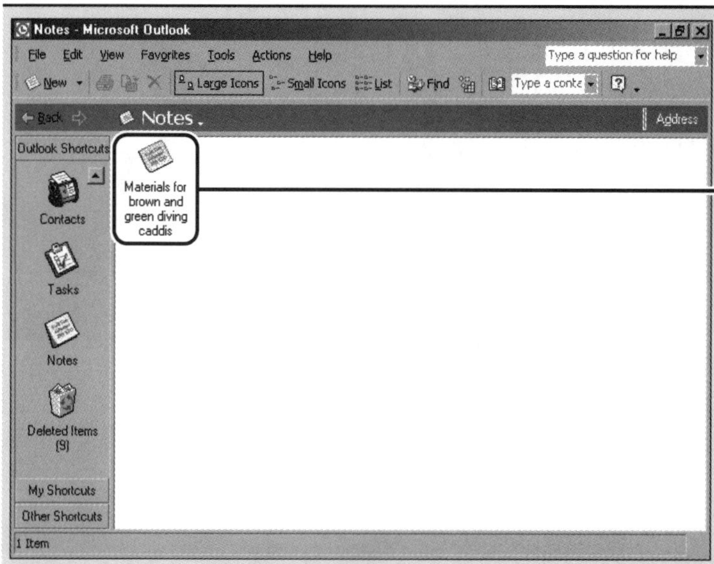

5 Double-click the note to open it.

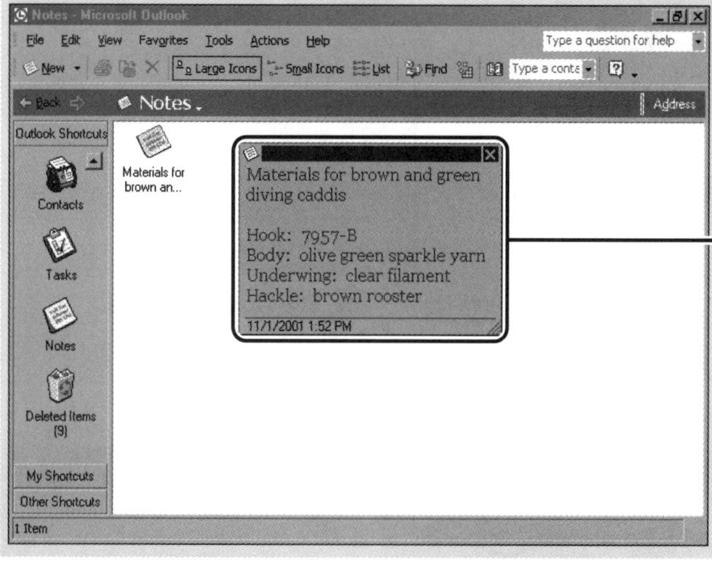

Materials for brown and green diving caddis

Hook: 7957-B
Body: olive green sparkle yarn
Underwing: clear filament
Hackle: brown rooster

11/1/2001 1:52 PM

● The color of the note is changed.

PRINT NOTES

You can easily print notes to take with you.

PRINT NOTES

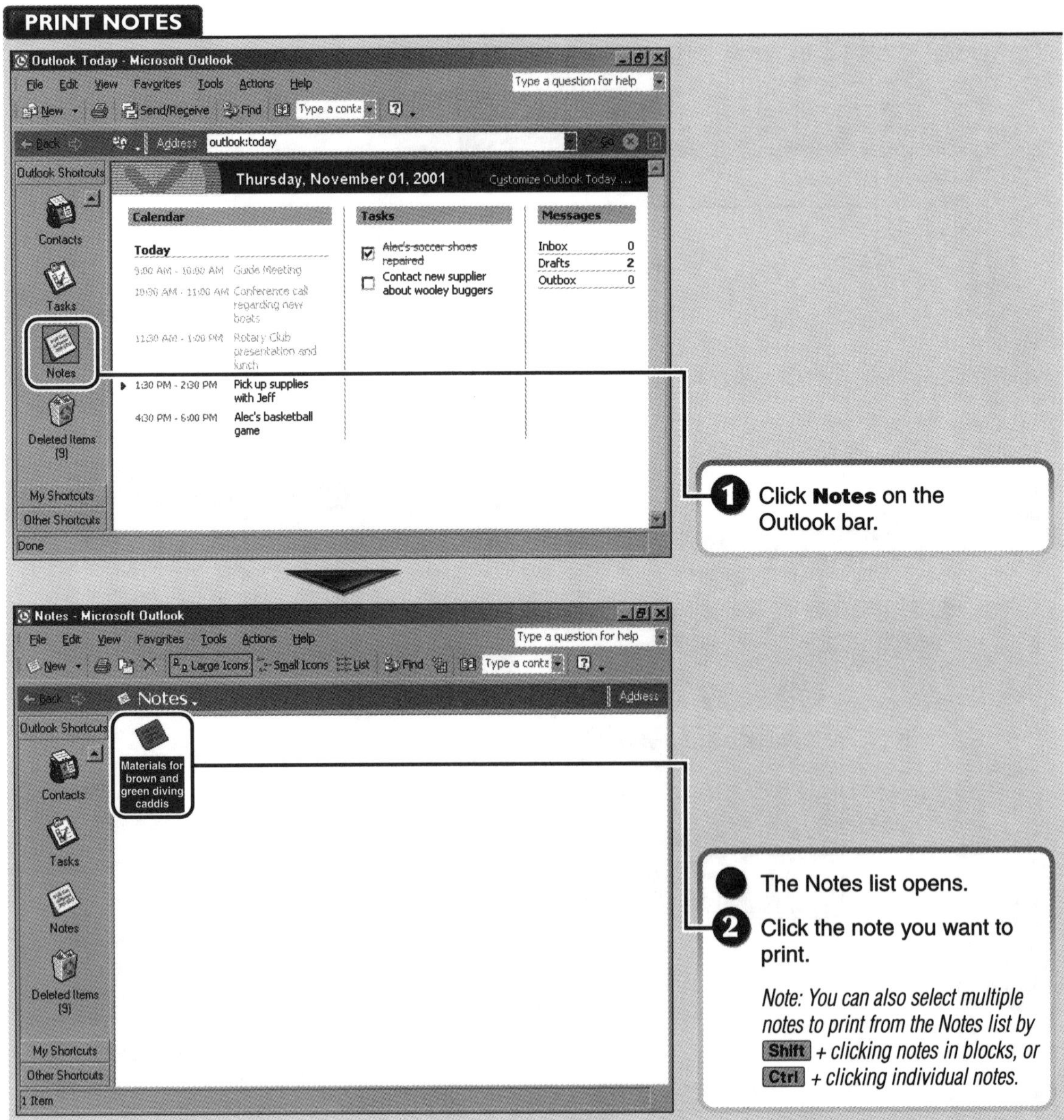

1. Click **Notes** on the Outlook bar.

- The Notes list opens.

2. Click the note you want to print.

Note: You can also select multiple notes to print from the Notes list by **Shift** *+ clicking notes in blocks, or* **Ctrl** *+ clicking individual notes.*

in an instant

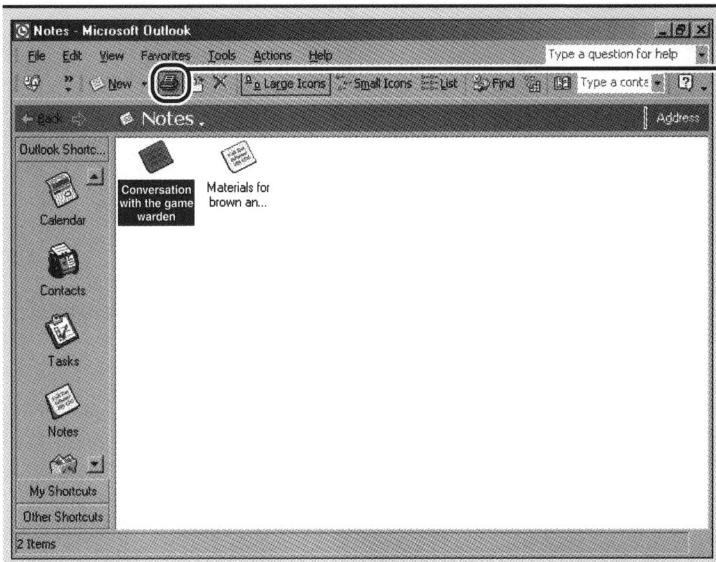

3 Click [print icon].

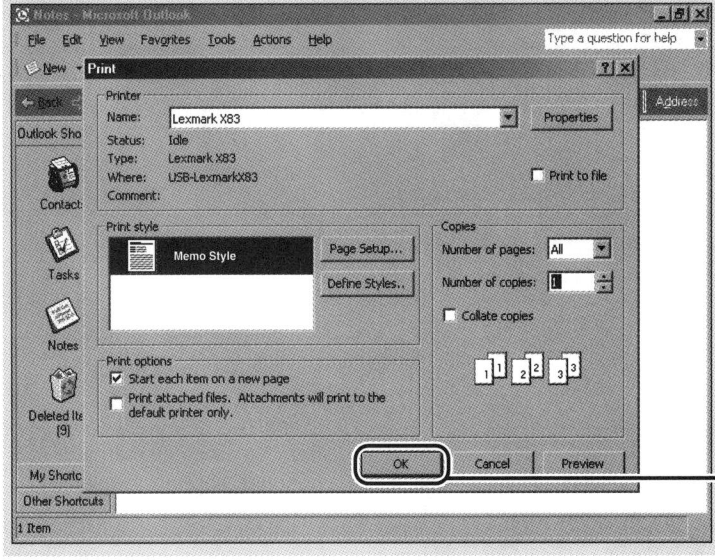

- The Print dialog box appears.

4 Make sure that the printing parameters are set the way you want them.

5 Click **OK** to print.

- Outlook prints the note.

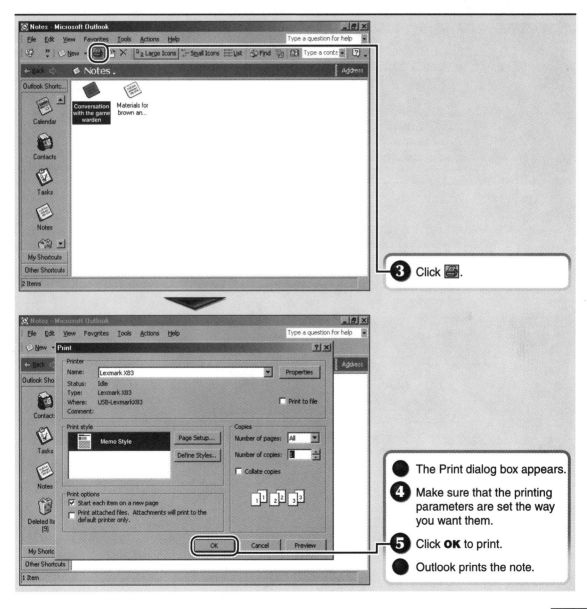

FORMAT A MESSAGE

You can format messages to get just the look you want. *HTML*, a worldwide standard for data interchange over the Internet, offers a wide variety of formatting and layout choices, and most of the e-mail based newsletters you receive today were probably authored using HTML. *Rich text* is another formatting standard with more formatting options than plain text.

FORMAT A MESSAGE

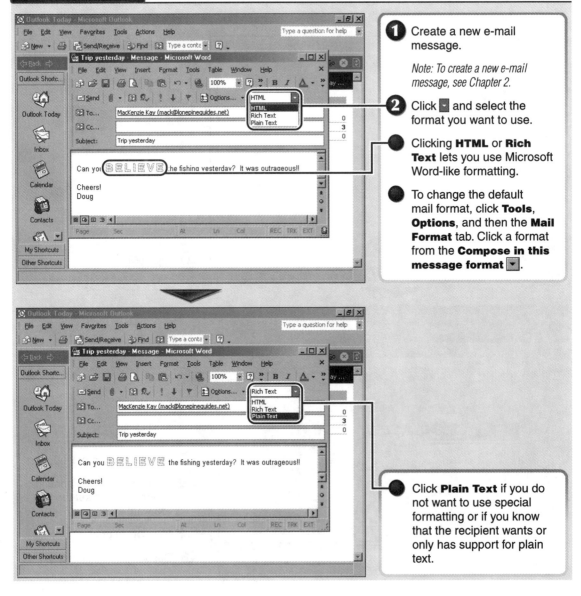

1. Create a new e-mail message.

   Note: To create a new e-mail message, see Chapter 2.

2. Click ▾ and select the format you want to use.

- Clicking **HTML** or **Rich Text** lets you use Microsoft Word-like formatting.
- To change the default mail format, click **Tools**, **Options**, and then the **Mail Format** tab. Click a format from the **Compose in this message format** ▾.

- Click **Plain Text** if you do not want to use special formatting or if you know that the recipient wants or only has support for plain text.

in an instant

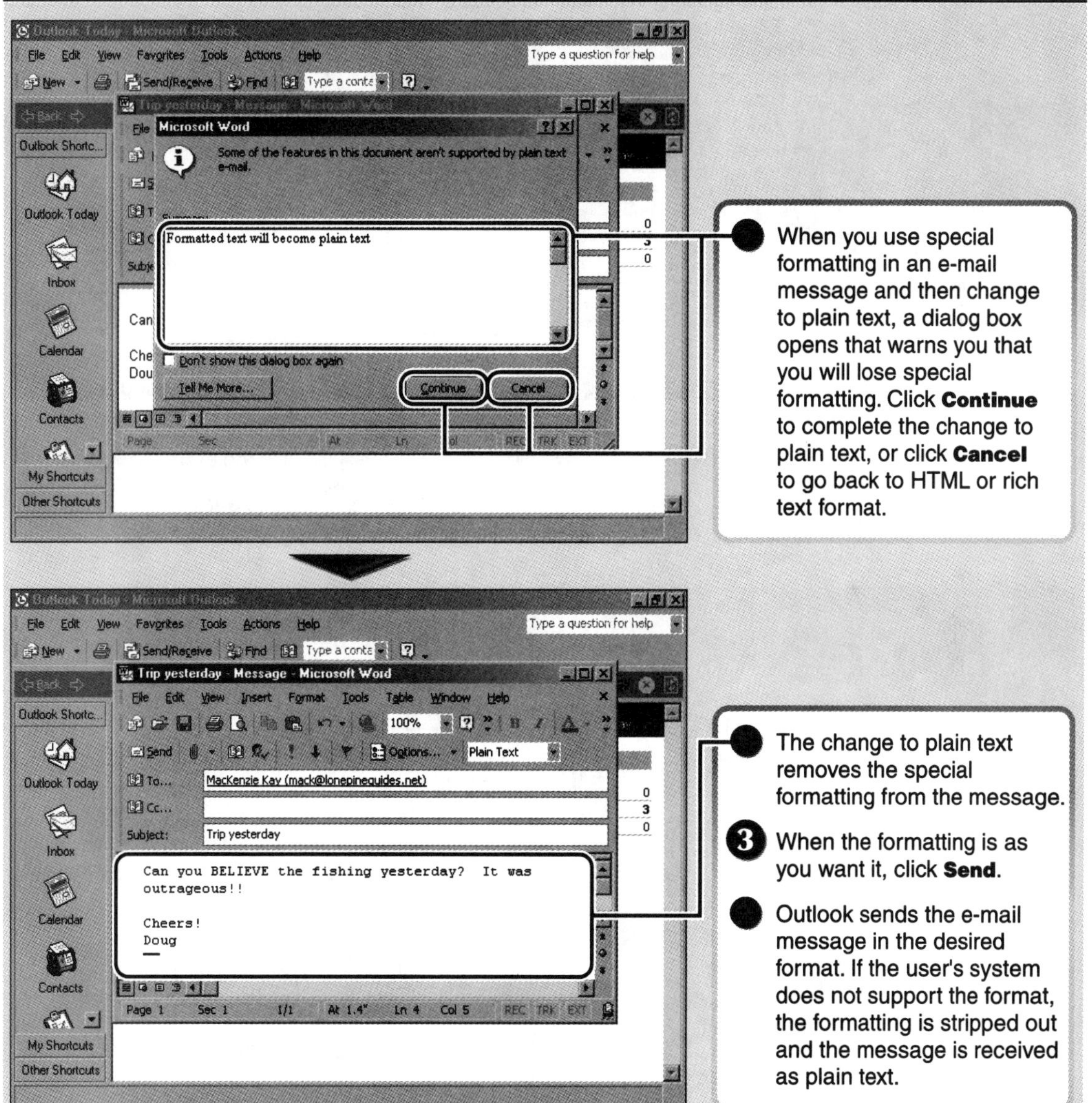

- When you use special formatting in an e-mail message and then change to plain text, a dialog box opens that warns you that you will lose special formatting. Click **Continue** to complete the change to plain text, or click **Cancel** to go back to HTML or rich text format.

- The change to plain text removes the special formatting from the message.

3. When the formatting is as you want it, click **Send**.

- Outlook sends the e-mail message in the desired format. If the user's system does not support the format, the formatting is stripped out and the message is received as plain text.

CHANGE DEFAULT FONTS FOR YOUR E-MAILS

You can change the default fonts you use when composing a new message, when replying or forwarding a message, and when composing and reading plain text.

CHANGE DEFAULT FONTS FOR YOUR E-MAILS

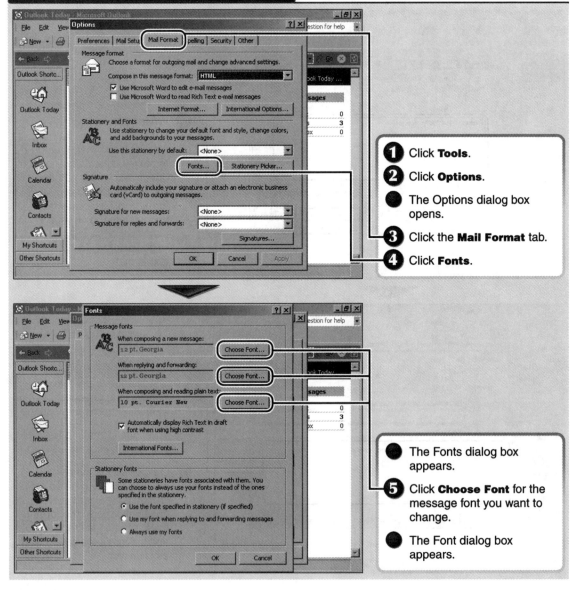

1. Click **Tools**.
2. Click **Options**.
- The Options dialog box opens.
3. Click the **Mail Format** tab.
4. Click **Fonts**.

- The Fonts dialog box appears.
5. Click **Choose Font** for the message font you want to change.
- The Font dialog box appears.

in an instant

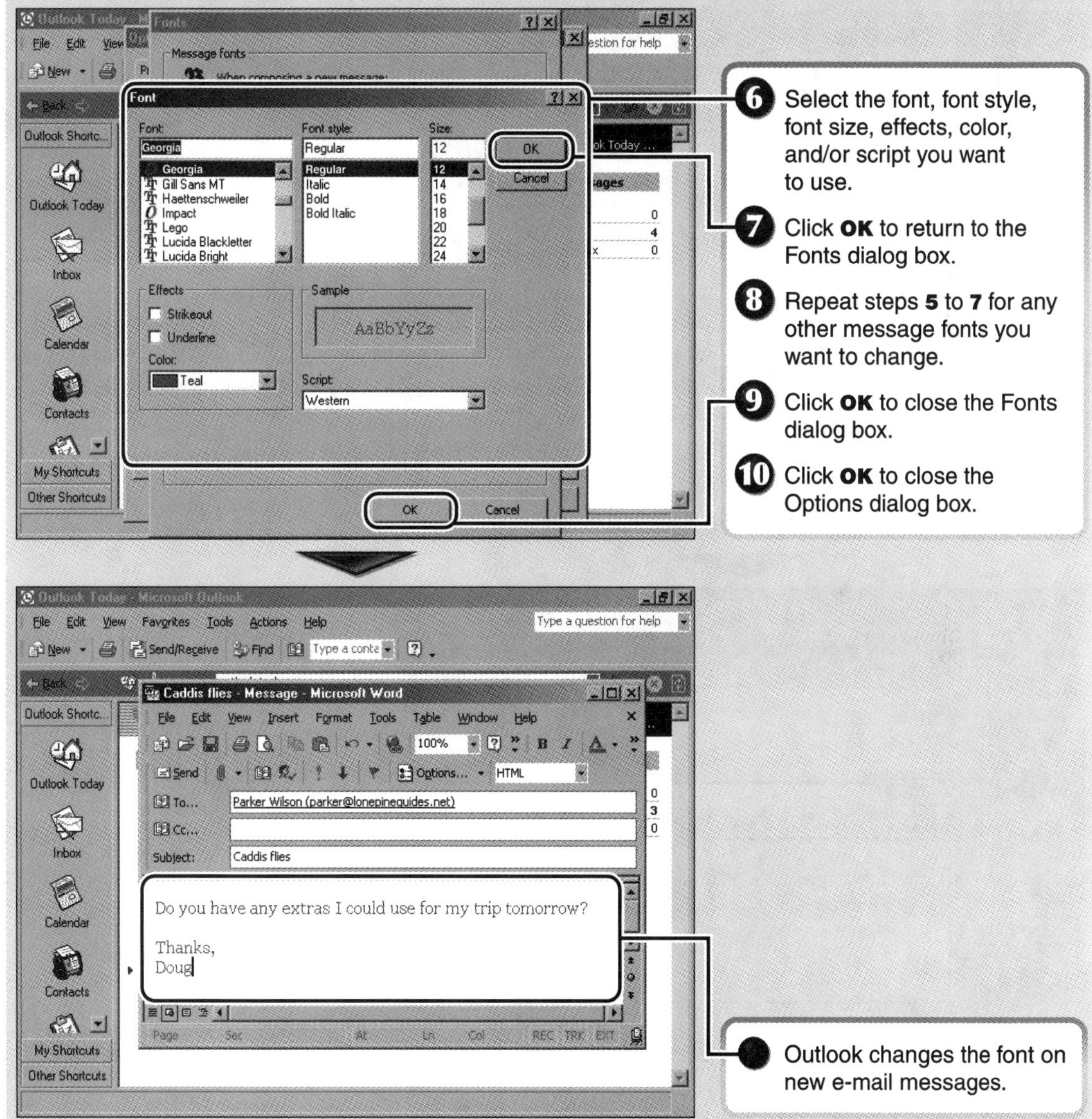

6. Select the font, font style, font size, effects, color, and/or script you want to use.
7. Click **OK** to return to the Fonts dialog box.
8. Repeat steps **5** to **7** for any other message fonts you want to change.
9. Click **OK** to close the Fonts dialog box.
10. Click **OK** to close the Options dialog box.

- Outlook changes the font on new e-mail messages.

USING STATIONERY

Outlook stationery gives the e-mail messages you send a special look, with colorful backgrounds and coordinated fonts. Creative backgrounds and graphics, however, increase the size of each e-mail message, and recipients with slow Internet connections may prefer faster e-mail over better looking e-mail. Also, recipients whose systems support only plain text cannot see the stationery.

USING STATIONERY

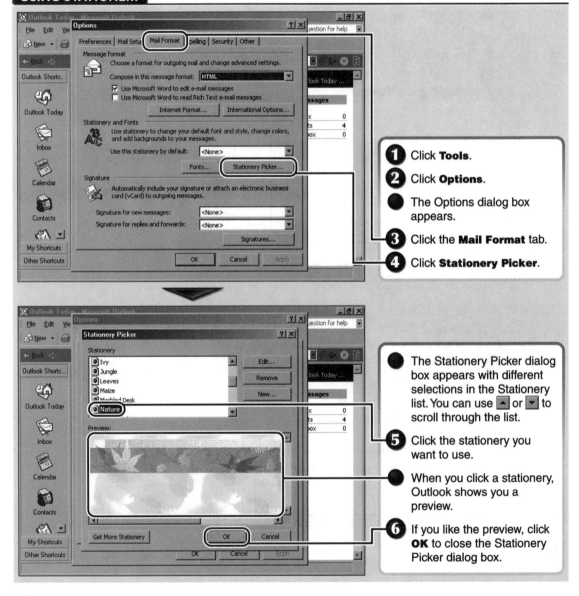

1. Click **Tools**.
2. Click **Options**.
- The Options dialog box appears.
3. Click the **Mail Format** tab.
4. Click **Stationery Picker**.

- The Stationery Picker dialog box appears with different selections in the Stationery list. You can use ▲ or ▼ to scroll through the list.
5. Click the stationery you want to use.
- When you click a stationery, Outlook shows you a preview.
6. If you like the preview, click **OK** to close the Stationery Picker dialog box.

in an instant

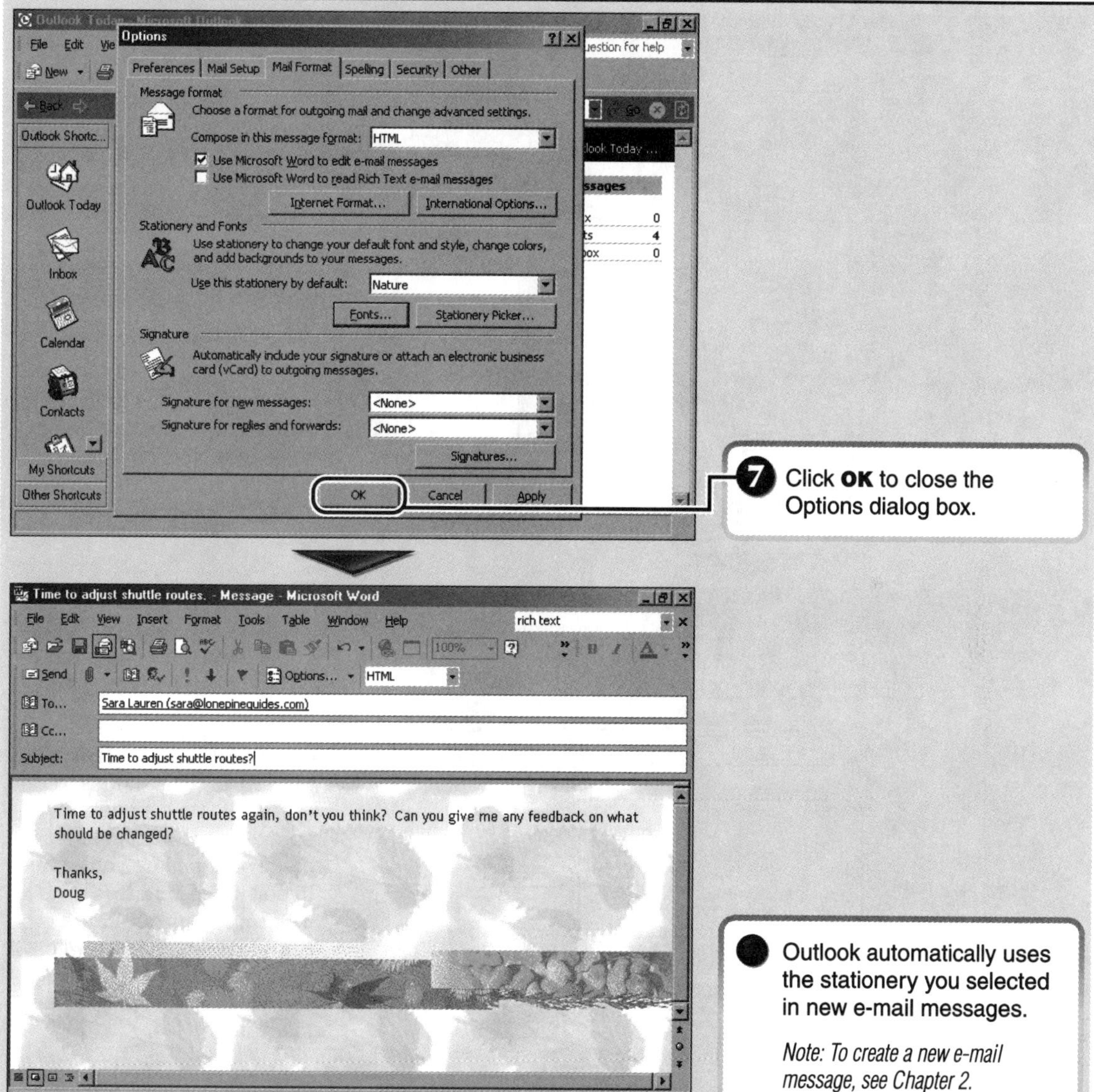

7 Click **OK** to close the Options dialog box.

● Outlook automatically uses the stationery you selected in new e-mail messages.

Note: To create a new e-mail message, see Chapter 2.

ADD SIGNATURE TEXT TO YOUR E-MAILS

You can make Outlook automatically add signature text such as company tag lines or slogans to your e-mail messages. Attaching a *vCard* — a communications standard for data interchange across communications applications like e-mail, contacts management, scheduling, and personal information management — lets recipients with vCard-compatible programs like Outlook store the card in their own address file.

ADD SIGNATURE TEXT TO YOUR E-MAILS

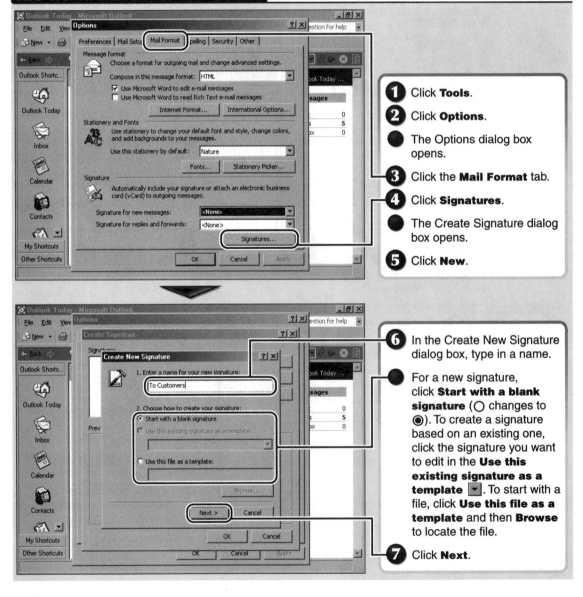

1. Click **Tools**.
2. Click **Options**.
   - The Options dialog box opens.
3. Click the **Mail Format** tab.
4. Click **Signatures**.
   - The Create Signature dialog box opens.
5. Click **New**.

6. In the Create New Signature dialog box, type in a name.
   - For a new signature, click **Start with a blank signature** (○ changes to ◉). To create a signature based on an existing one, click the signature you want to edit in the **Use this existing signature as a template** ▾. To start with a file, click **Use this file as a template** and then **Browse** to locate the file.
7. Click **Next**.

in an instant

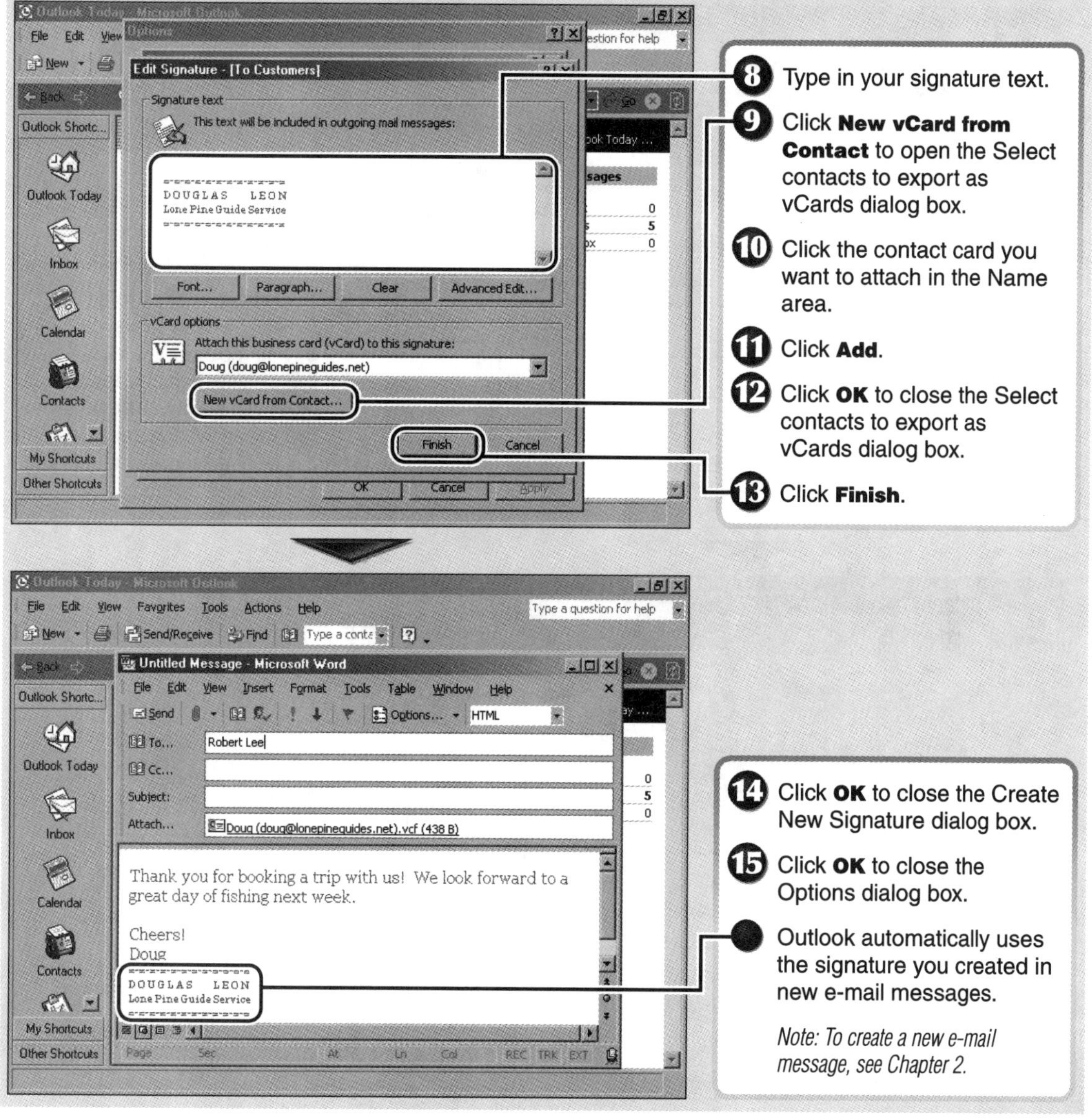

8. Type in your signature text.
9. Click **New vCard from Contact** to open the Select contacts to export as vCards dialog box.
10. Click the contact card you want to attach in the Name area.
11. Click **Add**.
12. Click **OK** to close the Select contacts to export as vCards dialog box.
13. Click **Finish**.
14. Click **OK** to close the Create New Signature dialog box.
15. Click **OK** to close the Options dialog box.

- Outlook automatically uses the signature you created in new e-mail messages.

Note: To create a new e-mail message, see Chapter 2.

REMOVE INDENTS FROM REPLIES AND FORWARDS

You can remove the default indents that Outlook adds to e-mail messages that you reply to or forward. Removing indents on replies and forwards is often a good idea, because if you have a long series of e-mail messages containing a lot of replies, the text ends up indented so far over that it is difficult to read.

REMOVE INDENTS FROM REPLIES AND FORWARDS

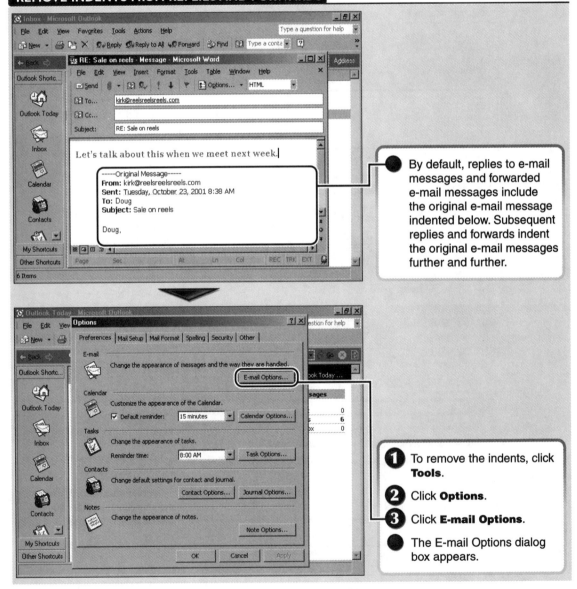

- By default, replies to e-mail messages and forwarded e-mail messages include the original e-mail message indented below. Subsequent replies and forwards indent the original e-mail messages further and further.

1. To remove the indents, click **Tools**.
2. Click **Options**.
3. Click **E-mail Options**.

- The E-mail Options dialog box appears.

in an instant

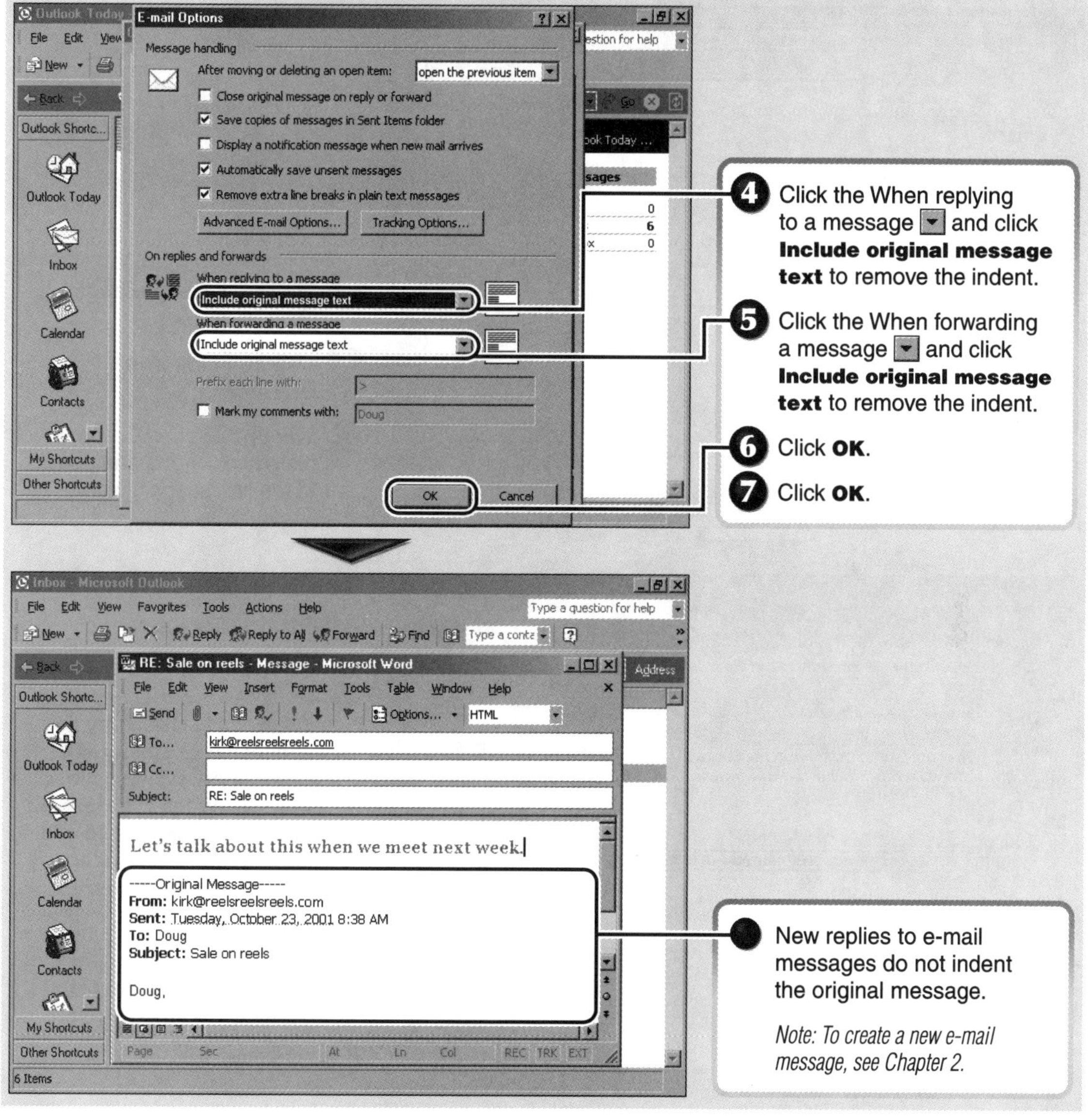

4. Click the When replying to a message ▾ and click **Include original message text** to remove the indent.
5. Click the When forwarding a message ▾ and click **Include original message text** to remove the indent.
6. Click **OK**.
7. Click **OK**.

- New replies to e-mail messages do not indent the original message.

Note: To create a new e-mail message, see Chapter 2.

USING THE SPELL-CHECKER AND AUTOCORRECT

Outlook has a spell-checker feature that you can use right before you send a message to avoid embarrassing mistakes. Outlook also has an AutoCorrect feature that you can use to correct mistakes as you go, saving precious typing time. You can also add entries to the dictionary that Outlook uses and select options for both the spell-checker and AutoCorrect.

CHECK SPELLING

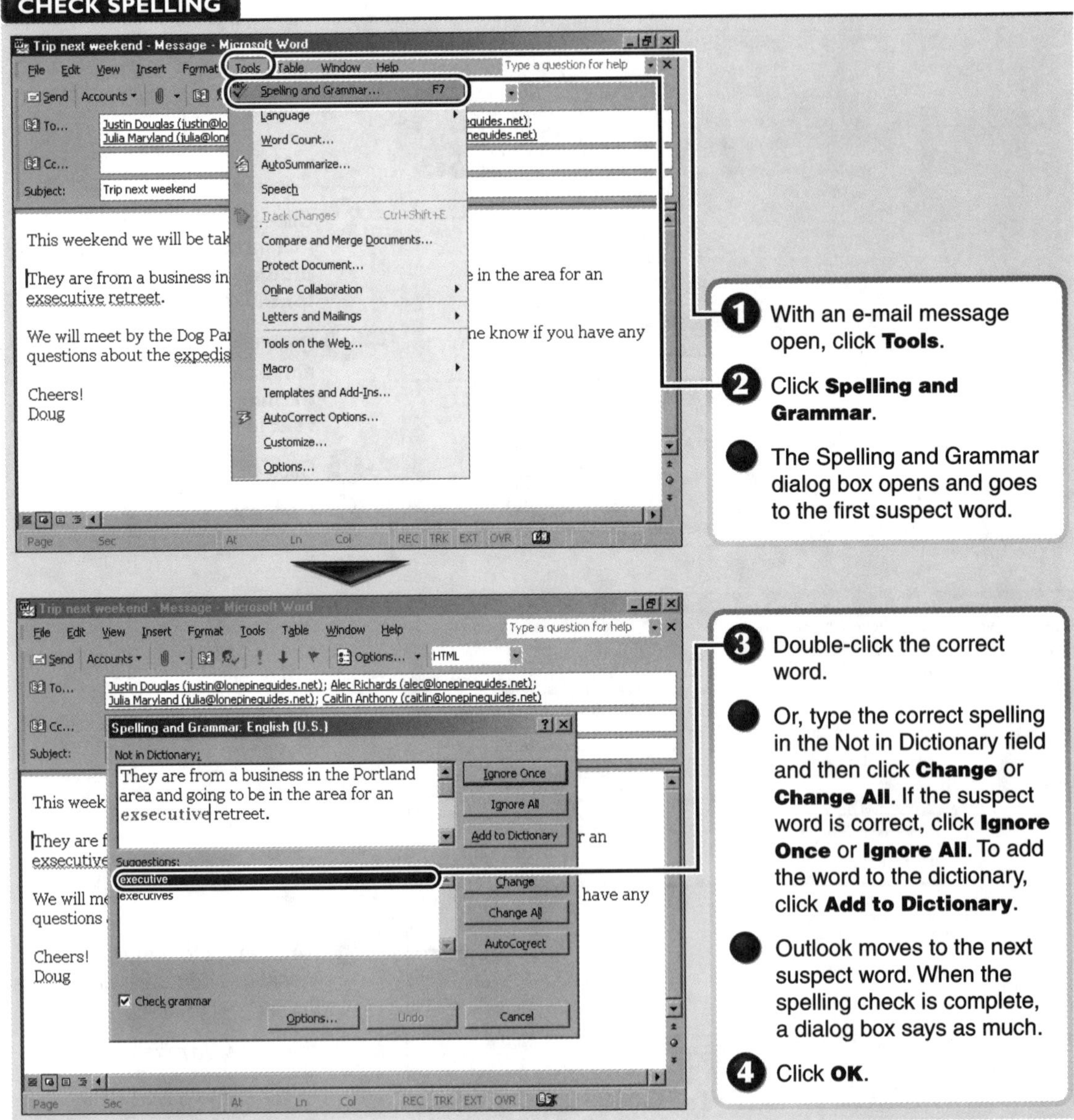

1. With an e-mail message open, click **Tools**.
2. Click **Spelling and Grammar**.

- The Spelling and Grammar dialog box opens and goes to the first suspect word.

3. Double-click the correct word.

- Or, type the correct spelling in the Not in Dictionary field and then click **Change** or **Change All**. If the suspect word is correct, click **Ignore Once** or **Ignore All**. To add the word to the dictionary, click **Add to Dictionary**.
- Outlook moves to the next suspect word. When the spelling check is complete, a dialog box says as much.

4. Click **OK**.

in an instant

SET SPELL-CHECKING AND AUTOCORRECT OPTIONS

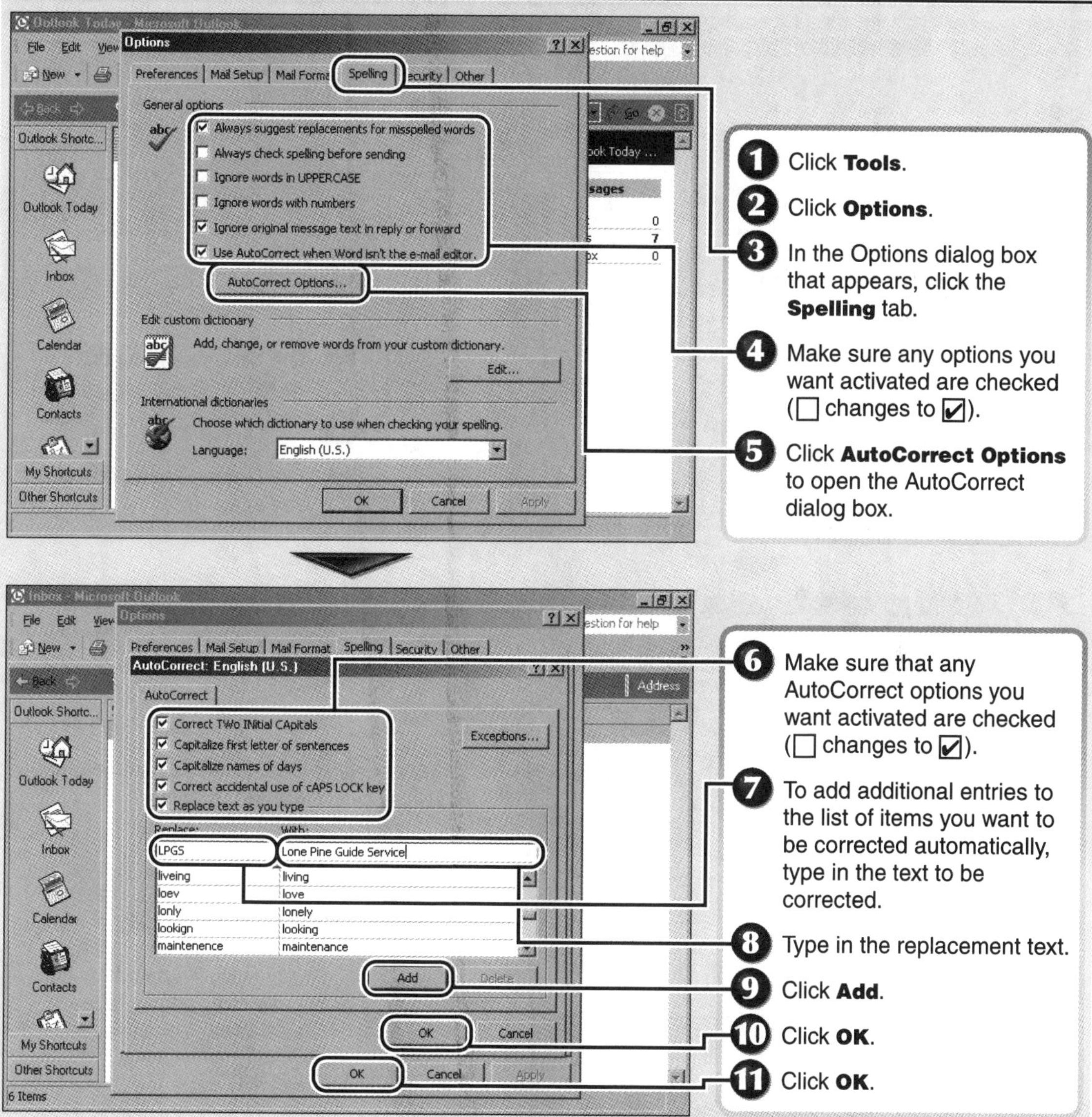

1. Click **Tools**.
2. Click **Options**.
3. In the Options dialog box that appears, click the **Spelling** tab.
4. Make sure any options you want activated are checked (☐ changes to ☑).
5. Click **AutoCorrect Options** to open the AutoCorrect dialog box.
6. Make sure that any AutoCorrect options you want activated are checked (☐ changes to ☑).
7. To add additional entries to the list of items you want to be corrected automatically, type in the text to be corrected.
8. Type in the replacement text.
9. Click **Add**.
10. Click **OK**.
11. Click **OK**.

MARK YOUR COMMENTS

You can reply to e-mail messages with inline comments. Inline comments are responses in the body of the e-mail message that was sent to you. Marking your comments allows the person receiving the message to easily tell the difference between your comments and the message body.

MARK YOUR COMMENTS

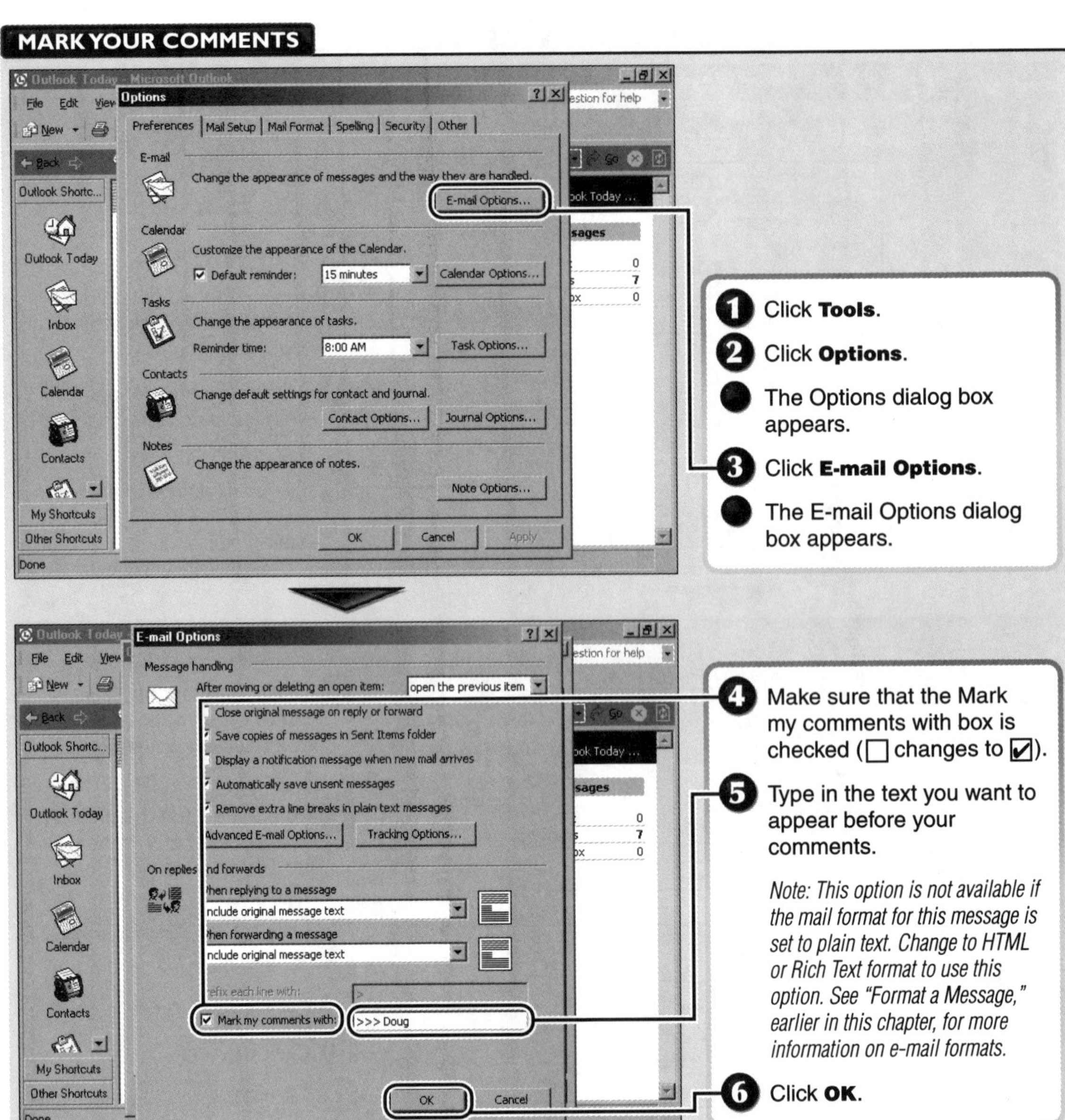

1 Click **Tools**.

2 Click **Options**.

- The Options dialog box appears.

3 Click **E-mail Options**.

- The E-mail Options dialog box appears.

4 Make sure that the Mark my comments with box is checked (☐ changes to ☑).

5 Type in the text you want to appear before your comments.

Note: This option is not available if the mail format for this message is set to plain text. Change to HTML or Rich Text format to use this option. See "Format a Message," earlier in this chapter, for more information on e-mail formats.

6 Click **OK**.

in an instant

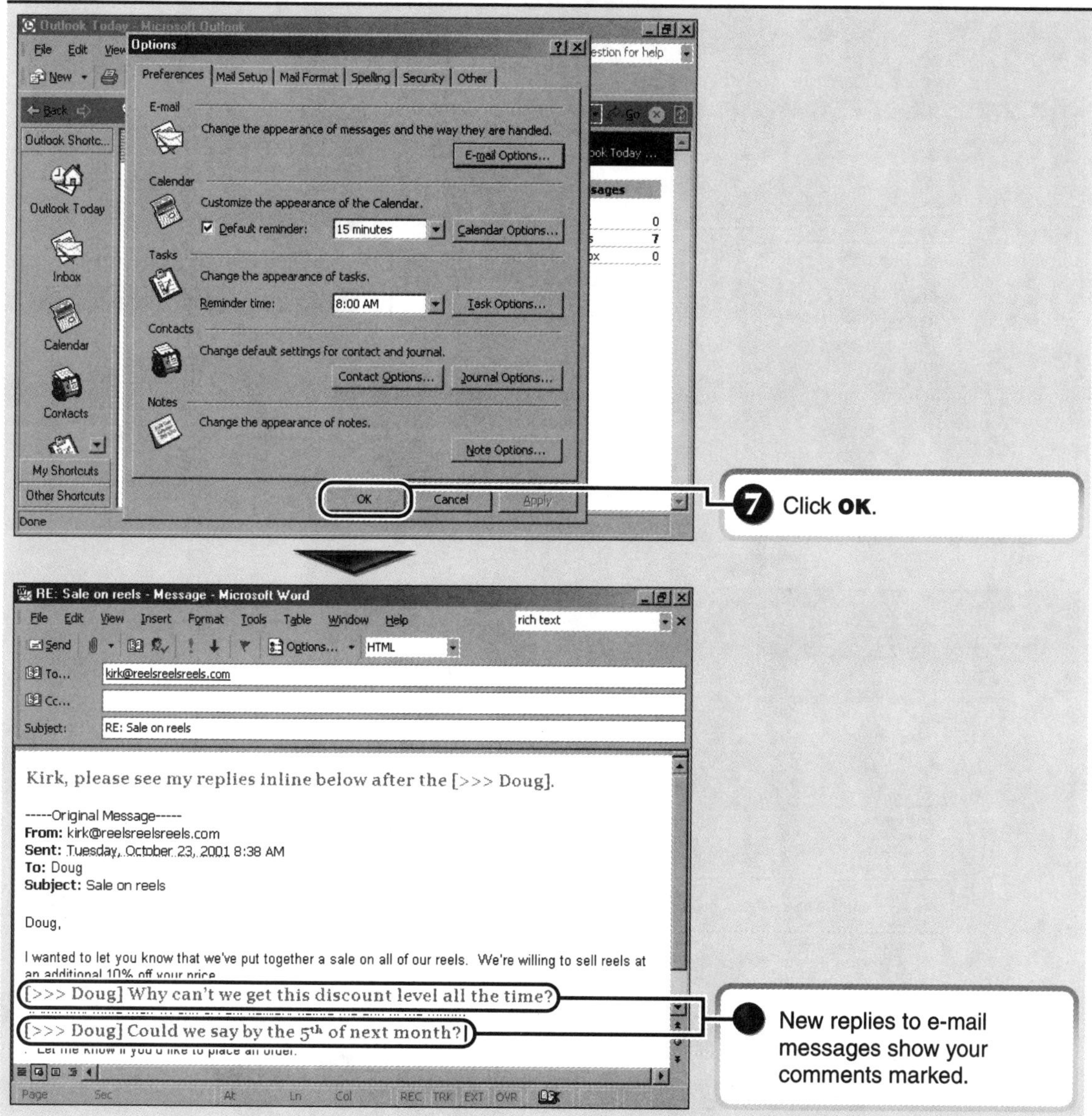

7 Click **OK**.

● New replies to e-mail messages show your comments marked.

ADD AND SEND FROM DIFFERENT E-MAIL ADDRESSES

You can use Outlook as your e-mail client for multiple e-mail accounts. After you have added the accounts to Outlook, you can select which e-mail account you want to send a message from while composing the message. Outlook 2002 gives you this capability, even with Web-based e-mail services like Hotmail.

ADD AND SEND FROM DIFFERENT E-MAIL ADDRESSES

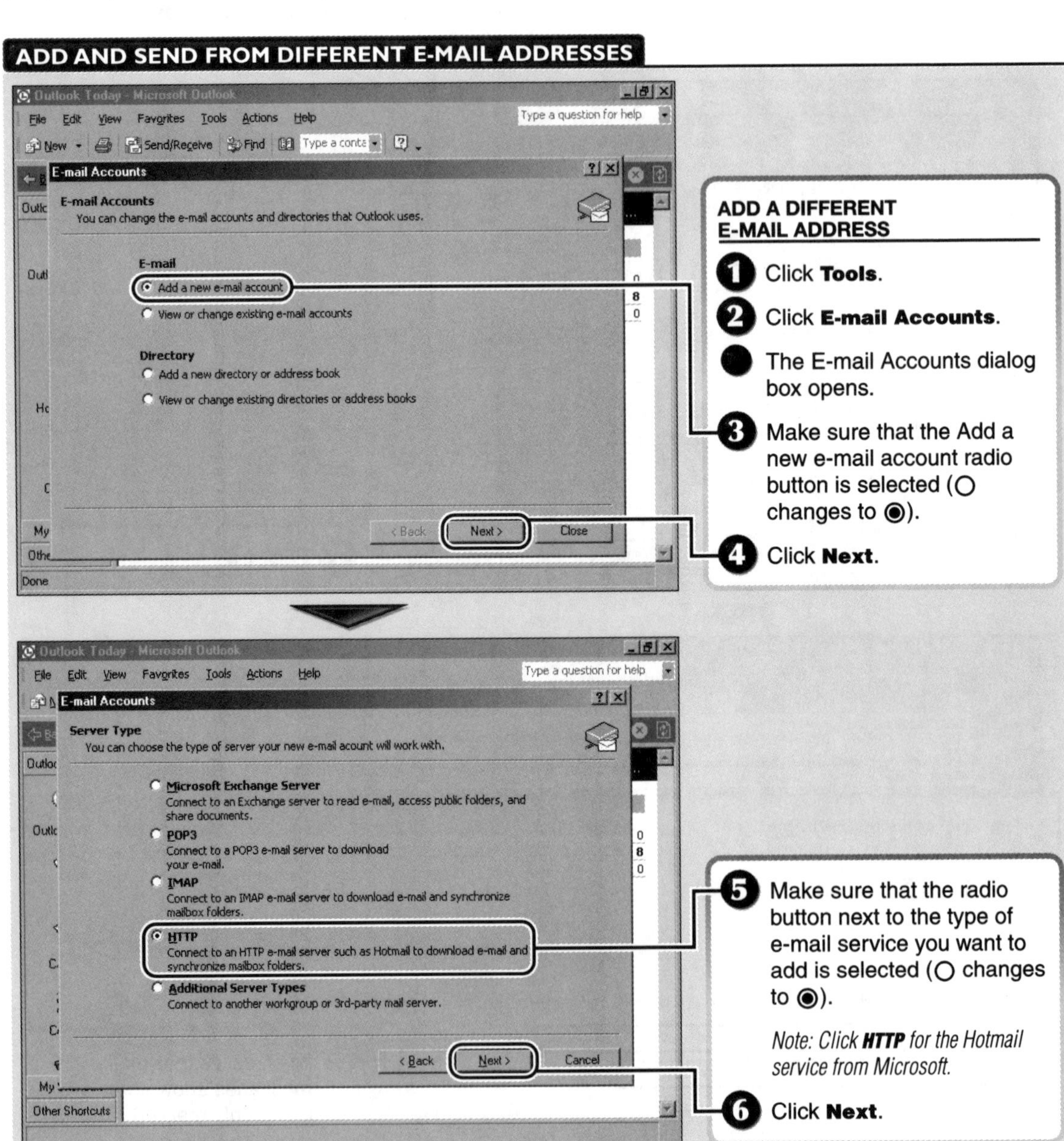

ADD A DIFFERENT E-MAIL ADDRESS

1. Click **Tools**.
2. Click **E-mail Accounts**.

- The E-mail Accounts dialog box opens.

3. Make sure that the Add a new e-mail account radio button is selected (○ changes to ◉).
4. Click **Next**.

5. Make sure that the radio button next to the type of e-mail service you want to add is selected (○ changes to ◉).

   *Note: Click **HTTP** for the Hotmail service from Microsoft.*

6. Click **Next**.

in an instant

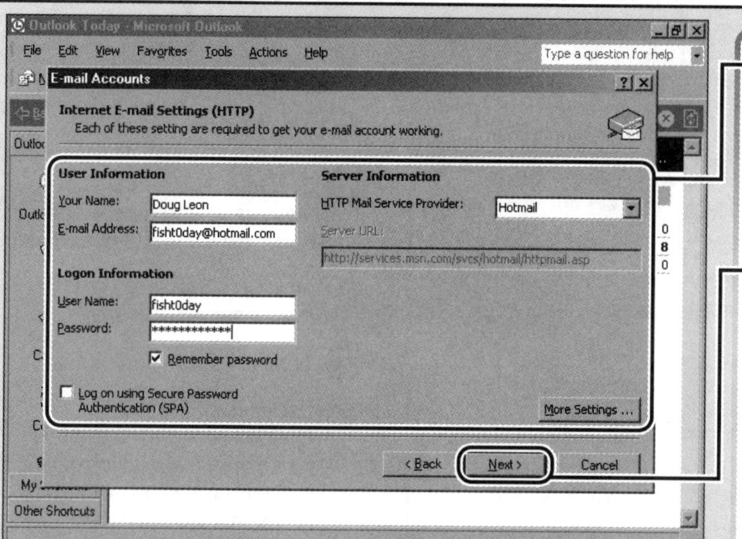

7 Complete the information about the service you want to add.

Note: For more information about setting up e-mail accounts, see Chapter 1.

8 Click **Next**.

- The E-mail Accounts dialog box opens.

9 Click **Finish**.

- The new e-mail account is set up. Now you can choose which e-mail account you want to send e-mail from.

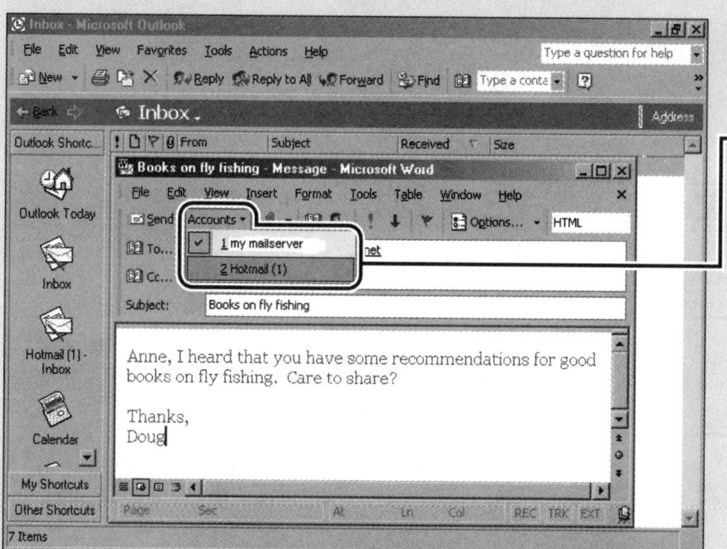

SEND FROM A DIFFERENT E-MAIL ADDRESS

- When you send an e-mail message, the Accounts ▾ enables you to choose which account to send the e-mail message from.

Note: The default account is the one in the top position in the E-mail Accounts dialog box. Even if you send an e-mail message from an account that is not the default account, the next e-mail message you send will be sent from the default account unless you specifically change it.

INCLUDE A LINK IN A MESSAGE

A hyperlink is a bit of text that, when clicked, displays another document, such as a Web page. You can add a hyperlink to a document or Web page in an e-mail message simply by typing the address. When you begin the hyperlink with a standard prefix like *http://*, *www.*, or \\, Outlook recognizes the text as a link and automatically formats it as such.

INCLUDE A LINK IN A MESSAGE

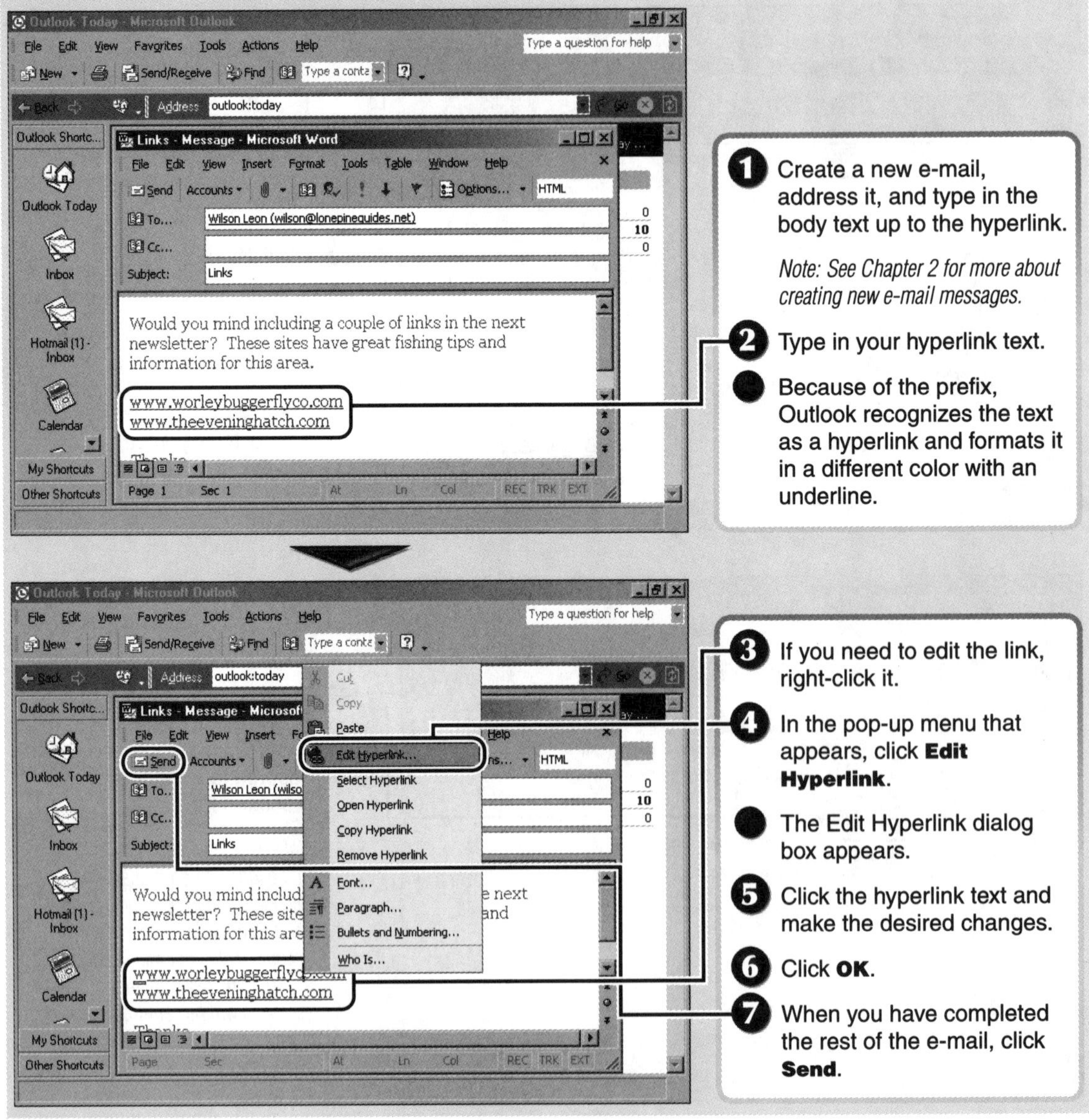

1. Create a new e-mail, address it, and type in the body text up to the hyperlink.

   Note: See Chapter 2 for more about creating new e-mail messages.

2. Type in your hyperlink text.

- Because of the prefix, Outlook recognizes the text as a hyperlink and formats it in a different color with an underline.

3. If you need to edit the link, right-click it.
4. In the pop-up menu that appears, click **Edit Hyperlink**.

- The Edit Hyperlink dialog box appears.

5. Click the hyperlink text and make the desired changes.
6. Click **OK**.
7. When you have completed the rest of the e-mail, click **Send**.

VIEW WEB PAGES FROM WITHIN OUTLOOK

You do not need to leave Outlook and go to a browser to view Web pages. You can view Web pages from directly within Outlook.

VIEW WEB PAGES FROM WITHIN OUTLOOK

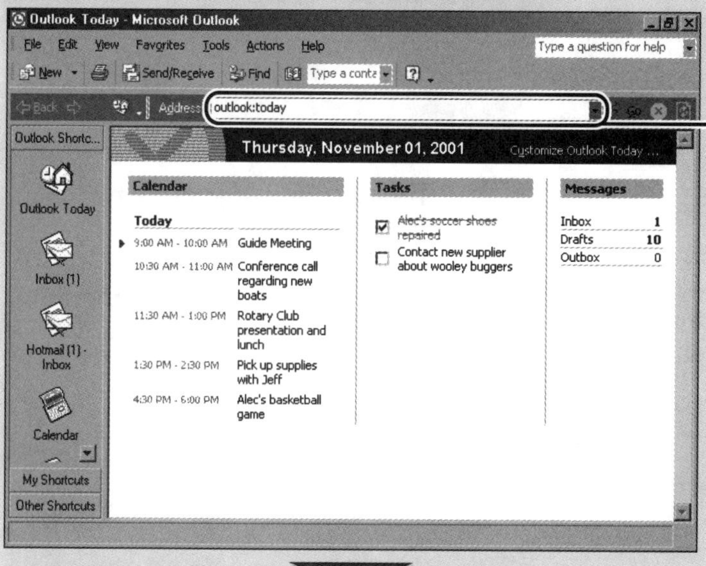

1. Make sure that the Web toolbar is visible.

- Click **View**, then **Toolbars**, and then **Web** to summon the toolbar.

2. Type in the Web site address.

3. Press Enter.

- You can also click the **Address** ▾ and select a Web site from the pop-up list of prior Web sites accessed that Outlook keeps.

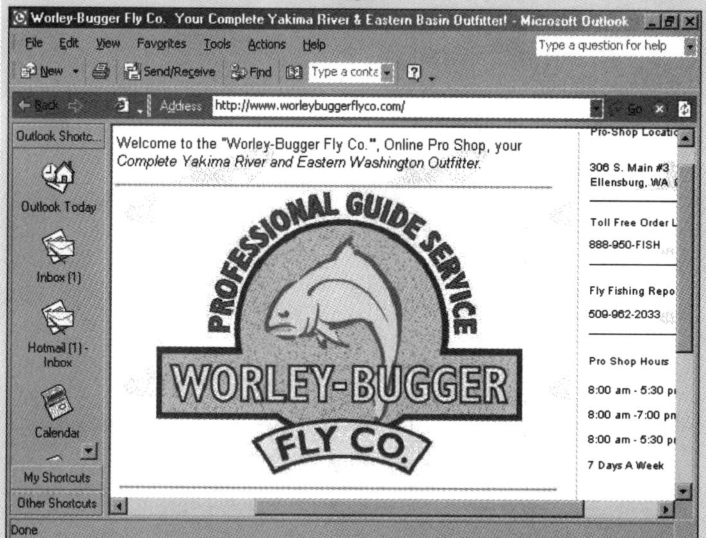

- Outlook displays the Web page.

ADD A SHORTCUT TO A WEB PAGE

Links in Outlook messages do not have to begin with standard hyperlink prefixes like *http://* or *www.* You can use Outlook to turn any text into a shortcut to a Web page. Turning a short piece of text into a hyperlink is especially convenient when you are linking to a very long Web site address and don't want the recipient to see an "ugly URL."

ADD A SHORTCUT TO A WEB PAGE

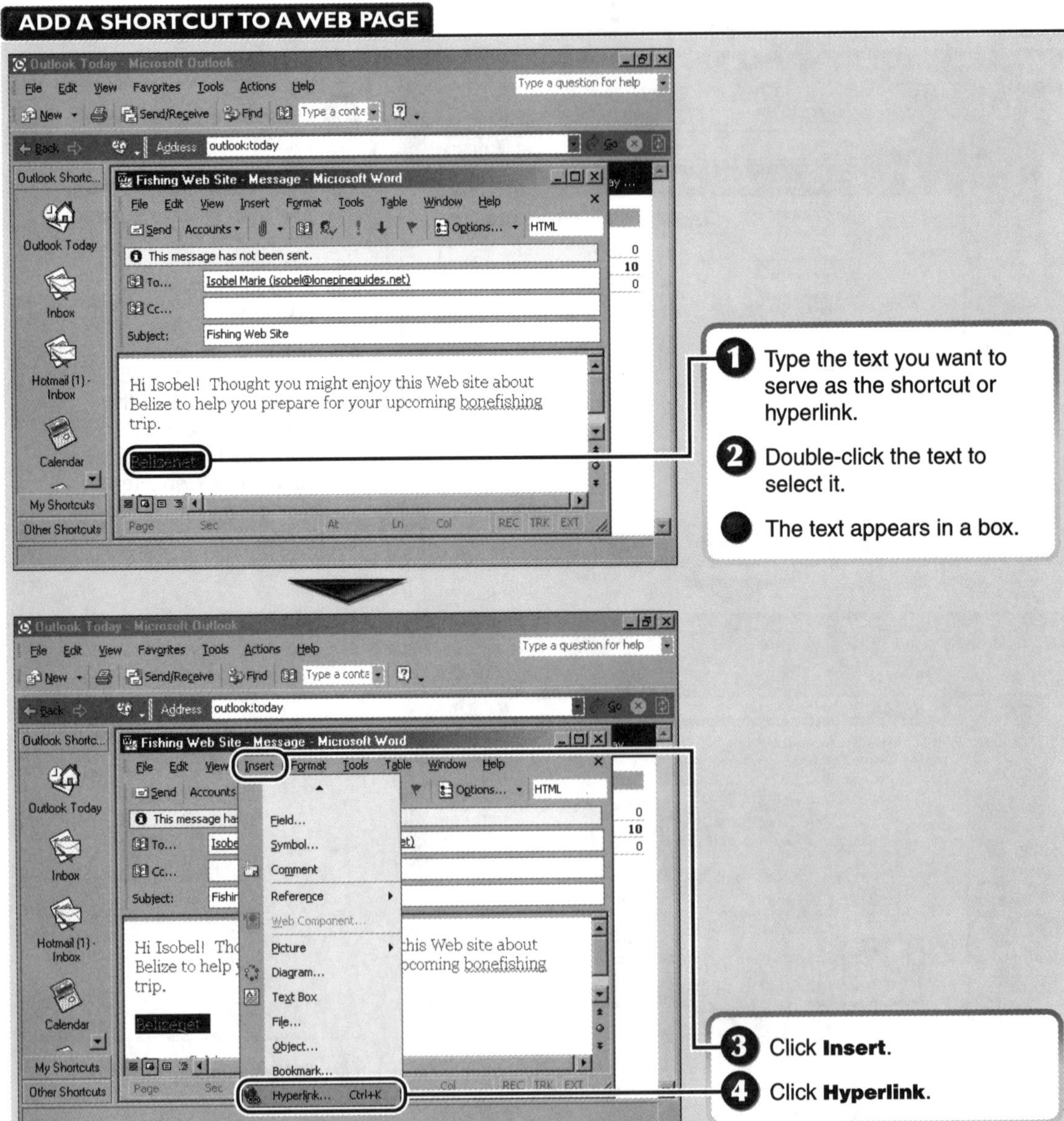

1 Type the text you want to serve as the shortcut or hyperlink.

2 Double-click the text to select it.

- The text appears in a box.

3 Click **Insert**.

4 Click **Hyperlink**.

in an instant

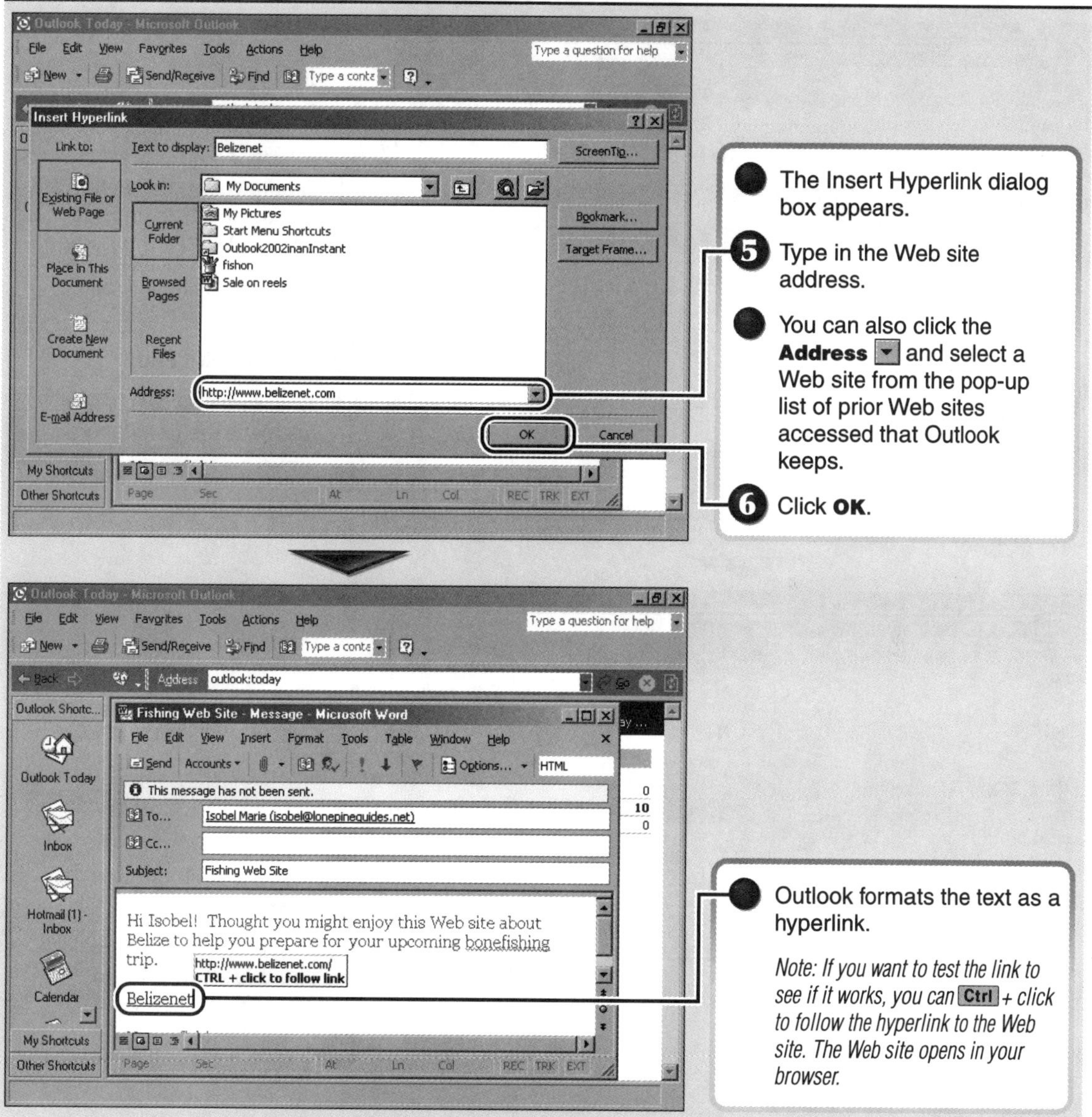

- The Insert Hyperlink dialog box appears.

5. Type in the Web site address.

- You can also click the **Address** ▾ and select a Web site from the pop-up list of prior Web sites accessed that Outlook keeps.

6. Click **OK**.

- Outlook formats the text as a hyperlink.

Note: If you want to test the link to see if it works, you can **Ctrl** *+ click to follow the hyperlink to the Web site. The Web site opens in your browser.*

SEND AN HTML-BASED NEWSLETTER

You can send your own professional-looking newsletters and e-mailings by using Outlook in combination with another Microsoft program, such as Word or FrontPage. One caveat: The process of sending the newsletter sends only the Web page text. Do not include graphics unless they are hosted on a Web server that all the recipients can access.

SEND AN HTML-BASED NEWSLETTER

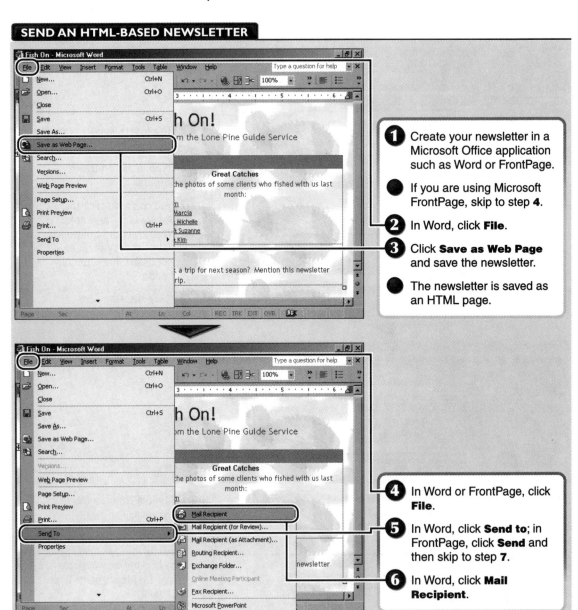

1. Create your newsletter in a Microsoft Office application such as Word or FrontPage.

- If you are using Microsoft FrontPage, skip to step **4**.

2. In Word, click **File**.
3. Click **Save as Web Page** and save the newsletter.

- The newsletter is saved as an HTML page.

4. In Word or FrontPage, click **File**.
5. In Word, click **Send to**; in FrontPage, click **Send** and then skip to step **7**.
6. In Word, click **Mail Recipient**.

in an instant

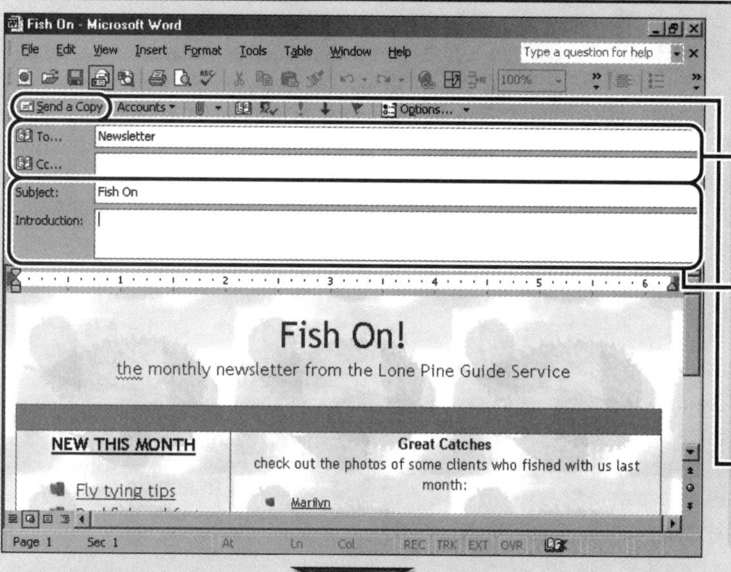

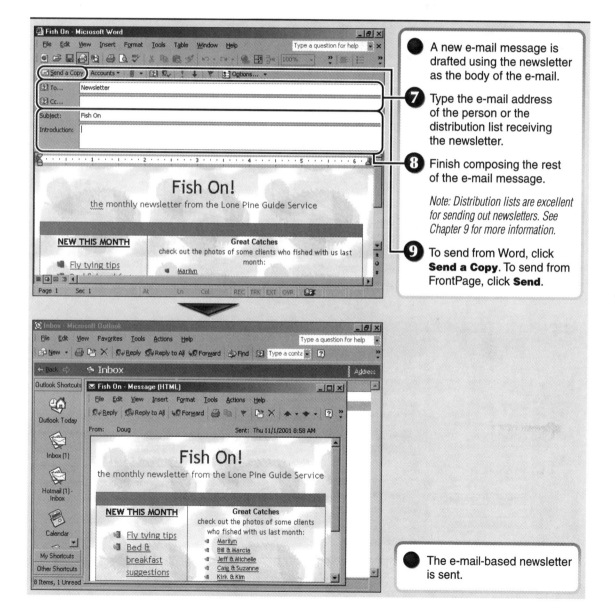

- A new e-mail message is drafted using the newsletter as the body of the e-mail.

7 Type the e-mail address of the person or the distribution list receiving the newsletter.

8 Finish composing the rest of the e-mail message.

Note: Distribution lists are excellent for sending out newsletters. See Chapter 9 for more information.

9 To send from Word, click **Send a Copy**. To send from FrontPage, click **Send**.

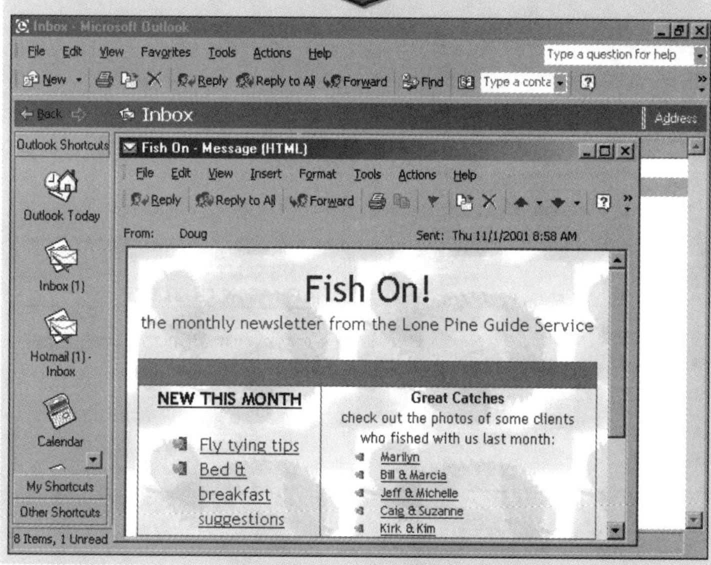

- The e-mail-based newsletter is sent.

USING INSTANT MESSAGING

If you subscribe to the MSN Messenger Service for Windows, you can open Outlook Contacts, see whether a contact is online, and, if so, send an instant message. One caveat: You must have the MSN Messenger Service, about which you can find more at http://messenger.msn.com/, installed to use this function. You must also enable Instant Messaging in Outlook.

USING INSTANT MESSAGING

ENABLE INSTANT MESSAGING IN OUTLOOK

1. Click **Tools**.
2. Click **Options** to open the Options dialog box.
3. Click the **Other** tab.
4. Make sure that there is a check mark next to the Enable Instant Messaging in Microsoft Outlook check box (☐ changes to ☑).
5. Click **OK** to enable Instant Messaging.

USING INSTANT MESSAGING IN OUTLOOK

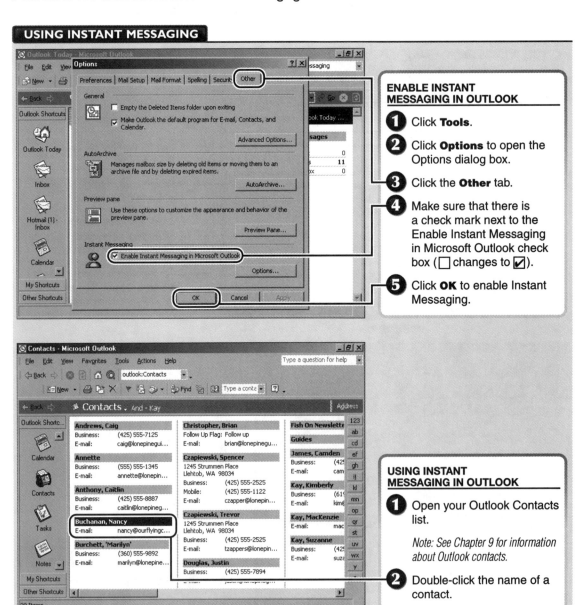

1. Open your Outlook Contacts list.

   Note: See Chapter 9 for information about Outlook contacts.

2. Double-click the name of a contact.

in an instant

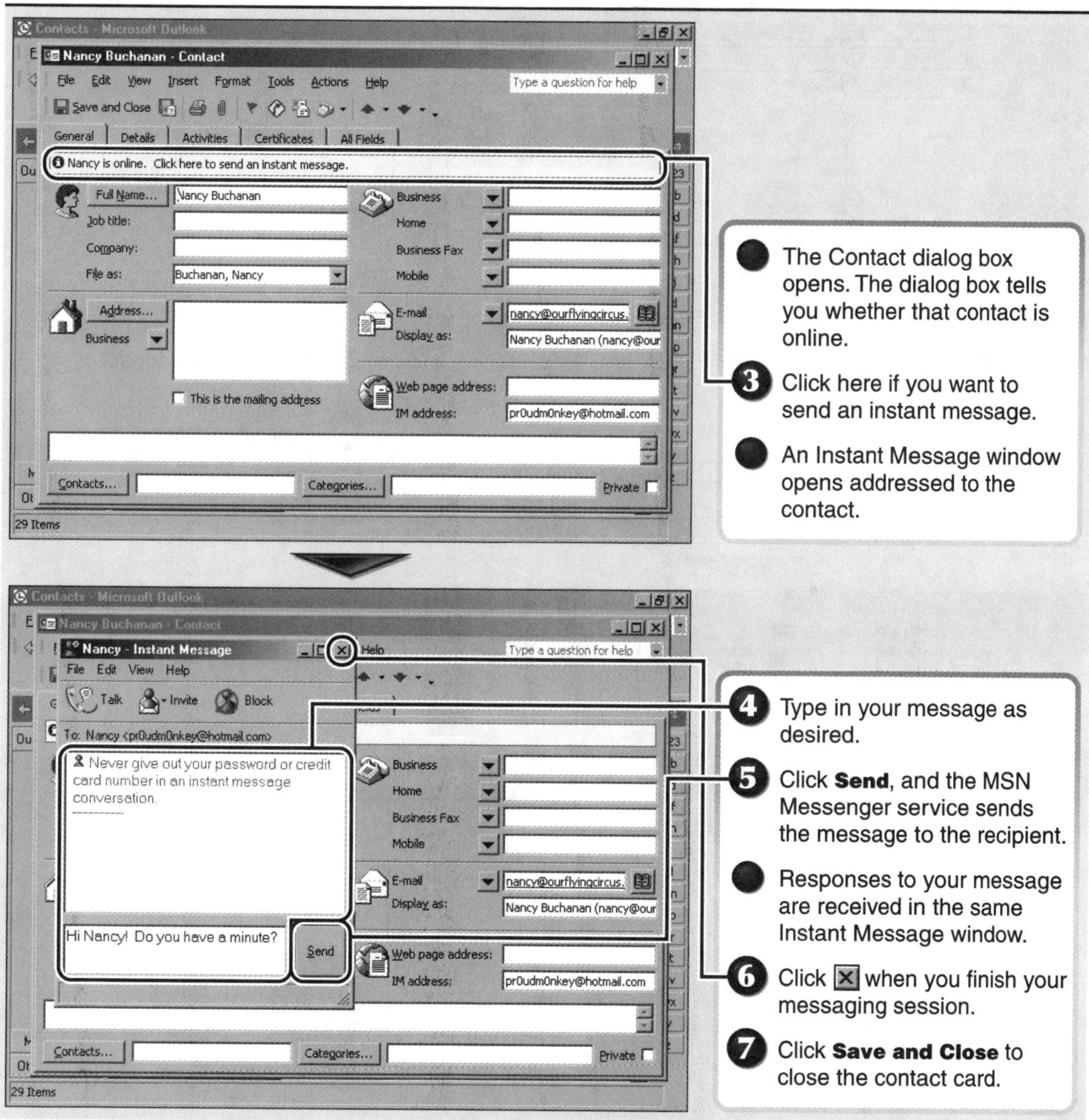

- The Contact dialog box opens. The dialog box tells you whether that contact is online.
3. Click here if you want to send an instant message.
- An Instant Message window opens addressed to the contact.
4. Type in your message as desired.
5. Click **Send**, and the MSN Messenger service sends the message to the recipient.
- Responses to your message are received in the same Instant Message window.
6. Click ☒ when you finish your messaging session.
7. Click **Save and Close** to close the contact card.

READING NEWSGROUP MESSAGES

You can use newsgroups to get product support and find out about many things across the Internet. Outlook 2002 includes Outlook Express, an excellent news reader that allows you to connect to newsgroups. Many companies use newsgroups to provide customer support for their products and services.

READING NEWSGROUP MESSAGES

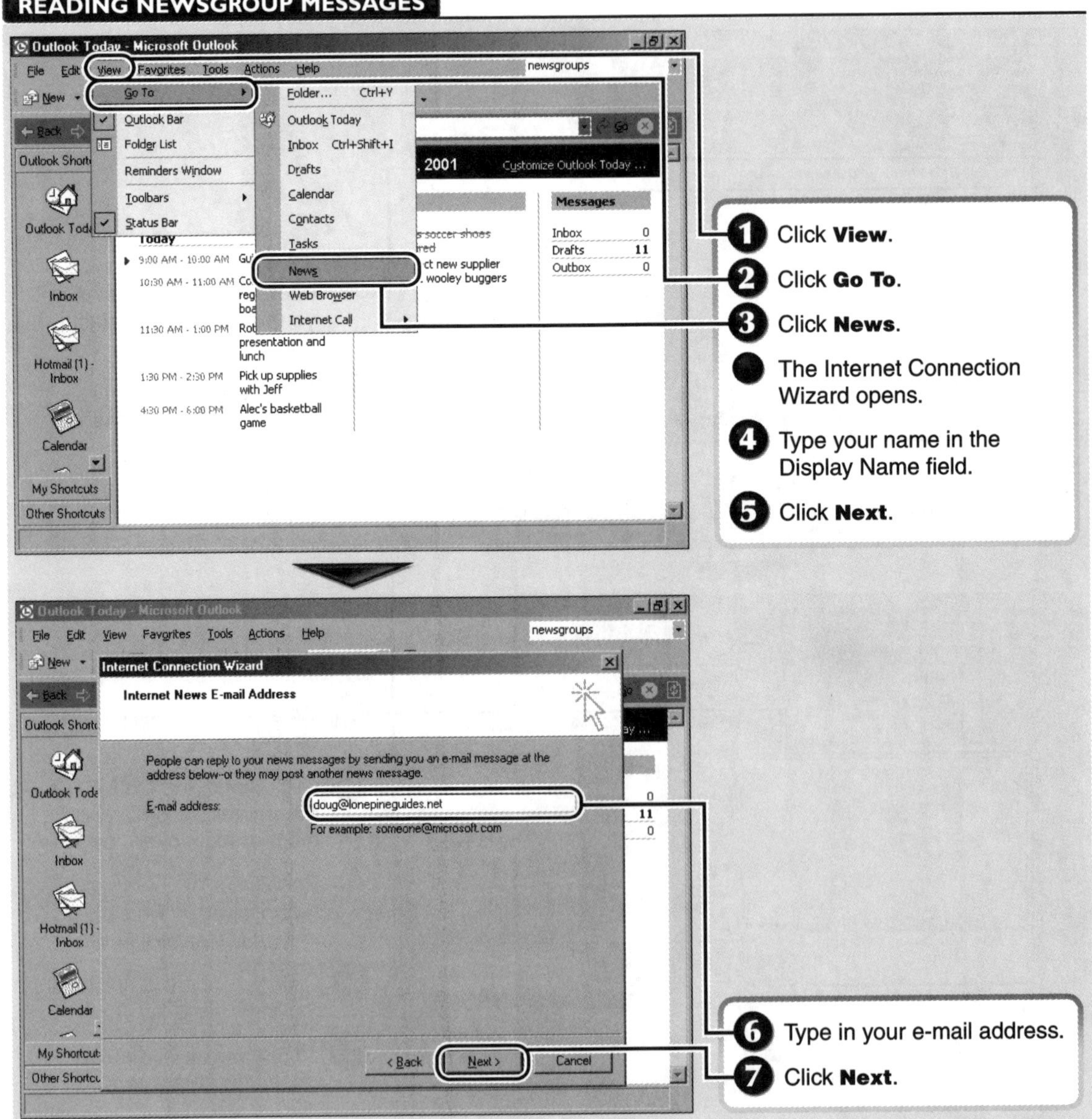

1. Click **View**.
2. Click **Go To**.
3. Click **News**.

- The Internet Connection Wizard opens.

4. Type your name in the Display Name field.
5. Click **Next**.
6. Type in your e-mail address.
7. Click **Next**.

in an instant

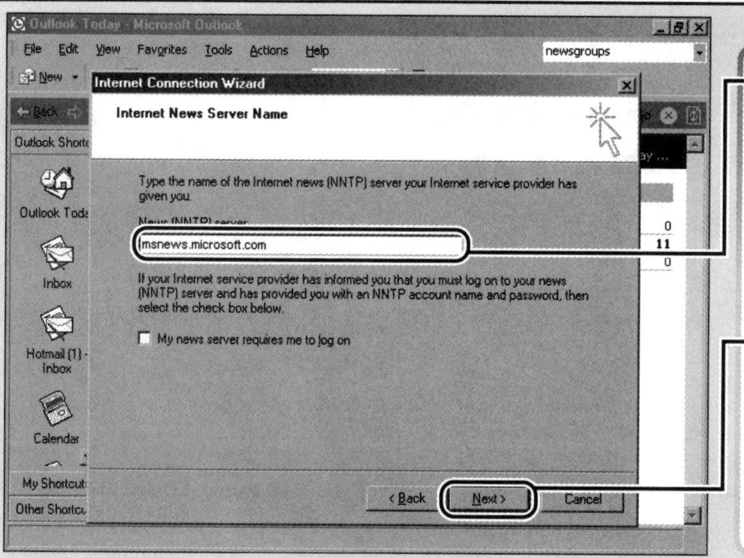

8. Type in the name of the news server to which you want to connect.

   Note: Newsgroups are commonly used by companies to provide support for products and services. Check company Web sites for the address of their newsgroups.

9. Click **Next**.

- A dialog box opens and says that you have successfully set up the newsgroup reader.

10. Click **Finish**.

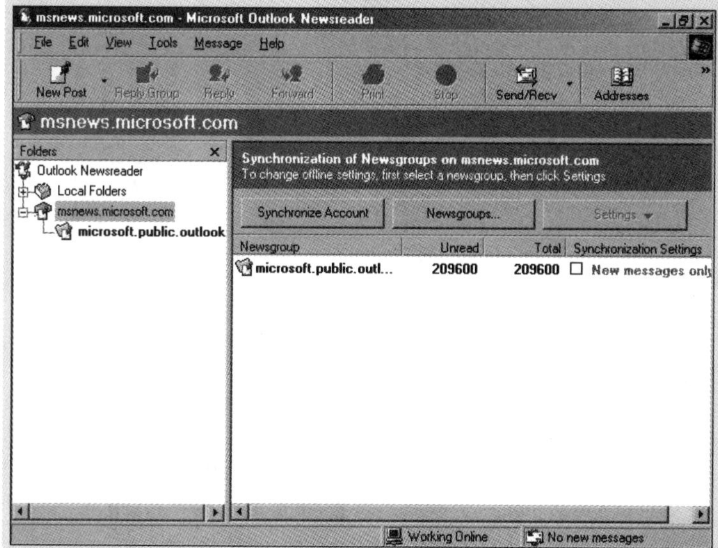

- Outlook Express opens and connects to the newsgroup you specified. The next time you want to access a newsgroup, just follow steps **1** through **3**. Outlook Express opens, and you simply click to open the newsgroup you want to access.

ADD YOUR INBOX TO YOUR FAVORITES

You can add your own list of favorites to Outlook to get from one place to another in the program very quickly. Adding your own favorites can be a good way to get to your favorite spots without using the Outlook bar or Folder List. Some users choose not to use the Outlook bar or Folder List to maximize the space on the screen for reading and writing e-mail messages.

ADD YOUR INBOX TO YOUR FAVORITES

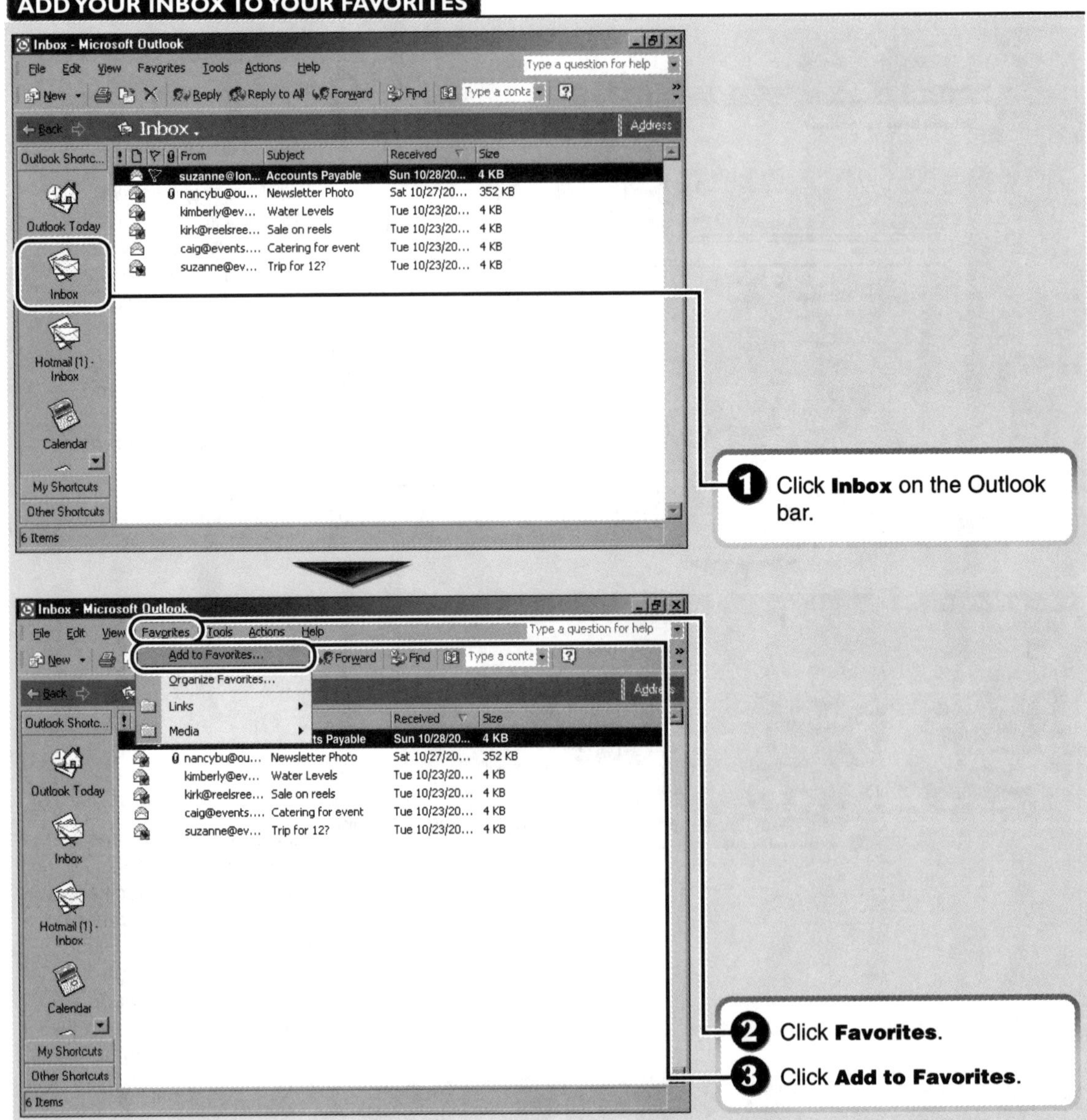

1 Click **Inbox** on the Outlook bar.

2 Click **Favorites**.

3 Click **Add to Favorites**.

in an instant

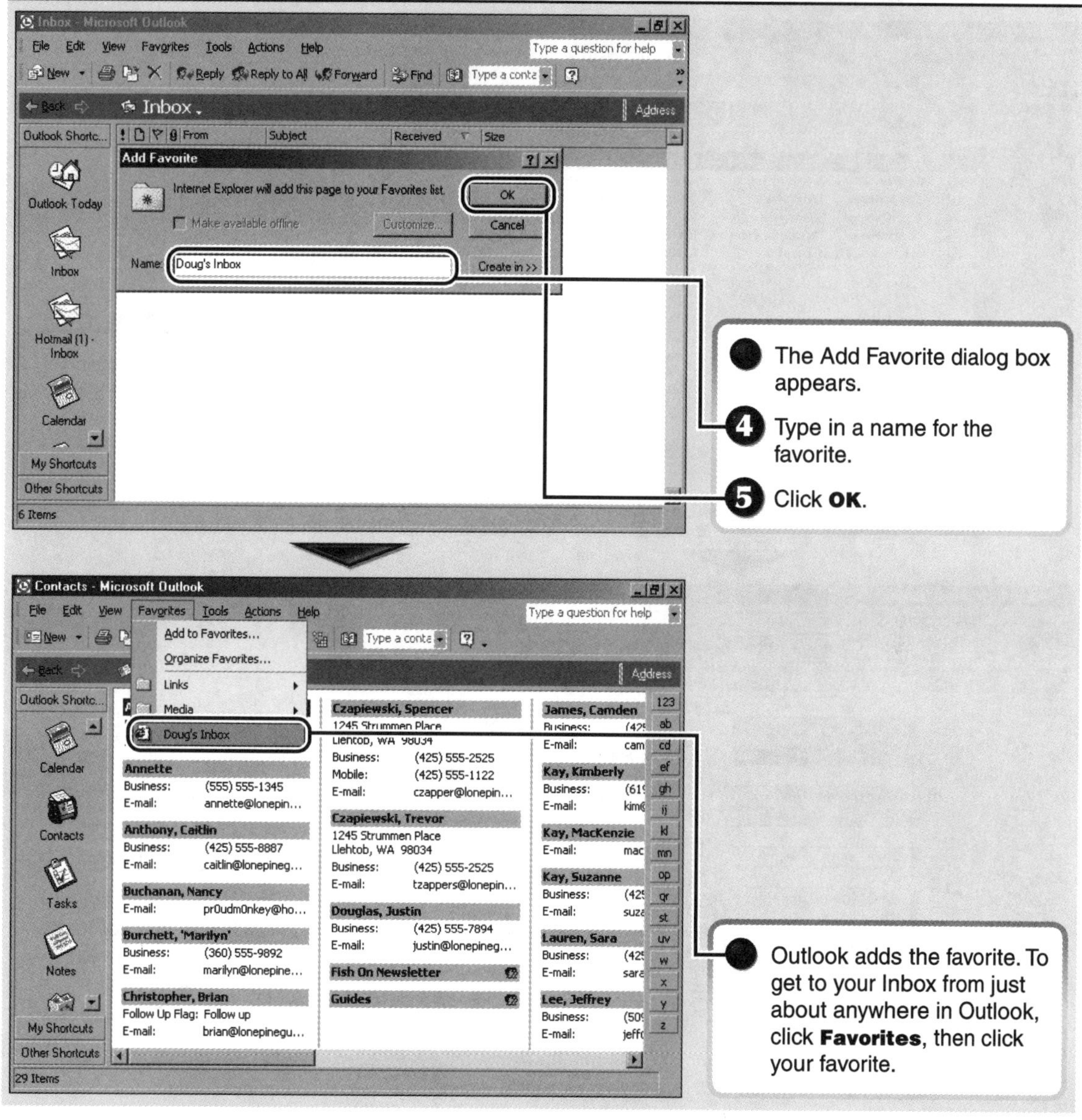
Add Favorite
Internet Explorer will add this page to your Favorites list.
OK
Cancel
Make available offline
Customize...
Name: Doug's Inbox
Create in >>
The Add Favorite dialog box appears.
4 Type in a name for the favorite.
5 Click OK.
Add to Favorites...
Organize Favorites...
Links
Media
Doug's Inbox
Outlook adds the favorite. To get to your Inbox from just about anywhere in Outlook, click Favorites, then click your favorite.

MICROSOFT EXCHANGE OVERVIEW

You can use Microsoft Exchange Server as your back-end e-mail, scheduling, collaboration, and instant messaging server software. Microsoft Outlook serves as the client or front-end to Exchange Server. You can either maintain a server computer running Exchange in your company or outsource Exchange-based hosting to a third party to manage for you.

MICROSOFT EXCHANGE OVERVIEW

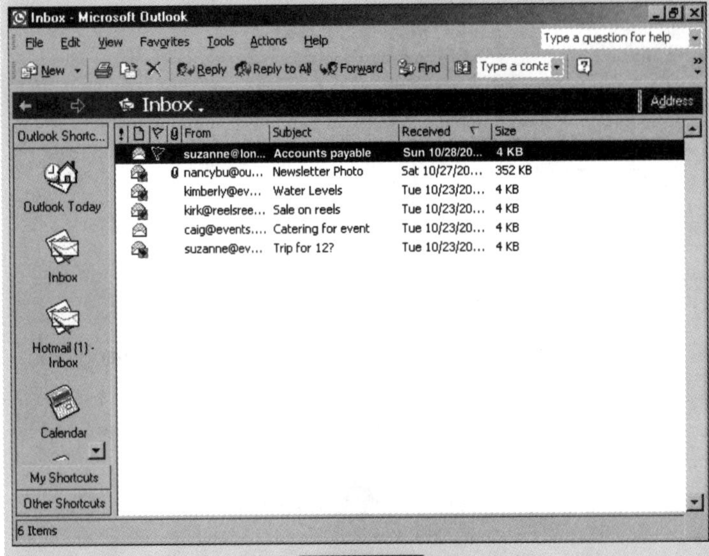

USING EXCHANGE E-MAIL

- Exchange Server stores and distributes e-mail messages, manages out-of-office messages, and maintains the Contacts list.

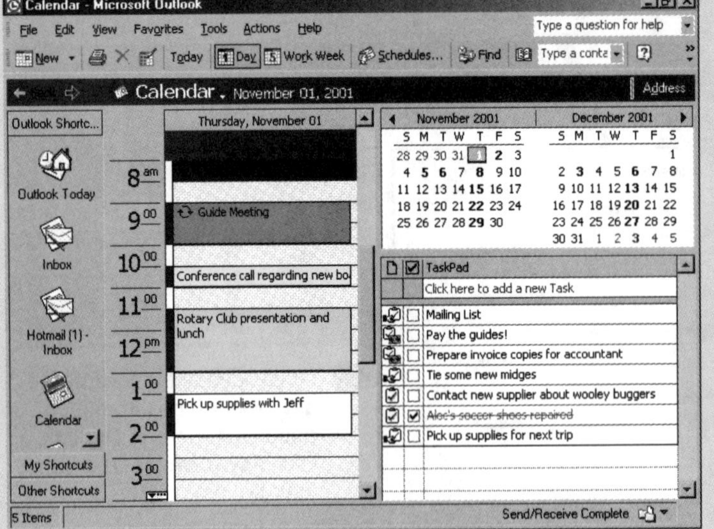

USING EXCHANGE SCHEDULING

- Exchange Server maintains schedules so that you can see free/busy times when scheduling appointments, keeps group schedules, and manages sending meeting requests and responses.

in an instant

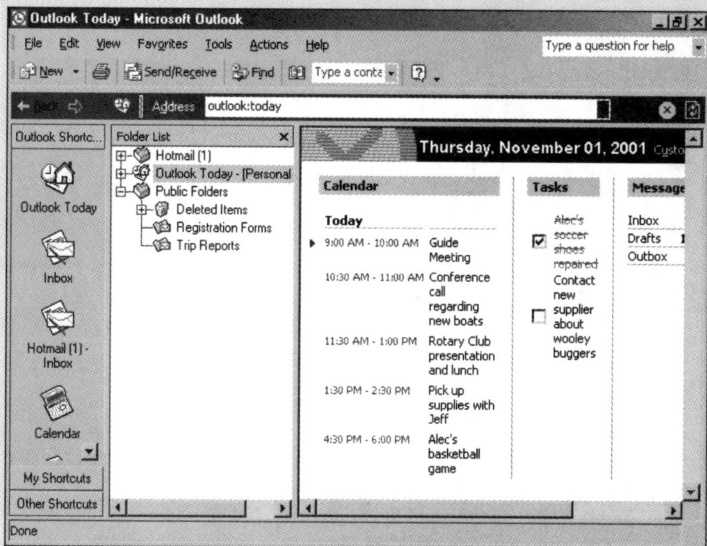

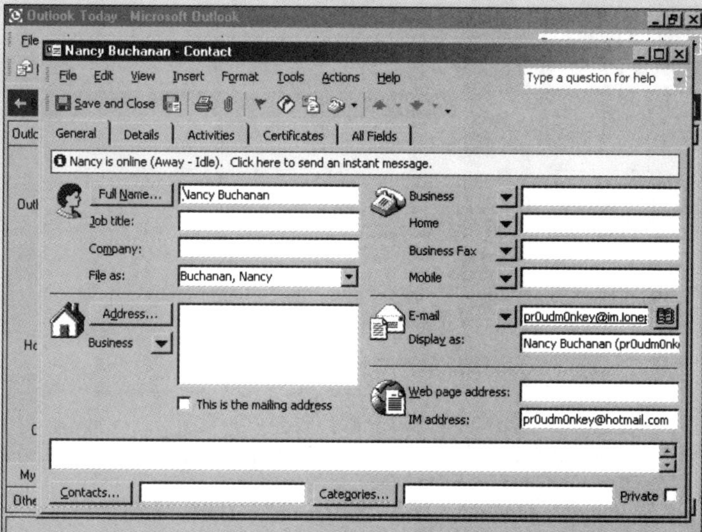

USING EXCHANGE COLLABORATION

- Exchange Server collaboration features such as public folders allow everyone to store information on the server as easily as they store it on their own hard drive.

USING EXCHANGE INSTANT MESSAGING

- Exchange Server's instant messaging service allows you to send and receive notes in real-time and see whether others are online without leaving Outlook.

CONNECT TO A MICROSOFT EXCHANGE SERVER

You can connect to a server running Microsoft Exchange as your default e-mail server, or you can add an account on an Exchange-based server in addition to previously set-up accounts. For more information on connecting to your mail server, see Chapter 1.

CONNECT TO A MICROSOFT EXCHANGE SERVER

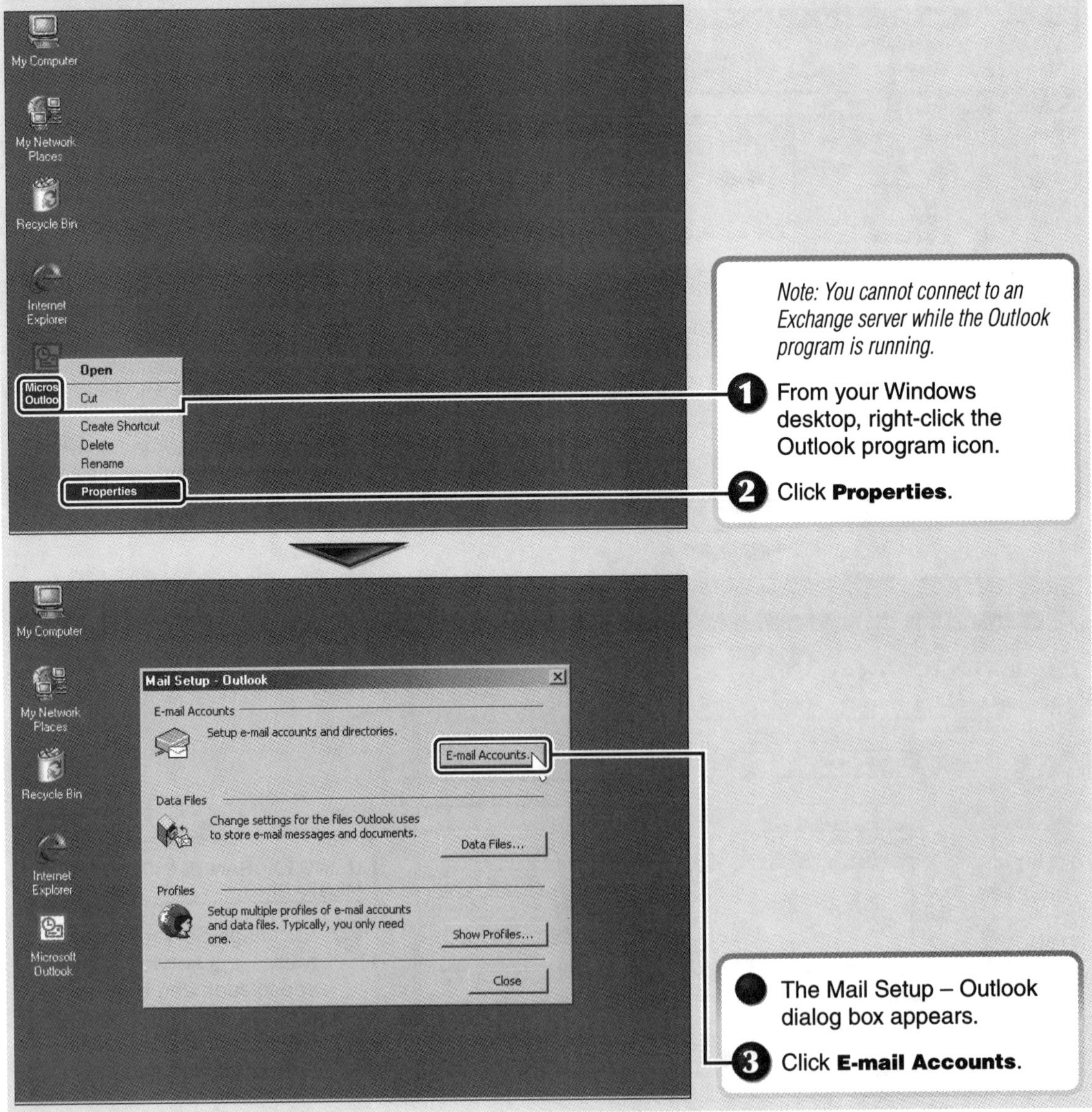

Note: You cannot connect to an Exchange server while the Outlook program is running.

1. From your Windows desktop, right-click the Outlook program icon.

2. Click **Properties**.

- The Mail Setup – Outlook dialog box appears.

3. Click **E-mail Accounts**.

in an instant

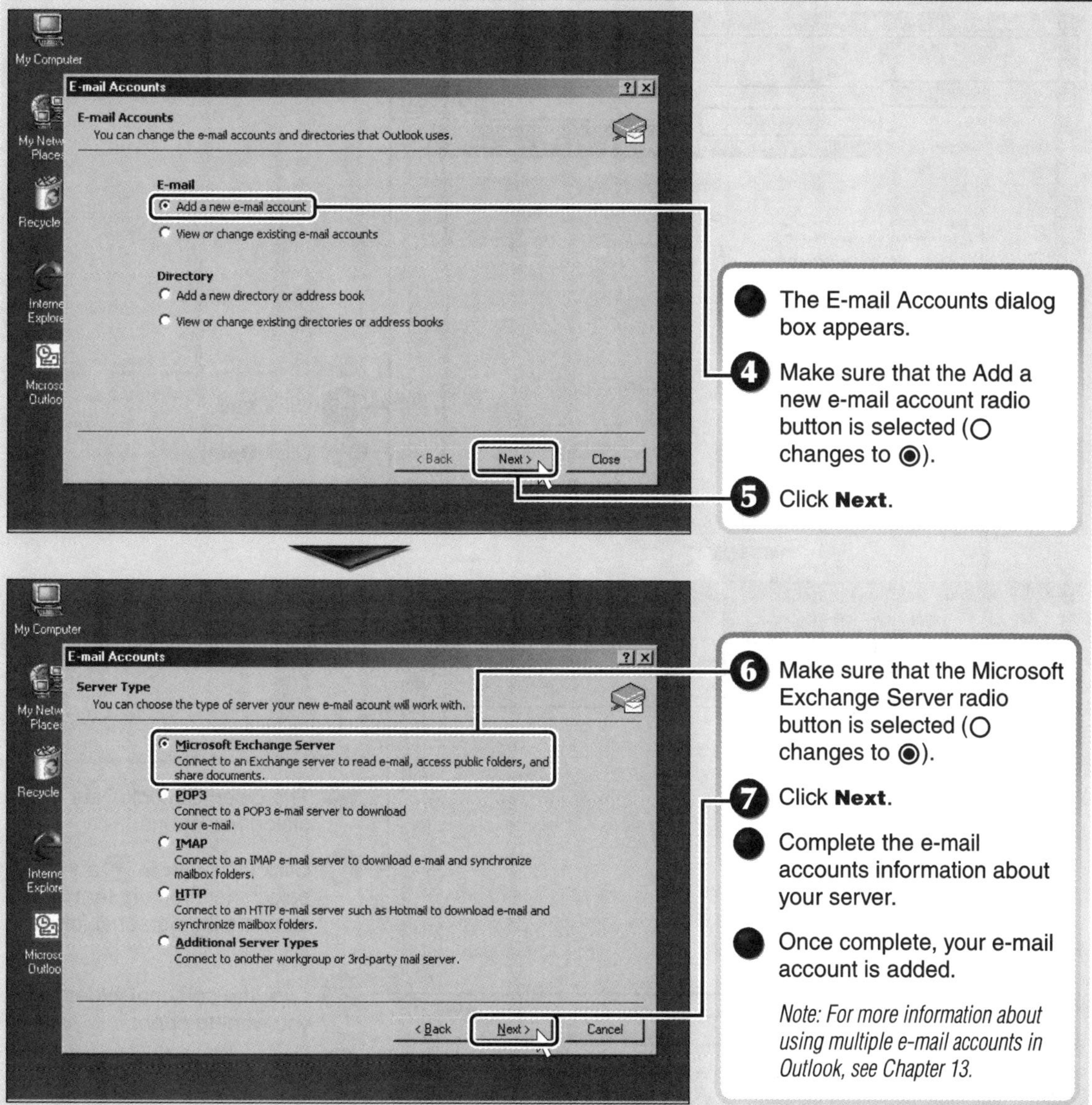

- The E-mail Accounts dialog box appears.

4. Make sure that the Add a new e-mail account radio button is selected (○ changes to ◉).
5. Click **Next**.
6. Make sure that the Microsoft Exchange Server radio button is selected (○ changes to ◉).
7. Click **Next**.

- Complete the e-mail accounts information about your server.
- Once complete, your e-mail account is added.

Note: For more information about using multiple e-mail accounts in Outlook, see Chapter 13.

WORK WITH FOLDERS THAT BELONG TO SOMEONE ELSE

You can store e-mail in personal folders to keep similar e-mail together and to save storage space on the e-mail server. You can also use personal folders as a way to transfer e-mail message collections from one person to another. For more information about personal folders, see Chapter 7.

WORK WITH FOLDERS THAT BELONG TO SOMEONE ELSE

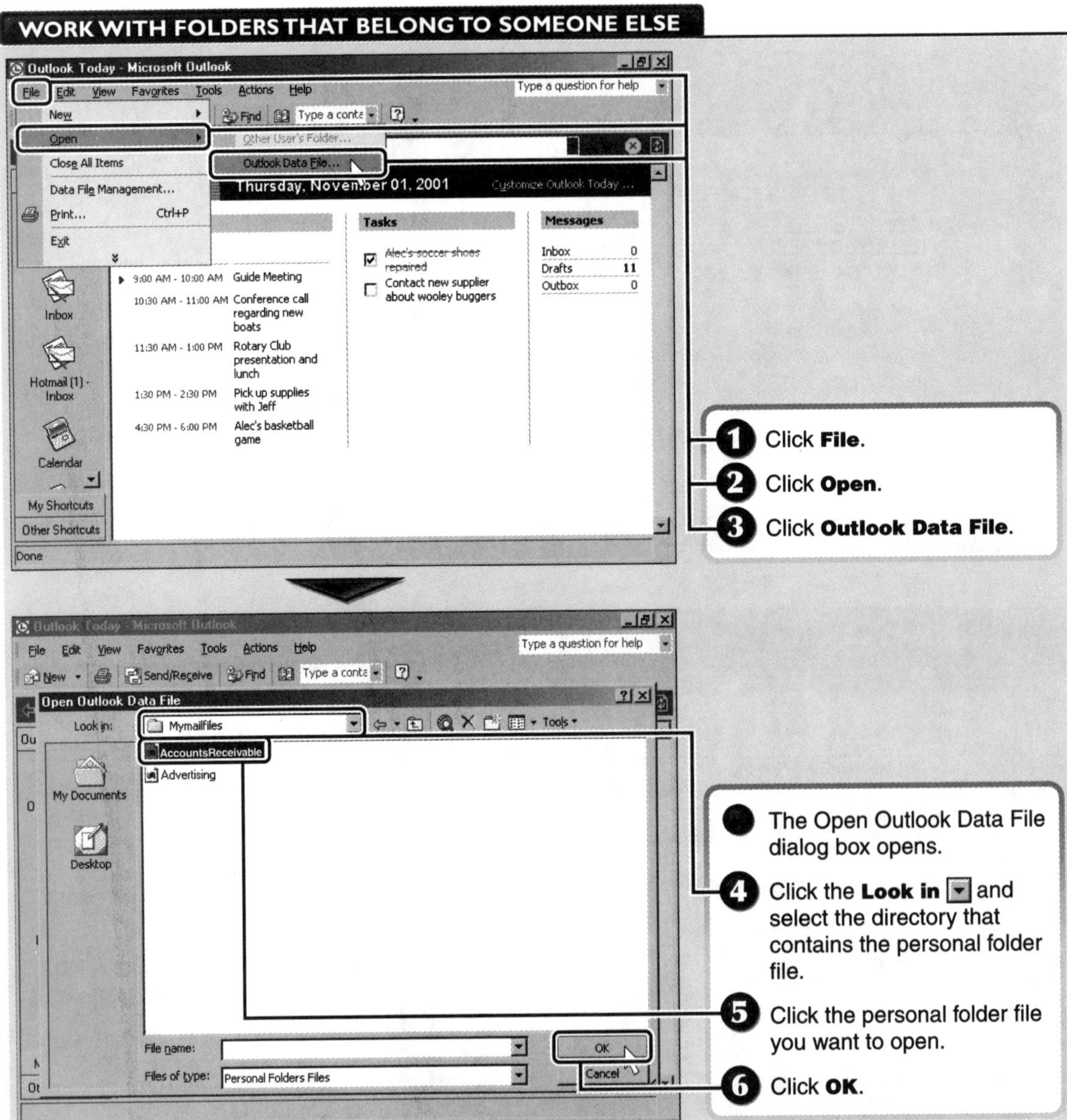

1. Click **File**.
2. Click **Open**.
3. Click **Outlook Data File**.

- The Open Outlook Data File dialog box opens.

4. Click the **Look in** ▾ and select the directory that contains the personal folder file.
5. Click the personal folder file you want to open.
6. Click **OK**.

in an instant

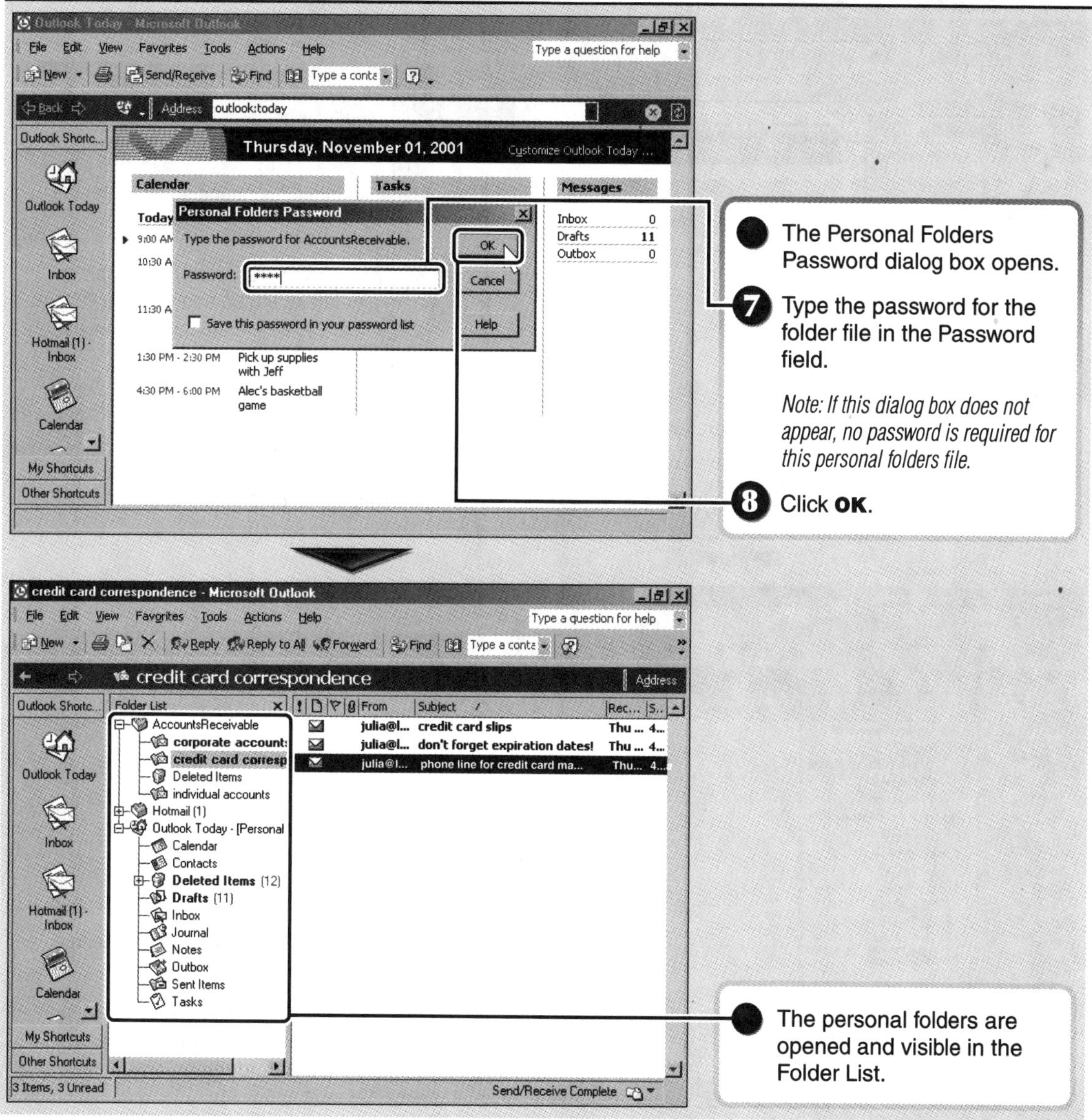

- The Personal Folders Password dialog box opens.
- **7** Type the password for the folder file in the Password field.

  Note: If this dialog box does not appear, no password is required for this personal folders file.
- **8** Click **OK**.

- The personal folders are opened and visible in the Folder List.

VIEW A PUBLIC FOLDER

You can use Exchange Public Folders as a central repository for e-mail messages that multiple people in your organization need access to. Public folders are similar to personal folders, but everyone granted privileges to the public folders can access them.

VIEW A PUBLIC FOLDER

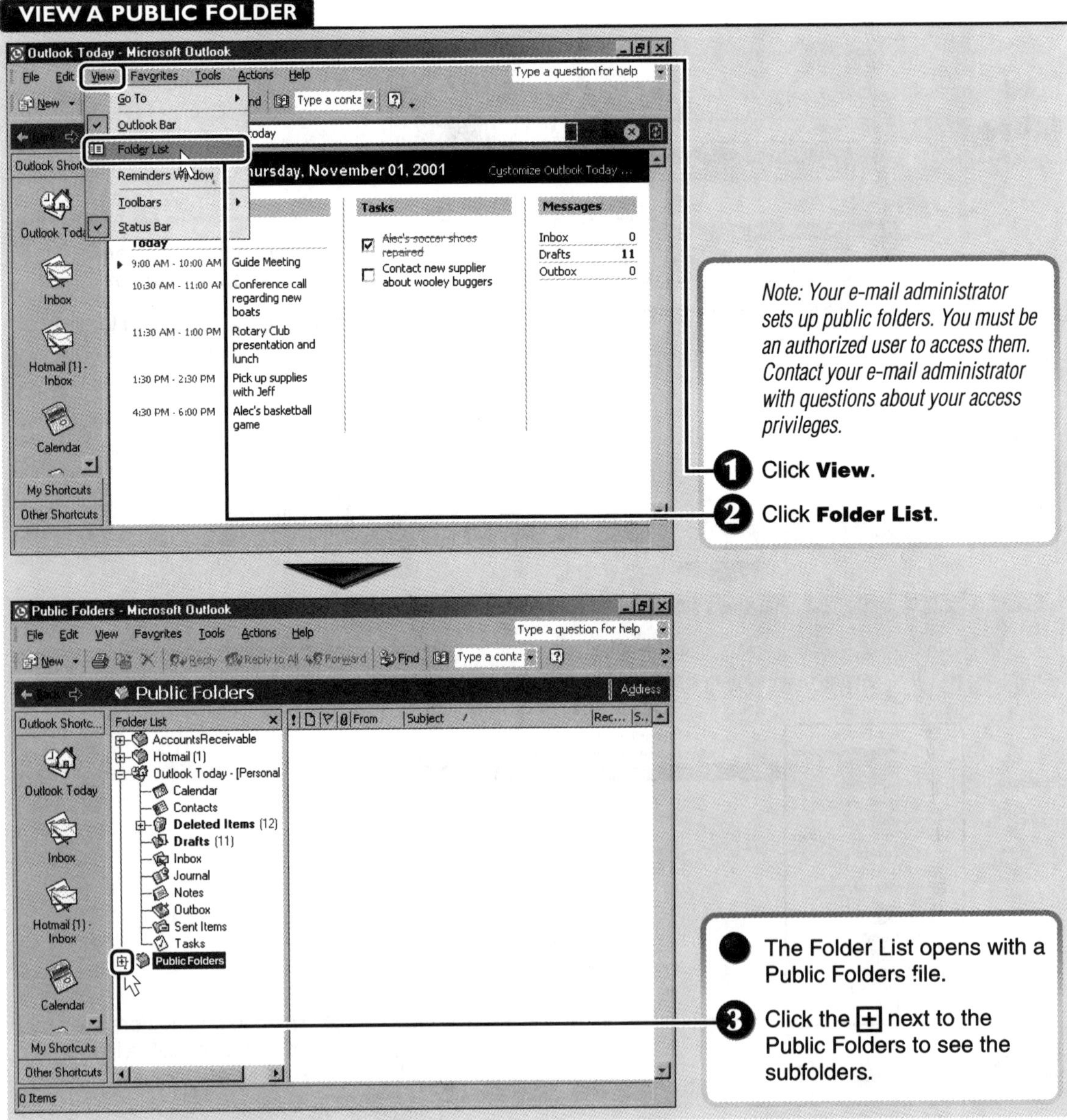

Note: Your e-mail administrator sets up public folders. You must be an authorized user to access them. Contact your e-mail administrator with questions about your access privileges.

1. Click **View**.
2. Click **Folder List**.

- The Folder List opens with a Public Folders file.

3. Click the ⊞ next to the Public Folders to see the subfolders.

in an instant

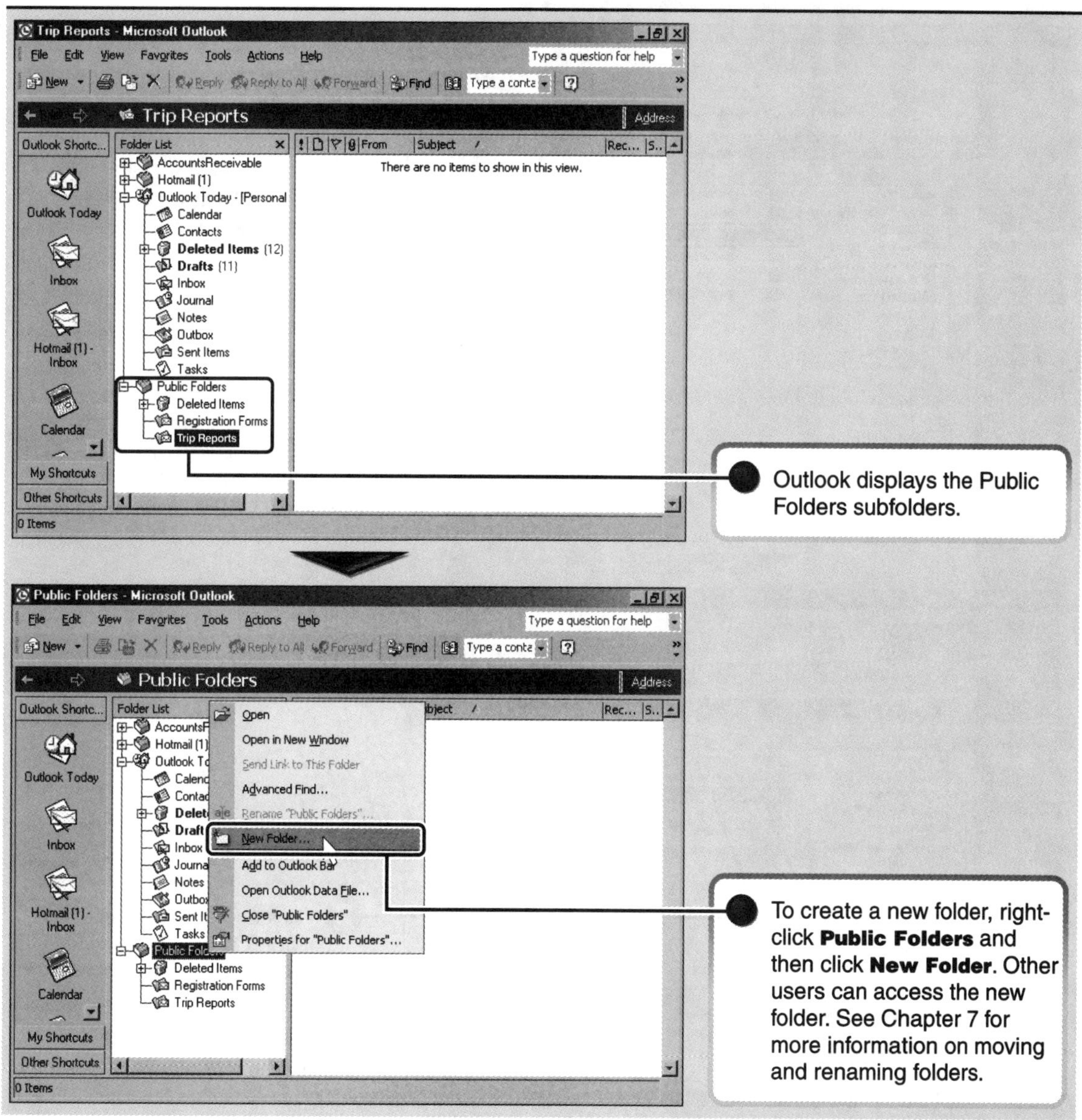

Outlook displays the Public Folders subfolders.

To create a new folder, right-click **Public Folders** and then click **New Folder**. Other users can access the new folder. See Chapter 7 for more information on moving and renaming folders.

MOVE MESSAGES TO PUBLIC FOLDERS

You can easily move e-mail messages and other Outlook items from your mailbox or Personal Folders to Exchange Public Folders. The easiest way to move e-mail messages is to click and drag them to the public folder. You can also move or copy e-mail messages, notes, tasks, and other Outlook items to public folders via the *Move to Folder* or *Copy to Folder* menu options.

MOVE E-MAIL MESSAGES TO PUBLIC FOLDERS

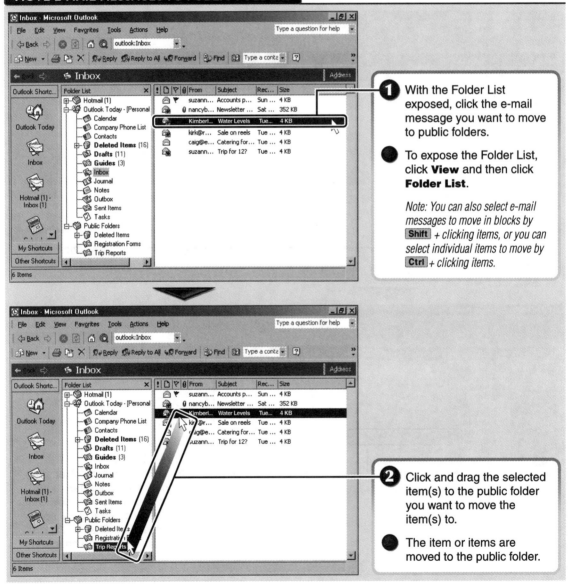

1. With the Folder List exposed, click the e-mail message you want to move to public folders.

- To expose the Folder List, click **View** and then click **Folder List**.

Note: You can also select e-mail messages to move in blocks by **Shift** *+ clicking items, or you can select individual items to move by* **Ctrl** *+ clicking items.*

2. Click and drag the selected item(s) to the public folder you want to move the item(s) to.

- The item or items are moved to the public folder.

in an instant

MOVE OR COPY E-MAIL MESSAGES OR OTHER ITEMS TO PUBLIC FOLDERS

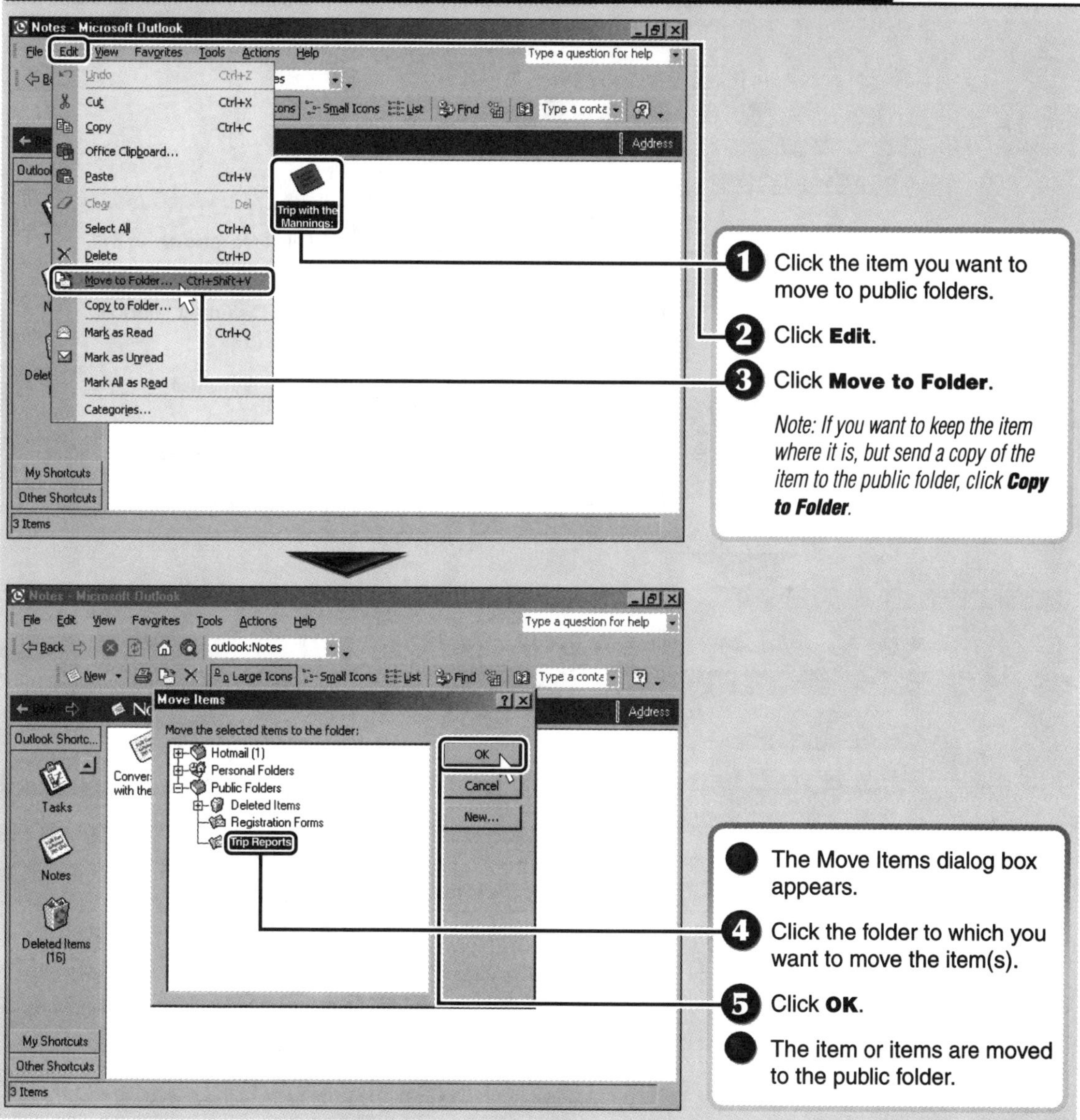

1. Click the item you want to move to public folders.
2. Click **Edit**.
3. Click **Move to Folder**.

*Note: If you want to keep the item where it is, but send a copy of the item to the public folder, click **Copy to Folder**.*

- The Move Items dialog box appears.

4. Click the folder to which you want to move the item(s).
5. Click **OK**.

- The item or items are moved to the public folder.

CREATE A GROUP CALENDAR

You do not have to schedule a meeting to check the availability of a group of people. Instead, you can create a group schedule that you can open any time you want to check free/busy times for that group. For example, you could create a group schedule for all the people working on a task force at work.

CREATE A GROUP CALENDAR

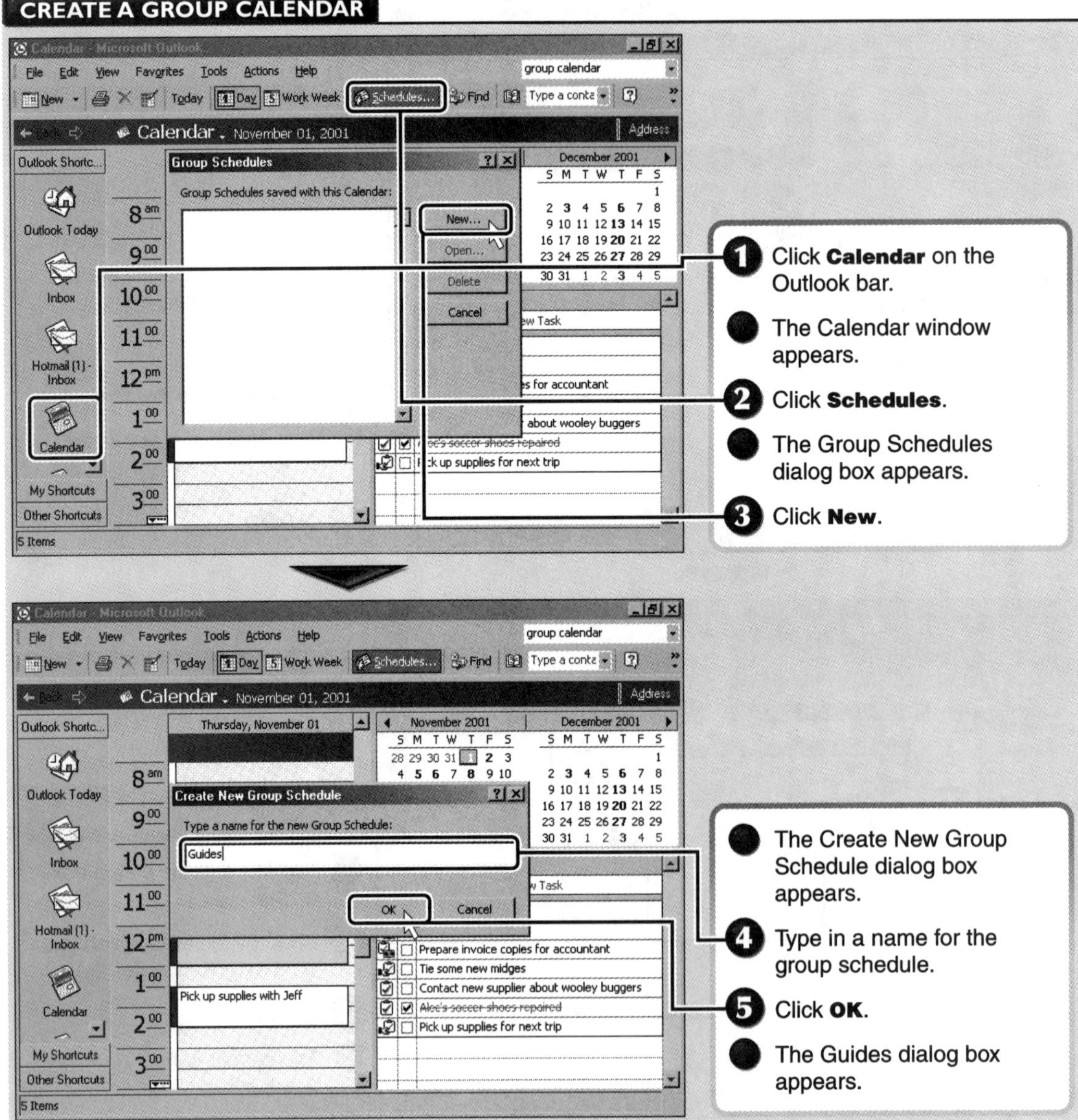

1 Click Calendar on the Outlook bar.
The Calendar window appears.
2 Click Schedules.
The Group Schedules dialog box appears.
3 Click New.
The Create New Group Schedule dialog box appears.
4 Type in a name for the group schedule.
5 Click OK.
The Guides dialog box appears.

in an instant

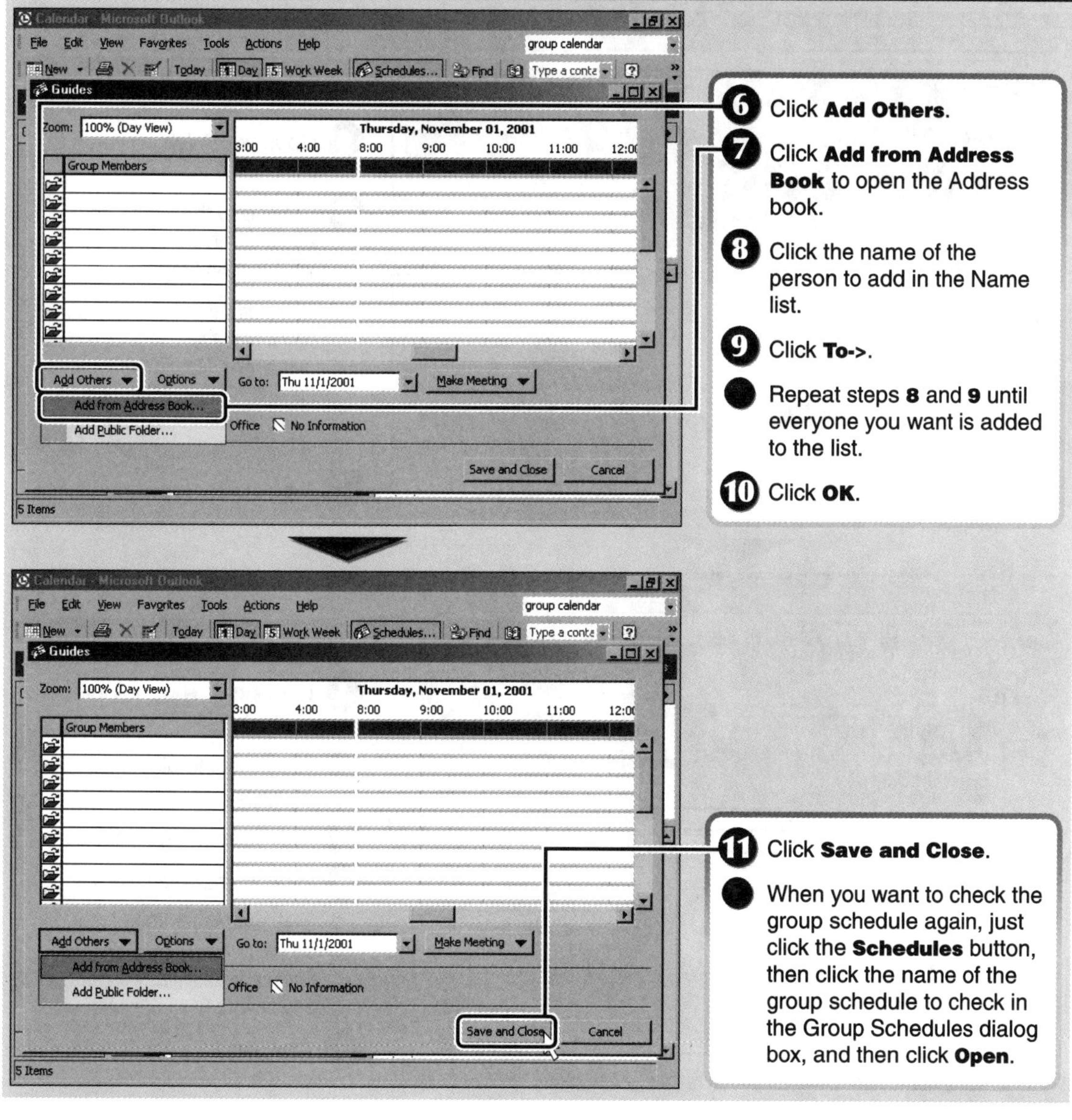

6. Click **Add Others**.
7. Click **Add from Address Book** to open the Address book.
8. Click the name of the person to add in the Name list.
9. Click **To->**.
- Repeat steps **8** and **9** until everyone you want is added to the list.
10. Click **OK**.
11. Click **Save and Close**.
- When you want to check the group schedule again, just click the **Schedules** button, then click the name of the group schedule to check in the Group Schedules dialog box, and then click **Open**.

ACCESS YOUR E-MAIL OVER THE INTERNET

You can use Outlook Web access to view your Microsoft Exchange Server-based e-mail over the Internet. The ability to see your e-mail Inbox from virtually anywhere is particularly convenient if you travel or change locations frequently.

ACCESS YOUR E-MAIL OVER THE INTERNET

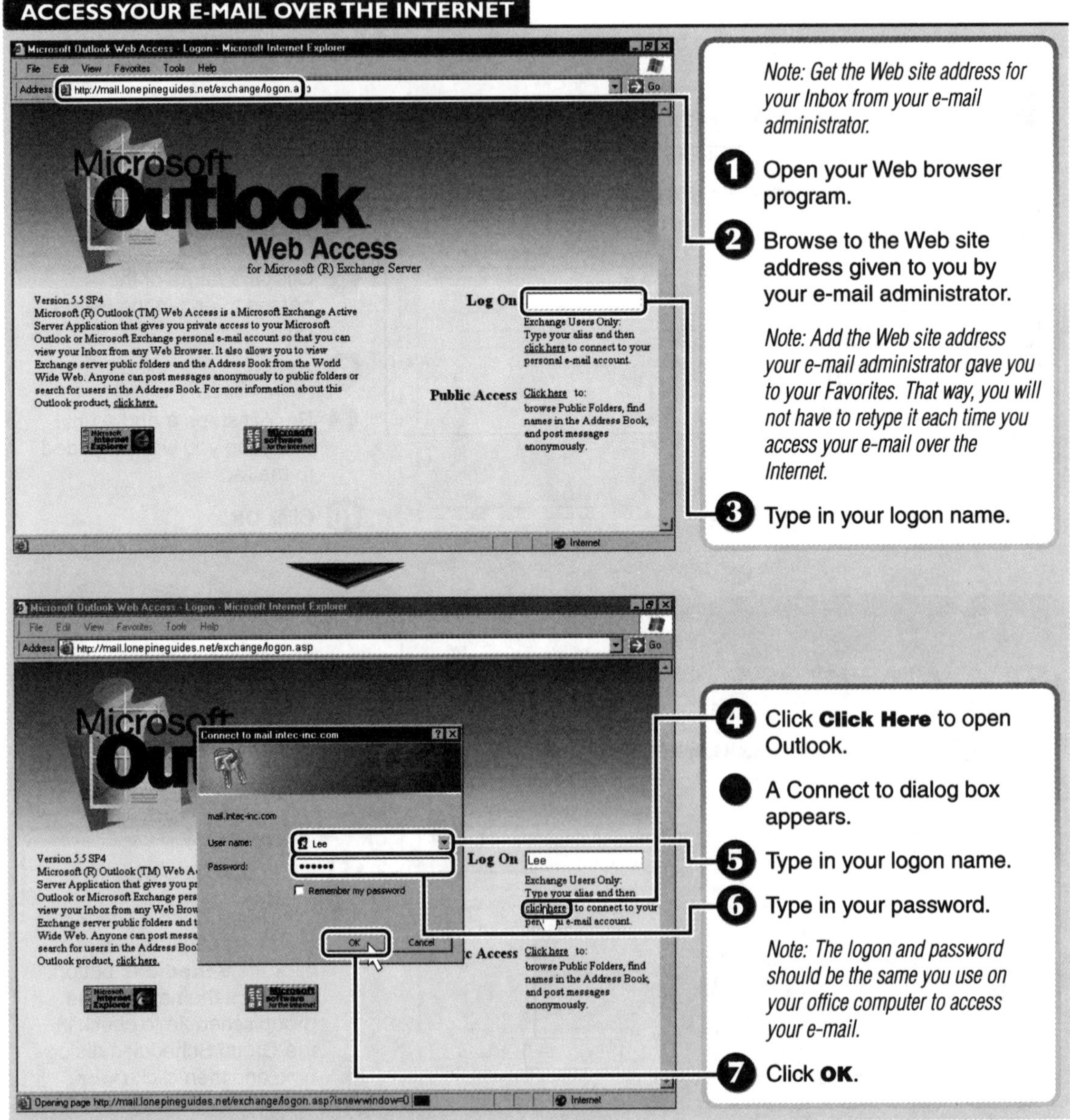

Note: Get the Web site address for your Inbox from your e-mail administrator.

1. Open your Web browser program.
2. Browse to the Web site address given to you by your e-mail administrator.

Note: Add the Web site address your e-mail administrator gave you to your Favorites. That way, you will not have to retype it each time you access your e-mail over the Internet.

3. Type in your logon name.
4. Click **Click Here** to open Outlook.

- A Connect to dialog box appears.

5. Type in your logon name.
6. Type in your password.

Note: The logon and password should be the same you use on your office computer to access your e-mail.

7. Click **OK**.

in an instant

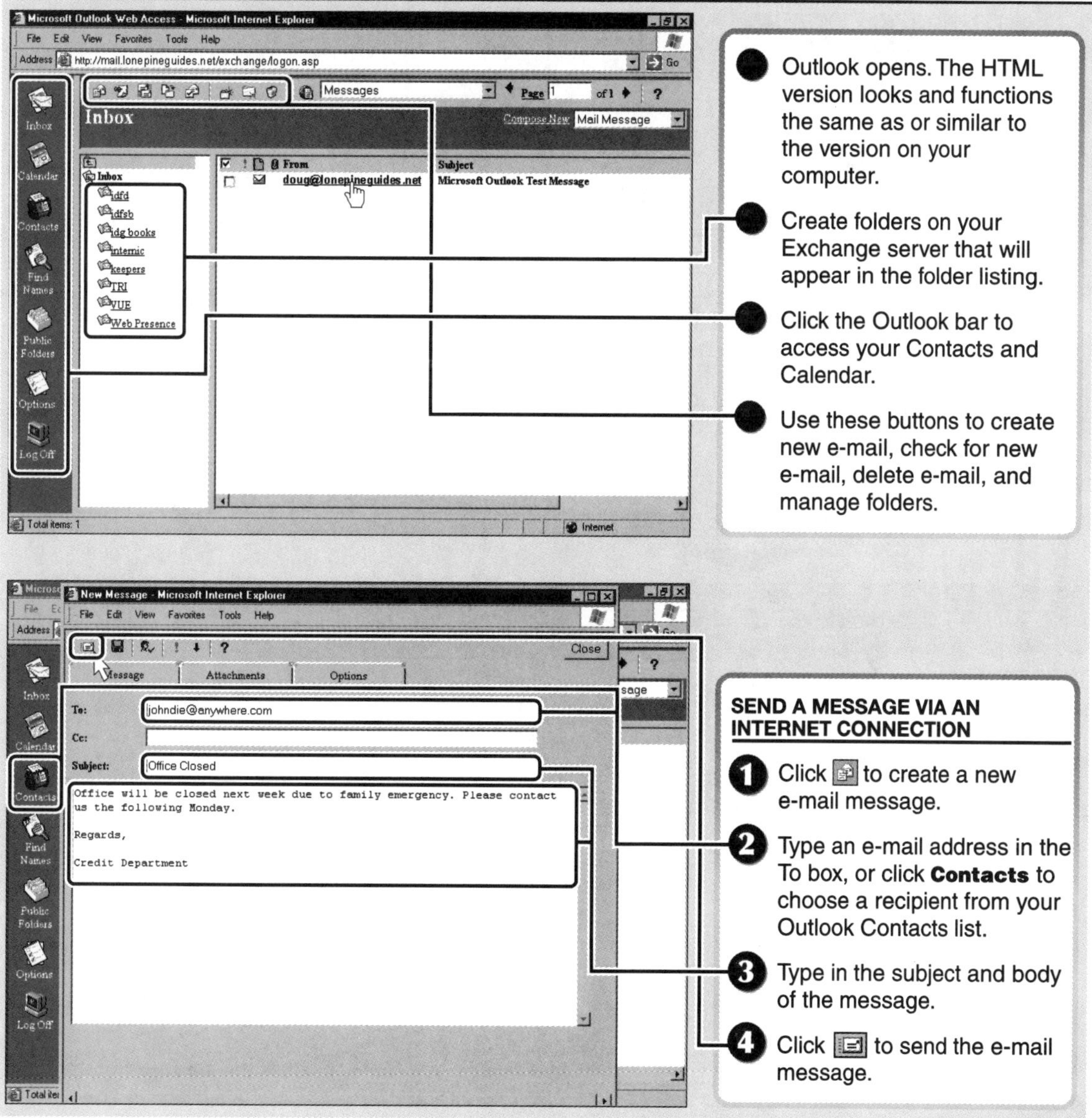

Outlook opens. The HTML version looks and functions the same as or similar to the version on your computer.
Create folders on your Exchange server that will appear in the folder listing.
Click the Outlook bar to access your Contacts and Calendar.
Use these buttons to create new e-mail, check for new e-mail, delete e-mail, and manage folders.

SEND A MESSAGE VIA AN INTERNET CONNECTION

1. Click [icon] to create a new e-mail message.
2. Type an e-mail address in the To box, or click **Contacts** to choose a recipient from your Outlook Contacts list.
3. Type in the subject and body of the message.
4. Click [icon] to send the e-mail message.

USING EXCHANGE-BASED INSTANT MESSAGING

You can use Microsoft Exchange instant messaging service to open Outlook Contacts and see whether the contact is online, and — if the contact is online — send an instant message to that contact.

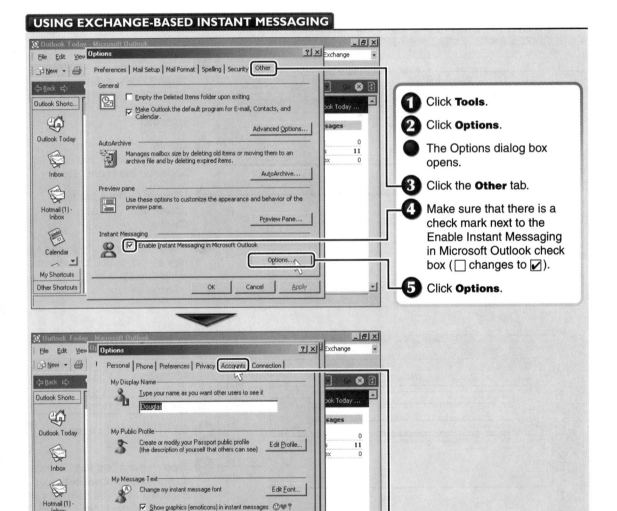

1. Click **Tools**.
2. Click **Options**.
- The Options dialog box opens.
3. Click the **Other** tab.
4. Make sure that there is a check mark next to the Enable Instant Messaging in Microsoft Outlook check box (☐ changes to ☑).
5. Click **Options**.

- The Options dialog box appears.
6. Click the **Accounts** tab.

in an instant

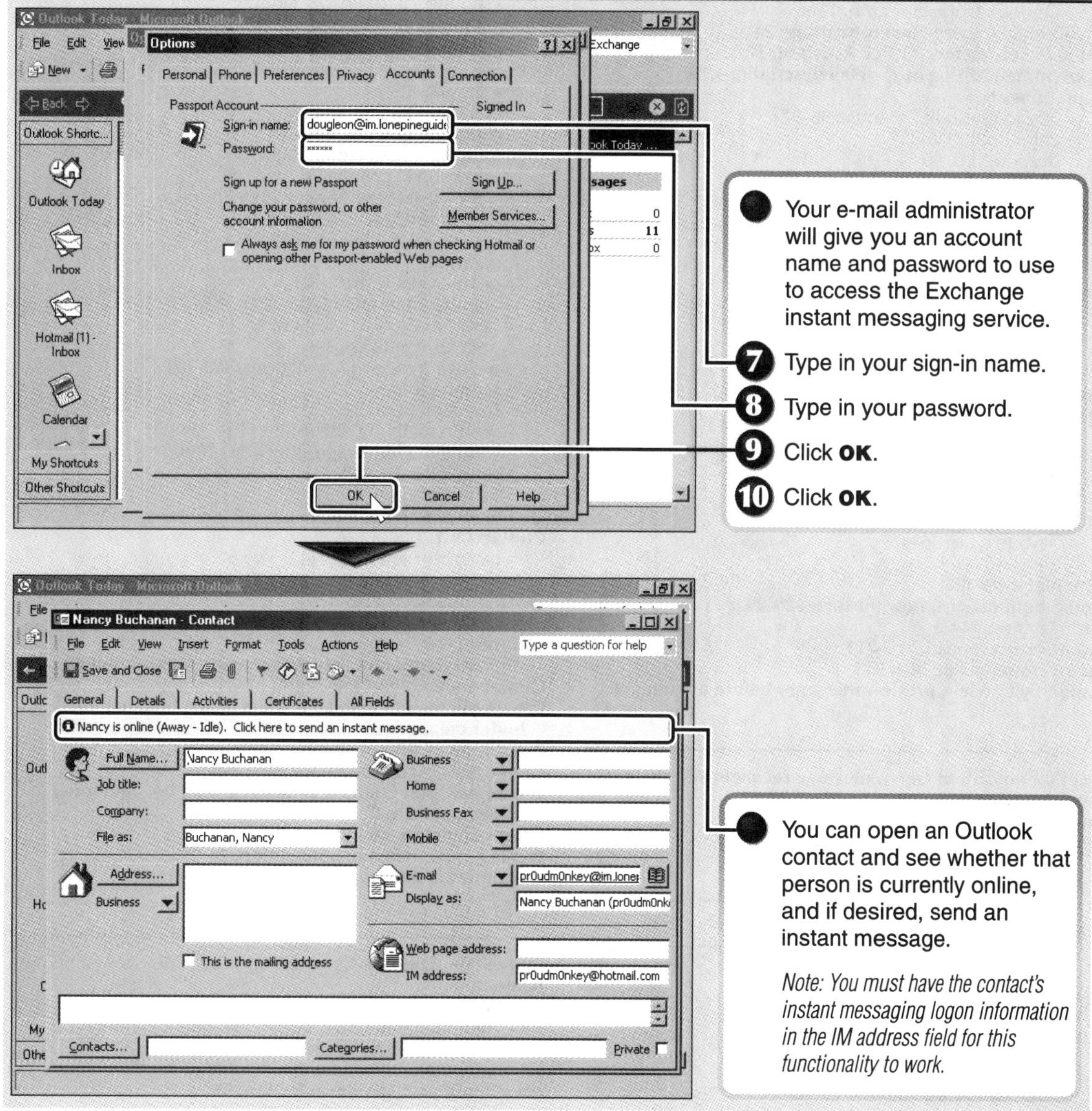

- Your e-mail administrator will give you an account name and password to use to access the Exchange instant messaging service.

7. Type in your sign-in name.
8. Type in your password.
9. Click **OK**.
10. Click **OK**.

- You can open an Outlook contact and see whether that person is currently online, and if desired, send an instant message.

Note: You must have the contact's instant messaging logon information in the IM address field for this functionality to work.

INDEX

E

F

M

N

INDEX

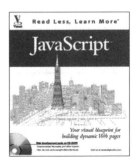

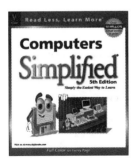